Royal Artillery Glossary

of Terms and Abbreviations (Historical and Modern)

ROYAL ARTILLERY GLOSSARY

OF TERMS AND ABBREVIATIONS (HISTORICAL AND MODERN)

Philip Jobson

The History Press

This book is dedicated to all gunners past, present and future.

And also to:

My wife, Carol, and my children, Louise, Hannah and Matthew
for their patience over the last twenty years.

First published 2008

The History Press Ltd.
The Mill, Brimscombe Port
Stroud, Gloucestershire, GL5 2QG
www.thehistorypress.co.uk

British Library Cataloguing in Publication Data.
A catalogue record for this book is available from the British Library.

ISBN 978 1 86227 476 1

Typesetting and origination by The History Press Ltd.
Printed in Great Britain

Contents

Introduction

I have produced this book as a consequence of my personal interest in the language of the Royal Regiment. I have taken the terms and abbreviations from documents, books and training manuals in my possession and also from discussions with serving and retired gunners of all ranks. I initially started out to list just the abbreviations, but it soon became apparent that there were many historical terms that meant little or nothing to me. I therefore embarked on the production of this *vade mecum* of the Royal Regiment of Artillery, little knowing what a major drain on my time and patience it would become.

It became necessary to include a number of non-artillery terms and abbreviations in the book, this has been occasioned by the diverse nature of the roles undertaken by the Regiment. I have, however, endeavoured to keep these to a minimum. There are also a number of Commonwealth Artillery terms included in this book. As with the non-artillery terms, I have tried to keep these to a minimum, as to have included all the commonwealth variations would have meant the book never coming to fruition.

When using this book, it should be borne in mind that the terms and abbreviations given may have had a relatively short usage life and indeed may have had different meaning at different times. I have endeavoured to indicate the period during which they were used, but this has not always proved possible.

Whilst details of many of the artillery pieces used by the Regiment are included in the book, I have not attempted to include every artillery piece ever employed. This would have made the book excessively large and changed the scope of it dramatically.

Acknowledgements

I must thank the staff at Firepower, the Royal Artillery Museum; in particular Paul Evans, the Librarian and Les Smith, the Keeper of Collections for their assistance and patience in answering my many and often, I am sure, to them obvious questions.

Thanks are also due to Major General Jonathan Bailey, Major Bruce McMillan, Nigel Evans, Peter Head, Lt Col Brian Reid, Don Graves, Jim Bryce, Arthur Burke, Chris Jobson, Richard Little, Geoff Coxhead, Kim McGarth, Maurice Harper, Keith Holderness, Mark O'Neill, Col Andrew Pinion, Lt Col Will Townend, Gerry Boyd, Mick Mortimer (Secretary 42 Regt Old Comrades Association), Andy Anderson, David Moore, webmaster of the Palmerston Forts Society, Tom Stimpson and the members of the Junior Leaders Regiment RA Old Comrades Association.

All illustrations used in this book have been supplied Courtesy of the Royal Artillery Historical Trust, unless otherwise indicted.

Obviously, partly due to the changeable nature of the subject, this title by no means contains all of the words and phrases used by the Royal Artillery. In order to improve this book I would welcome comments, suggestions, amendments and additions from readers. Please send these to me care of the Publishers: The History Press, The Mill, Brimscombe Port, Stroud, Gloucestershire, GL5 2QG.

Section Headings

The section headings are derived from the various phonetic alphabets used by the British Army since their first introduction in 1904. This first phonetic alphabet only covered the six commonly transposed letters. In 1914, DON was added for the letter 'D'. A full phonetic alphabet was not introduced into the British Army until 1927. A phonetic alphabet standardised across the Allied forces was introduced in June 1943, this was changed to the current NATO phonetic alphabet in March 1956. Each heading therefore consists of the phonetic pronunciations together with the date(s) of the alphabets they appeared in.

Philip Jobson

Foreword

Major General (Retd) J. B. A. Bailey CB MBE PhD

In the accurate application of lethal fire, accuracy of expression is as important as the precision of the data passed. Over the years, as the art and science of artillery and its employment at the operational as well as tactical level has developed, so too has its language.

This language has many parts, some change little but others are dynamic as practitioners keep pace with technical and tactical innovation on the piece, in the command-post, on the staff, in the mess and in the laboratory and factory. Some terms change their meaning, some their spelling, some enter the vernacular (stonk), some migrate from other armies (barrage), and others are adopted, along with new procedures, from the necessity to work with allies (Fire Direction Centre).

The development of indirect fire, counter-battery, anti-tank and anti-aircraft fire all required a novel lexicon as did advances in survey and locating. Changes in communication from shouts, to flags, to line, to radio, to compressed data transmission all left their mark on the language. The migration from 'foot' artillery, the employment of horses, the advent of motorized and armoured transport, let alone airborne and amphibious artillery all added to the language. Categorization at one moment can be misleading at another. Thus, terms such as 'heavy' have no immutable meaning over time. Not surprisingly, the language of calculation and fire orders used at Crécy, Waterloo, Le Cateau, Amiens, on D-Day and on operations today is very different.

What does not change is the human factor which dominates war and the organizations which wage it. Soldiers generate their own language, sometimes slang (full screw), often humorous or cynical, to match the technical dialect imposed upon them. This is even more transient than the authorized version, and strange evolutions can emerge in the small and self-contained communities that constitute military society, whether that be in a single battery or across the various messes.

How could one possibly grasp the enormity and complexity of the artillery lexicon, morphing as it does in so many ways for so many different reasons across the centuries? Philip Jobson has answered with an extraordinary *Glossary of Terms and Abbreviations* for those who need to know, and for those who are just plain curious.

Professions need to maintain a record of their practices and their expression lest this precious instrument of military capability be lost, or worse, misunderstood. Even the most expert Gunner would be likely to fail an unseen test based on this work. It will therefore be a pleasure to those who think themselves expert in some way to browse this volume; but more importantly it will serve as a reference for historians and researchers to ensure that they use the correct term and understand its true meaning.

This work is a labour of love which few would have dared to attempt. It is a triumph of assiduous research for which Gunners will be truly grateful, and a welcome contribution to the literature of the military profession.

Jonathan Bailey
Bratton

Numbers

0 See *Zero.*

0A See *Zero Alpha.*

1st Captain See *First Captain.*

1st Line ammunition See *First Line Ammunition.*

2.95 inch QF See *Millimetre Gun.*

2/Capt Second Captain. A rank between Captain and Lieutenant, it was abolished in 1872.

(2H) See *(H)* (Royal Canadian Artillery).

2IC Second In Command.

2-inch Mortar Introduced to infantry platoons during the 1930s, the 2-inch mortar was also issued to anti-tank batteries in the Second World War to provide smoke and illuminating rounds. Replaced by 51 mm Mortar during the 1980s.

(2L) See *(L).* (Royal Canadian Artillery).

2/Lieut Second Lieutenant.

2/Lt Second Lieutenant.

2nd Captain See *Second Captain.*

2-inch Medium Trench Mortar Not to be confused with the smaller infantry version 2-inch mortar, the 2-inch Medium Trench Mortar was introduced during the First World War. Consisting of a steel tube 2-inch internal diameter mounted upon a wooden base and supported by a bipod fitted with both elevating and traversing gears. As with a normal field gun, elevation was applied by means of a clinometer, whilst laying for line was achieved by using a tall periscopic sight attached to the piece. Regrettably, no details of this sight can be traced. Propellant charges consisted of packets of cordite weighing 1 and 1½ ounces (28 and 44 grams), used to make up charges of 1½, 2½, and 3½ ounces, which gave ranges of 100–220, 180–340, and 300–500 yards respectively. The 2-inch medium mortar was despite its name bigger than the Stokes 3-inch mortar for the simple reason that the Stokes was measured by the size of the bomb whilst the 2-inch was measured by the size of the 'stick' that went into the weapon. The much bigger bomb stayed on the outside. The bomb itself consisted of a spherical iron container filled with amatol or ammonal attached to a piece of pipe known as the 'stick' which fitted into the bore of the mortar, while the bomb sat on the muzzle. The total weight of the projectile was 60 lbs (27 kg) and it could be fitted with either a time or a simple percussion fuse. To load, the required packets of cordite were dropped down the barrel, the 'stick' of the bomb was inserted in the bore, and the detachment took cover. Ignition was achieved by means of a 'T' friction tube inserted into a vent at the breech or by a rifle mechanism firing a blank screwed into it. The Detachment fired the mortar with a long lanyard due to the fact that occasionally the packets of cordite did not burn completely and the bomb fell short, occasionally dangerously short!

Detachments were provided by personnel seconded from 18-pounder batteries, and used mainly for cutting barbed-wire entanglements. For transportation, the mortars could be moved over short distances using frames with perambulator wheels whilst for longer distances MT vehicles were used. See *3-inch Stokes Trench Mortar.*

2-pdr Anti-Tank Gun See *Ordnance QF 2-pounder.*

2-pounder Anti-Tank Gun See *Ordnance QF 2-pounder.*

3-inch Mortar Infantry weapon in service from the 1930s to the 1960s. During the Second World War it equipped mortar and anti-tank (as an alternative weapon) batteries in Burma. Replaced by 81 mm L16 Mortar.

3-inch Stokes Trench Mortar Developed during the First World War by Sir Wilfred Scott-Stokes, the Stokes Trench Mortar comprised a barrel, which was supported by a bipod and sat on a base plate. The mortar was fired by dropping an 11 lb shell down the tube onto a firing pin at the base of the tube. The action of dropping the bomb onto the firing pin activated a shotgun-like blank cartridge which in turn ignited propellant rings attached to the mortar shell. The range could be adjusted by changing the angle of the bipod.

Barrel	Length: 51 in
	Diameter: 3 in
	Weight: 43 lbs
Bipod	Weight: 37 lbs
Baseplate	Weight: 28 lbs
Range	Maximum: 800 yards
	Safe Minimum Distance: 100 yards

By 1918 each British division possessed 24 light Stokes mortars, 12 medium and several heavy models.

3.7-Inch QF AA Gun Entering front line service in 1937, the 3.7-inch AA gun remained in service with the Royal Artillery until replaced by guided missiles in the late 1950s. Both static and mobile versions of the 3.7-inch saw service with the Royal Artillery. The mobile mounting employed a cruciform set of legs for stability when deployed. In order to move, these legs were folded in and a pair of road wheels lowered to the ground. The gun towing vehicle used with the 3.7-inch was the AEC Matador.

Four production 'Marks' of the 3.7-inch existed, the first three having only slight differences, whilst the fourth variant had a longer barrel and utilised a different mounting. During its service life, the main improvements were the introduction of an automatic fuze-setter and an automatic loader. These improvements led to an increase in the rate of fire and the elimination of variation in loading speed and fuzes settings. The automatic fuze-setter and automatic loader also meant that the gun worked better with predictor data.

Whilst capable of operating in the anti-tank role, this was not considered to be a common role for this piece of ordnance owing to a number of factors. One reason for this was organisational, in that heavy AA regiments equipped with the 3.7-inch gun were controlled by either corps or Army Headquarters, or at even higher level HQs, and command of them was rarely devolved to the commanders at divisional levels.

Perhaps more importantly, the 3.7-inch gun mobile mounting was almost twice as heavy as the German '88', resulting in redeployment being a slower operation whilst the heavy AEC Matador gun tower could only operate on roads or hard surfaces.

The most significant reason for not employing it in the anti-tank role was probably the fact that prolonged firing at low elevations (which had not formed part of the original specification) caused unacceptable strain on the mounting and recuperating gear.

The variants comprised:

Mk I The original 3.7-inch HAA gun.

Mk II This varied slightly from the Mk I in the method by which the breech and barrel were built up. Manufactured in the UK by Vickers-Armstrong until 1943 when production was taken on by Canada as the 3.7-Inch AA Mark II C

Mk III This was a combination of a Mk I breech with a Mk III barrel. As with the Mk II it was built by Vickers-Armstrong but only in limited numbers.

Mk IV This was a prototype development of the 3.7 using the Naval QF 4.5-inch Mark V gun with a liner to allow the use a 4.5-inch shell cartridge case to drive the 3.7-inch shell. The project was dropped in favour of the Mk VI.

Mk V A further prototype developed at the same time as the Mk IV and using the same principle. It too was dropped in favour of the Mk VI.

Mk VI The final version of the 3.7-inch QF AA Gun employing a Naval 5.25-inch mount and a longer 3.7-inch barrel as a starting point. Its barrel differed from the usual 3.7-inch QF AA barrel in that over the last five calibres of the barrel before the muzzle, the rifling gradually disappeared. This has the effect of smoothing the driving bands of the shell flush, which in turn had the effect of providing superior aerodynamic shape and hence better ballistic performance. This type of rifling had been developed at the Royal Arsenal, by Colonel Probert. The ceiling for the gun was somewhere around 18,000 metres.

Due to the heavy 4.5-inch carriage, a towed version was too expensive to develop and they were deployed as static emplacements only. They were part of the UK's air defence in 1944 and were kept until 1959.

Specifications
Place of origin: UK
In service: 1937–1959
Weight: 20,541 lb (9,317 kg)
Length: 4.96 m
Barrel length: L50 185 in (4.7 m)
Detachment: 7
Shell: 28 lb (12.7 kg)
Calibre: 3.7 inches (94 mm)
Carriage: Mobile and static versions existed.
Rate of fire: Between 10 and 20 rpm
Muzzle velocity: 792 m/s
Maximum ranges:
Horizontal: 18,800 m

Slant range: 12,000 m
Ceiling: 9,000 m

4.2-inch Mortar Introduced in 1942, initially for Royal Engineers chemical warfare companies, it was later transferred to heavy mortar companies in infantry divisional machine-gun battalions. Post Second World War light regiments RA were equipped with the 4.2-inch Mortar until about 1960. It was last used by the Royal Artiullery in Borneo in 1966 by a section provided by the Kuching based Air Defence bty, drawn from 22 Lt AD Regt.

18/25-pounder See *Ordnance QF 25 Pounder.*

25-pdr See *Ordnance QF 25 pounder.*

25-pounder See *Ordnance QF 25 pounder.*

25/17-pounder See *Pheasant.*

100 percent zone See *Zone of the Gun.*

105-mm Abbot See *105-mm Field.*

105-mm Field The name given to a range of ammunition developed for use with the Gun QF L13 which was mounted on the Abbot self-propelled gun. The name was used to to distinguish it from the US 105-mm Howitzer M1 ammunition family then in service.

In the 105-mm field system, cartridge and shell are loaded separately with the primer being initiated electrically. The system comprises two marks of ammunition, the Mk I was used for the initial year's training while war stocks of Mk II were produced. The Mk I used high explosive and white phosphorus shells of the United States M1 design (L33 and L32) with reduced charges (L32 cartridge charges 1–4, L34 cartridge charge Super); thus giving a reduced maximum range of 15 kilometres. The Mk II ammunition uses L35 cartridge charges 1–5 (although Charge 5 has a separate 5th increment attached to the top of the cartridge case) and L36 cartridge charge Super which gives a maximum range of 17.4 kilometres. Initially, there were two sub-zones A and B (L1 cartridge), which were used to provide short range high angle fire. The L1 cartridge was however soon replaced by plastic spoilers fitted over the shell nose and used with charges 1 and 2. The L31 HE shell which is used with Mk II is 7% heavier and contains 20% more HE than the previously used US M1 shell design. Other shells in the family are the L43 illuminating, L36 Base Ejection white smoke, and the L37 (red) and L38 (orange) bursting coloured marker shells of the types originally designed for use with the 25-pdr. There is also a HESH round for direct anti-tank fire. The 105-mm L118 light gun uses the Mark 2 ammunition, but due to its slightly shorter barrel it achieves slightly less range. There is also a ½ charge increment for Charge 4 for use with the L118 to improve charge range overlap in high angle fire. 105-mm field cartridges are delivered in plastic containers, whilst fuzed shells are delivered in paperboard tubes, with either two cartridges or two fuzed shells being contained in a steel box. Due to being introduced for use with the Abbot self-propelled gun, the family is sometimes unofficially referred to as the 105-mm Abbot. See *Abbot* and *L118 Light Gun.*

105 mm L5 Pack How See *105mm Pack Howitzer (L5).*

105 mm Pack Howitzer (L5) No longer in service, the 105 mm Pack Howitzer served with the parachute and commando regiments of the Royal Artillery.

Equipment weight: 1308 kg.
Traverse Limits: 498 mils left and right (in low position with three leg sections)

Elevation Limits: Minus 89 mils to 1155 mils (in low position with three leg sections and with recoil pit).
Equipment positions:
(i) High – wheels narrow and with 2 or 3 leg sections.
(ii) Low – wheels wide and 3 leg sections.
Detachment: 7 (a sergeant detachment commander), bombardier (2IC), two layers (one for line and one for elevation) and three ammunition numbers).
Time into action: 2–3 minutes
Maximum range: 10000 m
Rates of fire:
(i) Burst for 1 minute – 6 rpm
(ii) Burst for 3 minutes – 5 rpm
(iii) Sustained – 3 rpm
Ammunition: Semi-fixed (hand rammed with fist)
(i) HE
(ii) HESH
(iii) Smoke (BE and WP)
(iv) Illuminating
Lethal frontage: 35 m
Ammunition supply – Carried on towing and ammunition vehicles, could be supplied on pallets as helicopter underslung loads.

155 mm SP, M40 — See *M40*.

180 Degree Throw-off Shoot — A form of anti-aircraft training used prior to the introduction of simulators, whereby the guns were 180 degrees (3200 mils) out of phase with the target. Thus if the target aircraft was being tracked by the battery instruments whilst flying to the north, the guns would in fact be pointing and shooting to the south. Both the target and the shell bursts could be seen superimposed simultaneously on a screen, as though the guns were in actual fact shooting at the target aircraft. This meant that the target aircraft, rather than sedately towing a target sleeve, could operate at operational speeds, climb and alter course as it would if it was actually being fired on.

50 Miserable — Derogatory nickname of 50 Missile Regiment RA

50 percent zone — See *Zone of the Gun*.

50 Tracksuit Regiment — Nickname of 50 Missile Regiment RA, who were known for their sporting achievements.

60-pounder Medium Gun — A medium 5-inch gun designed in 1904. It was the mainstay of British medium artillery during the First World War, being operated by batteries of the Royal Garrison Artillery and employed principally in the counter-battery role. It was capable of firing a 60 lb (27.3 kg) shell to a maximum range of 10,300 yards (9.4 km). Weighing 4.4 tonnes, the 60-pounder required a gun team of 12 horses to move it. The Mark II which came into service during 1918 had a new carriage and breech which effectively added another tonne to the gun's weight resulting in it no longer being capable of being drawn by horses, and from then onwards it had to be towed by a caterpillar tractor. The gun was one of only two types that could be carried by the Gun Carrier Mark I. The gun remained in use with the British Army until 1944. It last saw combat action in the Western Desert.
60-Pounder MK II Specifications
In service: 1918 – 1944
Weight: 5,400 kg
Barrel length: 37 Calibres

	Shell: HE Calibre: 127 mm Carriage: Wheeled, fixed trail Muzzle velocity: 648 m per second Effective range: 15 km
70 km Snipers	See *Seventy Kilometre Snipers*.
75mm Pack Howitzer	This American designed howitzer replaced the 3.7-inch Pack Howitzer, entering service with the 1st Airlanding Light Regiment RA in February 1943. Whilst capable of being parachuted into action (in nine separate sections), the preferred method of deployment was by Horsa glider. This allowed the howitzer to be delivered fully assembled and ready for immediate action. It required two Horsa gliders to deliver each gun detachment and its equipment. Typically, one glider would carry the howitzer, its jeep tower and an ammunition trailer, together with the number one and three members of the detachment. The second glider carried the remainder of the detachment, a second jeep and two ammunition trailers. The ammunition trailers carried a total of 137 rounds, made up of 125 high-explosive, 6 armour piercing and 6 smoke rounds. 1st Airlanding Light Regiment RA had a complement of 24 75 mm pack howitzers. Manufacturer: US Ordnance Dept Calibre: 75 mm Length: 12′ 0″ Width: 3′ 11″ Height: 2′ 10″ Weight: 1339 lbs Elevation: -5° to +45° Range: 9,760 yards Rate of Fire : 3–6 rounds per minute One of 1st Airlanding Regiment RAs' Pack Howitzers that was used at Arnhem can be seen at Firepower, The Royal Artillery Museum.
570 USAAG	570th United States Army Artillery Group. The United States Army unit that commanded all custodial detachments assigned to UK regiments and had custodial responsibility for reserve nuclear weapons assigned to 1 (BR) Corps. Supported by the Weapons Support Group. See *Weapons Support Group*.
1098	See *G1098*.
1151	The first four digits of a seven digit number issued to RA Boys at Woolwich during the period 1940–48 and prior to their moving to Rhyl (1948–1950) as Boys Battery. Numbers also started with 1157. The term is currently used to identify those who served as Boys during this period. See *1157*.
1157	See *AF 1157*. (ii) The first four digits of a seven digit number issued to RA Boys at Woolwich during the period 1940–48 and prior to their moving to Rhyl (1948–1950) as Boys Battery. Numbers also started with 1151. The term is currently used to identify those who served as Boys during this period. See *1151*.
90210 Battery	Derogatory nickname for 4/73 (Sphinx) Special Observation Post Battery RA.

A – Ack – 1904/1927
Able – 1943
Alpha – 1956

A	Add.
A	A First World War artillery abbreviation for 18-pounder shrapnel shell. The abbreviation was used in ammunition returns.
A Column	Ammunition Column.
A1 Echelon	Usually referred to as the Ammunition Control Point.
A13	See *Station Radio A13.*
A14	See *Station Radio A14.*
A41	See *Station Radio A41.*
A42	See *Station Radio A42.*
A43R	See *Station Radio A43R.*
A&ER	Ammunition and Explosive Regulation.
A&S Wagon RA	Ammunition and Store Wagon RA.
A&T	Assembly and Test.
AA	(i) Anti-Aircraft. (ii) Air Assault – used as part of a battery title, for example 21 (Gibraltar 1779-83) AA Battery. (iii) Avenue of Approach. (iv) Artillery code used during the First World War meaning 'Anti-aircraft guns'.
AAA	Air Avenue of Approach.
AAAD	All Arms Air Defence.
AAC	Army Air Corps.
AACC	(i) All Arms Commando Course. (ii) Army Air Control Centre.
AAD	Area Air Defence.
AADC	Anti-Aircraft Defence Commander.
AAdjt	Assistant Adjutant.
AADSC	Advance Air Defence Siting Computer.
AAES	Anti-Aircraft Experimental Section.
AALMG	Anti-Aircraft Light Machine Gun. (Second World War).
AALO	Anti-Aircraft Liaison Officer. (Second World War).
AAMG	Anti-Aircraft Machine Gun. (Second World War).
AAMTE	Anti-aircraft Mobilization Training Centre.
AAOD	Anti-Aircraft Ordnance Depot. See *EAM* and *IAD*.
AAOR	Anti-Aircraft Operations Room. (Second World War).
AAP	Allied Agreed Publication.
AAPPS	All Arms Pre-Parachute Selection.
AAR	After Action Review.
AASL	Anti-Aircraft Searchlight. (Second World War).
AASV	Assembly Area Support Vehicle.
AAT	Annual Alert Test.
AATE	Anti-aircraft Training Establishment.
AATTC	All Arms Tactical Targeting Course.
AAvn	Army Aviation.
AAW	Anti-Air Warfare.
AAWC	Anti-Air Warfare Commander.
AB 545	Army Book 545.
AB 548	See *Target Record Book.*
ABA	Amphibious Bombardment Association.
Abbot	Country of Origin: UK In Service: 1965 Type: Self-propelled Artillery Engine: Rolls Royce K60 Mk 4G 6-cylinder MF 6.57 litre; 240bhp at 3,750rpm Internal Fuel Capacity: 386 litres Speed: 48 kph

	Range: 390 km. Length: 5.709 m; 5.84 m with gun forward Width: 2.641 m Height: 2.489 m (with AA Machine Gun) Empty weight: 14,878 kg Combat weight: 16,556 kg Primary Gun Armament: 1x105 mm L13A1 Secondary Gun Armament: 1x7.62 mm machine-gun on the commander's cupola. Other Armaments: Three smoke dischargers on each side of turret. Ammunition Carried: 40 x 105 mm with six normally being anti-tank rounds; 1,200 x 7.62 mm rounds. Main Turret traverse horizontal: 360° Main gun traverse vertical: -5° to 70° Armour: 6–12 mm Detachment: 4 NBC protected Infra-red driving lights Maximum rate of fire was 12 rpm for short periods. Replaced by the M109 Self-Propelled Gun. Abbot was the field artillery component of the FV432 family of vehicles.
ABCA	American, British Canadian and Australian Standardisation Program.
ABEX	Airborne Exercise.
ABFAC	Airborne Forward Air Controller.
Abnormal (Non-Standard) Projectile Correction	A correction, normally common to all guns of a troop which compensates for differences in drift from the standard caused by the employment of a non-standard projectile. Sometimes referred to as a Non-Standard Projectile Correction.
Abnormal Projectile Correction	See *Abnormal (Non-Standard) Projectile Correction.*
ABR	Air Burst Ranging.
ABRO	Army Base Repair Organisation.
Abu Klea	Battery Honour Title of 176 (Abu Klea) Battery RA which was granted on 22 Jun 1955 under authority of 20/ARTY/6271/AG6a. See *Battery Honour Titles.*
Abu's	Nickname given to members of 176 (Abu Klea) Battery.
AC	(i) Army Code (Publications). (ii) Ammunition Column (First World War). See *Ammunition Column, BAC* and *DAC.* (iii) Adjusted Charge.
ACA	(i) Airspace Control Authority. (ii) Azimuth Crab Angle. (iii) Ammunition Container Assembly.
ACBO	(i) Assistant Counter Battery Officer. (ii) Assistant Counter Bombardment Officer.
ACC	(i) Air Component Commander. (ii) Airspace Control Cell.
ACCE	Air Component Coordination Element.
ACCT	Artillery Centre Canoe Team.
Accuracy	A measure of the precision with which the mean point of impact of a group of rounds can be placed on a target. If the mean point of impact is near the target, the accuracy is said to be good or the error in accuracy on that occasion is said to be small. Conversely, if the mean point of impact is far from the target, the accuracy is said to be poor or the error in accuracy is on that occasion said to be large.
ACE	(i) Army Certificate of Education. (ii) Allied Command Europe.

Achilles	Second World War self-propelled anti-tank gun, in service 1944–1950. Based on an American M10 self-propelled mounting, but with the original 76 mm gun replaced with the more powerful British 17-pdr mounted in a turret giving 360° traverse.
ACI	Army Council Instruction. Generally followed by the number identifying the relevant instruction.
Ack	(i) Assistant (as in OP Ack) derived from the original phonetic alphabet for A. (ii) Acknowledge communication on a radio net.
Ack-Ack	Anti-Aircraft.
Ack Ack Command	Formed on 1st April 1939, Ack-Ack Command, with General Sir Frederick Pile as General Officer Commanding, consisted of seven anti-aircraft divisions by the start of the Second World War. The Command was responsible for all aspects of the ground war against the Luftwaffe using heavy guns, light guns, rockets and searchlights. At its strongest, Ack Ack Command had over 350,000 personnel from the Royal Artillery, Royal Engineers, Auxiliary Territorial Service, Royal Marines and the Home Guard under command.
Ack-Adjt	Assistant Adjutant.
Ack IG	Assistant Instructor-in-Gunnery (now known as a SMIG or sergeant-major instructor-in-gunnery).
Ack I Sigs	Assistant Instructor Signals.
ACL	Apparatus Cable Laying.
ACLOS	Automatic Command Line of Sight. A missile guidance system.
ACM	Airspace Control Measures. An Air Defence term.
ACMB	Anti-Coastal Motor Boat. See *Anti-Motor Torpedo Boat.*
ACMO	Assistant Counter Mortar Officer (Second World War).
ACMR	Airspace Control Means Request.
ACO	(i) Airspace Control Order. (ii) Airspace Coordination Order.
ACOP	Approved Code of Practice.
Acorn	Radio appointment title. This title was used army-wide by the intelligence staff officer, however, in the Royal Artillery the following officers used the title. At HQRA level by the intelligence officer. At a regimental headquarters level by the intelligence officer. At battery level by the assistant command post officer. See *Appointment Titles.*
Acorn Gunners	Nickname by which 107 RHA (South Nottinghamshire Hussars Yeomanry)(TA) and 150 (South Nottinghamshire Hussars Yeomanry) Field Regiment RA (TA) were known due to the fact that they retained their original South Nottinghamshire Hussars cap badge instead of using the Royal Artillery one.
ACP	(i) Ammunition Control Point. (ii) Airspace Control Plan.
ACPO	Assistant Command Post Officer.
ACS	(i) Artillery Command Systems. (ii) Airspace Control System.
ACSAS	Army Command Support Application Suite.
ACSC	Army Command and Staff Course.
Action	(i) Guns are said to be 'in action' when they are in position and ready to fire, but not necessarily firing. (ii) An executive order given by the observation post to guns on the move, indicating that immediate fire support is required. On receipt of 'action', the gun position officer immediately deploys his/her guns in the nearest available

position. The gun position officer will lay the first gun into action on the appropriate centre of arc and open fire, leaving the troop leader to bring the remaining guns onto the centre of arc. See *Centre of Arc.*

Action Front — The order to bring guns 'into action' facing in the direction of advance. See *Action, Action Left, Action Rear* and *Action Right.*

Action Left — The order to bring guns 'into action' facing to the left of the direction of advance. See *Action, Action Front, Action Rear* and *Action Right.*

Action Rear — The order to bring guns 'into action' facing the opposite direction to the direction of advance. See *Action, Action Front, Action Left* and *Action Right.*

Action Right — The order to bring guns 'into action' facing to the right of the direction of advance. See *Action, Action Front, Action Left* and *Action Rear.*

ACV — Armoured Command Vehicle.

AD — Air Defence.

AD4 — Army tactical control radar. Used by light air defence units. The radar was not air portable. An S band radar with a range of 75 miles (121 km).

AD10 — The Ferranti Firelight coherent continuous wave radar used with the Thunderbird II Heavy Air Defence missile system. See *Thunderbird.*

AD11 — AMES Type 88. The surveillance element of the Thunderbird II Air Defence missile system. Air portable and known to troops as 'Big Ears'. See *Thunderbird.*

AD12 — Height finding element of the Thunderbird II Air Defence missile system. Air portable and known to troops as 'Noddy'. See *Thunderbird.*

ADA — Air Defended Area.

ADAC — Army Department Ammunition Code.

AD-ACA — Limit Between Divisional Artillery and Corps Artillery (FSCM).

ADAD — Air Defence Alerting Device.

ADC — Air Defence Commander.

ADCIS — Air Defence Command and Information System.

Add — A correction which is used by an observer to indicate that an increase in range along the observer target line is required.

ADDER — Artillery detection device for rapid effect forces.

Additional Gunners — During the eighteenth century, these were infantrymen, drawn from the supported infantry battalion, who were specially trained to work with the battalion gun detachments. They usually performed the role of the higher gun numbers and were employed in running up the carriage after firing and in hauling on the drag ropes. See *Battalion Guns.*

Additionals — See *Additional Gunners.*

Aden Troop — (i) Together with Gazala Troop, Hook Troop and Martinique Troop, one of the four troops in 74 Battery (The Battle Axe Company) Royal Artillery.

(ii) Originally one of the troops in 3rd Squadron Honourable Artillery Company, after 1994 transferred to Signal Squadron with Cassino Troop and Somme Troop. See See *Cassino Troop, Gaza Troop, Honourable Artillery Company, Rhine Troop, Somme Troop and South Africa Troop.*

ADEX — Air Defence Exercise.

AD-EXJAM — Artillery Delivered Expendable Jammers.

Ad Fines — Artillery range at Redesdale in Northumberland.

ADF(TF) — Air Defence Formation (Territorial Army).

ADGB — Air Defence of Great Britain.

ADGE	Air Defence Ground Environment.
Adj	(i) Adjust. (ii) Adjustment.
Adj FIRE	Adjust Fire.
Adjt	Adjutant.
Adjust	Adjusting fire is the process by which artillery rounds are corrected onto the target by observing the fall of shot. The initial round will be fired either from map data or from an estimation made by the OP. Once the initial fall of shot is observed, subsequent rounds are 'adjusted' until they are hitting the target, when 'Fire For Effect' will be given.
Adjust Fire	(i) A command or request to initiate the process of adjustment. (ii) A method of control transmitted in the call for fire by the observer to indicate that he will be controlling the adjustment.
Adjusting	See *Adjust* and *Ranging*.
Adjustment	The process used in artillery and naval gunfire support to obtain correct bearing, range and height of burst (if time fuzes are being used) when engaging a target by observed fire.
Adjustment for Future Engagement	See *Registration.*
Adjustment to Range for False Angle of Sight	An adjustment which enabled the Command Post to the range to the target if the correct Angle of Sight had been applied during registration. It was only really of any use when used with recorded targets.
Adjutant	The commanding officer's staff officer. In action the Adjutant is responsible, under the supervision of the second-in-command, for the organization and control of the regimental command post. Other duties include, the allocation of the guns of the regiment in response to calls for fire, the preparation of operation and movement orders, compilation of routine ammunition returns, the preparation of routine orders, reports and returns and in the absence of the intelligence officer, intelligence duties. See *Assistant Adjutant.*
ADLO	Air Defence Liaison Officer.
ADLT	Air Defence Liaison Team.
Adm	Administration.
ADM	Atomic Demolition Munition.
Admin	Administration.
Administrative Detachment RA	This unit, later known as the Administrative Wing RA, was based at Shoeburyness, Essex. It included a small mounted detachment who, using wagons similar to the Wagon GS, were responsible, at low tide, for the recovery of spent shells on Maplin Sands. The mounted detachment continued to perform this function until 1957, when after 108 years service, they were replaced by DUKWs.
Administrative Wing RA	See *Administrative Detachment RA*.
ADOLT	Air Defence Operations Liaison Team.
ADOS	Assistant Director of Ordnance Services.
ADP	(i) Army Doctrine Publication. (ii) Automatic Data Processing.
ADRA	Administrative Detachment Royal Artillery.
ADRM	Air Defence Range Manorbier.
ADS	Advanced Dressing Station.
ADT3	Air Defence Tactical Training Theatre.
Adv	Advanced. Used in relation to courses, as in OPA (Adv) – Observation Post Assistant (Advanced).

Advance Air Defence Siting Computer	A software application which has been designed to provide ground based air defence battery and troop command posts with a deployment planning tool capable of operating on a normal laptop computer via the Windows operating system. The AADSC gives operators the ability to conduct GBAD co-ordination for static tasks and the ability to import and display the Airspace Coordination Order data graphically by utilising an Airspace Coordination Order translator. The system also supports digital mapping, with the ability to create boundaries, edit location data together with an optimising GBAD site capability. See *Ground Based Air Defence*.
Advanced Observation Post	Used as part of the sound ranging organisation. See *Advanced Post* and *Long Base*
Advanced Post	A listening post comprising an NCO and six men, part of the sound ranging organisation. See *Advanced Observation Post*.
Advanced Sound Ranging Programme	A portable, passive, acoustic sensing system for detecting and locating the source of artillery fire and loud detonations. Once the system is fully deployed, the microphones at the sensor post are able to detect any acoustic disturbance caused by gunfire. The sensor posts are accurately surveyed in, and connected by RAVEN radio or D10 wire to the command post which is manned by a crew of four who in turn control the four microphone crews consisting of three to four soldiers. Detachment: 6 Detection Range: Greater than 15 km Accuracy: 50 m. Circular Error Probable at 15 kilometres Time into Action: 15 minutes *See Sound Ranging.*
AEC	Army Education Centre.
A/ECAs	Azimuth and Elevation Crab Angles.
A Echelon	See *Echelon*.
AEC Matador	A 4 x 4 medium artillery tractor powered by a diesel engine and fitted with a winch and a wooden body. The body consisted of a flat floor with doors at the front and a tailgate at the rear. Two forward facing wooden benches were fixed across the front of the body. A folding seat was fitted at the nearside of each row. Each row was capable of seating four men. If necessary, two additional seats could be fitted to the rear corners of the body. A ten rifle rack and a spare wheel carrier were fitted on the offside. Artillery shells were stowed in the centre of the body, whilst charges in boxes were located on either side and fuzes were carried under the rear seats. Racks for the detachments kit were located along each side under the roof. Early versions of the Matador had a metal roof, but this was later replaced by canvas. In both cases the sides consisted of canvas panels which could be rolled up and which had translucent panels in them. A hatch was provided over the cab for use by the anti-aircraft look out.
AEP	Army Equipment Policy.
AER	Ammunition and Explosive Regulation.
AES	Armoured Escort Services – A Northern Ireland procedure.
AESP	Army Equipment Support Publication.
AF	Army Form. This abbreviation would be followed by the relevant form number.

AF 1157 — Soldiers Kit list held by the Quartermaster which details all personal items of clothing and equipment issued to the soldier.

AFA — (i) Army Field Artillery. (First World War).
(ii) Australian Field Artillery. (First World War) (Royal Australian Artillery).

AFB 7111 — See *Bearing Picket Card.*

AFCT(PT) — Artillery Fire Control Trainer (Part Task).

AFDC — Artillery Fire Data Computer.

Affiliation — The normal relationship of direct support artillery with its supported arm. For example a battery with an infantry battalion/armoured regiment or a regiment with an infantry/armoured brigade.

Affix — A number which was added to a battery or regimental radio call sign to identify the role of the user. This system is no longer in use. Examples of affixes given in 'Artillery Training Volume II – Handling of Units in the Field – Pamphlet 1 – Field Artillery Branch – 1948' are listed here:

<u>Regimental Headquarters Affixes</u>

1 – Commanding Officer
2 – Second in Command
3 – Adjutant
4 – Intelligence Officer
5 – Survey Officer
6 – Air Observation Post
7 – Signals Officer
8 – Technical Adjutant
9 – REME
10 – Quarter master

Battery Affixes	P	Q	R
Battery Commanders	21	41	61
Battery Captain	22	42	62
Command Post Officer	23	43	63
Assistant CPO	24	44	64

Troop Affixes	A	B	C	D	E	F
Troop Commander	25	35	45	55	65	75
Troop GPO	26	36	46	56	66	76
Troop Leader	27	37	47	57	67	77

See *Link-Sign.*

AFM — Army Field Manual.

AFSOP — Army Formation Standard Operating Procedures.

AFTC — Army Field Training Centre.

AFV — Armoured Fighting Vehicle.

AG6 — The department which dealt with RA administrative matters at the War Office.

AGA — Australian Garrison Artillery.

AGAA — Artillery Group Administration Area. (Op Granby).

AGAI — Army General Administrative Instruction.

AGL — Above Ground Level.

AGLS — Automatic Gun Laying System.

AGM — Attack Guidance Matrix.

AGRA — Army Group Royal Artillery.

AGRA (AA) — Army Group Royal Artillery (Anti-Aircraft). See *Army Group Royal Artillery.*

AGRA (Fd) — Army Group Royal Artillery (Field). See *Army Group Royal Artillery.*

AGRA Trickle — The rapid movement of small numbers of vehicles, belonging to an AGRA, along a road jammed with traffic, without inconveniencing anyone. See *Army Group Royal Artillery.*

Agreed Point Method — This Second World War Arty/R shoot, was based on the assumption that all targets would be pre-arranged to a greater or lesser degree. The agreed point was, if its location was accurately known, the target, or if not, either a prominent feature within the area to be searched or the centre of the area, if no such feature existed. The initial salvo was fired onto the agreed point and the pilot of the Arty/R aircraft corrected the fire of the ranging troop onto the target. The system did not allow for impromptu shoots but was regarded as highly practical, especially if vertical photographs were available prior to the mission so that pilots could be briefed on target locations and identification. See *Artillery Reconnaissance.*

AH	Attack Helicopter.
Ahmed Khel Day	Battery day of F (Sphinx) Parachute Battery RHA.
AI	(i) Air Interdiction. (ii) Area of Interest.
AIG	Assistant Instructor Gunnery. (colloquially known as an Ack IG, pronounced Ack Eye-Gee).
AILO	Air Intelligence Liaison Officer. In use early in the Second World War.
Aiming Point	There are two types of aiming point, namely: Battery Aiming Points and Gun Aiming Points. A Battery Aiming Point is one selected by the gun position officer. All guns are laid on their original lines by means of an angle taken from the aiming point. A Battery Aiming Point could be a visible point on the landscape or a suitably placed director. Gun Aiming Points, originally referred to as Auxiliary Aiming Points, in contrast, are selected by the No. 1 of the gun for use after the gun has been laid on its original line. Where possible, a distant object, (the greater the distance, the better) is selected for a Gun Aiming Point. It can be a topographical feature or an 'artificial' one, such as the guns own aiming posts. Other examples of artificial aiming points include (i) a night picket or (ii) a parallelescope for each gun. See *Director, Night Picket* and *Parallelescope.*
Aiming Posts	Used to provide an aiming point for the guns when using indirect fire. They were used by each gun to compensate for the movement of the dial sight when the gun traversed or moved back ('bedded-in') during firing. They were used in pairs, the posts being planted at about 50 and 100 yards from the gun. Initially the posts were planted in line with the dial sight, as the sight moved a gap appeared between the two posts when viewed through the sight, the layer then looked for the pair of numbers on the cross bars that were closest and layed on the rear one. During the Second World War aiming posts were painted black and white, rather like a belisha beacon, and to reduce the scope for mistakes between guns in each section one gun had posts with circular tops the other with square tops. In the early twentieth century a battery commander would carry a special less cumbersome pattern of aiming posts in a saddle bucket.
Aiming Rifle	A 1-inch calibre rifle used by coast artillery for practice shoots in place of the main armament.
AINC	Accident and Incident Notification Cell.
AIO	Artillery Intelligence Operator.
Air	Air Force aircraft as opposed to Army Air Corps Helicopters.
AIR	Atmospheric Instrumentation Research.
Airborne Support Net	Developed initially by 1st Forward Observer Unit RA (Airborne) during the Second World War for use by

Airborne Observation Post parties, this was the main radio net which linked the various OP's with a control station and with rear links to the supported brigades, HQRA and liaison officers with the various supported regiments. Eventually, all Forward Observer Units RA (Airborne) adopted the same format of radio net. See *Forward Observer Unit RA (Airborne).*

Airburst
(i) Shells are fuzed, with either time or proximty fuzes, to explode above the target, thus causing shell fragments to be driven downwards to penetrate vertical cover, which would otherwise offer protection from ground bursts.
(ii) Airburst can also be used to verify the accuracy of the gun or to determine any corrections which may be required due to meteorological conditions. By using survey equipment the exact point of burst can be determined and comparison with the expected point of burst will allow suitable corrections to be made to the gun data.

Air Defence Alerting Device
A passive air defence alerting designed to work in conjunction with the HVM missile system. Operating as an infra red search and tracking system in the 8–14 micron waveband, it is designed to operate against low and fast moving fixed wing aircraft, as well as the latest generation of attack helicopters. The SP HVM has ADAD mounted on the Stormer vehicle, whereas the HVM LML detachments operate with the free standing version. See *HVM, Javelin* and *Stormer*.

Air Defence Command Information System
A computer system that permits AD command posts to carry out their procedures faster. When combined with the Clansman radio network, it is possible to have secure text communications between CPs and detachments. See *Clansman*.

Air Defence Formation (Territorial Army)
Formed in the 1920s to man the air defences of the London area, together with its searchlight belt. Commanded by a major-general, it worked under the operational control of the Air Defence of Great Britain RAF. It was converted into 1st Anti-Aircraft Division in the late 1930s.

Air Defence of Great Britain
Formed in 1925 as a Command of the Royal Air Force. It was replaced by Fighter Command in July 1936. However, in late 1943, Fighter Command ceased to exist, with much of its strength being transferred to 2nd Tactical Air Force. The units remaining adopted the old title of ADGB. None of these changes affected AA Command's position of being operationally part of a RAF Command. AA Command was always responsible for the recruitment, equipment and training of its own personnel.

Air Manoeuvre Training and Advisory Team
Part of the Joint Helicopter Command this team works directly with 16 Air Assault Brigade to give professional advice and guidance on air manoeuvre and attack aviation in the joint environment.

Air Observation Post
These units were squadrons in the Royal Air Force, although the pilots were all regular Royal Artillery officers. The ground crew were supplied by both the RAF and the Royal Artillery. The two RAF officers in a squadron fulfilled the roles of adjutant and equipment officer. RAF personnel provided the fitters, riggers, etc, whilst the Royal Artillery provided personnel to

maintain radio equipment and operate ground radio stations in addition to maintaining the unit's transport. The AOP role consisted of observing artillery fire, reporting information from ground observation, undertaking photographic aerial reconnaissance and taking senior officers on flights over sector fronts prior to future planned operations. AOP Squadrons were under the command of the Commander Corps Royal Artillery (CCRA), each AOP flight within the squadron was affiliated to an infantry or armoured division in the corps or theatre. Flights were under the command of the Commander Royal Artillery (CRA). Each flight was further divided into AOP sections with each section consisting of one Auster aircraft and pilot, one jeep and a 3-ton lorry. Personnel consisted of a driver-batman and a driver operator to look after the section commander, the vehicles and the wireless sets. An RAF engine mechanic and RAF air-frame mechanic were responsible for looking after the aircraft. Each RHA and field regiment (and where possible each medium and heavy regiment) had its own affiliated AOP section. The section could be placed under the command of the affiliated regimental commander. Following the Second World War, AOP squadrons were composed of a squadron headquarters and a varying number of self-contained flights, of either Type A or Type B. Type A flights performed normal AOP duties, whilst Type B flights were especially equipped for aerial photography missions.

Air OP — Air Observation Post.

Air-Photo Interpretation Section — From 1944 this section was part of the Counter-Bombardment organisation.

Air Route — An Airspace Control Measure/Air Defence term.

Air Troop — During the mid-1960s many RA and RHA regiments had their own air troop of 3 Bell Sioux observation helicopters which were employed in the air observation post and liaison roles. Pilots were either gunner officers or NCOs of at least acting sergeant rank. The technical ground crew, who provided first line servicing at the landing site, were provided by REME personnel and comprised an aircraft artificer (staff-sergeant or warrant officer) and from four to six aircraft technicians, (lance corporal to sergeant). The non-technical ground crew provided aircraft-crewmen, and driver-radio-operators were provided by the Royal Artillery. Each troop also had a Land Rover (fitted for radio) for landing site control and a cargo vehicle for transporting aircraft and REME stores. Air troops had a relatively short lifespan, only remaining part of the Royal Artillery regimental establishment until the beginning of the 1970s.

AI Sigs — Assistant Instructor Signals.

Air Vehicle Controller — The controller of an unmanned aerial vehicle.

A/L — Air Landing.

Alam Hamza — Battery Honour Title of 42 (Alam Hamza) Battery RA which was granted on 18 Feb 1974 under authority of 20/ARTY/6824/AG6a. See *Battery Honour Titles.*

Alanbrooke Medal — Awarded for the best honours degree achieved at the Royal Military College of Science.

Alanbrooke Troop — One of the troops in 39 Roberts Bty Junior Leaders Regiment RA. See *Ironside Troop, Porteous Troop* and *Ramsay Troop.*

ALES — Autonomous Link Eleven System. See *Link 11* and *Link 16.*

Alfred Burne Memorial Award — Awarded to the officer or soldier who, in the opinion of the Royal Artillery Historical Affairs Committee, had effected the best piece of work in the historical field preferably related to the Royal Artillery.

ALG — Advanced Landing Ground. (Second World War AOP).

Alkmaar Troop — With Ross Troop one of the two troops forming A Battery (The Chestnut Troop) RHA.

All Arms Staff Officers Liason and Watchkeepers Group — One of the three pools which comprise CVHQ RA, members of the pool provide individual reinforcements to HQ ARRC and Formation HQs at all levels and as such comprises both ex-Regular and experienced TA Officers of Capt rank and above with the experience and maturity to enable them to be accepted by their regular peer group. See *CVHQ RA, RA Specialist Pool (V)* and *LCSP (V).*

All Arms Tactical Targeting Course — Run by the Targeting Section of the Royal School of Artillery and aimed at those holding the rank of sergeant through to lieutenant colonel.

All Available — A command or request to obtain the fire of all artillery capable of delivering effective fire on a given target.

All burnt — The point expressed in time and distance at which the propellant is completely ignited as the round makes its way up the tube.

All Gone — Only used in response to the observers order 'Report All Gone' given during fire for effect. The Gun Position Officer will make this report when the last round ordered has been fired. See *Fire For Effect*.

Allied Command Europe (ACE) Mobile Force (Land Component) — The AMF(L) was the NATO multinational force for operations on NATO's flanks. It was formed in the mid 1960s with units and sub-units from several nations. The artillery component comprised 105 mm batteries from several nations including the UK, who in addition supplied the Force Artillery Commander and HQ including meteor and survey detachments.

Alma — Battery Honour Title of 8 (Alma) Commando Battery RA which was granted on 26 April 1954 under authority of 20/ARTY/6271/AG6a. See *Battery Honour Titles.*

ALND — Alignment Degraded. See *ALNF*.

ALNF — Alignment Full. See *ALND*.

ALO — (i) Army Liaison Officer – title originally given to officers fulfilling the role of Bombardment Liaison Officer on RN Warships. (Second World War)
(ii) Air Liaison Officer.

ALS — (i) Automatic Laying System (Part of the MLRS system)
(ii) Apparatus Loud Speaking. Generally followed by the model number, for example, ALS 23.

Alt — Altitude.

Alternate Headquarters — An alternative to Main Headquarters with limited staff and able to take-over from Main if it goes out of action. Permanent Alt Headquarters were adopted when brigade and divisional Headquarters in 1(BR) Corps were 'hardened and reduced' in 1980–81. See *Battery Headquarters, Main Headquarters, Rear Headquarters, Regimental Headquarters Step-Up* and *Tactical Headquarters*.

Alternative NATO Task Table — A task table similar to a Divisional Task Table, used by allied artillery headquarters when allotting tasks to

	British artillery firing in support of allied operations. See *Monster*.
Alternative Position	When a regiment occupies a new gun area, a number of positions, in addition to the main position, are reconnoitred and prepared. These are used if the main position, due to enemy action or for any other reason becomes unusable. See *Main Position, Roving Position* and *Temporary Position*.
Altitude	The vertical distance of a point measured from mean sea level.
Alvis Stalwart	High mobility, amphibious, load carrying vehicle based on the same chassis as the Saracen Armoured Personnel Carrier/Command Vehicle and the Saladin Armoured Car. The normal crew consisted of a driver and two passengers. See *FV643*.
Alvis Stalwart Mk 2 Limber Vehicle	See *Alvis Stalwart* and *FV643*.
AMA	Artillery Manoeuvre Area.
Amatol	An explosive composition consisting of Ammonium Nitrate and Trinitrotoluene which was used as a filling for High Explosive shells.
Ambrose Pratt Memorial Prize	Awarded to the Young Officer who has shown the greatest improvement in all-round officer qualities on the course for newly-commissioned Artillery officers at the Royal School of Artillery, but excluding holders of the Tombs, Benson and Earl Roberts Memorial Prizes. See *Benson Memorial Prize, Earl Roberts Memorial Prize, Tombs Memorial Prize* and the *Tombs-Benson Memorial Prize*.
AMC	At My Command. See *Fire by Order*.
AMDU	Auxiliary Map Display Unit.
American, British, Canadian and Australian Standardisation Program	Its purpose is to achieve interoperability between coalition forces, whilst accepting that it is unrealistic to expect member nations to standardise equipment, ABCA seeks to develop procedures to enable a multi-national coalition force to operate effectively.
AMES	Air Ministry Experimental Station. See *AMES Type 86 Radar* and *AMES Type 89 TCR*.
Amesbury Roundabout Battery	A derogatory nickname for 22 Locating Battery RA.
AMES Type 88 Radar	See *AD11, Indigo Corkscrew* and *Thunderbird*.
AMES Type 89 TCR	The surveillance radar used with the Thunderbird II Heavy Air Defence missile system. See *TCR* and *Thunderbird*.
AMETS	Artillery Meteorological System.
AMF(L)	(i) Allied Command Europe (ACE) Mobile Force (Land component). (ii) Ain't My Fight, a derogatory nickname, which derived from the initials of the Allied Command Europe (ACE) Mobile Force (Land component).
AMM	Air Mission Message.
Ammunition	Derived from the Latin word *Muniri*, which originally meant, to protect by a wall, but later evolved to mean fortify, and more recently, to supply all that is necessary for defence. Ammunition has over time come to mean all missiles and devices used both offensively and defensively. The term covers both explosive and non-explosive components and generally embraces all forms of military stores which contain some type of explosive, incendiary or chemical hazard, together with

those items used for training purposes, whether inert or otherwise.

Ammunition and Store Wagon RA — Part of a battery's integral horse drawn vehicle establishment during the late nineteenth and early twentieth century. The Ammunition and Store Wagon RA was a heavy wagon with small front wheels which increased its heaviness in draught. It was found to be unsuitable for use over rough ground.

Ammunition Carriers — Used during the First World War these waterproof canvas carriers were fastened at the front with a strap and buckle. The Ammunition Carrier enabled one man to bring four complete rounds of ammunition to the gun. On either side of the carrier were two pockets, each designed to carry one round. Two lifting handles, secured to each side, catered for men of different heights. The percussion primer on the base of the cartridge was protected by a cruciform clip. Similar carriers existed for pack animals, being provided in eight or six shell versions for both the 18-pdr and the 4.5-inch Howitzer.

Ammunition Column — Every horse and field artillery brigade, certainly until the end of the First World War, and probably later, would have its own ammunition column, which in addition to carrying ammunition for the brigade, would carry small arms ammunition for the infantry. During the Boer War an ammunition column consisted of two portions, the first line consisting of horsed ammunition wagons and mule drawn buck carts, whilst the second line was made up of ox-drawn wagons. See *Brigade Ammunition Column* and *Divisional Ammunition Column.*

Ammunition Column Officer — In the late nineteenth and early twentieth century India, these officers were appointed in each brigade, to take charge of the reserve ammunition mules of the batteries, and to arrange for the replenishment of the ammunition supply from the Ordnance Field Parks. See *Ordnance Field Park.*

Ammunition Dumping — See *Dumping.*

Ammunition Entrance — The entrance to a Magazine for ammunition, not used for personnel.

Ammunition Group — One of the tactical groups of a battery (Second World War).

Ammunition Park — During the Boer War, an Ammunition Park was formed directly under the control of the GOCRA. The ammunition park in addition to supplying ammunition to all arms, formed a reserve of officers, men, horses and stores to provide immediate replacement for casualties.

Ammunition Passage — In Coast Artillery a passage along which all types of ammunition were transported. See *Powder Passage* and *Shell Passage*

Ammunition Refilling Point — The point where the Corps Ammunition Parks or Sub Parks transferred Ammunition to the Divisional Ammunition Columns. See *Divisional Ammunition Column.*

Ammunition Trailer — See *Limber.*

Amn — Ammunition.

Amphibious Bombardment Association — The Old Comrades Association for members of 148 (Meiktila) Commando Forward Observation Battery and its forerunners.

Amphibious Ready Group — A Task Group of ships with a RM Commando embarked together with their affiliated RA Battery, a troop of Commando engineers, a support and light helicopter

	force operated by the RN and RAF, plus all the small boats and landing craft required to put the commandos ashore.
AMSL	Above Mean Sea Level.
AMTAT	Air Manoeuvre Training and Advisory Team.
AMTB	Anti-Motor Torpedo Boat.
AMV	Adopted Muzzle Velocity.
AN501	Shortened form of AN/USD-501, see *AN/USD-501* and *Midge.*
Anchor OP	An Observation Post which does not move during an assault involving a large, Battle Group etc. level Fireplan. The Anchor OP's job is to control the fire of the guns during the assault and amend the Fireplan if necessary. There will also be other OPs moving with the combat teams, these will be responsible for calling down fire on opportunity targets. See *Observation Post.*
Anderson Troop	Anderson Troop is the name given to a troop within 53 (Louisburg) Battery Royal Artillery.
Anderson's Cupola	A ponderous and complicated blast furnace which was used to heat pig-iron to a molten state in order to fill Martin's Liquid Iron Shell, in Coast fortifications during the late 1850s. A supply of pig-iron and a dedicated squad of men was required in each battery. Battery Commanders were somewhat apprehensive about having a machine full of red-hot coke in the middle of their position whilst in action. As a result, its use was short-lived. See *Martin's Shell.*
Angle of Departure	The angle between the horizontal plane and the gun bore when fired. Quadrant Elevation and Jump are incorporated within the Angle of Departure. See *Jump* and *Quadrant Elevation.*
Angle of Descent	The angle formed between the horizontal plane and the line of arrival of the shell as it impacts the ground.
Angle of Elevation	The angle which the line of sight makes with the axis of the gun.
Angle of Impact	See *Impact Angles.*
Angle of Incidence	The angle between the line of arrival of a projectile and the surface of a target. In British practice the angle is considered to be 'Normal' (0°) when the target is struck at a perfect right-angle, the angle increases as the line of arrival becomes more oblique. Current NATO practice considers a shot striking at a perfect right-angle to strike at 90°. The angle being measured from the face of the target.
Angle of Projection	The angle formed between the line of sight and the axis of the bore when the gun is fired. The angle consists of Tangent Elevation plus Jump. See *Jump* and *Tangent Elevation.*
Angle of Sight	The angle between a sight line connecting the gun to the target and the horizontal plane. This may be an angle of elevation or depression.
Angle T	The (interior) angle formed at the target by the intersection of the gun-target line and the observer-target line. Formerly referred to as the Apex Angle.
Angular Deviation due to Drift	The horizontal angle between the plane of departure and the vertical plane containing the gun and the projectile at any point on the trajectory. See *Drift.*
Animal Pack	A transportation method whereby equipment or supplies are carried on pack mules.
Annual Operational Test	Tactical test exercise for nuclear units, it replaced the Annual Training Test. Assessors from other NATO nations, RA officers attended AOT of other NATO nations. See *Annual Training Test.*

Annual Training Test — Tactical test exercise for nuclear units, the Annual Training Test was replaced by the Annual Operational Test. See *Annual Operational Test.*

AN/MMQ-1B — See *Wind Set.*

ANR — Active Noise Reduction.

Anti-Aircraft Defence Commander — First created in 1916, the officer holding this post was responsible for the protection of an area from attack from the air.

Anti-Aircraft Experimental Section — Formed by the Ministry of Munitions at the Royal Naval Gunnery School, Whale Island, during the First World War. The section was established to conduct systematic testing of all aspects of Anti-Aircraft gunnery.

Anti-Aircraft Mobilization Training Centre — The Centre was formed in 1942 to provide training to Anti-Aircraft units prior to their deployment overseas.

Anti-Aircraft Ordnance Depot — During the Second World War, these supplied ammunition to Intermediate Ammunition Depots for onward transmission to Equipment Ammunition Magazines and ultimately to Gun Sites. See *Equipment Ammunition Magazine* and *Intermediate Ammunition Depot.*

Anti-Aircraft Training Establishment — Formed in 1941, it comprised many training units tasked with training new recruits and converting non-RA units to the Anti-Aircraft role.

Anti-Coastal Motor Boat — A classification for coastal defence guns such as the 12-pdr QF. See *Anti-Motor Torpedo Boat.*

Anti-Motor Torpedo Boat — A classification for coastal defence guns, The example given by Denis Rollo in *The Guns and Gunners of Malta* is the twin 6-pdr. See *Anti-Coastal Motor Boat.*

AN/USD-1 — Original US designation for complete drone system, known in UK as SD-1 and later, after change in US designation, as MQM 57. See *MQM 57.*

AN/USD-501 — NATO designation for Midge drone. See *Midge.*

AO — (i) Amphibious Observation.
(ii) Area of Operations.
(iii) Army Order. Generally followed by the number identifying the relevant order.
(iv) Ammunition Obturated. See *BO.*

AOB — Air Order of Battle.

AOCC — Air Operations Coordination Centre.

AOCC(L) — Air Operations Coordination Centre (Land).

AoD — Angle of Departure.

AoE — Area of Effect.

A of D — Angle of Departure.

AoI — Area of Interest.

A of S — Angle of Sight.

AoP — Angle of Projection, a ballistic angle.

AOP — (i) Air Observation Post.
(ii) Armoured Observation Post.
(iii) Advanced Observation Post.
(iv) Air Observation Party.

AOPA — Amphibious Observation Post Assistant.

AOP Carrier — See *Armoured Observation Post Carrier.*

AOR — Area Of Responsibility.

AORG — Army Operational Research Group. (Second World War).

AOT — Annual Operational Test.

AOV — Armoured Observation Vehicle.

AP — (i) Armour Piercing (Projectile).
(ii) Advanced Post.

	(iii) Anti-Personnel. (iv) Ammunition Point. (v) Aim Point.
APA	Advance Post Alpha. See *Advanced Post* and *APB*.
APB	Advance Post Bravo. See *Advanced Post* and *APA*.
APBC	Armour Piercing Ballistic Capped.
APC	(i) Armour Piercing Capped. (ii) Armoured Personnel Carrier (iii) Abnormal Projectile Correction. See *Abnormal (Non-Standard) Projectile Correction.* (iv) Army Personnel Centre.
APCBC	Armour Piercing Capped Ballistic Capped.
APCBCHE	Armour-Piercing Cap, Ballistic Cap, with delayed-action High Explosive charge.
APCNR	Armour Piercing Composite Non-Rigid.
APCR	Armour Piercing Composite Rigid.
APCU	Advanced Post Control Unit. Part of the Sound Ranging organisation.
APDS	Armour Piercing Discarding Sabot.
APES	Azimuth, Position and Elevation System, used in Warrior OPV. See *Warrior OPV*.
Apex Angle	The angle at the target formed by the line of fire and the observer's view to the target. It is now referred to as Angle T.
APFSDS	Armour Piercing Fin Stabilised Discarding Sabot.
APIS	Air-Photo Interpretation Section.
APM	Air Purity Module.
APOD	Airports of Disembarkation.
Apparatus Loud Speaking	The successor to the Second World War tannoy used between Command Posts and guns with lights in the Command Post to represent acknowledgements. The abbreviation ALS is generally followed by the model number, for example, ALS 23.
Apple Pie Shoot	A shoot undertaken by heavy anti-aircraft regiments during the Second World War. This type of shoot involved the suppression of enemy Flak positions by the employment of airburst ammunition, whilst RAF aircraft conducted missions in the area.
Appointment Titles	A defunct radio scheme, since replaced by BATCO, whereby officers in specific appointments were given code names to identify them during radio traffic. The army-wide scheme was further utilised within the Royal Artillery with each appointment title being used to identify specific posts at HQRA, RHQ and Battery levels. See *Acorn, Batco, Conrod, Cracker, Molar, Pronto, Seagull, Seagull Minor, Sunray* and *Sunray Minor*.
APPU	Air Position Plotting Unit (Based at Kidlington; now defunct).
Apricots	Nickname for 6/36 (Arcot) Battery RA.
April Foolers	Nickname given to the now disbanded 87 HAA Regiment RA. The name originated from the fact that 87 Regiment was formed on 1 April 1939.
Apron of lead	In early muzzle-loading cannon this was a lead cover used to prevent damp entering the vent. It was often placed over the fid. See *Fid* and *Vent*.
APS	Automatic Positioning System (on Light Gun replaces Dial Sights). See *Dial Sight, Light Gun* and *LINAPS*.
APSO	Artillery on Peace Support Operations.
AP-T	Armour Piercing – Tracer. An artillery round.
APV	Anti Powerlock Valve.
APWT	Alternative Personal Weapons Test.
AQSM	Artificer Quartermaster Sergeant.

AR (i) Air Route.
(ii) Aiming Rifle.
(iii) Artillery Code used during the First World War meaning 'Sir'.

A/R Aiming/Ranging.

ARA Artillery Reserved Area.

Archer The Archer was a 17-pdr anti-tank gun mounted on a Valentine tank chassis. The 17pdr A/T gun was mounted pointing to the rear on a limited-traverse mounting. It was used as a 'tank-killer' from late 1944 onwards, and proved a popular and useful weapon.
Specifications
Weight: 15 tonnes
Length: 6.7 m
Width: 2.76 m
Height: 2.25 m
Detachment: 4 (Commander, gunner, loader, driver)
Armour: 60 mm maximum
Primary armament: QF 17 pounder Anti-Tank gun
Ammunition carried: 39 rounds
Secondary Armament: .303 Bren Ligt Machine Gun
Engine: GMC 6-71 6-cyl diesel 192 hp
Operational Range: 200 miles
Speed: 20 mph (off road: 8 mph)

Archibald See *Archie*.

Archie Nickname given to anti-aircraft fire during the First World War. Said to derive from a British pilot who reacted to enemy anti-aircraft fire by shouting the punch-line from a music hall song, 'Archibald-certainly not'. This soon caught on and was inevitably shortened to Archie. The name endured until 1939.

Arcot 1751 Battery Honour Title of 6/36 (Arcot 1751) Battery RA which was granted on 30 December 1969 under authority of 20/ARTY/6824/AG6a. See *Battery Honour Titles*.

Arcots Nickname for 6/36 (Arcot 1751) Battery RA.

ARF Aviation Reconnaissance Force. Part of 16 Air Assault Brigade.

ARFAS Adjustment to Range for False Angle of Sight.

ARG Amphibious Ready Group.

ARH Ammunition Railhead. Second World War and earlier.

ARI Assistant Regimental Instructor.

ARLO Assistant Range Liaison Officer.

ARM Anti-Radiation Missile.

Armament Artificer A member of the Army Ordnance Corps assigned from 1905 to Artillery Brigades, (other than Horse Artillery Brigades), to maintain the Ordnance. In 1906 Armament Artificers were assigned to the Horse Artillery Brigades.

Armament Battery The Armament Party was formed in 1940 to mount coast guns all around the coasts of UK. It later became 245 Armament Battery. There was another one in the Middle East for the same purposes. On the demise of Coast Artillery, the Armament Batteries were responsible for the dismantling of Coast Artillery Ordnance. (Note: During the late-1940s and early-1950s 245 Armament Battery wore a Red lanyard in place of the usual White RA Lanyard).

Armament for General Defence See *Movable Armament*.

Armament for the Protection of Land Fronts See *Movable Armament*.

Armament Major A field officer of the RGA who was accountable for the armaments in the area allotted to him. This position was instigated as part of a Special Regimental Order dated

28 July 1891. The position was however, short-lived, as it was abolished by a Regimental Order of 1891, except for a few officers who were located in places where no RGA Company was stationed.

Armament Party See *Armament Batter.*

Armament Pay Payment proposed by a select committee in the 1880s to be made to officers of the RGA, in order to render service in that Branch of the Royal Artillery more attractive. These payments were implemented in 1891.

Arm of Service Stripe See *Tactical Recognition Flash.*

Armour Piercing Ballistic Capped An Armour Piercing round fitted with a streamlined ballistic cap, this reduced in-flight loss of velocity and increased penetration.

Armour Piercing Capped An Armour Piercing round fitted with a cap of specially hardened steel to prevent it shattering at oblique impact angles.

Armour Piercing Composite Non-Rigid An anti-tank round used with the Littlejohn adapter. See *Littlejohn Adapter.*

Armour Piercing Composite Rigid This anti-tank round was introduced very briefly for the 6-pdr, and does not seem to have ever reached units in action. It utilised a solid alloy body, highly tapered in shape, around a tungsten steel core.

Armour Piercing Discarding Sabot Introduced in 1944. This anti-tank round had a tungstencarbide sub-calibre core in a light metal casing that fell apart and dropped away from the core when it left the muzzle.

Armoured Observation Post Carrier A universal carrier (commonly referred to a Bren Gun Carrier) modified for use by the Royal Artillery, as an observation post vehicle. The various Mk III versions were used in NW Europe during the Second World War. These carried a detachment of four consisting of a driver, a forward observation officer, an observation post assistant and a Signaller. The front housing, which was normally used for a Bren gun, was in this role, plated over and fitted with an observation shutter. Several variants saw service in NW Europe, namely:

No 1 Mk IIIw. Based on the Universal carrier No 1 Mk III. The 'w' indicated a welded hull. The engine was a British built Ford V8 of 65bhp.

No 2 Mk III. Based on Universal carrier No 2 Mk III. Powered by the more powerful American built GAEA V8 engine of 85 bhp.

No 3 Mk III. This version was based on the Universal carrier No 3 which was Canadian built.

The AOP Carrier was intended to carry the observation party to its observation post, unlike the ram observation post, it was not intended to be used as an actual observation post itself. In normal circumstances, the forward observation officer and his assistant would leave the carrier and move to a suitable concealed point from which to carry out their observation duties. A cable would be laid from the carrier to the observation post and the Wireless set No19 would be employed in the remote control mode. The observer could then communicate with his own gun position officer or battery command post by wire or wireless. However, the carrier could be used as a mobile observation post, advancing with the infantry and communicating with them via the Wireless set No 18. Later this was replaced by the Wireless set No 38.

The Wireless set No 19, together with its batteries were carried in the front of the offside compartment. It was possible to demount this set for ground use but this was not a usual procedure. A charging engine for the Wireless set No 19 batteries was carried on the rear platform, outside the body. A Wireless set No 18 was carried at the rear of the nearside compartment. The No 18 set could readily be carried by one man and would be set up in the observation post in order to communicate with the supported infantry battalion or company headquarters. There were cable reels at the front and rear to allow remote operation.

Following the D-Day landings in 1944 it became apparent that the OP carriers were no longer suitable for their tasks. It had become impracticable for them to carry the amount of equipment and personnel required to fulfill their role. At first, in order to overcome this problem, extra vehicles in the form of jeeps or scout cars were added to the observer's team. When working with armoured units however an OP tank was made available by the armoured regiment. See *Command Tank, Forward Observation Officer, Ram Observation Post, Wireless Set No 18, Wireless Set No 18* and *Wireless Set No 38.*

Armoured Vehicle Multiple Rocket Launcher

An alternate, and little used name for the Multi Launch Rocket System, sometimes incorporated into the full title for the system as the M270 AVMRL MLRS. See *Multiple Launch Rocket System.*

Armt S/Sgt — Armament Staff Sergeant. (Rank no longer in use).

Army Book 545 — The Task Table which is used to assist in fire planning, known as the TIDDLER for ease of recognition on the radio and telephone. The form contains columns for the following information: The originator, fire plan nickname, tasks in support of..., H-hour, date time of origin, serial, timings, target numbers, grid reference and height or description, batteries to engage, ammunition, rate, column and ammunition expenditure.

Army Department Ammunition Code

The ADAC is made up in the following manner. The first figure defines the user group, (Royal Artillery), the second and third figures the nature of the ammunition packaged (155 mm Artillery), fourth and fifth figures the type of ammunition (HE or Smoke) whilst the sixth and seventh (if used) define a specific mark or model. A suffix letter may be added which defines the method of packaging used. Examples of the groups are given in brackets, these are not definitive.

Army Equipment Policy — A directorate within MOD, the particular branch is identified by a numerical suffix, for example: AEP6.

Army Field Artillery — During the First World War, these were Royal Field Artillery Brigades which operated under Army as opposed to Corps or Divisional command.

Army Form B2596 — See *Sands Graph.*

Army Form Blank — Toilet Paper.

Army Form G904 — Form used to certify that ordnance is Free From Explosives.

Army Group Royal Artillery

AGRAs were in essence artillery brigades, they were 'army troops' that were usually assigned to corps. The number and type of regiments in an AGRA was not fixed, but typically consisted of five or six regiments, most of which would have been medium regiments. An AGRA was commanded

	by a CAGRA, who was a brigadier. Note: the organisation used for study purposes on war time staff college courses was one army field regiment (self-propelled), four medium regiments and one heavy regiment. The break down by type was 24 field (25-pounder or 105mm), 64 medium (4.5- or 5.5-in) and eight each of 7.2-in howitzers and 155 mm guns. Not only did the AGRA provide artillery additional to divisional artilleries, it also provided appropriate command and staff personnel together with facilities for control and administration.
Army Planks	Skis.
Army Staff Duties	A Directorate within MOD, the particular branch is identified by a numerical suffix, for example: ASD6.
Army Test and Evaluation Programme	Originally a US Army programme. Custodial units were subject to it but it did not involve the Royal Artillery Regiment they were assigned to.
ARO	Assistant Reconnaissance Officer.
ARP	(i) Ammunition Refilling Point. (First and Second World Wars.) (ii) Aviation Reconnaissance Patrol.
Arras Troop	One of the Troops in 1st Squadron Honourable Artillery Company. See *Honourable Artillery Company, Somme Troop* and *Ypres Troop*.
ARSA	Artillery Raid Staging Area.
Arracan	Battery Honour Title of 88 (Arracan) Battery RA which was granted on 23 July 1930 under authority of 20/ARTY/4735/AG6a. See *Battery Honour Titles*.
Arracan Day	29 March – Battery day of 88 (Arracan) Battery RA.
ARRC	Allied Command Europe Rapid Reaction Corps.
Arrol-Withers Platform	A prefabricated steel platform designed to enable the standard 6-inch coast defence gun to be mounted in an Emergency Battery. See *Emergency Battery*.
ART	Artillery Code used during the First World War meaning 'Artillery'.
ARTAT(FD)	Artillery Training and Advisory Team (Field) Formerly known as RAGTE.
ARTEP	Army Test & Evaluation Programme.
ARTHUR	Artillery Hunting Radar (Manufacturer's name for the precursor to MAMBA (qv) ARTHUR was deployed to both Iraq on Operation Telic and Afghanistan.)
Artificer Quartermaster Sergeant	A senior non-commissioned officer in the light aid detachment. (Royal Electrical and Mechanical Engineers.) See *Artificer Sergeant-Major*.
Artificer Royal Artillery	In 1923, the appointment of Artificer Royal Artillery was created by combining the trades of Fitter, Wheeler and Smith. Artificers were trained in the trades of blacksmithing, woodworking, painting and lettering. In order to qualify as an Artificer RA, it was necessary to pass the appropriate trade tests.
Artificer Sergeant-Major	A Senior Non-Commissioned Officer in the Light Aid Detachment. (Royal Electrical and Mechanical Engineers.) See *Artificer Quartermaster Sergeant*.
Artificial Moonlight	See *Movement Light*.
Artillery Board	First used in 1917, an Artillery Board was up to 30 inches square covered with gridded paper (either 1:25,000 or 1:50,000 scale). A brass pivot represented the pivot gun with a steel range arm rotating about it along a steel bearing arc. It enabled map data (range and switch) to be measured accurately. It could be placed on a flat(ish) surface or mounted on Stands, Instrument No 27.

Artillery Centre	The name given to the amalgamated Headquarters Director Royal Artillery and Royal School of Artillery. However, the Royal School of Artillery still exists as a separate entity responsible for the technical training of the regiment.
Artillery Code	Two or three letter groups which were used for all fire order terms and also for other instructions, transmitted in Morse Code. Artillery Code was possibly introduced in the First World War, it was certainly in use well before the Second World War, during which there was also a Reconnaissance Code which was used for reporting information about the enemy. Similarly, there was a Coast Artillery Code used by Coast Batteries.
Artillery Command Systems	One of four branches within the Royal Artillery. Artillery Command Systems branch is responsible for the communication and computation functions. See *Strike, Targeting* and *Artillery Logistics*.
Artillery General Store	In Coast Artillery, a store for spare gun stores of all natures and wedge wads.
Artillery Delivered Expendable Jammers	Electronic warfare jammers delivered to the required area of operations via a 155 mm artillery carrier shell.
Artillery Fire Data Computer	A hand held computer which was used for the computation of field artillery ballistic data. Computation for various natures of field artillery equipment could be carried out by changing the clip in modules. It had the facility to run some basic survey routines. Due to its being ruggedized and waterproofed in a thermoplastic carrying case the AFDC with a battery life of 80 hours, and capable of storing 9 observation post locations, 18 registration points and 47 target records was used for light role deployments and as a back-up to other systems.
Artillery Fire Plan Table	A presentation of planned targets giving data for engagement. Scheduled targets are fired in a definite time sequence. The starting time of any target may be on call, at a prearranged time, or at the occurrence of a specific event. (Royal Canadian Artillery.)
Artillery Locating Radar	Artillery Locating Radar detects an incoming shell or mortar bomb at two points during its flight, and quickly calculates the position of the enemy battery, so that the Artillery can engage enemy guns or mortars with counter-battery fire, before the enemy has time to move.
Artillery Logistics	One of four branches within the Royal Artillery. Artillery Logistics branch is responsible for combat service support functions. See *Artillery Command Systems, Strike* and *Targeting*.
Artillery Manoeuvre Area	A large area in which Close Support and General Support artillery units deploy and in which they do not remain in static fighting positions, but use a number of different locations. Unlike the Artillery Reserved Area, it is not exclusively reserved for artillery units. See *Artillery Reserved Area*.
Artillery Meteorological System	Entered service in 1972 and provided meteorological messages in a standard NATO format. Its main drawback was that there was only one system per division, which resulted in a high radius of data application. AMETS also used an active radar, which made the entire system vulnerable to enemy counter-measures. Replaced by BMETS in 1999. See *BMETS*.
Artillery Mounted Rifles	Formed during the Boer War in South Africa, originally from two howitzer brigades. Later, other batteries were

also converted to the mounted infantry role. Commanded by a Lt Col, the brigades and batteries retained their own organisations and nomenclature. Each of the corps, or columns, as they were usually known, was self-contained, having its own pom-pom section, scouts and signallers. A column would usually have a strength of 750 men, with 20 mule wagons for baggage. A supply column would also normally be attached to the column. All ranks were armed with rifles and bayonets, a total of 350 rounds per man was carried in the following allotment: 150 rounds per man in a bandolier, two boxes per section on a pack horse with a further 14 boxes per company carried in a scotch cart. Interestingly, whilst the howitzers and equipment of the batteries was returned to ordnance stores, the columns retained their range-finding instruments. The three A&S wagons RA and the water cart which formed part of the battery equipment were also retained. Also known as the Royal Artillery Mounted Rifles, they were immortalised by Rudyard Kipling in his poem 'Ubique', in which one line reads 'Ubique means the R.A.M.R. Infantillery Corps!'

Artillery Net — The Royal Artillery Radio Communications net. Reputed to be the most reliable of any radio net in the British Army.

Artillery Punch — Believed to have originally been devised by the American Army, this drink consisted of the following: rye whiskey, red wine, strong black tea, various fruits, cloves and sugar.

Artillery Reconnaissance — Artillery observation and ranging conducted by RAF aircraft by means of special procedures established prior to the Second World War. The procedure was itself a successor to the First World War Zone Call system.

Artillery Reserved Area — An area reserved for the exclusive use of an artillery unit or sub unit. See *Artillery Manoeuvre Area.*

Artillery Strike — See *Strike*.

Artillery Store — In Coast Artillery, a store in a battery for the sights, elevating arcs, and other stores which belonged to the guns and were required for their immediate service.

Artillery Survey — In the UK this was divided into two distinct forms, RA Survey, conducted by Survey Units and Regimental Survey, conducted by the regimental surveyors of the gun regiments. See *RA Survey* and *Regimental Survey*.

Artillery Target Indication — The procedure by which officers of other Arms call for artillery fire. It is used when there is no personal contact with a Battery Commander, Observation Post Officer or Forward Observation Officer.

Artillery Targeting — See *Targeting*.

Arty — Artillery.

ArtyCen — Artillery Centre.

Arty Int — Artillery Intelligence.

Arty INTSUM — Artillery Intelligence Summary. (Royal Canadian Artillery)

Arty Net — Artillery Net.

Arty/R — Artillery Reconnaissance.

Arty SUPINTREP — Artillery Supplementary Intelligence Report. (Royal Canadian Artillery)

AS90 — AS90 is a 155 mm self-propelled gun which fires the NATO L15 unassisted projectile out to a range of 24.7 kms. Fitted with a long (52 Calibre) barrel the gun can reach out to 30 km using standard ammunition, and 60–80 km with Extended Range Ammunition. Fitted with the Autonomous navigation and Gun Laying System, AS90 can work independently of external sighting references. Central to the system is an inertial Dynamic Reference Unit. All main turret functions are controlled by a Turret

	Control Computer. These systems allow AS90 a burst fire capability of 3 rounds in 10 seconds. Detachment: 5 Length: 9.07 m Width: 3.3 m Height: 3 m Armour: 17 mm Calibre: 155 mm Range: (39 calibre barrel): 24.7 kms (52 calibre): 30 kms Rate of Fire: 3 rounds in 10 secs (burst), 6 rounds per minute (intense), 2 rounds per minute (sustained) Secondary Armament: 7.62 mm machine-gun. Ammunition Carried: 48 x 155 mm projectiles and charges (31 in the turret and 17 in the hull) Engine: turbo-charged V8 diesel 600 hp Max Speed: 53 kph; Road Range 420 kms
A/S	Angle of Sight.
ASACS	Air Surveillance and Control Systems.
Asbury Mechanism	The mechanism used to close and lock a BL breech. The upward movement through about 90° of the breech mechanism lever swung the breech block though about 90° into the breech ring then rotated it though about 40° to lock it in position; the reverse motion was to open it.
ASC	Army Service Corps. Later the Royal Army Service Corps.
ASCC	Airspace Coordination Centre (Royal Canadian Artillery.)
ASD	Army Staff Duties.
ASG	Automotive Servicing Guide.
ASM	(i) Artificer Sergeant-Major. (ii) Azimuth Servo Motor.
ASMT	Artillery Survey Mathematical Tables.
ASOC	Air Support Operations Centre.
ASP	(i) Advanced Sound Ranging Programme. (ii) Ammunition Sub Park. (iii) Ammunition Supply Point. See *WSG*.
Assaye	Battery Honour Title of 10 (Assaye) Battery RA which was granted on 18 October 1926 under authority of 20/ARTY/4544/AG6a. Awarded for service at the Battle of Assaye 23 September 1803 under Arthur Wellesley (Later Duke of Wellington), a famous victory against the Maharatta army. See *Battery Honour Titles*.
Assembly and Test	The troop in Honest John and Lance batteries responsible for holding warheads and motors, mating them and delivering them to firing sections. See *Honest John* and *Lance*.
Assistant Adjutant	The Adjutant's deputy and relief, with particular responsibilities for the detailed administration of Regimental Headquarters. See *Adjutant*.
Assistant Computer	A member of an Artillery Survey Computing Centre. An assistant to the Chief Computer. See *Chief Computer* and *Computing Centre*.
Assistant Counter Battery Officer	During the Second World War ACBOs formed part of Counter Battery Office staff, normally deployed to divisional Headquarters. After the Second World War this role became the Divisional Counter Bombardmant Officer and the Assistant Counter Bombardment Officer (B at this time becoming 'Bombardment') seems to have been located at brigade Headquarters replacing the wartime Assistant Counter Mortar Officer. See *Assistant Counter Mortar Officer* and *Divisional Counter Bombardment Officer*.
Assistant Counter Bombardment Officer	See *Assistant Counter Battery Officer* and *Assistant Counter Mortar Officer*.

Assistant Counter Mortar Officer	A position introduced into brigade headquarters in 1944, it later became known as the Brigade Artillery Intelligence Officer. The position was often filled by an infantry officer.
Assistant Instructor in Gunnery	A graduate of the Long Gunnery Staff Course (NCOs), a Warrant Officer whose duties included the instruction of both officers and other ranks, of both the regular and territorial units of the Royal Artillery, in units or on courses, in the drills and handling of equpments used by the Royal Artillery. Some Assistant Instructors in Gunnery were posted permanently to the Master-General of the Ordnance Department of the War Office as Experimental Battery Sergeant-Majors or Experimental Sergeant-Majors. This rank no longer exists, having been replaced by the rank of Sergeant-Major Instructor in Gunnery (SMIG). See *Experimental Battery Sergeant-Major* and *Experimental Sergeant-Major.*
Assistant Instructor Signals	A Senior NCO responsible for radio and telephonic communications within a Battery.
ASSU	Air Support Signals Unit.
Asten	Battery Honour Title of 59 (Asten) Battery RA which was granted on 24 Jan 1951 under authority of 20/ARTY/6271/AG6a. See *Battery Honour Titles.*
ASTOR	Airborne Stand-off Radar.
ASV	Azimuth Servo Valve.
Asymptote Plotter	This device was fitted onto a plain gridded board. Strings passed through gaps with asymptote curve shaped guides to plot microphone time differences in sound ranging. Ideal plot would be exact meeting of strings at a grid point. In practice, usually a small cats cradle. The curves only came into play on oblique strings, straight down the grid lines ahead of base, just a plain gap for straight plotting string.
AT	(i) Anti-Tank. (ii) Ammunition Technician. (iii) Artillery Training. Usually followed by the number of the volume referred to.
AT2 Scatmin	The AT2 Scatterable Mine is dispensed by the 277 mm MLRS system, each rocket contains 28 mines. Therefore, one round Fire For Effect from a single launcher (12 rockets) will deliver 336 mines. See *Multiple Launch Rocket System.*
ATACMS	Army Tactical Missile System. Part of the MLRS system. *See Multiple Launch Rocket System.*
ATD	Army Training Directive.
ATE	Army Training Estate.
ATEP	Army Test and Evaluation Programme. (Royal Australian Artillery.)
ATESP	Army Training Estate Salisbury.
ATF	Airborne Task Force.
ATGW	Anti-Tank Guided Weapon.
ATI	Artillery Target Indication.
ATk	Anti-Tank.
At My Command	The command used when controlling the exact time of delivery of fire is desired. Designated fire units will only engage when given the executive order 'Fire' or 'Cancel at my Command' from the authorising call sign. Previously known as 'Fire by Order'. See *Fire By Order.*
ATO	(i) Air Tasking Order. (ii) Ammunition Technical Officer.

ATP	Allied Tactical Publication.
At Priority Call	A modification to a tactical mission to assign a different priority for calls for fire. The term must always be linked with a specific authority; i.e., guns will be assigned 'At Priority Call To (e.g., a specific Artillery Intelligence Officer, Forward Observer, or other authority)', and will immediately answer calls for fire from that authority. Introduced after the Second World War the control order lasted into the 1990s.
ATS	Auxiliary Territorial Service.
ATT	Annual Training Test.
Attending man	Of the gunners detailed for guard duty, the attending man collected meals and drinks for the guard from the cookhouse.
Attitude	The position of a body as determined by the inclination of the axis to some frame of reference. If not otherwise specified, this frame of reference is fixed to the earth.
ATU	Advanced Training Unit.
AU	Aiming Unit. (Part of the Javelin/HVM shoulder launched system.)
Aural Adjustment	The practice of adjusting artillery fire by sound alone.
AUSOP	Army Unit Standard Operating Procedures.
Auster AOP	Various Marks of Auster were flown by gunner officers in the air observation post squadrons of the RAF. Specification for three of the Marks are given below.
Auster AOP Mk 3	Description: Two seat, composite wood and metal structure, fabric covered. Power Plant: One 130 hp DH Gypsy Major 1 Wing Span: 36 ft; Length: 23 ft 5ins; Height: 8 ft Weights: Empty: 1100 lb; Loaded: 1,700 lb Maxium Speed: 130 mph; Cruising Speed: 108 mph; Initial Climb: 950 ft/min Ceiling: 15,000 ft Range: 250 miles Armament: none
Auster AOP Mk 6	Description: Two seat, composite wood and metal structure, fabric covered. Powerplant: One 145 hr Gypsy Major 7 Wing Span: 36 ft; Length: 23 ft 7 in. Weights: Gross: 2,204 lb Maximum Speed: 121 mph Ceiling: 12000 ft Armament: none
Auster AOP Mk 9	Description: Two seat, composite wood and metal structure, fabric covered. Powerplant: One 180-hp Blackburn Cirrus Bombardier 203 Inline Piston Engine. Weight: Empty 1,590 lbs; Maximum Takeoff 2,330 lbs Wing Span: 36 ft 5 in; Length: 23 ft 8.5 in; Height: 8ft 11 in. Maximum Speed: 127 mph; Cruising Speed: 110 mph. Ceiling: 19,500 ft Range: 242 miles Armament: none. See *AOP*.
Authorized Observer	An officer who is authorized to order fire from specific fire units in addition to his own unit, for the engagement of any target he feels suitable. He/she may issue orders directly to the units concerned without reference to any higher authority. (Royal Canadian Artillery).
Auto-frettage	A method of increasing the strength of a gun barrel by creating additional radial tension to counteract the internal pressures created when the gun fires.

Automatic Command Line of Sight — A missile guidance system. See *SACLOS*.

Automatic Gas-Check — See *Gas-Check*.

Automatic Sight — See *Autosight* and *Gun Auto-Sight*.

Automatic Weapon Data Transmission System — Connected to FACE in the Battery Command Post with a data display at each gun connected by line or radio link. See *FACE*.

Autonomous Link Eleven System — A tactical data link system unique to 20 Commando Battery, which allows the Battery to receive the recognised air picture from ship, AWACS and ground radar out to 500 kms. See *Link 11* and *16*.

Autosight — Telescopic sighting system used in Coastal Artillery for range finding. The term is a contraction of 'Automatic Sight'. The sight incorporated cams which allowed for the height of the gun above sea level, and were also capable of allowing for the rise and fall of the tide. This resulted in the layer only having to keep his telescopic pointer on the target and the gun being automatically given the appropriate elevation. The longer the range the greater the movement of the gun in relation to the sight, this was known as the ratio of movement. See *Gun Auto-Sight*.

Auxiliary Aiming Point — The original name given to the Gun Aiming Point. The title was changed between the First and Second World Wars. See *Aiming Point*.

Auxiliary AP — Auxiliary Aiming Point.

Auxiliary Force — Pre-1908 collective term for Yeomanry, Volunteers and Militia.

Auxiliary Force (India) — The equivalent of the TA enlisting local Europeans. Its artillery element comprised thirteen batteries throughout India and Burma. Only the battery in Rangoon mobilised in the Second World War.

Auxiliary Territorial Service — The forerunner of the Women's Royal Army Corps, the ATS consisted of about 20,000 women who performed operational support tasks such as driving, postal work, food preparation and ammunition inspection. Many served in Mixed anti-aircraft units and wore gunner badges together with the Royal Artillery white lanyard.

AV — Air Vehicle. See *Desert Hawk, Phoenix, UAV* and *Watchkeeper*.

AVB — Aim Verification Bracket.

AVC — (i) Air Vehicle Controller.
(ii) Artillery Volunteer Corps.

Avenger Battery — Nickname given to 216 Battery RA(V) The Bolton Artillery.

Aviation — Army Air Corps Helicopters.

Aviation Reconnaissance Patrol — Composed of both observation and armed helicopters, the Aviation Reconnaissance Patrol is tasked with conducting helicopter reconnaissance missions whilst in contact with the enemy. In this role the observation helicopters move in tactical bounds whilst being covered by the armed helicopter. It is normal practice to have artillery on call during such missions. A typical ARP might consist of two gazelle observation helicopters and one TOW armed Lynx helicopter, although other combinations are possible. This composition will have changed with the introduction of the WAH-64 Apache Attack Helicopter. ARP's are fully capable of acting in the Air Observation Post role when required. See *Air Observation Post, Gazelle, Lynx* and *TOW*.

Aviation Tactical Group — Part of 7 Para Regt RHA, the Aviation Tactical Group was formed in 2001 to support 3, 4 and 9 Regiments Army Air Corps and any Joint Helicopter Forces deployed on operations. The group consists of eighteen personnel and specialises in directing and coordinating Air, Aviation and Offensive Support assets, together with the associated Battlespace Management. The Aviation Tactical Group is organised into five units, namely the Command Cell, a Fire Panning Cell and three Fire Support Teams. The Fire Support Teams are able to supply Forward Observation Officers and their Assistants provide Air Observation Posts operating from Lynx and Gazelle helicopters in addition to the normal ground based roles of Forward Observers. See *Air, Aviation, Battlespace Management, Fire Support Team* and *Forward Observation Officer.*

AVM — Azimuth Valve Module.

AVMRL — Armoured Vehicle Multiple Rocket Launcher.

Avn — Aviation.

AWDATS — Automatic Weapon Data Transmission System; connected to FACE in the BCP with a data display at each gun connected by line or radio link.

AWES — Area Weapons Effects Simulator.

AWIFM — A mnemonic representing the five principles of organizing field artillery for combat; adequate weight of fire, weight the main effort, immediate response, facilitate future operations, and maximum feasible control. (Royal Canadian Artillery.)

AWO2 — Acting Warrant Officer Class 2.

AWT — (i) Arctic Warfare Training.
(ii) Alternative Weapons Test.

AX — First World War artillery abbreviation for 18-pounder High Explosive shell. The abbreviation was used in ammunition returns.

Axletree — A transverse beam which supports the gun carriage, and on the ends of which the wheels are fitted.

Axis of the bore — A line which passes through the centre of the barrel along its longitudinal axis from breech to muzzle.

Axis of the Trunnions — The axis about which the barrel rotates during elevation and depression. The axis of the trunnions is at right angles to the axis of the bore. See *Axis of the Bore.*

AYT — Army Youth Team.

Az — Azimuth.

B – Beer – 1904/1927
Baker – 1943
Bravo – 1956

B — Artillery code used during the First World War meaning 'Are you receiving my signals?'

B43/R220 — See *Station Radio B43/R220.*

B44 — See *Station Radio B44.*

B47 — See *Station Radio B47.*

B48 — See *Station Radio B48.*

BAA — Brigadier Anti-Aircraft. (Second World War.)

BAC — Brigade Ammunition Column. See *AC, Ammunition Column* and *Divisional Ammunition Column.*

Back Bearing — The bearing of a line observed in the opposite direction to that of the original observation. That is to say plus or minus 3600 mils. See *Mils.*

Back Door Training Area — A military training area located near Topcliffe.

Backup Alert Force	Part of the security force at a field storage site or a special ammunition supply site.
BACP	Battery Ammunition Control Point.
BADC	Brigade Air Defence Cell.
BADCOM	Brigade Air Defence Command.
BADCOMD	Brigade Air Defence Commander.
Badgie	(i) Slang term for a trumpeter, said to derive from the Hindustani word Bhudgie meaning time. The day being controlled by the Trumpeter sounding calls at set times during the day. (ii) Used by the Kings Troop RHA when referring to ex-soldiers of 65+ years who wear regimental badges on their blazers.
BADLO	Brigade Air Defence Liaison Officer.
Bad Ram	A 'bad ram' occurs when the gun number ramming the projectile does not ram the shell with sufficient power to ensure it is engaged into the rifling and at the full depth of ram. This can normally be ascertained from a mark on the rammer. If the projectile isn't rammed properly the gap between the back end of the shell and the propellant will not allow for the correct amount of pressure to build up in the chamber, thus causing the round to fall short or range too long.
BAF	Backup Alert Force.
BAI	(i) Battlefield Air Interdiction. (ii) Brigade Artillery Intelligence.
BAI SNCO	Brigade Artillery Intelligence Senior Non-Commissioned Officer.
Bail Battery	These were heavy batteries in India in the 1890s comprised of elephant drawn guns. Due to the concerns about the steadiness of elephants under fire, they were, whenever possible, replaced by bullocks when the battery came into action. Normally the gun teams comprised two elephants harnessed in tandem, whilst the wagons were drawn by bullocks. The establishment of a heavy battery in India in the 1890s consisted of a European garrison company, a native establishment of 213, 18 elephants, 262 bullocks not to mention the ponies for the staff sergeants, farrier and trumpeters. At the beginning of the twentieth century, with the introduction of breech-loading guns for the heavy batteries, the elephants and bullocks were replaced with teams of eight heavy horses. To prevent the elephants bolting, regulations specified that in addition to hobbling the elephants forelegs in action, a long chain should be attached with drag ropes to their hind legs – to be manned by the detachment should the need arise. The last recorded action involving a bail battery was during the battle of Kandahar in 1880. Bail is Hindustani for oxen.
BAIO	Brigade Artillery Intelligence Officer (1960s–1980s).
Balaclava Day	Battery day of C Battery RHA, celebrated each year on 25 October.
Ball Cartridge Brigade	The mid-Nineteenth Century term for an Ammunition Column. Sometimes referred to as a a Ball Cartridge Division. See *Brigade Ammunition Column* and *Divisional Ammunition Column*.
Ball Cartridge Division	See *Ball Cartridge Brigade*.
Ballistic Aerial Target System	A type of remote controlled 'model' aircraft used as a target for Air Defence training.
Ballistic Angles	These are angles which are associated with trajectory. Vertical ballistic angles include: Angle of Departure; Angle of Sight; Angle of Projection; Angle of Descent; and

Angle of Arrival. Horizontal ballistic angles include: Map Bearing; and Angular Deviation due to Drift.

Ballistic coefficient — The ability of a projectile to overcome air resistance. A high coefficient will mean that the velocity of the projectile will drop off slower than one with a low coefficient. Generally, the ballistic coefficient increases with the weight of the shot, but decreases as the diameter of the projectile increases.

Ballistic Memorandum of Understanding — A 1963 agreement between Germany, Italy, the United Kingdom and the United States for a 155 mm 39 calibre barrel and a standard shell shape based on the US M549 Rocket Assisted Projectile. It led to the development of the FH70 and the 155 mm L15 shell in Europe and the M109A1 and M198 in the United States. See *FH70, Joint Ballistic Memorandum of Understanding* and *M109A1*.

Ballistic Point of Graze — See *Point of Graze.*

Ballistics — The science dealing with the motion of a projectile both inside and outside of the gun. Gunnery is the practical application of the science of ballistics.

Ballistic Sensor Fused Munition — A 155 mm artillery munition.

Ball of Fire — All available guns are concentrated on one point, with the intention of delivering a heavy weight of fire on that location. (Second World War.)

BALO — Brigade Air Liaison Officer. An RAF Officer.

Bamboo Cane — Carried by SMIGs, this 24-inch cane was originally used to check the breech of the gun was clear during training. See *SMIG*.

Banana Battery — Nickname of 31 (Headquarter) Battery RA.

Banderole — A six foot survey pole, marked in twelve alternate black and white segments. It is used to mark the position of the Director. An alternate version of the stadia rod. See *Stadia Rod*.

Bangy Boards — Slang for Canadian army skis. (Royal Canadian Artillery.)

Bankrupters, The — Derogatory nickname given to MLRS equipped Regiments. Said to have originated from their rate of fire outstripping the available logistical support.

Banshee — Unmanned Target Drone for Air Defence Missile training.

BAOR — (i) Battery Area Of Responsibility.
(ii) British Army of the Rhine.

BAP — (i) Battery Aid Post.
(ii) Battery Ammunition Point.
(iii) Breech Alignment Plunger.

Barney — Nickname given to Barnard Castle, Durham.

Barrage — Often incorrectly used to mean 'heavy artillery fire'. In practice a barrage has precise meaning, it is a moving or stationary ('standing') belt of fire providing a protective screen behind which the attackers can advance or defenders are positioned. It is applied in a series of lines in lanes. A barrage is not aimed at specific targets but at an area. In a creeping barrage the fire of all units remains in the same relative position throughout, whilst in a rolling barrage the fire of the units involved is leap-frogged. See *Fire Plan.*

Barrage Key Lines — These are lines of a barrage for which predicted gun data is deduced. Gun data for other lines in the barrage being calculated by interpolation. The first and last line of a barrage will always be key lines.

Barren Rocks of Aden, The — Regimental March of 19 Regt RA. (The Highland Gunners.)

BARRT — BATUS Alternative Replacement Red Top.

Bas — Basic (As in Sigs (Bas) course).

BAS Battle Attrition Study.

Base Defence Zone An Airspace Control Measure / Air Defence term.

Base Details During the First World War in France, this term was used to indicate Pool gunners, who were not assigned to any particular battery, and were used for relief or replacement as required.

Base Ejection Coloured Flare Shell Such shells were normally used for marking targets for aircraft at night. They were of the carrier type and contained a number of canisters, filled with flare composition. The shell was fuzed for airburst. On activation, the canisters were ejected and fell to the ground where they burnt with a brilliant coloured light. See *Carrier Shell.*

Base Ejection Shell A form of Carrier Shell. These are the most common type of carrier shell in service. Activated at the appropriate point in its flight by a time fuze, the burster charge blows out the base of the shell and ejects its contents. The burster charge also, where appropriate, ignites the contents prior to ejection, for example in a smoke shell. See *Bursting Shell* and *Carrier Shell.*

Base Ejection Smoke Shell A carrier type smoke shell fitted with either a time or time and percussion fuze. The shell contains a number of canisters filled with a smoke making substance. In use, the fuze is set to cause the shell to burst, whilst still in the air. The canisters ignite and fall to the ground where a dense cloud of smoke is emitted for approximately 1½ minutes. See *Carrier Shell.*

Base Ring In muzzle-loading artillery, this is the part of the breech which defines the end of the bore. It was usual to find the base ring marked by a raised moulding that around the circumference of the breech. The maker's name and the date of casting were often inscribed on the moulding.

Basic Structure That part of a carriage or mounting that provides a stable support for the ordnance. With a carriage, this includes trails and wheels.

BASO Brigade Air Support Officer.

BAT Battalion Anti-Tank Gun. See *MOBAT* and *WOMBAT.*

BATCO British Army Tactical Code.

BATES Battlefield Artillery Target Engagement System.

BATLSK British Army Training Staff Kenya.

Batman An officer's servant, the name is said to derive from the Spanish mules used during the Peninsular War to carry officers' baggage. These mules were known at Bats, hence the soldier detailed to drive the mule became a Batman.

BATS (i) Biological Antibiotic Treatment Set.
(ii) Ballistic Aerial Target System.

Batsim Battle Simulation.

BATSM Battlefield Simulation.

BATSUB British Army Training Sub Unit Belize.

Batt An early abbreviation of Battery but also used for a Battalion (During the early nineteenth century RA units were known as Battalions). See *Battalion* and *Bty.*

Battalion Prior to 1859 a Battalion was the equivalent of a present day Regiment. Battalions were renamed Brigades in 1859, and were given their current title of Regiment in 1938. See *Company.*

Battalion Guns During the eighteenth century, each infantry battalion was provided with either two 3-pdr or two short 6-pdr light field pieces. These artillery pieces were served by detachments from Royal Artillery Companies. The detachments normally consisted of a Subaltern, two

Non-Commissioned Officers, two Gunners and up to six Mattrosses. The RA Personnel were assisted by Additional Gunners, drawn from the supported infantry battalion. See *Additional Gunners* and *Mattross*.

Battery — The basic unit of the Royal Artillery. The word battery derives from the French *battre* (to beat), which is itself derived from the Latin *battuere*. A battery was a 'fixed' fortified structure in which artillery pieces were placed. Artillery in the field, however, were grouped into troops and companies. In 1722 gunner companies were organized into a regiment and it became known as the Royal Regiment of Artillery. In the late 1850s, companies of guns became known as battalions, then with another name change, they became regiments; over the same period troops of artillery came to be referred to as batteries. The term battery was adopted by the Royal Artillery in 1859, when it replaced 'company' in field and garrison artillery and 'troop' in the Royal Horse Artillery. The composition of a battery has changed a number of times over the years, *Field Artillery Training 1914* defines the various types of battery as: A battery of horse, field or mountain artillery consists of two or three sections, each of two guns with their complement of ammunition wagons. At that time heavy and territorial batteries consisted of two sections only.

Battery, The — The title by which 148 (Meiktila) Commando Forward Observation Battery RA is referred to by the Royal Marines.

Battery Aiming Points — See *Aiming Point.*

Battery Angle — The angle to the right or the left of a visible observation post which indicates the Zero Line of guns in action. See *Zero Line.*

Battery Area — An area which contains either troop or section gun positions, local defence posts and the battery echelon. One or more battery areas may be contained within a gun area. See *Gun Area, Gun Platform* and *Gun Position.*

Battery Captain — When in 1874 the rank of the Battery Commander was increased to Major, one of the four subaltern officer positions was raised from Lieutenant to Captain. This Officer then became known as the Captain. However, in 1938 when troop commanders were created in batteries they also held the rank of captain. During the same period vehicles started carrying 'tac_signs', that for the Captain being 'K'. It therefore became the practice to refer to the Captain as the Battery Captain or more colloquially the 'BK'.

The Battery Captain is the Battery Commander's deputy. In action his responsibilities are:

(i) Selection of battery areas, if ordered to do so.

(ii) Coordination and planning of local defence of the battery area.

(iii) Command of the battery in the event of an enemy attack.

(iv) Maintenance of servicing records of the guns.

(v) All Quartermaster, supply and Motor Transport matters.

At Battery level, the battery captain also performs the role of gun area commander.

See *Battery Commander, Gun Area Commander, Gun Area* and *Subaltern.*

Battery Centre — Located at the approximate geometrical centre of the guns of the battery. Battery Centre is used in setting up the plotters in the Battery Command Posts, and all measurements of line and range to targets are calculated from it.

	Introduced in 1956 to replace the pivot gun when calculating firing data. See *Pivot Gun* and *Troop Centre.*
Battery Column	A battery with the sections in open column. See *Battery Quarter Column.*
Battery Commander	The officer commanding a Battery. After 1874 the Battery Commander has been a major, prior to that date the position was held by a captain. Commonly referred to as the BC. See *Battery Captain.* Battery Commanders' Assistant The Tac Group's Senior Non-Commissioned Officer, whose prime responsibility is the coordination of targets for the Battery Commander's Fire Plan. Whilst in camp, the Battery Commander's Assistant is responsible for the technical training of all Forward Observation Officers and their Assistants. Generally referred to as the BC's Ack. See *Forward Observation Officer* and *Tactical Group.*
Battery Commander's Reconnaissance Group	Once orders have been received from the regimental commanding officer, and having conducted a reconnaissance with him, the Battery Commander carries out his own reconnaissance with his troop commanders. Once this has been accomplished he remains close to the headquarters of the unit being supported by his Battery. Orders are then transmitted directly to the troops and to the officer in charge of administration and supply.
Battery Commander's Staff	The signallers and specialists required who assist the Battery Commander in controlling the Battery. Use of the term seems to have died out when troop commanders were introduced. It existed prior the First World War when the Battery Commander was both the primary observing officer and at or near the gun position. BC's Party would seem the modern equivalent.
Battery Fire	At Battery Fire the guns are fired in rotation from the right, with an interval as specified in the fire orders. Battery fire continues until the requested number of rounds have been fired.
Battery Grid	Fixation and orientation of the guns which originated and was used in a battery. It was achieved by using basic survey methods, such as magnetic compass and map resection. See *Fixation, Orientation, Regimental Grid* and *Theatre Grid.*
Battery Guide	The Battery Guide, usually a WO2, accompanies the Gun Position Officer during the reconnaissance of the battery area and assists in reconnoitring routes and wagon lines. The Battery Guide then leads the various parties of the battery onto the gun position and assists the Battery Sergeant-Major in dispersing the vehicles. He/She can also assume the duties of a section commander. See *Section Commander.*
Battery Headquarters	Depending on the type of battery, may only be used for the peacetime location. In the field it generally ceased to be used by field artillery batteries, particularly those in direct support, between the First and Second World Wars because the Battery Commander and the Gun Group were increasingly widely separated. Not all field artillery batteries are direct support. See *Alternate Headquarters, Main Headquarters, Rear Headquarters, Regimental Headquarters, Step-Up* and *Tactical Headquarters.*
Battery Headquarters Group	A term used prior to and during the early part of the Second World War to describe the combined O and G Parties.
Battery Honour Titles	Titles awarded to batteries in recognition of certain outstanding actions performed during their history.

Not to be confused with battery nicknames, these are official titles which form part of the battery name. A full explanation of each battery honour title can be found in *Honour Titles of the Royal Artillery* by Major-General B. P. Hughes.

Battery Leader — The Battery Officer who was responsible for the movement and positioning of the Battery, he led guns between positions from the early 1900s until the troop organisation was introduced in 1938. After the Second World War the Battery Leader was responsible for leading the Battery gun group during a move. The role, at that time, was generally undertaken by the troop leader of the leading troop, although if he was available, the Battery Captain would undertake the role. See *Battery Captain* and *Troop Leader*.

Battery Left — A method of fire in which weapons are discharged from the left, one after the other, at five second intervals unless otherwise specified. See *Battery Right, Section Left* and *Section Right*.

Battery Manoeuvre Area — A Battery of nine MLRS launchers will be assigned a Battery Manoeuvre Area, within which will be allocated three Troop Manoeuvre Areas. In a typical day, an MLRS Battery may move to one or two different Battery Manoeuvre Areas. See *Troop Manoeuvre Area* and *MLRS*.

Battery Plotting Room — In Coast Artillery, a room in which information regarding the range, bearing, course and speed of target was received and from whence ranges and bearing suitably corrected were passed to the guns.

Battery Power Management — Part of the L118 Light Gun Capability Enhancement Package, the BPM is a 24v, 115Ah lithium-ion based series parallel battery, with its own integral management system. See *L118 Light Gun* and *L119 Light Gun*.

Battery Quarter Column — A battery with the sections in quarter column. See *Battery Column*.

Battery Quartermaster Sergeant — A staff sergeant, who amongst other things is responsible for the provision of rations and material support for his/her battery. As with other Staff Sergeants the BQMS is frequently addressed as 'Staff'. During the 1920s BQMS were often addressed as 'Quarter'. See *BQ, Quarter* and *Quarterbloke*.

Battery Reconnaissance Officer — An Officer or Senior Non-Commissioned Officer who is responsible for reconnaissance and deployment procedures within a gun battery. He/she is also capable of supervising battery and troop level continuation training both in the field and in barracks. The title was first used during the First World War, and subsequently resurrected during the 1990s.

Battery Reconnaissance Officers' Course — A five-week course at the Royal School of Artillery which aims to develop the skills and knowledge of selected Officers and SNCOs in order to train them in this role. See *Battery Reconnaissance Officer*.

Battery R Group — Battery Commanders Reconnaissance Group.

Battery Right — A method of fire in which weapons are discharged from the right one after the other, at five second intervals unless otherwise specified. See *Battery Left, Section Left* and *Section Right*.

Battery Smoker — A social gathering of all members of a Battery.

Battery Survey Data	The grid reference or co-ordinates of the battery centre on the current grid are recorded in the AB 548 Target Record Book. On a change of grid or a change of position the old details are struck through. See *Target Record Book*.
Battery Surveyor	A gunner trained to use the survey equipment held within the regiment. The title Battery Surveyor was used to distinguish them from the specialist surveyors in the Royal Artillery Survey Regiments.
Battery Target	A target on which the fire of all guns within a single battery are concentrated.
Battery - Target Line	Imaginary line drawn between the Battery and the Target. See also *TOB*.
Battle Attrition Study	Along with the Review of Ammunition Rates and Scales, this study was completed in 1981 and resulted in recommendations for large increases in Daily Ammunition Expenditure Rates for all natures of artillery. In the case of the M109, it was recommended that the Daily Ammunition Expenditure Rates be trebled. See *Review of Ammunition Rates and Scales* and *Daily Ammunition Expenditure Rates*.
Battle Axe Company, The	Battery Honour Title of 74 Battery (The Battle Axe Company) RA which was granted on 18 October 1926 under authority of 20/ARTY/4544/AG6a. The Battery is addressed when on parade as 'Company', the BC is referred to as the 'Company Commander' and the Battery is always referred to (at least within the Battery) as 'The Company'. See *Battery Honour Titles*.
Battleaxe Day	Battery day of 74 Battery (The Battleaxe Company). Celebrated on 24 February.
Battle Dress	Khaki serge all-ranks temperate climate uniform which was in the process of being introduced at the start of the Second World War. It was worn until the end of National Service when combat suits were introduced and Service Dress re-introduced for other ranks. See *Jungle Greens* and *Khaki Drill*.
Battlefield Air Interdiction	This is conducted between the Fire Support Coordination Line and the Reconnaissance and Interdiction Planning Line. See *Close Air Support*.
Battlefield Artillery Target Engagement System	Developed by the Target Engagement Automation Working Party, the system was named after Major General Sir Jack Bates. The acronym being constructed around his surname. BATES provides a computerised Command, Control, Communications and Information (C^3I) system capable of connecting to all non-Air Defence Artillery assets. Initially developed to enable multiple batteries to rapidly and effectively engage large enemy formations. Designed to reduce the need for voice traffic to a minimum, data is processed and passed rapidly through the artillery network ensuring speedy responses to calls for fire from observers. The system consists of a number of processing cells and data entry devices linked by secure communications equipment. During local elections in Bosnia, BATES was used to provide a secure 'fax' system.
Battlefield Meteorological System	A fully stand-alone meteorological system capable of producing computer and ballistic meteorological data for artillery surface to surface weapons, target acquisition meteorology and local Nuclear Biological and Chemical reports to a height of 20,000 metres and to a radius of

10,000 metres. With a detachment of five for Close Support Regiments and six for General Support Regiments, both of which are increased by one during war or operations, the system is transported in a Reynold Boughton 44 (RB44). BMETS came into service in 1999 as a replacement for AMETS. See *Artillery Meteorological System, Close Support* and *General Support.*

Battle Group Thermal Imaging — Mounted in Warrior Observation Post Vehicles this gunner's sight, manufactured by Thales Optronics has replaced the former image intensifying sights. The system includes a laser rangefinder, GPS navigation system and associated display screens. See *Warrior OPV.*

Battlespace Management — The means and measures by which the dynamic synchronisation of activity throughout the six dimensions of land, sea, air, space, electromagnetic spectrum, computer generated space and time are achieved. The three key components of Battlespace Management are Landspace Management, Airspace Management and Battlespace Spectrum Management.

BATUS — British Army Training Unit Suffield (Canada).

Bayliss Troop — Bayliss Troop is the name given to B Troop within 53 (Louisburg) Battery Royal Artillery.

BB — (i) Mustard Gas. A First World War British gas shell filling. The abbreviation is derived from the chemical name, beta, beta-Dichlorethylsulphide.
(ii) Base Bleed.
(iii) Battery Box.

BC — (i) Battery Commander. Usually a major.
(ii) Boom controller. Part of the MLRS system. See *Multiple Launch Rocket System.*

BCA — (i) Battery Commander's Assistant, often referred to as the BC Ack.
(ii) Boots, Combat, Assault.

BC Ack — See *BCA.*

BCC — Basic Communications Course.

BCC 46U — See *Station Radio BCC 46U.*

BCD — (i) B Coast Defence.
(ii) Battlefield Coordination Detachment.

BCD(A) — Battlefield Command Detachment. (Army).

BC Divn — Ball Cartridge Division.

BCFT — Basic Combat Fitness Test.

BCH — Boots, Combat, High.

BCHQ — Bombardment Control Headquarters. (Royal Navy).

BCIP — Bowman/ComBAT (Common Battlefield Application Toolset) Infrastructure Platform. May be followed by a number denoting the software version, for example BCIP5.

B Class — See *Black Class.*

BCM — Bottom Charge Module. See *TCM.*

B Coast Defence — A type of Coast Artillery gun mounting for the Naval 15-inch B gun. This was in fact a cover name for the Breech Loading 18-inch Mk I. Only three were ever constructed, being completed in 1918. After the First World War, two of the mounting were sent to the Experimental Establishment at Shoeburyness. During the Second World War these mountings were moved to Dover, where they were used to mount the cross-channel 14-inch guns which were known by the titles of 'Winnie' and 'Pooh'. After the Second World War the mounting were returned to Shoeburyness.

BCOE	Bowman Common Operating Environment.
BCP	Battery Command Post.
BCPO	Battery Command Post Officer.
BCPP	Battery Command Post Processor.
BCR	Battle Casualty Replacement.
BCRGA	Bermuda Contingent Royal Garrison Artillery.
BC Staff	Battery Commanders Staff.
BCV	Battery Commanders Vehicle, a Warrior variant.
BCW	Bombardment Calling Wave.
BD	Battle Dress.
BDA	Battlefield Damage Assessment.
BDD	British Defence Doctrine.
Bde	Brigade.
Bdr	Bombardier.
Bdry	Boundary.
BDTA	Back Door Training Area.
BDTS	Bowman Data Terminal System.
Bdy	Boundary.
BDZ	Base Defence Zone.
B Echelon	See *Echelon*.
B+E	Driving qualification allowing holder to drive a Land Rover and Trailer.
BE	Base Ejection Shell.
Beanies	Nickname for members of 57 (Bhurtpore) Battery RA. See *Beany Battery*.
Beany Battery	Nickname for 57 (Bhurtpore) Battery RA said to derive from the Heinz 57 varieties Baked Beans advertisements. Members of the Battery are referred to as Beanies. See *Beanies*.
Bearing	The clockwise angular measurement in the horizontal plane from a reference line, normally grid north. It is measured from 0 to 6400 mils (0 to 360 degrees). If measured from the map, or obtained by computation the bearing is referred to as the Map Bearing. If obtained by shooting, it is referred to as the Reduced Bearing. See *Fired Bearing*.
Bearing Picket	Originally known as a Survey Picket, the Bearing Picket, commonly known as a peg, consists of a steel stake driven into the ground with a card affixed to it giving accurate bearings to Aiming Points. The co-ordinates of the Bearing Picket are also given on the card. The Battery Director is set up over the Bearing Picket and orientated using the aiming points. A bearing and distance from the Bearing Picket can be used to fix the location of the gun selected as the pivot gun. See *Aiming Point*.
Bearing Picket Card	AFB 7111, the Bearing Picket card is used to record details of: (i) The title and particulars of the grid on which the relevant Bearing Picket has been established. (ii) The Bearing Pickets' name and number. (iii) The Bearing Pickets' co-ordinates. (iv) The grid bearing to three or more Reference Objects. (v) Diagrams of the Reference Objects, showing the exact point of lay, with a written description of the Reference Point and its location. (vi) The estimated distance to each of the specified Reference Objects. (vii) A diagram showing the location of the Bearing Picket and its relation to local topographical details. See *Bearing Picket, Grid* and *Reference Object*.
Bearing Picket Round	The measurement of horizontal angles, taken at a bearing picket, to Reference Objects whose bearings are to be recorded on a bearing picket card. See *Bearing Picket, Bearing Picket Card* and *Reference Object*.

Bearing Recess	That part of the gun carriage where the trunnions sit. See *Trunnions.*
Bearing Report Trace	A trace that can quickly be positioned over the Hostile Battery chart. It is used to determine locations of enemy weapon systems, record areas shelled or mortared and indicate times of firing from information contained on Shell and Mortar Reports. It has a secondary role of preventing the Hostile Battery chart from being disfigured for these purposes. See *Shelling Connection and Activity Trace, Shelling Plot, Hostile Battery* and *Hostile Battery Chart.*
Beat-up	Name by which the four week Pre-Commando Course is known.
BECA	Boom Electrical Control Assembly. Part of the MLRS system. See *Multiple Launch Rocket System.*
BE Coloured Flare Shell	See *Base Ejection Coloured Flare Shell* and *Carrier Shell.*
Bedblock	Folded bedding.
Bed Down	To prepare a bed of clean dry straw for a horse before finishing work. (The King's Troop RHA.)
Bedicopter	See *Heli-Bedford.*
Begbie Signalling lamp	A signalling lamp that was used by RA Signallers during the early part of the First World War, it was rapidly superseded by the 'Lucas' electrical signalling lamp which was vastly more portable and therefore better suited to operational conditions.
Behenna's Fuse	Introduced between 1817 and 1867 the Behenna's Fuse was designed to be used when firing rockets. It consisted of a nine-inch fuse, inserted into a cone-shaped boxwood plug which was designed to fit into one of the vents of a rocket. It had a burning time of fifteen seconds. The fuse was named after Quartermaster Behenna, the proposer of the design.
Belson's Blazers	See *Blazers, The.*
Bengallers	Nickname given to members of 132 (The Bengal Rocket Troop) Battery RA.
Bengal Rocket Troop, The	Battery Honour Title of 132 Battery (The Bengal Rocket Troop) RA which was granted on 18 October 1926 under authority of 20/ARTY/4544/AG6a. See *Battery Honour Titles.*
Benson Memorial Prize	Awarded between 1903 and 1939 to the cadet commissioned from the Royal Military Academy, Woolwich with the highest marks in War Material, Tactics and Riding. Between 1948 and 1973 it was awarded to the cadet commissioned into the Royal Artillery who had shown himself most deserving on the grounds of general efficiency and character at the Royal Military Academy, Sandhurst. Intakes 1–52. Between 1987 and 1993 the award was revised and re-allocated to the student officer RA on the Standard Graduate Course who had the best all-round performance. See *Tombs-Benson Memorial Prize.*
BER	Beyond Economic Repair.
BE Shell	See *Base Ejection Shell* and *Carrier Shell.*
BE Smoke	See *Base Ejection Smoke Shell* and *Carrier Shell.*
BE Smoke Shell	See *Base Ejection Smoke Shell* and *Carrier Shell.*
BF	Artillery Code used during the First World War meaning 'Battery fire'.
BFA	(i) Balloon Filling Area. Part of the BMETS system. (ii) Blank Firing Attachment.
BFCS	Battery Fire Control System. (Royal Canadian Artillery).
Bfg	Briefing.
BFS	Battery Fitter Section. (REME).
BFT	Basic Fitness Test, introduced in 1970s.
Bg	Bearing.

BG — (i) Battle Group.
(ii) Battery Guide. A Warrant Officer class 2 who, along with the battery leader assists with the reconnaissance of the new gun positions and guides the guns, when they arrive, to their firing platforms.

BGRA — Brigadier General Royal Artillery.

BGTI — Battlegroup Thermal Imager System. An upgrade for the Warrior OPV STA and Navigation systems.

Bhail Battery — See *Bail Batter.*

BHQ — Battery Headquarters. See *RHQ* and *THQ*.

BHTIK — Bottled Hydrogen Trailer Installation Kit. (Part of the BMETS system.)

Bhurtpore — Battery Honour Title of 57 (Bhurtpore) Battery RA which was granted on 18 October 1936 under authority of 20/ARTY/5040/AG6a. See *Battery Honour Titles.*

BID 150 — First generation voice encryption device used with the Larkspur C42Z and C45Z radios on formation command radio nets, entered service in the mid-1960s.

BID 250 — Lamberton voice encryption device used with Clansman UK/VRC 353. The original intention had been for a UK/VRC354 to be designated as '353Z', however, a late decision was made to build all 353 to 'Z' standard.

BID 460 — Data encryption used in BATES SANIE, the first software based encryption adopted by the British Army. See *BATES* and *SANIE*.

BIF — Battlefield Information Features.

BIFU — Blindfire Interface Unit. (Part of the Rapier FSB2 AD system.)

Big Ears — See *AD11*.

BILA — Balloon Inflation Launching Area. (Part of the BMETS system.)

BILD — Balloon Inflation and Launch Device. (Part of the Viasala system.)

Birch Gun — The first true Self-Propelled gun to be trialled by the Royal Artillery. The Mark I had the following specifications:
Weight: 12 tons
Engine: The Armstrong Siddeley 8 cylinder engine provided 90hp which developed a top speed of 15 mph
Armament: 18-Pdr gun
Detachment: 6
Ammunition: Approximately 75 rounds
Maximum Elevation: Between 80° and 90°
Traverse: 360°
Length: 19 feet
Breadth: 6 feet 9 inches
The gun and its detachment on the Mark I was unprotected, however, this was rectified in the Mark II with the addition of a shield and the provision for the detachment to be carried around with the gun when it traversed. Both Marks of the Birch Gun were capable of being employed in the ground support role and in an anti-aircraft role.

Bird Gunners — Slang used by both the Royal Australian and Royal Canadain Artillery for Air Defence artillery.

Bishop — The Bishop was an early attempt to provide a Self-Propelled gun to support to British armoured divisions. The official name for the Bishop was Ordnance QF 25-pdr Mk II or III on Carrier Valentine 25-pdr Gun Mk1. It consisted of a 25-pdr gun in an armoured box mounted on a Valentine tank chassis. Due to the armoured housing, the 25-pdr had a limited elevation which reduced its range considerably. In order to compensate, its detachments would often build large ramps out of the earth so

that the vehicle could be tilted. Its high silhouette was also a disadvantage. The Bishop was not a great success and was replaced at the earliest opportunity by the M7 Priest 105mm gun. Between 80 and 100 Bishop SP guns were produced but after 1943 they were withdrawn from service.
Weight: 17.5 tons
Length: 5.53 m
Width: 2.63 m
Height: 2.83 m
Detachment: 4 (Commander, gunner, loader, driver).
Armour:
Hull: 8–60 mm
Superstructure: 13–51 mm
Primary Armament: QF 25 pounder gun-howitzer with 32 rounds.
Secondary Armament: 0.303 inch Bren machine-gun
Engine: AEC A190 diesel 131 hp (98 kW)
Power/weight ratio: 7.4 hp/tonne
Suspension: coil sprung three-wheel bogies
Operational range: 145 km
Speed: 24 km/h

BIT — Built In Test.

BITE — Built In Test Equipment.

BK — Battery Captain.

BKI — Batch Key Indicator.

BL — (i) Breech Loading.
(ii) Battery Leader.
(iii) Bomb Line.

BL 4.5-inch Medium Gun — Introduced at the start of the Second World War, the initial supply of modern 4.5-inch guns was made by converting existing 60-pounders to the required calibre. However, it was found that few of these were suitable for conversion. Therefore a new gun was designed which was capable of utilising the same carriage as that used for the 5.5-inch gun. Production started in 1940, and the 4.5-inch remained in service throughout the war. Following the end of hostilities in 1945, the gun was relegated to training purposes and ultimately declared obsolete in 1959. Two Marks of the 4.5-inch Medium Gun were produced, the Mark I which comprised the converted 60-pounders, which were declared obsolete in 1944 and the Mark II.
Mark II Specifications:
Calibre: 4.5-inch
Length: 41 calibres. (4.6 metres)
Weight: 1.93 tonnes
Muzzle velocity: 686 metres per second
Detachment: 9
Shell Weight: 25 kg
Range: 18 km
See *BL 5.5-inch Medium Gun.*

BL 5.5-inch Medium Gun — A specification was issued in January 1939 for a replacement for the 60-pounder guns and 6-inch howitzers then in use. The BL 5.5-inch Medium Gun entered service in May 1942, being used for the first time in the Western Desert Campaign. Due to the weight of the shell when first introduced the range was disappointing, but with the introduction of a new shell, which was 20 lbs (9 kg) lighter the range obtainable improved dramatically. A 4.5-inch calibre version was also developed, using the same carriage. This had a longer range but suffered from poor lethality due to the low grade steel used in the production of its projectiles. The 4.5-inch was retired shortly after World War II.

Both the 5.5-inch and the 4.5-inch were generally teamed with the AEC Matador artillery tractor during the Second World War, however, from the 1950s, the 5.5-inch was typically towed by an AEC Militant Mk 1 6x6 truck.

The 5.5-inch remained in service with the Royal Artillery until replaced by the FH-70 155 mm towed howitzer in 1978. It was in service from 1942 until 1978.

Specifications:
Weight: 5.8 tons
Detachment: 9
Shell: HE 45.5 kg
Calibre: 5.5 inch (140 mm)
Carriage: Split trail
Rate of fire: 3 rounds per minute
Muzzle velocity: 517 metres per second
Effective range: 14 km
See *BL 4.5-inch Medium Gun* and *FH70.*

BL 6-inch 26cwt howitzer — See *Ordnance BL 6-inch 26cwt howitzer.*

Black Battery, The — Nickname said to have been given to 8 (Alma) Commando Battery RA following the Battle of the Alma owing to the powder stains covering the faces and chests of the men at the end of the Battle. See *Black Eight.*

Black Class — Blister Gas filled munitions. (Second World War and later.)

Black Eight — Nickname of 8 (Alma) Commando Battery RA. See *Black Battery, The.*

Black Knights — The Royal Artillery Parachute Display Team.

Black Powder — A form of propellant used extensively in the Royal Artillery. From the middle of the eighteenth century, the proportions of its constituents were 75% saltpetre, 10% sulphur and 15% charcoal. Originally a very fine powder, it was found that its propellant qualities could be enhanced by manufacturing the powder as gravel or pebbles. This slowed the rate of combustion and made possible the projection of heavier projectiles for a given calibre. This necessity being brought about by the introduction of rifling and the elongated projectile. Also known as gunpowder.

Black Rain — Nickname given to the bomblets dispensed by MLRS by the Iraqi forces during the First Gulf War.

BL Ammunition — Breech Loading Ammunition.

Blank Charge — A charge filled with quick burning cordite or gunpowder.

Blazers, The — Unofficial, but generally accepted nickname of the 1st Battery RA. The name has been the subject of some controversy over the years with at least three claims being made as to its origin. The most plausible reason is that while under command of Captain Belson (1829–1841) the Battery spent ten years at Woolwich (1831–1841). While there, Belson's Company regularly trained on the common 'blazing' away vast quantities of ammunition; it is reputed that this was done with the intention of impressing the local maidservants. 'Belson's Blazers' became a household name in the area and although Belson's name was dropped the Battery still continued to use their unofficial title, 'The Blazers'. However, at least two other candidates for the title exist, the first originates from the siege of Sebastapol in the Crimean War, where it is alleged a General is to have said 'Wait until I bring up my Blazers, that will shift them', whereupon the Battery came into action with great dash and in spite of their heavy guns, fired to such good effect that the opposition was soon cleared allowing the attack to continue. The third justification for the title is said to have originated at the battle of Dettigen in 1743 where the gunners served with such bravery and tenacity that, in spite of heavy casualties, they still managed to keep their guns firing. King George II remarked on it and declared that the Battery should henceforth be named 'The Blazers'. However, a report from the RA Historical Committee of 1950 said 'the title "Blazers" appears to be no more than a canteen nickname and that not one piece of solitary evidence of any historical value has been advanced to support the claim'.

Blazers Day Battery Day of 1st Battery RA (The Blazers).

BLC Breech Loading Converted.

BL Cartridge See *BL Ammunition*.

Bliff To polish leather with shoe polish until it shines, the term would appear to be used exclusively by the King's Troop RHA.

Blind A projectile where, after firing, the fuze has failed to function. Once the projectile has been fired, the forces of firing etc., will have rendered the safety devices in the fuze non-functional resulting in the projectile being liable to function if handled. During peacetime on the ranges, if an Observation Post can positively see the 'splash' of a blind, they will have to report it to range control with an accurate grid of it's location, type of projectile and fuze. Range control then list it as a blind and it's location for future reference (if practicable, an Ammunition Technical Officer might go and investigate it and blow it up). As most ranges are open to the public during non-firing weekends, blinds can become a hazard to 'ramblers' etc.

Blindfire Target Tracking Radar (Part of the Rapier FSB2 AD system), also known as DN 181 and Radar Tracker.

Blitz An artillery fire mission used during the early part of the Second World War, which eventually developed into the Stonk. See *Stonk*.

BLO (i) Bombardment Liaison Officer.
(ii) British Liaison Officer.

Blocked Up Slide In fortifications and coast artillery batteries this was a traversing carriage raised up on a central pivot which enabled the gun to fire over the parapet rather than through an embrasure.

Blokes, The Derisive nickname given to members of the Frontier Garrison Artillery. See *FGA*.

Blowpipe Very short range air defence missile system, replaced by Javelin. See *Javelin*.

BLR Breech-Loading, Rifled.

BLUEFOR Blue Forces – the good guys in exercises.

Blue Fuze The common name by which the No 57 fuze was known. They were sent to South Africa in 1900 to increase the range of shrapnel from horse and field guns. The No 57 fuze increased the range by 1800 yards.

Blue List, The Annual list of officers, serving and retired, of the Royal Regiment of Artillery. So called owing to the blue cover.

Blue Noses Nickname given to 29 Battery RA.

Blue on Blue An accidental contact between friendly forces, which may or may not result in casualties. The term appears to derive from the NATO practice of marking friendly forces on maps in blue and enemy forces in red.

Blue Water A developmental air-portable, mobile tactical nuclear missile mounted on a 3-ton Bedford lorry. With a range of 55 miles, Blue Water was to have had the ability to 'shoot

	and scoot'. Development started in 1957, but the project was cancelled in 1962.
Blythe Gunners, The	Nickname of 203 (Elswick) Battery RA (TA).
BM	Battlespace Management. See *BSM.*
BMA	(i) Battery Manoeuvre Area. (ii) Battle Management Application. See *GBAD BMA.* (iii) Brigade Maintenance Area. (iv) Bermuda Militia Artillery.
BMAT	British Military Advisory Team.
BMATT	British Military Advisory and Training Team.
BMD	Ballistic Missile Defence. British Military Doctrine.
BMDT	Bowman Management Data Terminal – part of the Bowman communications system. See *Bowman.*
BMETS	Battlefield Meteorological System.
BMHA	Brigade Major Heavy Artillery.
BMOU	Ballistic Memorandum of Understanding. See *JBMOU.*
BMRA	Brigade Major Royal Artillery. Staff officer to a CRA.
BMS	Battlespace Management System.
Bn	Battalion. See *Batt.*
BNG	British National Grid.
BNSSS	Battle Noise Simulation Safety Supervisor.
BO	Breech Obturated. See *AO.*
Board of Ordnance	A government body created in the 15th century. The Board of Ordnance was responsible for the design, testing and production of armaments and munitions for the entire British Army. In respect of artillery, the Board was responsible for providing artillery trains for armies and the maintenance of coastal fortresses. Another of its responsibilities was the production of maps for military purposes, a function which was later taken over by the Ordnance Survey. The Headquarters of the Board were located in the Tower of London. In addition to the Land Armament, the Board was responsible for Naval munitions, including cannon, shot, muskets, and gunpowder up until approximately 1830. The Board consisted of the following members: Master-General of the Ordnance, Lieutenant-General of the Ordnance, Surveyor-General of the Ordnance, Clerk of the Ordnance, Storekeeper of the Ordnance, Clerk of the Deliveries of the Ordnance and Treasurer of the Ordnance. In 1855 an Act of Parliament incorporated the Board of Ordnance into the War Office as the Department of the Master-General of the Ordnance. From this date the Board of Ordnance was effectively abolished. However, following the Second Boer War, and the perception that the British Army had been ill-equipped to fight the conflict, a new Board of Ordnance was created under the new title of the Ordnance Board. See *Clerk of the Deliveries of the Ordnance, Clerk of the Ordnance, Lieutenant-General of the Ordnance, Master-General of the Ordnance, Ordnance Board, Principal Storekeeper of the Ordnance, Surveyor-General of the Ordnance* and *Treasurer of the Ordnance.*
Boche-Buster	The name given by 471 Siege Battery RGA to a 14-inch, 270 ton Railway Gun, capable of firing a three-quarter ton shell to a range of twenty miles during the First World War. The first round fired by Boche-Buster was fired in the presence of King George V and caused immense damage to Douai railway station. This round became popularly known as 'The King's Shot'. See *Scene-shifter.*
BOEX	Battery Office Exercise.

Bofors A Swedish Arms manufacturer. The name was used colloquially to refer to the 40 mm Light Anti-Aircraft gun manufactured under licence by many nations. The Bofors had an effective altitude range of 12000 feet, and this combined with a 360° traverse and 90° elevation meant it was capable of tracking targets rapidly and without interruption. The Bofors was loaded four rounds at a time via chargers which were stacked into an automatic loader above the breech. The 2-lb projectiles could be fired at a rate of 110 rounds per minute, at a muzzle velocity of 2450 feet per second. Both the L40/60 and L40/70 (introduced in the 1950s) in various marks were used by the Royal Artillery. During the Second World War, a self-propelled version was employed by some batteries. The details given above are for earlier variants of the Bofors.

Bogues Troop One of the Troops in O/Headquarters Battery 'The Rocket Troop' RHA. See *Mains Troop.*

Bolster (i) In muzzle-loading artillery, a block of wood placed over the axletree of a gun.

(ii) A support for a black powder mortar barrel.

Bolton Wads Introduced into service in the mid-nineteenth century and constructed from a pulp made up of 75% old rags, known as 'tammies' or 'woollens' and 25% old tarred rope, the wads were formed in a mould and varnished when dry. They were intended to reduce windage in rifled ordnance, however, they proved useless and were withdrawn from service in favour of the copper gas-check. See *Gas-Check* and *Windage.*

Bolt Vent Axial Used to secure the obturation pad in Breech Loading ordnance.

Bomb (i) See *Bomb Vessel.*

(ii) An abbreviated reference to Bombardier. Usage is similar to the word Sarge for Sergeant. See *Bombardier.*

Bombard (i) An early artillery piece. Used by the British at the Battle of Crecy in 1346. The first battle in which the English employed artillery. There were problems with the Bombards; at times they could be just as deadly to the detachments as they could be to the enemy, for they were known to blow up as the charge was ignited, as a result the dangerous task of firing the piece fell to the most junior NCO, hence the rank Bombardier. See *Bombardier.*

(ii) The engagement of enemy batteries shown on the Hostile Battery (HB) list using predicted fire. The engagement was usually in the form of a scheduled or on-call fire plan. (Second World War.)

Bombarders Name given to members of Bombardment Troops. See *Bombardment Troop.*

Bombardier In 1920 the rank of Bombardier in the Royal Artillery, then denoted by a single chevron, was upgraded to replace that of corporal, the latter being abolished. Prior to that date the rank fell between that of Gunner and Corporal, and was denoted by a single chevron. At the same time the rank of Lance Bombardier was introduced. Thus from 1920 the Lance Bombardier wore a single chevron, whilst the Bombardier wore two chevrons.

This rank of Bombardier was introduced into the artillery in 1686, the rank being so named because he was trained in the use of the mortar which fired bombs and bombarded its targets.

The position was introduced owing to the substantial number of mortars added at that date to the to the equipment scales, the King approved the appointment of one Chief

Bombardier (a commissioned rank) and 12 Bombardiers who were to be specialists in the use of mortars.

From that time, whenever mortars formed part of any artillery train a proportion of Bombardiers accompanied them. Although the Bombardier was created to specialise in mortars it was not long before he added guns to his repertoire. By 1697 the guns of a long train were in general worked by ordinary troops of the line under the direction of Bombardiers, Petardiers, and Gunners. Bombardiers also served on Royal Navy bomb vessels which were equipped with a main armament of two heavy mortars.

Both the ranks of Corporal and the Sergeant appeared in the Royal Artillery after the Bombardier. (The Corporal first appeared in 1692 on the same rate of pay, and the Sergeant in 1702 on 6*d* more, but did not achieve their status as layer and Number One respectively until much later.) The Bombardier is therefore the oldest existing non-commissioned rank after Gunner and Master Gunner. See *Bomb Vessel, Bombard* and *Petardier.*

Bombardment Calling Wave	A wireless frequency common to all FOOs FOsB, BLOs and the Headquarters Ship.
Bombardment Fire	A concentration of fire onto a target. (Royal Canadian Artillery.)
Bombardment Liaison Officer	An RA Officer aboard a naval vessel who assisted in co-ordinating naval gunfire support during the Second World War.
Bombardment Troop	Second World War unit comprising sixteen gunner officers, seven OPA's and fourteen Naval Telegraphists, each Tp supported one division on a beach landing. The Major commanding the Tp, supported by a Capt, operated in the Divisional HQ Ship, Seven Capts each with an OPA and two Naval Telegraphists formed Forward Observers Bombardment (FOBs) and seven Capts, known as Bombardment Liaison Officers (BLO) were allocated to Naval vessels supporting the landings. FOBs moved ashore with the attacking units whilst BLOs took over the warship's guns when the ships were answering calls for fire from a FOB.
Bombardment Unit Association	Formed in 1945 the Association was subsequently replaced by the Amphibious Bombardment Association.
Bombardos	A Second World War term use to describe a number of Bombardment Units.
Bombing Up	Replenishing on-board stocks of ammunition.
Bomblet	Generic name applied to ammunition natures designed to dispense explosive sub-munitions.
Bomb Line	The term used during the Second World War for what is now known as the Fire Support Coordination Line. See *Fire Support Coordination Line.*
Bombr	Bombardier. Used during the Anglo-Boer War. See *Bombardier.*
Bomb Service	That branch of the Royal Artillery which served on bomb vessels. Part of the detachment was accommodated on the bomb vessel itself to tend the mortars and their beds (made from huge baulks of timber). The remainder of the detachment lived on the bomb vessels' tender and were responsible for looking after the ammunition. Shells were stored empty and were filled with powder on the tender just prior to use. A separate magazine was usually provided for this. This work was not without its

risks, especially at the hands of inexperienced ammunition numbers. Occasionally a special long boat crewed by watermen was provided, by the Board of Ordnance, to assist in ferrying ammunition and stores from the tender to the bomb vessel whilst in action. See *Board of Ordnance, Bomb Vessel* and *Detachment.*

Bomb Vessel

Commonly referred to at the time by the shortened title of Bomb, it is known that Bomb Vessels served with the Royal Navy from the late 17th century, however, more detail is available for those which existed during the early part of the nineteenth century. These Royal Navy ships were intended for the bombardment of cities, coast defences or anchored shipping. And as such were equipped with one or two smooth bore muzzle-loading iron or bronze 13-inch mortars, although 10-inch mortars were sometimes used. The mortars were mounted on a central pivot bed which permitted 360° traverse. During action it was necessary to ensure that the rigging was kept wet so that it was not ignited by the muzzle flash. Bomb vessels were normally accompanied by a tender carrying the necessary tools and equipment, including fuses, priming tubes, portfires and quick match. Three unidentified Bomb Vessels which were fitted out in 1738 were equipped as follows; one 13-inch and one 10-inch howitzer with 400 shells and 40 carcasses per mortar and howitzer. The mortar, with 30 lbs of powder would throw a 240 lbs shell 4000 yards whilst the howitzer using a 12 lbs powder charge could throw a 96 lbs shell the same distance.

During the Napoleonic period, a typical ammunition supply for a bomb vessel would be, 24 Carcasses, 24 Common Shell and 106 5 lb flannel cartridges for each mortar. A further 152 Carcasses, 352 empty shells and 4000 lbs of iron shot, together with 150 half barrels of gunpowder would be carried by the tender. The mortars were initially served by members of the Royal Artillery. RA Detachments carried on Bomb Vessels were shown on the ships books as 'Supernumeraries'. They were struck off the muster roll of their own company and instead shown on Detachment Muster Rolls. The vacancies created in the Companies by this action were filled by promotion and recruitment. These gunners were borne on the ship's books in the same way as Royal Marines, an arrangement which continued until 1804, when they were withdrawn after disagreements between the Royal Artillery subalterns in charge of them and the RN Officers who tried to make them carry out ships' duties. The Royal Marine Artillery was then formed to take the place of the RA detachments.

Bomb Vessels and their tenders (where identified), on which members of the Royal Artillery are known to have served:

Bomb Vessel	**Tender**
Aetna	
Alderney	*Pompey*
Basilisk	
Blast	
Bulldog	
Carcass	
Comet	*Sea Nymph*
Discovery	
Drake	

	Explosion
	Firedrake
	Furnace
	Fury
	Granado
	Hecla
	Infernal
	Lightning
	Mortar
	Perseus
	Salamander
	Solebay
	Strombolo
	Sulphur
	Tartarus
	Terrible *Goodley*
	Terror
	Thunder
	Triumph
	Vesuvius Rover
	Viper
	Volcano
	Warren
	Zebra
	A model of a Bomb Vessel can be seen in Firepower, The Royal Artillery Museum at Woolwich. See *Carcass, Common Shell* and *Portfire.*
Bomrep	Bombing Report.
BONCO	Battery Orderly Non-Commissioned Officer. See *RONCO.*
Boots and Socks	Nickname for the Quartermaster (Maintenance).
Boots CWW	Cold and Wet Weather boots originally issued for wear during the Korean War.
BOP	Battery Observation Post.
BOR	British Other Rank.
Border Ridge Position X	A permanent position manned during the CLARET operation in the 5 Division of Sarawak during 1965–6 by 51 Gurkha Infantry Brigade. It was located astride the border ridge and was occupied by an infantry platoon, a mortar section and a single gun section which rotated every two weeks.
Bore	The interior of an artillery piece down which the shell travels on firing. The size of the gun, known as its calibre, is measured across the lands of the barrel. See *Calibre.*
Bore Premature	See *Premature.*
Bore Safe	A fuze is said to be 'Bore Safe' if it is so designed that it is prevented from arming whilst in the bore of the gun. It is a requirement that all fuzes used by the Royal Artillery are Bore Safe.
Borgard Troop	One of the Troops in 33 Campbell Bty Junior Leaders Regiment RA. See *Gunn Troop, Shrapnel Troop* and *Wingate Troop.*
Boring	The process by which the bore of a gun is made. A metal bit or tool is forced down the length of a gun removing the excess metal and forming the cavity which is known as the bore.
Borneo Troop	One of the Troops in 88 (Arracan) Battery RA. See *Kairouan Troop.*
Bouche a Feu	Name given to the small iron trough carried by one man in each three-man section of the Rocket Troop RHA during the Napoleonic period. It is described by Congreve as being a small iron trough 18 inches long,

	fitted with four prongs at the bottom so that it could be heeled into the ground. For transport purposes it was carried in a small leather case, strapped above the valise at the rear of the saddle.
Bouncing How	Nickname given to the 7.2" Mk IV How which was fitted with huge pneumatic tyres.
Bourrelet	A carefully machined portion to the rear of the shoulder of a projectile which is designed to centre the front of the projectile in the gun. Together with the driving band it provides a 'Wheelbase' on which the projectile travels in the bore of the gun. See *Driving Band.*
Bowman	Bowman is the Army's new tactical communications system. Bowman provides a tactical, secure voice and data communication system, replacing the Clansman series and taking over the headquarters part of the Ptarmigan trunk communications system. Bowman is a component of Land Digitisation, which will include future battlefield information systems. See *Clansman* and *Larkspur.*
Bowman ComBAT Infrastructure and Platform Team	The BCIP team at the Royal School of Artillery provides instruction and training on the applications associated with the BOWMAN communications system. These applications include ComBATand FC BISA. See *ComBAT* and *FC BISA.*
Bowman Common Operating Environment	Part of the Bowman communications system. See *Bowman.*
Bowman Data Terminal System	Part of the Bowman communications system. See *Bowman.*
BOWO	Brigade Ordnance Warrant Officer.
BOWTAG	Bowman Training and Advisory Group.
BOWTAG(S)	Bowman Training and Advisory Group (South).
Box Trail	The trail of a gun which in this instance is designed in the shape of a hollow box. See *Trail.*
Boyes Anti-Tank Rifle	0.55-inch anti-tank rifle used in the first half of the Second World War, it was issued to Royal Artillery units for local anti-tank defence.
BP	Bearing Picket.
BPC	Basic Parachute Course.
BPFA	Basic Physical Fitness Assessment.
BPI	Ball Powder Igniter.
BPM	Battery Power Management.
BPR	Battery Plotting Room.
BP Round	Bearing Picket Round. See *Bearing Picket, Bearing Picket Card* and *Reference Object.*
BP Trophy	See *Thales Shield.*
BRA	Brigadier Royal Artillery.
Bracket	Two rounds, one of which is an over and one which is short of the target. A target round is the equivalent of a Bracket. See *Over, Short, Target Grid Corrections* and *Target Round.*
Bracketing	See *Bracket.*
Bradbury Troop	One of the three troops in L (Nery) Battery RA. See *Dorrell Troop* and *Nelson Troop.*
BRASCO	Brigade Royal Army Service Corps Officer.
Breast loop	In muzzle-loading artillery this was an iron loop embedded in the breast transom.
Breech	The rear part of a gun, where in Breech-Loaders the ammunition is inserted.
Breech Clinometer Plane	An accurately machined plane surface on the top of the breech ring. Most of the angular measurements and adjustments made on the gun are based on this plane. Within

certain limits of tolerance the breech clinometer plane is parallel to both the axis of the bore and to the axis of the trunnions. See *Axis of the Bore* and *Axis of the Trunnions.*

Breech Loading A form of ordnance where obturation is provided by the breech mechanism and the propellant was bagged and not supplied in a metal cartridge case. The number of bags could be varied to increase or decrease the explosive power of the charge. See *Obturation* and *QF.*

Breech Loading Ammunition In Breech Loading ammunition, the charge is contained in a fabric bag, an 'igniter' being sewn on one or both ends. Obturation is not a function of the cartridge, but is achieved by an 'obturation pad' on the breech mechanism. Ignition is achieved by means of a 'tube' (either percussion or electric), which is inserted into the breech mechanism and ignites the igniter by way of a flash. The projectile and charge are loaded separately. An example of a gun using BL ammunition is the 5.5-inch gun. See *Obturation* and *QF Ammunition.*

Breech Loading Cartridge See *Breech Loading Ammunition.*

Breech Loading Converted Some earlier Breech Loaders were modernised by the fitting of a faster operating breech. Bagged charges were however still used. See *Breech Loading.*

Breech-Loading, Rifled The original nomenclature given to the Armstrong Rifled Breech Loaders, which was afterwards changed to RBL.

Breech Ring The portion of the Breech into which the Breech block fits.

Bren Light Machine Gun .303 light machine-gun introduced just before the Second World War, converted to 7.62 mm in 1950s (as L4 LMG), it was widely used by Royal Artillery units until 1980s.

BRG Bearing.

BRI Brightness.

Brigade Prior to 1938, a Lieutenant Colonels' command consisting of a number of Batteries. After 1938, the title was changed to Regiment.

Brigade Ammunition Column At the beginning of World War I, Royal Artillery manned Ammunition Columns were responsible for the third line ammunition supply, not only of artillery ammunition, but also for infantry and cavalry ammunition as well. A Brigade Ammunition Column, commanded by a Captain, was attached to each field artillery brigade with the responsibility of distributing the ammunition brought up to the Ammunition Refilling Point by the Divisional Ammunition Column to the batteries of the brigade. Brigade Ammunition Columns were disbanded in France during 1916. The task then, in Royal Garrison Artillery brigades became the responsibility of the Royal Army Service Corps. However, in India, the Royal Army Service Corps/Royal Indian Army Service Corps did not take over this responsibility until the mid/late 1930s. See *Divisional Ammunition Column.*

Brigade-Division In 1885 Batteries in the same station would be grouped into Brigade-Divisions, this title was abolished in 1903 when the title Brigade was introduced. A Lieutenant Colonel's command. Between 1881 and 1885 such formations were known as Divisions.

Brigade of Artillery In 1914 this consisted of two batteries of horse artillery or three batteries of field artillery. In both cases an ammunition column was also attached.

Brigade of Guns An early nineteenth century term for a Battery. Guns would be drawn from the Artillery Park and manned by a Company RA.

Brigade Survey Officer	See *Regimental Survey Officer.*
Brigade TAC	Comprises a small group of armoured fighting vehicles that deploy forward of the brigade headquarters when the Brigade Commander wishes to see what is happening himself. Brigade TAC normally consists of the Brigade Commander, the Artillery Commander and the Royal Engineers Commander together with a close protection section. See *Regimental TAC* and *TAC Party.*
BRITARTYBAT	British Artillery Battery. (UN Bosnia Deployment.)
British Army Tactical Code	A means of encrypting messages using a daily code, sometimes referred to as a Battle Code.
British Defence Doctrine	A unified tri-service doctrine which was first introduced during the 1990s. It was based mainly on British Military Doctrine which had been introduced some years earlier. See *British Military Doctrine.*
British Liaison Officer	Royal Artillery officers posted to foreign artillery schools are usually British Liaison Officers.
British Military Doctrine	Formal top level army doctrine first issued during the 1980s it established the manouvrist approach. See *British Defence Doctrine.*
British Other Rank	A definition used to differentiate between British and Indian Other Ranks in mixed units prior to Independence in 1948. See *Indian Other Rank.*
BRO	Battery Reconnaissance Officer.
BROC	Battery Reconnaissance Officers Course.
Broken Wheel, The	Battery Honour Title of 171 (The Broken Wheel) Battery RA which was granted on 18 October 1926 under authority of 20/ARTY/4544/AG6a. See *Battery Honour Titles.*
Brooke's Troop	One of the two troops in N Battery (The Eagle Troop) RA. Named after the FM Alan Brooke who served in the battery. Not currently in use (2007) due to N Battery (The Eagle Troop) RA being reduced to Troop size. See *Leslie's Troop.*
BRP	Bore Riding Pin – part of the Javelin AD missile system.
BRPC	Beyond Repair Provisionally Condemned.
BRT	Bearing Report Trace.
BRX	Border Ridge Position X.
BQ	Abbreviated form of BQMS. See *Quarter* and *Quarterbloke.*
BQMS	Battery Quartermaster Sergeant. See *BQ, Quarter* and *Quarterbloke.*
BS	Battery Surveyor.
BSA	Base Support Area.
BSCP	Battery Safety Command Post.
BSD	(i) Burst Safe Distance. (ii) Burst Safety Distance.
BSFM	Ballistic Sensor Fused Munition.
BSM	(i) Battery Sergeant-Major. (ii) Battlespace Management.
BS Major (IG)	Battery Sergeant-Major (Instructor-in-Gunnery). Rank no longer in use.
BSM(IG)	Battery Sergeant-Major (Instructor in Gunnery). Rank no longer in use.
BSM(I)	Battery Sergeant-Major (Instructor).
BST	Basic Science and Technology.
BT	Battery – Target. See *Battery – Target Line.*
Bty	Battery.
Bty L	Battery Left.
Bty Ldr	Battery Leader.
Bty R	Battery Right.
Bty Tgt	Battery Target.
BUA	Bombardment Unit Association.

Bubble Line Bubble Line Bubble	On guns where the same sight serves for both bearing and elevation, as the gun is elevated, if there is any tilt at all on the trunnions, and of course there generally is, the gun barrel and sight do not raise on a true vertical. It is necessary therefore to level the sight in a number of steps to compensate for this and ensure that the bearing and elevation the gun is layed at is true in the horizontal and vertical planes. The sequence to achieve this is correct the elevation (bubble) correct the bearing (line) then the elevation again (bubble) then the bearing a second time (line) and finally give the elevation the final touch (bubble).
Buffer	The apparatus used to check and control the recoil of a gun when firing. This is usually achieved through the use of springs or hydraulics.
Built-up Barrel	A built-up barrel consists of an inner tube enclosed by one or more outer tubes. This type of construction may be met in some large ordnance. The tubes are prevented from rotating, each within the other, by shrinkage, and forward movement is prevented by shoulders in the tube walls. The breech ring is screwed onto the outer tube and may incorporate a breech bush to secure the rear of the tubes. See *Loose Barrel* and *Monobloc Barrel.*
Bull	To polish leather with shoe polish until it shines. See *Bliff.*
Bull's Troop	Battery Honour Title of I Parachute Battery (Bull's Troop) RHA which was granted on 18 October 1926 under authority of 20/ARTY/4544/AG6a. See *Battery Honour Titles.*
Bullock Field Battery	Up until the time of the Mutiny a number of Field Batteries in India remained bullock-drawn, these were distinguished in the Army Lists as No ** Bullock Field Battery. See *Horse Field Battery.*
Bullocks	Derogatory nickname given to members of the Royal Marine Artillery. This formation is no longer in existence, having been disbanded in 1923.
Budge barrel	In the muzzle-loading artillery period, this was a wooden gunpowder barrel which had a leather liner. Its purpose was to provide a supply of powder near the gun. The leather inner could be tied up when not in use.
Bursting Shell	A type of carrier shell which generally bursts on impact by means of a percussion fuze. The small bursting charge breaks open the shell and releases the contents. Its main disadvantage, over a Base Ejection Shell, is that, even with a direct action fuze, the contents are carried by their remaining velocity into the ground and their effectiveness is reduced. See *Base Ejection Shell* and *Carrier Shell.*
Bush Artillery	Name applied by the Australian forces during the Second World War to captured artillery reused against its former owners, usually by infantry men. (Royal Australian Artillery).
Bustard Carpark	No need for a map.
Buster	An American mini UAV constructed from carbon fibre and launched via a small portable rail. Buster provides 32 Regiment RA with the ability to fully support UK based training for those units about to deploy to an operational theatre by giving them an insight into UAV capabilities, whilst at the same time ensuring all operational resources remain available to the batteries currently deployed.
Buttsman	A person employed in the Proof Butts. See *Proof Butts.*
BVA	Bolt Vent Axial.
BWR	Basic Wind Report. A meteorological message.

BWX — Beeswax. Used as an additive in certain types of artillery shell.

BX — (i) Battery Exchange – mainly a telephone exchange. (First World War).
(ii) First World War artillery abbreviation for 4.5-inch Howitzer High Explosive shell. The abbreviation was used in ammunition returns.

Byle Battery — See *Bail Battery.*

BZ — Beaten Zone.

C – Charlie – 1927/1943/1956

C — Carbon.

C/A — Centre of Arc.

C11/R210 — See *Station Radio C11/R210.*

C42 — See *Station Radio C42.*

C45HP — See *Station Radio C45HP.*

C2 — Command and Control.

C2W — Command and Control Warfare.

C3 — Command Control and Communications.

C4I — Command Control Communications Computers and Intelligence.

CA — (i) Coast Artillery.
(ii) Course Acquisition.

CAAD — Composite Anti-Aircraft Demonstration Battery RA. (Now defunct).

Cab Yard — An apocryphal name for the Riding Establishment Royal Artillery. Probably a misrepresentation of the more common Tan Yard.

CAD — Close Air Defence.

CADC — (i) Command Air Defence Centre.
(ii) Corps Air Defence Cell. See *DADC* and *FADC.*
(iii) Coastal Artillery Displacement Calculator. Second World War and later.

CADDET — Close Air Defence Detachment Trainer.

CADWS — Close Air Defence Weapons System.

CAEE — Coast and Anti-Aircraft Artillery Experimental Establishment.

Caffin's Grape Shot — Similar to ordinary Grape Shot, but in this guise, the lead balls were confined in layers between metal plates. See *Grape Shot.*

CAFTG(G) — Combined Arms Field Training Group (Germany).

CAGRA — Commander Army Group Royal Artillery. See *AGRA.*

CAGRA Representatives — Commander Army Group Royal Artillery Representative. See *Commanders Representative.*

CAIO — Corps Artillery Intelligence Officer.

Cal — Calibre.

CAL — Critical Assets List.

Calculator, Displacement, Field Branch Artillery — See *Displacement Calculator.*

CALFEX — Combined Arms Live Firing Exercise.

Calibrating Sights — These are sights which have an integrated gun rule that corrected the range for the gun's MV and in effect calculated Tangent Elevation. See *Dial Sight Carrier, Gun Rule* and *Reciprocating Sights.*

Calibration — This procedure determines the actual muzzle velocity of the gun, the difference between the actual muzzle velocity and the standard muzzle velocity for the nature of gun is applied as a correction to the guns firing data.

Calibre	The diameter of the bore measured across the lands. The term 'calibre length' means the length of the bore expressed in calibres. The clearance between the maximum diameter of the shell (excluding the driving band) and the calibre is known as the 'windage'.
Calibre Length	The length of the bore express in calibres. See *Bore* and *Calibre*.
Calibre Radius Head	A mathematical way of describing the shape of the nose of a shell, whether it be blunt, rounded, pointed etc.
Call For Fire	A request for fire containing the necessary data for obtaining the required weight of fire on a target.
CALM	Crane Articulated Lorry Mounted.
Cam	Camouflage.
CAM	Chemical Agent Monitor, 1980s and later.
CAMC	Cancel At My Command. See *At My Command*.
Camming Up	Applying camouflage.
Cam Up	Apply camouflage.
Canberra Winchman	A term commonly used at the Royal Artillery Range Hebrides to lure gullible nigs into thinking they'd get a ride in a Canberra aircraft with the job of winching in and out the target. Occasionally referred to as a Target Winchman. See *NIGs*.
Canc	Cancel.
Cancel	An order which when coupled with another order other than one specifying quantity or type of ammunition, rescinds that order.
Canned Drop Shots	Derogatory nickname given to members of self-propelled gun regiments of the Royal Artillery.
Cannon Pig	Derogatory nickname for a member of a gun detachment. See *Gun Bunny*.
Cannot Observe	A type of fire control which indicates that the Forward Observer will be unable to adjust fire, but believes a target exists at the given location and is of sufficient importance to justify firing upon it without adjustment or observation.
Canteen Cowboy	Derogatory nickname given to the Regimental Orderly NCO.
CAOC	Combined Air Operations Centre.
CAP	Course Assessment Plan.
CAPC	Coast Artillery Practice Camp.
Cap Composition	An igniferous initiator used in the caps of tubes and small arms cartridges. See *Igniferous Initiator*.
Capped Piercing Ballistic Capped	A projectile used for attacking armour, concrete etc.
Capt	Captain.
Captain, The	Second in command of a battery when there was only one captain per battery, became Battery Captain (BK) during the Second World War.
Captain General, The	The title now held by Her Majesty Queen Elizabeth II. The title, which was taken into use in 1951, superseded that of the Colonel-in-Chief of the Royal Artillery. It was His Majesty King George VI, whilst dining in the Royal Artillery Mess at Woolwich, in December 1950, who expressed his wish to be known by the title of Captain General. The title had previously been used in the 17th & 18th Centuries and at that time was the most senior of the General Officer ranks.
Captain-Lieutenant	Prior to 1827 this was a rank between Captain and Lieutenant, at that time the title was changed to Second Captain.
Capt-Lt	See *Captain-Lieutenant*.
Carcass	An incendiary projectile. This was a container made of layers of paper which was filled with 'composition'

which was heated and poured into the container and allowed to harden. The container was pierced with holes so that the flash of the charge could ignite it and the burning composition could escape on contact with the target. Carcasses were only fired from howitzers and mortars. See *Composition*.

Cardinal — Nickname for the M44 155 mm Self-Propelled Howitzer.

Carnous — A term used by some 17th Century commentators to describe that part of the gun breech which is behind the behind the base ring. Also found spelt as Carnouz.

Carnouz — See *Carnous*.

CAROT — Committee on Army Regular Officer Training.

Carriage — The structure of the gun that supports the ordnance and has wheels in contact with the ground when firing.

Carriage, Garrison, Rear Chock — A Garrison Standing Carriage where the rear trucks have been replaced with chocks. See *Garrison Standing Carriage* and *Chocks*.

Carriage-Smith — In 1904, one of the two Battery Wheelers then on the strength of each Battery was replaced by a Carriage-Smith.

Carrier Shell — A carrier shell contains a small bursting charge for the purpose of opening the shell and liberating its contents. Carrier shells may function on impact or as an air burst. There are two types of carrier shell, namely bursting and base ejection. Typical fillings are:
Smoke (White or Coloured)
Flare (Coloured)
Illuminating (Parachute)
See *Base Ejection Shell, Base Ejection Smoke Shell* and *Bursting Shell*.

Carrier, Observation Post — See *Armoured Observation Post Carrier*.

Cartouche — During the era of muzzle-loading artillery, this was a waterproof canvas bag for holding gun charges.

Cartridge Filling Room — In Coast Artillery, a chamber in a laboratory where cartridges were made up. See *Laboratory*.

Cartridge Issuer — In Coast Artillery a hatch or opening in a wall through which cartridges were passed. See *Shell Issuer*.

Cartridge Lift — In Coast Artillery the lift up which cartridges are hoisted from the cartridge store to the cartridge serving room. See *Shell Lift, Cartridge Store* and *Cartridge Serving Room*.

Cartridge Passage — In Coast Artillery a chamber on the same level as the gun into which the cartridge lift leads. See *Cartridge Lift* and *Shell Passage*.

Cartridge Recess — In Coast Artillery a small receptacle for the storage of a few cartridges for the immediate service of the gun. See *Shell Recess*.

Cartridge Store — In Coast Artillery a chamber where filled cartridges were stored.

CAS — (i) Close Air Support.
(ii) Commander's Alerting Sight.

Cascable — The part of a gun behind the vent. It is in fact, the button on the end of the breech of a gun. The cascables from two Russian guns captured at Sevastapol during the Crimean War are used to provide the metal for the Victoria Cross.

Cascable Button — A button at the rear extremity of a muzzle-loading gun. When no elevating screw was available it was often used as a leverpoint for elevating the gun.

Case I — One of three methods used in Coast Artillery to lay the guns onto a target. In Case I, which was the simplest method, the layer used the guns own sights to lay for both line and elevation, having been informed from the rangefinder (either Depression Range Finder or Position Finder) of the range to the target. It was rarely employed due to the problems associated with judging the elevation to be set on the gun sight, particularly at night. See *Case II, Case III, Depression Range Finder* and *Position Finder.*

Case II — The most widely practiced and preferred Coast Artillery method of laying guns onto a target. In Case II, the layer laid the gun for line, whilst the rangefinder detachment found the range, using either a Depression Range Finder or a Position Finder and applied corrections to a dial located at the rangefinder post. These corrections were then transmitted, either to the Battery Commander, who would make further corrections for each gun in the battery, or directly to a dial on the gun. In the latter case, another member of the detachment would read the gun dial and set the correct elevation from below the gun. See *Case I, Case III, Depression Range Finder* and *Position Finder.*

Case III — The third and final method used to lay Coast Artillery guns onto a target. In many ways similar to Case II, with the exception that laying for line was calculated by a Position Finder and transmitted directly to a second dial on each gun. When using Case III, the guns own sights were not used at all. Case III became the preferred method when the Fortress Plotting was introduced, although at that time corrections were calculated in the Battery Plotting Room. When Coast Artillery adopted Radar laying, all engagements were made using Case III. See *Case I, Case II* and *Position Finder.*

Case Shot — The initial version of case shot consisted of langridge placed in a suitable container, however, it was soon improved by the addition of a bursting charge and a short fuze. An early form of anti-personnel projectile. See *Grape Shot* and *Langridge.*

Casevac — Casualty Evacuation.

CASL — Coast Artillery Search Light.

Cassino Troop — (i) The OP Troop in 28/143 Battery (Tomb's Troop) RA. See *Hills Troop* and *Skeddys Troop.*
(ii) Originally one of the Troops in 2nd Squadron Honourable Artillery Company, after 1994 transferred to Signal Squadron with Aden Troop and Somme Troop. See *Aden Troop, El Alamein Troop, El Hamma Troop, Honourable Artillery Company, Somme Troop* and *South Africa Troop.*

CAST — Command and Staff Trainer.

Castlemartin — Artillery Range in Pembrokeshire now adapted for Ground Based Air Defence firing with both the Rapier and HVM systems. See *HVM* and *Rapier.*

Cat — Caterpillar Tractor – used to tow heavy artillery (i.e. 9.2 Hows) in the First World War.

CATAQ — Catalogue of Army Qualifications.

CATC — Coast Artillery Training Centre (Second World War). Consisted of three Training Regiments and an OCTU.

CATF — Commander Amphibious Task Force.

CATT — Combined Arms Tactical Trainer.

CAV — Artillery Code used during the First World War meaning 'Cavalry'.

CB — (i) Counter Battery.
(ii) Counter Bombardment.

CBA — Combat Body Armour.

CB Chart — (i) Counter Battery Chart.
(ii) Counter Bombardment Chart.

CBI	Clean Burning Igniter.
CBLO	Chief Bombardment Liaison Officer (Second World War).
CBO	Counter Battery Officer.
CB Perintrep	Counter Bombardment Intelligence Report. Used during the 1950s.
CBR	(i) A First World War British gas shell filling consisting of arsenious chloride. (ii) Counter Battery Radar.
CBSO	Counter Battery Staff Officer (First World War).
CBT	Computer-Based Training.
CBU	(i) Commander Bombardment Units (Second World War). (ii) Cluster Bomb Unit.
CC	(i) Collective Call. (ii) Chalk Commander. (iii) Column Commander.
CC1	Collective call sign for all Command Posts on the Regimental Net. See *Collective Call.*
CC11	Collective call sign for all Observation Posts on the Regimental Net. See *Collective Call.*
CC3	Collective call sign for all Command Post Officers on the Regimental Net. See *Collective Call.*
CCA	(i) Close Combat Attack. See *CAS* and *CIFS*. (ii) Commander, Coast Artillery. Now defunct.
CCAs	Circuit Card Assemblies.
CCBO	Corps Counter-Bombardment Officer. A Lieutenant Colonel commanding a Counter-Bombardment Troop. See *Counter-Bombardment Troop.*
CCC	(i) Radio Code indicating that a transmission was about to be sent using Artillery Code. See *Artillery Code.* (ii) Commando Conditioning Course.
CCF	(i) Computer and Communication Facility (Part of RARH). (ii) Course Correcting Fuze. (iii) Crest Clearance Factor. (iv) Crest Confidence Factor.
CCCA	Corps Commander Coast Artillery.
CCD	Commander of Coast Defences. (Royal Garrison Artillery.)
CCIS	Command, Control and Information System(s).
CCMA	Corps Commander Medium Artillery.
C Co-ordinates	Corrected co-ordinates. See *U Co-ordinates*.
CCRA	Commander Corps Royal Artillery.
CCRA Representative	Corps Commander Royal Artillery's Representative. See *Commanders Representative.*
CCRF	Civil Contingency Reaction Force.
CCS	Casualty Clearing Station.
CCSOD	Cloth, Camouflage, Synthetic, Olive Drab.
CCU	Command and Control Unit. Part of the Rapier FSC system. See *Rapier FSC.*
CD	Coast Defence.
CDB	Cast Double Base.
CDD	Coder Digital Data. Part of FACE.
Cdo	Commando.
CDR	Chemical Downwind Report. A meteorological message.
CDS	Chief of the Defence Staff.
Cdt	Cadet.
CDU	Chassis Distribution Unit.
C+E	Driving qualification allowing the holder to drive vehicles up to and including Light Goods Vehicles.
CE	(i) Composition Exploding. Used in fuzes as part of the explosive train. (ii) Chemical Energy.

Cease Firing — This order is given by the officer in command of the gun position immediately before the guns are to come out of action. Before 'Cease Firing' is given, the officer must have received an executive order to move the guns and he/she must be satisfied that the Empty Guns drill has been carried out. It should not be confused with Cease Loading. See *Cease Loading* and *Empty Guns.*

Cease Loading — No further rounds to be loaded, although any rounds which have already been loaded may be fired. The order should not be confused with Cease Firing. See *Cease Firing, Check Firing* and *Empty Guns.*

CEFO — Complete Equipment Fighting Order. This equipment is now obsolete and has been superseded by Personal Load Carrying Equipment.

CEFO/AO — Complete Equipment Fighting Order/Assault Order.

CEFO/CO — Complete Equipment Fighting Order/Combat Order.

CEI — Communications Electronic Instruction.

CEMO — Complete Equipment Marching Order.

Centenary Cup — Presented by Major-General F. T. Lloyd CBE in 1895 to commemorate the centenary of the appointment of the first DAGRA. The Centenary Cup was a challenge cup for good shooting to be awarded in alternative years to the best shooting battery of Field Artillery or Company of Garrison Artillery. In 1901 the Field Artillery gave up competitive practice, and the award of the cup became confined to the RGA. However, in 1905 the competition ceased and in 1907 the Cup was handed to the School of Gunnery, Shoeburyness, for safe keeping. See *DAGRA.*

Central Pivot Mounting — A mounting for a gun, whereby a pivot is constructed around a shaft, sunk into the ground. Generally used for Coast Artillery.

Centres — Horses which work in the middle of a Gun Team; usually the youngest horses of the Team. (The King's Troop RHA.)

Centre of Arc — A grid bearing which replaced the Zero Line in the 1950s. The CP was then able to order line as a bearing in relation to grid North. See *Zero Line.*

Centre-to-Centre Data — This consists of the bearing, angle of sight and range, corrector or fuze setting from the battery centre to the centre of the target, or other given point. See *Battery Centre.*

CEP — (i) Circular Error Probable, sometimes given as Circular Error Probability.
(ii) Capability Enhancement Package.

CEPA(R) — Charging Equipment Pure Air (Regenerative).

CERR — Cyprus Emergency Reinforcement Regiment.

Cervantes — An improved version of the Cymbeline mortar locating radar, it proved unsuccessful and the project was cancelled. See *Cymbeline.*

CES — Complete Equipment Schedules.

CESO(A) — Chief Environmental and Safety Officer (Army).

CET — Combat Enhancement Training.

CF — Covering Fire.

CFA — (i) Commander Force Artillery (Commander of the AMF(L) Artillery.)
(ii) Canadian Field Artillery.

CFD — Commander Fixed Defences.

CFF — Call For Fire.

CFL — Coordinated Fire Line. See *FSCM.*

CFOV — Centre Field of View. A Phoenix Unmanned Aerial Vehicle turret position. See *Phoenix.*

CFSP — Continuous Fire Support Plan. (Royal Canadian Artillery.)

CFT — (i) Combat Fitness Test.
(ii) Commanders Functional Test.

CFU — Commanders Firing Unit.

CG — Collongite–Phosgene. A First World War British gas shell filling, the name was derived from the source of the original supplies, the French town of Coulogne.

CGA — Canadian Garrison Artillery.

CGI — Corrugated iron.

Ch — Charge. The propellant, charges are usually made up of various bags, combinations of which are used to achieve differing ranges.

CH — Close Hide.

CHA — Commander Heavy Artillery. (First World War).

Chamber — (i) The smooth portion of the Bore which is shaped to take the propellant charge. See *Bore*.
(ii) A small piece of ordnance, without a carriage, which was used for firing salutes.

Change of Grid — The process by which the fixation and orientation of gun positions and recorded targets are updated when higher level survey data becomes available. An example of this would be changing from regimental grid to theatre grid.

Chapperton Down Artillery School — Located at Chapperton Down on Salisbury Plain in Wiltshire, the school was later renamed the School of Artillery and later still the Royal School of Artillery. See *Royal School of Artillery*.

Charge — A propelling charge is made up of several bags of propellant. In breech loading ordnance, the charge is loaded in a charge bag, whilst in Quick Firing ordnance, the charge is contained in a brass cartridge. In the British system, the various charges/increments are denoted by colour coding of the bags. For example, the charges for the 25-pdr comprised three increments which were colour coded in the following manner:
Increment 1: Red
Increment 2: White
Increment 3: Blue

Charge 1 consisted of increment 1 only, Charge 2 of increments 1 and 2 and Charge 3 consisted of all three increments.

Charge Super was, however, a separate cartridge giving the 25-pdr a range of 13,400 yards.
This system is still in use with the L118/L119 Light Gun, although with an increased number of increments and charges.

Charges for breech loading ordnance however, were loaded directly into the breech, without recourse to a cartridge case. This system was used on the 5.5-inch gun and is still in current use with the AS90. Increments for the AS90 are still colour coded.

Charges also used different types of propellant, in which the cordite granules or sticks varied in the composition and shape.

Chargers — Officers' Horses.

Charge Super — See *Charge*.

Charlie Charlie 1 — See *CC1* and *Collective Call*.

Charlie Charlie 11 — See *CC11* and *Collective Call*.

Charlie Charlie 3 — See *CC3* and *Collective Call*.

Charlie Tank Crossing — One of the Triangulation Exercise Stations on the now defunct RA Survey Course.

Chaser	An Air Defence Missile which engages its target from behind and therefore has to chase it, as opposed to one which is only capable of engaging an approaching target.
ChCOORD	Chief Fire Coordination.
Check Firing	Stop firing. Guns may not be fired, however, loading may continue. See *Cease Firing, Cease Loading* and *Empty Guns.*
Check Reading	See *Closing.*
Check Round	A round fired in order to detect any mistake which has been made whilst ranging of the gun.
Check Zero Lines	Normally conducted at first and last light, before fire plans and on any other occasions it was considered necessary. This procedure involved each gun reporting their angle to a director where it would be compared to the director's angle to the gun, and if different a new angle would be ordered and GAPs would be re-recorded. See also *Zero Line.*
Cheeks	The sides of a gun carriage.
Cheese – Possessed	Slang term used to describe the tins of processed cheese found in ration packs.
Chequerboard Flag	The Battery flag of B Battery RHA. The chequerboard design was first seen painted on the Battery Guns at the time of mechanization in 1936. A Battery flag was first introduced in 1944, the original design being blue with a gold Cypher which had a blue gothic B, in place of the GR, in the centre, on a red background. At that time it was also decided to fly a black and white chequerboard pennant below the battery flag in order to make it distinguishable from the similar E Battery flag. It is not currently known when the chequerboard flag itself was first introduced.
Chestnut Troop, The	Battery Title of A Battery (The Chestnut Troop) RHA which was granted under authority of Army Order 135 of 1902. This is not an honour title and should not be confused with such titles, however it is an officially granted title and as such forms part of the battery name.
Chestnuts	Shortened name by which both the battery and members of A (The Chestnut Troop) Battery RHA are known.
Chevron Barrage	Anti-aircraft barrage devised and used in Malta during the Second World War. The Chevron Barrage was comprised of two adjoining sides of a hexagon barrage, the shape of which had been arrived at by way of mathematical calculations. The sides selected would depend on the direction from which the hostile aircraft were approaching. Although initially successful, there was no depth to the barrage and it was eventually replaced by the Xmas Barrage. See *Xmas Barrage.*
Chief Computer	A member of the Computing Centre, in Artillery Survey, who is responsible for the organising of the work undertaken by the computing centre. He/She is assisted by another member of the team who is referred to as the Assistant Computer. See *Assistant Computer* and *Computing Centre.*
Chief Inspector of Armaments	Responsible directly to the Director of Artillery for the suitability for service of all warlike stores. The Chief Inspector of Armaments controlled four divisions; Ammunition, Guns and Carriages, Small Arms and Optical Stores. The position is no longer in existence.
Chimney Pot	Nickname given, by 27/28 Battery of 7 Medium Regiment RA during 1942, to the American M1 155 mm howitzer. The name derived from the distinctive rim around the muzzle.
Chinagraph Queen	Derogatory nickname for a Battery Clerk.

Chinese Bombardment	A short, intense artillery bombardment which was not followed up by an infantry attack. (First World War.)
Chin-Kiang-Foo day	The official Battery day of 127 (Dragon) Battery Royal Artillery celebrated on 21 July.
Chin Troop	One of the troops, together with Kiang Troop, of 127 (Dragon) Battery RA.
Chocks	Blocks which replaced the rear trucks on some Garrison Standing Carriages thereby transforming them, into Carriage, Garrison, Rear Chock. See *Garrison Standing Carriage* and *Trucks*.
Chore Horse	The 300-watt charging set for radio batteries.
Ch Temp	Charge Temperature.
Ch Tp	Chestnut Troop. As in A Battery (The Chestnut Troop) RHA. This abbreviation is used in internal documents, such as the 1 RHA Regimental Journal, but not in external communications. See *Chestnut Troop, The*.
Chunk	New gunner/recruit (The King's Troop RHA).
Chunky	A derogatory term used to denote a soldier in the Royal Pioneer Corps.
Chunky Ride	Recruits' Ride (The King's Troop RHA).
CI	Chief Instructor.
CIA	Chief Inspector of Armaments.
CIFS	Close-in Fire Support.
CIG	Chief Instructor Gunnery.
CI Gny	Chief Instructor of Gunnery.
CIM	Classroom Instructional Model.
Circular Error Probable	The radius of a circle within which half of a weapon systems projectiles are expected to fall. It is used as an indicator of the weapon systems delivery accuracy and as a factor in determining probable damage to a target.
CIS	Communication and Information Systems.
CL	Coordination Level.
CL89	Another name for the AN/USD 501 Midge. See *Midge*.
Claggnuts	Nickname given to A (The Chestnut Troop) Battery RHA.
CLAK	Cable Layer Adapter Kit.
Clansman	A system of battlefield radios which replaced Larkspur and other radios in 1980–2 and has subsequently been replaced with Bowman. See *Bowman* and *Larkspur*.
Clerk of the Deliveries of the Ordnance	Reporting to the Master-General of the Ordnance, this officer was responsible for full records of the number and kind of stores issued from the stocks of ordnance. A member of the Board of Ordnance from its constitution in 1597 until the position was abolished in 1830. See *Board of Ordnance* and *Master-General of the Ordnance*.
Clerk of the Ordnance	Reporting to the Master-General of the Ordnance and a member of the Board of Ordnance from the time of its constitution in 1597. The Clerk of the Ordnance was responsible for the correspondence and for financial bookkeeping of the Board. The position was abolished in 1857. See *Board of Ordnance* and *Master-General of the Ordnance*.
CLF	Commander Landing Force.
CLFSU	Control Logic Firing Sequence unit. Part of the Javelin AD missile system.
Clino	See *Clinometer*.
Clinometer	An instrument used to lay a gun in elevation, its bubble was levelled by elevating the barrel. A sight clino was part of the dial sight carrier and was set with the Angle of Sight (all guns used the same A of S, zero was usual for observed fire). The field clino, was used for laying in elevation instead of the gun-rule when maximum

precision was required. It was set with the Quadrant Elevation (Tangent Elevation plus Angle of Sight). See *Gun Rule.*

CLM — Career Leadership Management.

Clock Code — Introduced during the First World War the clock code was used to assist Royal Flying Corps aircraft in directing artillery fire. This was achieved by details being sent by wireless to Royal Flying Corps operators attached to the battery. The observer in the aircraft had a transparent sheet attached over his dashboard map with a number of concentric circles radiating out at distances of 10, 25, 50, 100, 200, 300, 400 & 500 yards, the centre of these circles was placed over the target. Each of these circles was lettered, Y, Z, A, B, C, D, E, and F respectively. The circle was then divided 1 to 12 as per a clock face. 12 o'clock was due North, with 3 o'clock being East, six o'clock being South and 9 o'clock being West. A direct hit on the target would be transmitted by the observing aircraft as 'OK'. Twenty five yards from the target was signalled as 'Y', 50 yards was 'A', 100 yards 'B', 200 yards 'C', etc. Therefore an aircraft reporting a hit at 'B6' would in fact be indicating that the shell had fallen 100 yards south of the target. The clock code continued to be used by Mountain Artillery to indicate targets well into the 1930s.

Close Air Defence Detachment Trainer — As HVM supersonic surface to air missile can only be fired live on special purpose missile ranges, it has proved necessary to develop the CADDET to provide realistic training for Missile Operators. Using computer equipment, projectors and replica equipment in order to simulate exercise scenarios and permit both the Operator and the Tactical Controller to train in a classroom environment without the need for large and expensive live training areas and real aircraft targets. Both fixed wing and rotary wing aircraft can be simulated together with terrain panoramas in both summer and winter guises. The system is available in two types, Type A having a 120 degree azimuth display screen for semi-permanent installation and the Type B which has a 60 degree azimuth screen for deployable use. The system is capable of holding at least 1000 scenarios, each of 90 minutes duration, and each containing at least 50 realistic target profiles. These target profiles can consist of both FW and RW aircraft. It is possible for each target profile to be assigned to a different target type if required. The system has twenty pre-set 'library' scenarios and the Instructor has the capability to generate many more. A library of forty-five 3D aircraft types, with the capacity to add more, is provided. See *SPADDET.*

Close Air Support. — Close support provided by fixed wing aircraft against ground targets. Close Air Support is conducted in the area between our own troops and the Fire Support Coordination Line. See *Battlefield Air Interdiction, Close Combat Attack, Close-In Fire Support* and *Fire Support Coordination Line.*

Close Combat Attack — Air support provided by attack helicopters. See *Close Air Support* and *Close-In Fire Support.*

Close-in Fire Support — Support provided by Attack Helicopters of the Army Air Corps being guided onto their target by RA Forward Observation Officer's using the gunner radio net.

Close Support — Close Support Regiments normally deploy in support of formations involved in the close battle. A Close Support

Regiment is comprised of a Tactical Group and a Gun Group. Close Support Regiments are equipped with either AS90 or the Light Gun. See *AS90, Direct Support, General Support, General Support Reinforcing, Gun Group, Light Gun* and *Tac Group.*

Closing	An operation used to detect any accidental movement of the director during use. At the completion of every operation, the director is turned on to the point on which it was first laid and a note made of the reading obtained. This check reading should be within specified parameters of the original reading. See *Director.*
Cloudpuncher	Nickname by which members of Air Defender units are known. See *Gun-Bunny.*
Clover	Name given to a three round ammunition container, the cross-section of which resembled a three leafed clover.
CLR	Clear.
CLU	Central Loading Unit. Part of the Rapier FSB2 Air Defence system.
CM	(i) Cruise Missile (ii) Control Module. (iii) Counter Mortar.
CMA	(i) Corps Maintenance Area. (ii) Corps Medium Artillery. Early Second World War and before.
CMCDB	Composite Modified Cast Double Base.
CMETS	Computerised Meteorological System.
CMG	Composite Maintenance Group.
CMO	(i) Civil Military Operations. (ii) Counter Mortar Officer.
CMP	Communications Processor. Part of the MLRS system. See *Multiple Launch Rocket System.*
CMRGA	Ceylon and Mauritius Battalion Royal Garrison Artillery.
CMS(R)	Common Military Syllabus (Recruit).
CNR	Combat Net Radio.
CNTDN	Countdown. (MLRS).
Co	Carrying Power.
COA	Course of Action.
Coast Artillery Code	Similar to the Artillery Code, but with particular relevance to Coast Batteries. See *Artillery Code.*
Coast Artillery Practice Camp	Formally located at Llandudno, North Wales. The Coast Artillery Practice Camp was responsible for training coast batteries in the latest techniques. There were two touring batteries associated with the Coast Artillery Practice Camp which were responsible for relieving the coast batteries so they could go to Llandudno for training. Each touring battery would relieve a different coast battery every week for about a three month period and then return to Llandudno for refit, leave and the latest drills. The Practice Camp was closed on the disbandment of Coast Artillery in the 1950s.
Coast Artillery School	Located at Shoeburyness, Essex, during the Second World War the school comprised Gunnery, Searchlight, Radar and Administration Wings, Workshop and Coast Training Regiment. Later relocated to Plymouth in Devon, as the School of Coast Artillery, the school closed on the disbandment of Coast Artillery in the 1950s.
Coast Artillery Search Light	The name adopted in 1940 for those searchlights used to illuminate targets for engagement by Coast Artillery batteries. Formerly known as Defence Electric Light. See *Defence Electric Light.*

Coast Battery	A position from which guns could protect the entrance to a harbour or port.
Coast Defence	Describes the guns used to defend harbours etc., against attack from ships.
Coaster	Nickname by which members of coast artillery units were referred to, particularly by themselves!
COB	Contingency Operating Base.
COBRA	(i) Combined Operations Battery RA (267 COBRA). (ii) Counter Battery Radar, FR/GE/UK system introduced in 2005. COBRA uses an active radar to detect multiple batteries of indirect fire systems. This includes mortar bombs, artillery and rockets. The system is capable of detecting forty targets within two minutes and displaying both their location and classification. Being mounted on the Foden improved medium mobility load carrier, the system is highly mobile. Mounted on a flatrack, COBRA can be lowered to the ground so as to occupy a less conspicuous position. Detachment: 3 Detection Range: 40 km Time into Action: 15 minutes Accuracy: 50 metres Circular Error Probable at 15 km Ability: Locate 40 batteries in 2 minutes Target Capability: 120 projectiles per minute Prime Mover: Foden IMMLC
COBU	Combined Operations Bombardment Unit.
Coburn Graphs	Used in calibration of coast artillery.
COE	Contemporary Operating Environment.
Coeff	Coefficient.
C of A	Centre of Arc.
C of M	Correction of the Moment.
C of R	Commencement of Rifling.
CoG	Centre of Gravity.
Cog Up	Insert small studs into a horse's shoes to improve grip. (The King's Troop RHA).
COL	Artillery Code used during the First World War meaning 'Column'.
Colenso	Battery Honour Title of 159 (Colenso) Battery RA which was granted on 14 August 1957 under authority of 20/ARTY/6271/AG6a. See *Battery Honour Titles.*
Cole's Kop	Battery Honour Title of 14 (Cole's Kop) Battery RA which was granted on 16 August 1928 under authority of 20/ARTY/4544/AG6a.
Collar-Maker	The Royal Artillery equivalent of the Cavalry Saddler. So named due to the almost continual struggle to keep horse collars correctly fitted to the gun teams.
Collective Call	A call from a single station to a pre-designated group of stations disguised by a collective Callsign. Transmitted on radios as 'Charlie Charlie', followed by a numerical suffix to identify the recipients. For example: CC1 on the Regimental net means that all command posts should answer (1, 2, 3 and 4 if there are 4 gun batteries). Therefore, if Zero (Regimental Headquarters) sends the message 'Hello CC1 this is Zero radio check over', the responses would be '1 OK over, 2 OK over, 3 OK over, 4 OK over'. If Zero sent 'Hello CC11 (all OP's) this is Zero radio check over', the responses would be '11 OK over, 12 OK over, 21 OK over, 22 OK over, 31 OK over, 32 OK over'.
Collective Protection	A defence against Nuclear, Biological and Chemical weapons.
Collective Ranging	Introduced in *Field Artillery Training 1912*, this type of ranging was conducted by using alternative fire from half-batteries.

Collie	Colchester.
Colonels Commandant	The Colonels Commandant Royal Artillery are appointed to assist the Master Gunner in his duties. There is an establishment of 24 Colonels Commandant, however a voluntary limit of 10 was adopted in 1996 of whom two may be Colonels Commandant Royal Horse Artillery. See *Representative Colonel Commandant* and *Honorary Colonels Commandant.*
Colours	The Regiment's guns and guided Weapons are its Colours. When on a ceremonial parade the Guns and Guided Weapons are accorded the same compliments as the Standards, Guidons and Colours of the Cavalry and Infantry.
COLPRO	Collective Protection.
Column of Batteries	Batteries moving in open column.
Column of Sections	A formation, described in *Field Artillery Training 1914*, as being used in brigade drill, when all the sections were in open column.
Column of Sub Sections	A column of single guns, each with a wagon to the right or left of it, moving at full intervals unless otherwise ordered.
Column of Route	A unit moving with the guns and wagons in single file.
COMAJF	Commander Allied Joint Forces.
COMARRC	Commander ARRC.
ComBAT	Common Battlefield Application Toolset.
Combined	Activities involving the activities of two or more allies. During the Second World War the UK use of 'combined' meant 'joint' in the modern sense. The term was also used in armies as 'combined arms' to indicate actions involving more than one arm (formerly 'all-arms' in UK).
COMBRITCON	Commander, British Contingent.
COMCAOC	Commander Combined Air Operations Centre.
Comd	(i) Command. (ii) Commanded. (iii) Commander. (iv) Commanding. (v) Commands.
Comdt	Commandant i.e. Comdt RSA is the Commandant of the Royal School of Artillery.
COMD-TGT POL	Commander's Target Policy.
Command	The artillery implication of command, is that the officer in who it is vested has authority to move guns and indicate where they should deploy. See *Control.*
Commandant	In Indian Mountain Artillery the Battery Commander was known as the Commandant.
Commander Fixed Defences	The officer commanding Coastal Artillery within a specified area.
Commander Royal Artillery	During the First World War this was usually a Brigadier-General commanding the artillery of a Division. See *Commander Royal Horse Artillery.*
Commander Royal Horse Artillery	A term used in the First World War and earlier for the artillery commander in a cavalry division where all artillery was RHA. See *Commander Royal Artillery.*
Commander's Representative	An officer, who could be a battery or regimental commander from a non-divisional artillery regiment (but in practice any officer can be so designated), who is authorised to order fire to all the units under the represented commander's control and who has radio com-

munications to all the units and Headquarters under that command.

Commando Training Wing Part of 29 Commando Regt RA which runs the Pre-Commando Training Course.

Command Post Officer The term was introduced in 1938. During the Second World War the Command Post Officer was responsible for the Battery Command Post and had overall technical control of the battery. With the reversion in the late 1950s to six gun batteries the term has come to be applied to the officer, warrant officer or senior NCO who is in charge of one of the Battery Command Posts. See *Command Post Officer's Party* and *Gun Position Officer*.

Command Post Officer's Party During the late 1940's the Command Post Officer's party comprised the Command Post Officer, together with the personnel and equipment required to reconnoitre and prepare the battery position and, where line was being used, to lay line between the battery and troop command posts. The size of the party depended on the movement restrictions in place in the forward areas. See *Command Post Officer.*

Commando Conditioning Course This three-week course is designed to fine tune the physical fitness and build on the military skills preparation of recruits to 29 Commando Regiment. The course instructors have a wide range of experience in all aspects of commando warfare and teach candidates survival skills, assault course techniques, weapon handling and close quarter battle procedures.

Command Tank During operations in North West Europe during the Second World War armoured brigades held eight command tanks for use both by Royal Artillery observers and RAF forward control officers. In order to blend in with the supported formation, these Command Tanks were of the same type as used by the supported brigade and had a crew provided by one of the armoured regiments within the brigade. Therefore, in armoured divisions where the gun tanks were normally Shermans the Command Tank was also a Sherman. However, in 7th Armoured Division the gun tanks were Cromwells and therefore the Command Tanks were either Cromwells or Centaurs. Command tanks were standard gun tanks and whilst some retained the normal armament but with reduced ammunition stowage, others had the main armament removed and replaced with a dummy gun. The space thus made available was used for the installation an additional Wireless set No 19, thus providing one for communication with the Royal Artillery troop and/or battery and one for liaison with the supported armoured regiment. A Wireless set No 38 was also carried for communication with infantry platoons. See *Wireless Set No 19* and *Wireless Set No 38*.

Commencement of Rifling The point within the bore of a barrel at which the grooves first reach maximum depth and marks the end of the shot seating. See *Depth of Rifling, Development of Rifling* and *Shot Seating*.

Common Abbreviated description of Common Shell.

Common Lyddite A steel High Explosive shell, also known as Lyddite Common.

Common Pointed Unlike the Common Shell, the Common Pointed Shell had a sharply pointed tip and was filled with gunpowder with the fuze located in the base of the shell. They were used against light targets which they penetrated prior to bursting. See *Common Shell.*

Common Shell circa 1880s this term referred to hollow shells filled with a bursting charge of Black Powder. Common Shell was so called because of its use against 'common' targets rather than armoured ones. During smoothbore days, these shells were spherical and employed a wooden fuze, whilst those used with RML guns were elongated and fitted with a nose fuze for use against troops and light targets on land. It was removed from service with field guns in the 1890s, when it was replaced in its entirety by Shrapnel. See also *Common Pointed, HE Common Shell* and *Ring Shell.*

Commonwealth Artillery Training Centre Based at Kure, Japan during the Korean War, the Centre provided additional training to gunners, both officers and other ranks, en-route to active service in Korea during the 1950s. The school had an Instructor in Gunnery and an Assistant Instructor in Gunnery who were responsible for directing the courses. Other instructors were found from within the Commonwealth Division and came from the RA, RCA, RNZA and the RAA. Courses consisted of Officers Refresher Courses, TARA courses and Signalers courses. Additionally Gun Number and NCO Cadres for 25-pdr, and 4.2-inch mortar were held. Some training was also provided to Infantry Gun Numbers for the 17-pdr anti-tank gun.

Common Weapon Sight A third generation Image Intensification night sight for use with the L85 Individual Weapon and the L86 Light Support Weapon.

Comms Communications.

Company, The See *Battle Axe Company, The.*

Company (i) Prior to 1859 Batteries of the Royal Artillery were known as Companies, the title was changed at the same time that Battalions were renamed as Brigades. See *Battalion.*
(ii) Under the terms of the Special Regimental Order dated 28 July 1891 Royal Garrison Artillery Batteries were retitled 'Companies'. However, The title Company was only applied to static units, such as Coast Artillery, whilst the title Battery was retained within the RGA for mobile units such as Mountain Batteries.

Company Sergeant This rank was introduced on 13 September 1813, and equated to that of a Colour Sergeant in other Regiments. Indeed, even in official correspondence, the term Colour Sergeant was frequently used within the Regiment. The rank insignia for a Company Sergeant comprised a Regimental Flag supported by two swords worn above the standard sergeants chevrons. This badge was initially worn on the right arm only, with a standard set of sergeants stripes on the left arm. However, by 1836 it was being worn on both arms, and finally disappeared from use when the tunic was introduced in 1856. The rank was equivalent to the present day Battery Sergeant-Major.

Company Sergeant-Major The non-artillery equivalent of a Battery Sergeant-Major. The rank was however used in the Royal Garrison Artillery. See *Company.*

Comparator Used in sound ranging, a mechanical computer calculating first order differential equations introduced in the 1930s to compare the location of a target with the location of the fall of shot and produce a correction for the guns.

Comparator Ranging The process by which a survey unit used the comparator to compare the sound of the fall of shot of friendly artillery to that of hostile batteries firing in order to adjust the friendly artillery fire onto the hostile battery. See *Comparator*.

Composite Charge — A multiple charge in which the propellant in at least one portion differs in size and/or shape and/or composition from that in the remaining portions.

Composite-Rigid — A type of artillery round.

Composition — Also referred to as Incendiary Composition, this was a mixture of saltpetre, sulphur, resin, sulphide of antimony, turpentine and tallow. Composition was used during the 18th and early-19th centuries as the filling for incendiary shells and carcasses. See *Carcass*.

Computing Centre — In Artillery Survey, this is the location where the field observations are sent and where the computing is carried out. This work is normally carried out by two personnel, one of whom is referred to as the Chief Computer, whilst the other is referred to as the Assistant Computer. It is their role to compute and compile the entire scheme. See *Assistant Computer* and *Chief Computer*.

COMSEC — Communications Security.

Con — (i) Control.
(ii) Converge.

Conc — Concentrate.

Concentrated — When two or more batteries 'concentrated' their fire, each gun was aimed at the same point instead of, as is normal, firing with barrels parallel or at individual aim-points such as would be the case when firing along barrage lines, in stonks, or laying smoke screens. The term 'converged' is now used in place of concentrated. See *Concentration*.

Concentration — (i) Instead of using a barrage, two or more batteries 'concentrated' their fire on a particular target.
(ii) A fire discipline term for switches passed to individual guns in a troop to correct for their layout in order that all guns were aimed at a common aimpoint or to spread their aimpoints along a line. See *Field Battery Linear Target, Linear Concentration, Medium Battery Linear Target, Heavy Battery Linear Target* and *Simple Concentration*.

Concentration and Positon Correction Chart — See *Sands Graph*.

Concrete Gunners — Nickname given to gunners serving in coast artillery.

CONFIG — (i) Configure.
(ii) Configuration.

Conker — Nickname for A (The Chestnut Troop) Battery RHA.

Connect Firing Lines — Order given on Rapier Air Defence Missile sub-sections instructing the detachment No.1 or No.4 to connect the missile firing lines to the launcher prior to firing. See *Rapier*.

Connolly Troop — A troop name sometimes used by L (Nery) Battery RA. See *Bradbury Troop, Dorrell Troop* and *Nelson Troop*.

Conrod — Radio appointment title used by the Air Defence representative. See *Appointment Titles*.

Consistency — A measure of the spread of a group of rounds all fired at the same data. It is measured, not about the target, but about the Mean Point of Impact. Thus, if a spread of rounds about the Mean Point of Impact is great, the consistency is said to be poor. Conversely, if the spread of rounds about the Mean Point of Impact is small, the consistency is said to be good.

Contingent Component Requirements — Title given to trained reinforcements from the Territorial Army who deploy on operations with Regular close support regiments.

Continuous Fire — A fire order whereby loading and firing continues at a specified rate or as rapidly as possible consistent with accuracy within the prescribed rate of fire for the weapon. Firing will continue until terminated by the command 'End of Mission' or temporarily suspended by the commands 'Cease Loading' or 'Check Firing'. See *Thirty Seconds* and *Continuous Illumination*.

Continuous Fire, Thirty Seconds — Part of a fire order which specifies the type of fire to be used, together with the interval between rounds from individual guns. See *Continuous Fire* and *Continuous Illumination*.

Continuous Illumination — Part of Fire Order which specifies that illumination rounds should be fired continuously until further notice. The order is normally accompanied by a time frame or a rate of fire. See *Coordinated Illumination, Continuous Fire* and *Continuous Fire, Thirty Seconds*.

Contradiction — The term used if, when ranging, verifying rounds do not correspond with initial ranging rounds when the same line and elevation are used. Contradiction may be caused by bad ramming or changes in temperature. See *Bad Ram* and *Check Round*.

Control — In the artillery sense, control implies control of artillery fire, it relates to the shells, as opposed to Command, which applies to the guns. See *Command*.

Control Post System — An anti-aircraft system introduced during the First World War, whereby aircraft were tracked by a single instrument located in the centre of the gun group. Once a future position for the aircraft had been calculated, fuze length, elevation and azimuth were determined and passed to the guns. They would then set their elevation and traverse scales to the figures ordered. Fuzes would be set to the ordered length and rounds then loaded and fired as quickly as possible. As the sight setters were no longer located at the guns, there was more room for the loaders and as a consequence a higher rate of fire was achieved.

Control Tank — See *Command Tank*.

Converge — A command used in a call for fire to indicate that the observer desires planes of fire to intersect at a point. See *Converged*.

Converged — A type of fire where each gun is aimed at the same point, instead of each gun having its barrel parallel to the others as would be normal. Or instead of being aimed at individual aiming points as would happen in the case of barrage lines, or when laying a smoke screen. See *Converge*.

Converted Gun — A smooth bore cast iron gun which has been rifled using the Palliser system of rifling.

Cookhouse Battery — Nickname given to 66 Battery Royal Artillery, now 159 (Colenso) Battery Royal Artillery for which at least two possible explanations exist. The first refers to an incident in the Battery's history, when during the First World War the Battery managed to fire a shell through their own cookhouse. The second explanation purports to relate to an incident during operations against the Mohmand tribesmen on the North West Frontier during 1935. When during a night alarm, part of the charge fell unobserved from the cartridge case during loading, resulting in the round falling short and ending up under the bed of a cook sergeant fom the 2nd Battalion, Duke of Wellington Regiment.

Co-op — Co-operation.

Coordinated Illumination A type of fire mission in which the firing of high explosive/bomblet and illuminating projectiles is coordinated in order to provide illumination of the target and surrounding area only at the time required for spotting and adjusting the fire of high explosive/bomblet rounds. See *Continuous Illumination.*

Coordination Level An Airspace Control Measure/Air Defence term.

COP (i) Common Operating Picture. (Royal Canadian Artillery.)
(ii) Covert Observation Platoon.

COPF Special type of depression Rangefinder. (Coast artillery.)

Coppering The fouling by deposition of copper from the driving bands of shells onto the rifling of a gun.

CoR Commencement of Rifling.

Cordite A form of propellant introduced in 1893 as a 'smokeless powder', it replaced black powder, although black powder continued to be used for some natures of RML. Cordite was formed into chords or sticks, hence its name. Cordite is composed of 58% nitroglycerine, 37% gun-cotton and 5% mineral jelly and is virtually smokeless. As with gunpowder (black powder), where the size of the grain, pebble, cube or prism governs the burning rate, the diameter of the sticks of Cordite governs its burning rate. Some sticks are made tubular. See *Cordite W* and *Cordite WM.*

Cordite MD See *Cordite WM.*

Cordite W A flashless propellant comprising 65% Nitrocellulose, 29% Nitroglycerine and 6% Carbamite.

Cordite WM Cordite (Waltham Abbey – Modified). A variation of Cordite, developed at the Royal Gunpowder Mills, at Waltham Abbey. It remained in British service until the demise of the 25-Pdr and the 5.5-inch gun. See *Cordite.*

Corporal (i) MGM-5. A first generation corps level tactical nuclear missile using liquid fuel with a maximum range of 75 miles. Equipped 27 and 47 Missile Regiments in support of 1 (BR) and 1 (GE) Corps. Entered service in the late 1950s, left service in mid 1960s.
(ii) A rank denoted throughout the British Army by two stripes, although the rank is now known within the Royal Artillery as Bombardier. Prior to 1922, the rank of Corporal existed within the Royal Artillery and at that time fell between that of Bombardier and Sergeant. See *Bombardier.*

Corpl Corporal.

Corps Artillery Intelligence Officer Replaced Corps Counter Bombardment Officer in the 1960s and was in turn replaced by SO2 Arty (Int) in the early 1980s. The post was held by a Major.

Corps Counter-Bombardment Officer A Lieutenant Colonel commanding a Bombardment Troop, (post Second World War) until the 1960s, when the role was downgraded in rank to a Major and renamed the Corps Artillery Intelligence Officer. See *Counter-Bombardment Troop.*

Corps of Captains, Commissaries and Drivers See *Corps of Royal Artillery Drivers.*

Corps of Gunner Drivers See *Corps of Royal Artillery Drivers.*

Corps Heavies Term used for Corps Heavy Artillery Headquarters. Responsible to a Corps Commander for all the Heavy Artillery in a Corps (First World War).

Corps of Royal Artillery Drivers From its formation until 1793 the Royal Artillery hired drivers and horses to move their guns but this was not a satisfactory situation. As a result a permanent corps of

'Captains, Commissaries and Drivers' was established, however, this was a separate entity to the Royal Artillery. Men and horses of this corps were attached to field artillery batteries both at home and abroad. Disbanded in 1801 the Corps was replaced by a similar body, the 'Corps of Gunner Drivers'. This in its turn was disbanded in 1806 and replaced by the Corps of Royal Artillery Drivers. It was at this time that the artillery style of dress was adopted. This Corps only supplied Drivers to the Field Artillery, the Drivers for the RHA, were, and always had been part of the establishment of the unit.

Whilst serving in the field, The corps had no officers of its own but answered to officers of the unit to which they were attached. Officers of RHA were often appointed to command the drivers when in barracks. The Senior NCOs of the Corps were all ex-artillerymen, and instances exist where Sergeants of the Corps took charge of gun detachments when their own No. 1 had been killed or disabled. The Corps of Royal Artillery Drivers was disbanded in 1822 and their role incorporated into the Royal Artillery in the form of gunner-drivers. Known by the nickname the 'Wee Gee Corps' members of the Corps of Royal Artillery Drivers were not highly regarded by the artillery with whom they served. Artillery personnel often resented the similarity of dress. The uniform changed several times during the early part of the nineteenth century.

Corps Training Centre — A generic term for special to arm and service training units (Second World War).

Corr — Corrector.

Correct Round — During registration a round which is observed as being correct is one which falls so close to the target that only a precision shoot would be likely to place the mean point of impact closer to the target.

Corrected Co-ordinates — These are standard in all respects and are, in fact, map data.

Corrected Line — See *Line*.

Corrected Range — An alternative name for Map Range. See *Map Range*.

Correction — (i) Any change in firing data to bring the Mean Point of Impact or Burst closer to the target.
(ii) A communication proword to indicate that an error in data has been announced and that corrected data will follow. See *Proword*.

Correction of the Moment — Corrections which are applied to the sights of a gun or to firing data before the gun is fired to take account of the various conditions which could affect the shell in flight. These include wind, drift, barometric pressure, the temperature of the propellant and of the air and variations in the weight of the shell.

Correction to Range for the Non-Rigidity of the Trajectory. — See *Non-Rigidity Correction*.

Corrector — The Corrector is a means of changing the time duration set on a time fuze. The corrector is set on the fuze indicator and so changes the fuze length for a given range. It is used to compensate for non-standard conditions and to range the height of burst.

Corrector Sight — A sight which automatically displaced the gun layer's view in order to afford the correct amount of aiming off required for a moving target. Mainly employed in anti-aircraft gunnery.

Corrn — Correction.

Corunna	(i) Battery Honour Title of 17 (Corunna) Battery RA which was granted on 16 April 1936 under authority of 20/ARTY/5023/AG6a. (ii) Battery Honour Title of 29 (Corunna) Battery RA which was granted on 16 April 1936 under authority of 20/ARTY/6824/AG6a. Battery now amalgamated with 3 Battery RA to form 3/29 (Corunna) Battery RA.
Corunna Troop	Named after the battle of Corunna, which took place on 16, 17 and 18 January 1809 in Spain, it is together with Downman's Troop, El Tamar Troop and Sahagun Troop, one of the four troops in B Battery Royal Horse Artillery.
COS	Chief of Staff.
COT	Close Observation Troop.
COTAT	Close Observation Training and Advisory Team.
Counter Balance Springs	Springs on L118/L119 Light Gun to relieve stress on elevation clutch gear.
Counter Balance Weight	Weight just forward of the breech on a 25-pdr to relieve stress on elevation gear.
Counter-Battery	A type of Fire Mission which is used to neutralise or destroy enemy artillery. The term is also applied to the target acquisition, intelligence, fire planning and target engagement activities employed to defeat the enemy's artillery. The Counter-Battery Officer (CBO) at corps level was responsible for all intelligence about hostile artillery and the collection, coordination and dissemination of Counter Battery information. The First World War term 'Counter Bombardment' was often used synonymously with counter battery and following the Second World War was readopted when the counter battery and counter mortar fire missions were combined. The term has since been replaced with Counter Fires. See *Counter Fires.*
Counter Battery Chart	In use during the Second World War, this was a map on which all enemy artillery locations were recorded, together with friendly locating assets. With the merger of Counter Mortar and Counter Battery, the chart became known as a Counter Bombardment Chart and continued in use into the 1960s.
Counter Battery Officer	During the Second World War this post was held by a major, who commanded the Corps Counter Battery Section.
Counter Bombardment	This term was used to describe Counter Battery work (including Counter Mortar) during the period 1940s to 1969 when the term Counter Battery was re-introduced. See *Counter Battery.*
Counter Bombardment Chart	See *Counter Battery Chart.*
Counter Bombardment Troop	A counter-bombardment troop formed the counter-bombardment staff at Corps level. Each troop was commanded by a Corps Counter-Bombardment Officer. See *CCBO.*
Counter Fires	This term has replaced Counter-Battery in current usage. Presumably as counter fire work is not necessarily directed at hostile artillery, but includes all hostile indirect fire systems. See *Counter-Battery.*
Counter Mortar	An organisation introduced in 1944 to deal with the mortar threat. Post war it merged with Counter Battery to become Counter Bombardment.
Counter Mortar Officer	A position introduced into divisional Headquarters in 1944.
Counter Preparation	A Fire Mission designed to cause casualties and damage to enemy forces and to disorganise and break up imminent attacks. It was dropped from British doctrine in 1941

as it was considered to be, for all intents and purposes, no different to a Defensive Fire Mission.

Counterweight Carriage — A disappearing gun carriage. The term being synonymous with 'Moncrieff mounting'. Also known as a Counterweight Gun. See *Moncrieff Carriage* and *Disappearing Gun.*

Counterweight Gun — See *Counterweight Carriage, Disappearing Gun* and *Moncrieff Carriage.*

Course Shooting — Course shooting takes place at the Royal School of Artillery (RSA) and the training establishment in Germany. Throughout the year courses are run at these establishments, and to practise and confirm the training they carry out live firing on the ranges (course shooting). This can incorporate a number of courses at one time i.e. survey courses (survey in the guns for live firing), command post courses (passing firing data to the guns and firing the guns live), observation post courses (directing live rounds onto the target) and of course gun courses (firing the guns live after learning the drills dry).

Coventry Clock — Named after its inventor, Major Coventry, these clocks were used during the run-in shoot on D-Day 6 June 1944 to control the fire of the guns. The clock consisted of a dial and a wooden hand, the dial being inscribed with the range from 13000 yards to 1000 yards. Having been set to move at a rate which corresponded with that of the speed of the Landing Craft (Tank) carrying the guns, and by using the following simple procedure, it was possible by using these clocks to ensure that the guns fired at the correct ranges. When the decreasing range shown on the face of the clock matched that of one of the thirty fire plan serials allocated to the troop, the troop lieutenant was able to give the order to fire, confident that his guns were at the correct range. The Canadian Artillery units participating in the run-in shoot used a variation of the Coventry Clock, known as the Vickers Range Clock.

Covered position — A covered position is used for indirect fire, and is usually located behind hills and/or woods as these features provide screening from enemy ground observers, though not from air observers. See *Open Position* and *Semi-covered Position.*

Coverer — Sub Section Second in Command, usually a bombardier.

Covering Fire — A Fire Mission used to neutralise the enemy during the assault using either barrages, concentrations or smoke.

COW — (i) Coventry Ordnance Works.
(ii) A $1^{1}/_{2}$-pdr artillery piece developed in the First World War by the Coventry Ordnance Works, initially as an aircraft gun. In its Mark IV version it was used as an Anti-Aircraft weapon for the defence of airfields during the First World War. See also *Cow Guns.*

Cow and Castle — Nickname of 46 (Talavera) Battery RA. Derived from their Battery crest which shows two bulls and a tower.

Cow Guns — Slang for Oxen-drawn artillery, for example the 4.7-inch gun which required 14 pairs of oxen, especially used during the Second Anglo-Boer War. (Royal Canadian Artillery.)

Coy — Company.

CP — (i) Command Post.
(ii) Common-Pointed shell.
(iii) Counter preparation.
(iv) Critical Point.
(v) Centre Pivot. In this type of mounting, the equipment is traversed on a central pivot.

CPA	Command Post Assistant, 1970s–80s. See also *CPOA.*
CPBC	(i) Capped Printed Ballistic Capped. This definition was given in an issue of *The Gunner* magazine. (ii) Capped Piercing Ballistic Capped.
CPDC	Command Post Detachment Commander.
C Pen	Counter Penetration.
CPF	Counter Preparation Fire.
Cpl	Corporal.
CPM	Critical Performance Monitoring.
CP Mounting	See *Central Pivot Mounting.*
CPN	Counter Preparation (First World War).
CPO	Command Post Officer.
CPOA	Command Post Officer Assistant (Second World War). See *CPA.*
CPSF	Command Post Shooting Form.
CPSO	Command Post Safety Officer.
CPSU	Controller Power Supply Unit. Part of the Rapier AD system.
CPTA	Cinque Ports Training Area.
CPU	Central Processing Unit.
CPX	Command Post Exercise.
CR	(i) Combat Ready. (ii) Composite-Rigid. (iii) Control Room. Coast artillery Second World War and later.
CRA	Commander Royal Artillery.
Cracker	(i) Radio appointment title. This title was used army-wide by a Counter Bombardment representative, however, in the Royal Artillery the following officers used the title: At HQRA level by the Corps or Divisional Counter Bombardment Officer; at a Regimental Headquarters level by the Assistant Counter Bombardment Officer. See *Appointment Titles.* (ii) Name by which a tour with Cracker Battery was known. See *Cracker Battery.*
Cracker Battery	In the early 1970s it was decided to provide artillery support to the Sultan of Oman. This support took the form of Officers, NCOs and Technical Staff (21 personnel in total) on 3 month tours, with each tour being known as a Cracker. The guns, logistic support and gun detachments were supplied by Oman. The guns used were 25-pdrs. A total of 12 Crackers were provided, with the first arriving 'in Country' in September 1971. The 25-pdrs were supplied to the Omani's by the King of Jordan, who also arranged for the Omani gunners to be trained at the Jordanian School of Artillery. The name Cracker had been derived from the code name for Counter-Bombardment.
Crack Track Flak	Nickname of 11 (Sphinx) Bty RA when during 1984 it was the only Battery equipped with Tracked Rapier. It is believed that this nickname was given to the Battery by its Battery Commander at the time, and that it remained in use for a few years only.
Cradle	The part of the superstructure of the carriage or mounting that carries the recoil system and ordnance.
C-RAM	Counter Rocket, Artillery and Mortar. Phalanx 20 mm close in weapons system radar directed Gatling gun mounted on a trailer for deployment on land.
CRA Representative	Commander Royal Artillery's Representative. See *Commanders Representative.*
Crash Action	Emergency deployment to meet an immediate threat.
CRBBO	Catch Retaining Breech Block Open.
CRC	Control and Reporting Centre.

Creeping Barrage — The creeping barrage was a later development of the lifting barrage. In a creeping barrage the lines of fire moved across the landscape, irrespective of identified enemy locations, at a rate calculated to stay just ahead of the advancing friendly troops. More ammunition was required than for the lifting barrage, but the creeping barrage was technically simpler to fire and covered all enemy positions, even those not located in trench lines. See *Barrage* and *Lifting Barrage.*

Crest — A terrain feature of such altitude that it restricts fire or observation in the area beyond, resulting in dead space, or limiting the minimum elevation possible for the weapon system, or both. See *Crested.*

Crest Clearance — The Gun Position Officer is responsible for selecting, and if necessary, changing the charge to clear intervening crests. See *Crest Clearance Table* and *Target Crested.*

Crest Clearance Table — A table which was used to ensure that the firing data provided sufficient clearance when firing over crests (hilltops, ridges, etc) occupied by friendly troops.

Crest Confidence Factor — The percentage chance of rounds expected to clear a crest. The factor was introduced with FACE. See *FACE.*

Crested — A target is said to be crested if it cannot be engaged by the guns using any charge fired in any trajectory. See *Crest Clearance, Crest Clearance Table* and *Target Crested.*

CRGA — Commander Royal Garrison Artillery.

CRH — Calibre Radius Head. The precise description, whether it be rounded, sharply pointed, etc., by mathematical formula, of the shape of the nose of a shell. The shape of the shell plays an important part in determining the characteristics of the shell in flight.

CRHA — Commander Royal Horse Artillery.

CRMA — Commander Royal Malta Artillery.

Cr-Mr — Collar-Maker.

Croix De Guerre Day — Battery Day of 5 (Gibraltar 1789–1793) Battery RA. See *Pontavert Day.*

Crossing Plate — When guns were mounted in casemates close together, the rear racers often intersected and special crossing plates had to be used to allow full lateral training. Crossing plates were thick plates of steel prolonging the form of the racers, which were roughened to improve foothold. See *Racers.*

Cross Observation — The use of optical instruments from two different points to locate a single distant object.

Crow — Nickname for a new soldier.

Crusader Gun Tractor Mk I — Introduced during the Second World War the Crusade Gun Tractor was developed with the intention of giving the 17-pdr anti-tank gun greater mobility. Due to the 17-pdr's heavy weight it was difficult to move across country and it was hoped that a fully tracked gun tower would be the solution. In order to achieve this the crusader tank was heavily modified. Everything forward of the engine compartment was removed to create a large open space used to accommodate a detachment of eight, plus 30 rounds of 17-pdr ammunition in boxes. A gun spare wheel and gun planks were carried on the engine deck. A disadvantage of this large open space was that there was no overhead protection and whilst the Crusader's armoured lower hull remained, the thinly armoured sides offered little protection. Towing hooks were fitted to the front and rear. Despite the developmental work, the US halftracks proved

	adequate as Gun Towing Vehicles for the 17-pdrs. As a result of this the Crusader was used by Corps anti-tank regiments. They proved to be very powerful and fast, although they were governed to 28 mph. In point of fact it was found that they were too fast across country and unless drivers exercised caution the guns could be damaged by driving over obstacles or rough country at speed. The Crusader Tractor also found favour as a battery commander's reconnaissance and command vehicle.
CRW	Counter Revolutionary Warfare (1960s–1970s).
Crypto	(i) Cryptograph. (ii) Cryptography.
Crystal Ball	Part of the collation system used by the Counter Bombardment Staff during the Korean War. It was one of two charts to be found in the Counter Bombardment Office. The Crystal Ball showed every battery that had been located, irrespective of whether they were active or not, whilst those displayed on the current Counter Bombardment chart were limited to those batteries currently listed on the Hostile Batteries list.
c/s	Callsign.
CS	(i) Close Support. (ii) Command Station.
CSA	Corps Supply Area.
CS BC	Close Support Battery Commander.
CSC	Centre Section Commander (The King's Troop RHA).
CSG	Close Support Group.
CSM	Company Sergeant-Major.
CSM(IG)	Company Sergeant-Major (Instructor-in-Gunnery). (Royal Garrison Artillery.)
CsRA	Commanders Royal Artillery.
CSR	Chief Superintendent of Ranges.
CSS	(i) Combat Service Support. (ii) Covert Static Surveillance.
CSSG	Combat Service Support Group.
CST	Combat Net Radio State.
CSU	Commanders Switch Unit.
CSups	Combat Supplies.
CT	(i) Counter-Terrorism. (ii) Communist Terrorist (Malaya).
CTA	Command Transmitter Assembly.
CTB	Common Trailer Base.
CTC	(i) Console Tactical Control. (Part of the Rapier FSB2 AD system.) (ii) Corps Training Centre.
CTO	Collective Training Objectives, introduced in 1990s.
CTP	Course Training Plan.
CTR	Close Target Reconnaissance.
CTT	Console Target Tracking. (Part of the Rapier FSB2 AD system.)
CTW	Commando Training Wing.
CUCCT	Compendium of Unit Collective Training Tasks.
Cuckoo	Codename given to experimental sound locating equipment during the Second World War. The equipment was employed by 1 Searchlight Regiment RA in France during 1940 and also by a heavy anti-aircraft regiment in Tobruk during the Western Desert campaign.
CUL	Charge Unit Load.
Curtain Shoot	A concentration of fire by light anti-aircraft guns during the Second World War. Whereby the concentration was fired in a given directional sector. It was not considered

to be very effective and was also wasteful in ammunition. See *Umbrella Shoot.*

Cuthbert — Name given to the 8-inch version of the Toby trench mortar. See *Toby.*

CVHQ — Central Volunteer Headquarters.

CVHQ RA — Central Volunteer Headquarters Royal Artillery was originally established to manage the RA Specialist Pool (V). However, on the reorganisation of the Territorial Army in 1967 it assumed responsibility for the All Arms Watchkeepers and Liaison Officers Pool (V). CVHQ RA is also took responsible for the administration of the Land Command Staff Pool (V) which was formed in 1995.

In April 2001 with the change in command status of Woolwich from a Garrison to a Station, the Headquarters assumed the role of Station Headquarters and with it responsibility for the command and administration of the Station and Station troops.

The CVHQ RA mission is to:

(i) Provide administration and the support infrastructure for Woolwich Station including effective estate development planning.

(ii) Recruit, train and administer TA officers and soldiers of the RA Specialist Pool.

(iii) Recruit, train and administer officers of the All Arms Staff Officers Group.

(iv) Provide training and administer officers in the Land Command Staff Pool.

(v) Provide individuals for long or short term commitments to the Regular Army both during training and on operations.

See *All Arms Staff Officers Liaison & Watchkeepers Group, LCSP (V)* and *RA Specialist Pool (V).*

CVR(T) — Combat Vehicle Reconnaissance (Tracked).

CVR(W) — Combat Vehicle Reconnaissance (Wheeled).

CVT — Controlled Variable Time (Fuze).

CW — (i) Continuous Wave.
(ii) Cold Weather.
(iii) Chemical Warfare.

CWR — Charge to Weight Ratio.

Cwrt-y-Gollen Training Camp — Training Camp located in Wales.

CWS — Common Weapon Sight.

Cymbeline — Thorn EMI Radar FA No. 15 Mortar Locating Radar. The No. 15 Mk I was carried on a trailer from which it could operate or be removed and placed on the ground. The Mk 2 was permanently mounted on FV432 and had a memory that allowed trajectory replay. In service with the close support artillery regiments of 1 (UK) and 3 (UK) Divisions. Cymbeline detects the flight path of the mortar bomb at two points in its trajectory, as it passes through the radar beam. From the information obtained, it is then possible to identify the grid reference of the enemy base plate so that it can be engaged with artillery. Subsequently replaced by MAMBA. See *MAMBA.*

D – Don – Introduced 1914/1927
Dog – 1943
Delta – 1956

D	Drop.
D&M	Driving and Maintenance.
D10	See *Don 10*.
D3	A field telephone used during the First World War, which was connected by a single line utilising an earth return. The conductivity of the signal could be improved in dry weather by pouring water, form a water bottle or a more 'natural' source over the earth return.
D3A	Decide, Detect and Track, Deliver and Assess.
DA	(i) Divisional Artillery (First World War). (ii) Direct Action, term used for a PD fuze in the First World War and 2. See *PD.* (iii) A First World War British gas shell filling, Diphenyl Chlorarsine. (iv) Danger Area.
DAA & QMG	Deputy Assistant Adjutant and Quartermaster-General.
DAC	Divisional Ammunition Column. See *AC, Ammunition Column* and *Brigade Ammunition Column.*
DADC	Divisional Air Defence Cell. See *CADC* and *FADC.*
DADR	Deputy Assistant Director Remounts.
DAER	Daily Ammunition Expenditure Rate.
DAG	Divisional Artillery Group.
DAGEX	Divisional Artillery Group Exercise.
DAGRA	Deputy Adjutant General Royal Artillery.
DAHQ	Divisional Artillery Headquarters (First World War).
Daily Ammunition Expenditure Rate	The predicted consumption of ammunition in terms of the required rate of flow, expressed in rounds per gun per day. By the late 1980s, this prediction was seen to have little relevance in terms of timed rate of expenditure, and ammunition was accounted for in simple terms of pre-packed loads.
DAIO	Divisional Artillery Intelligence Officer (1960s–1970s).
DALO	Divisional Air Liaison Officer.
Danger	Information contained in a Naval Gunfire Support fire order message which indicates that friendly forces are within 600 to 1000 metres of the target. (Royal Canadian Artillery.)
Danger Close	A type of fire mission where fire needs to be brought down in close proximity to friendly forces. The internationally agreed definition of a Danger Close fire mission is one delivered within 600 metres of friendly troops.
DAP	Divisional Ammunition Park.
DART	Disappearing Automatic Retaliatory Target.
DASC	Divisional Air Support Cell.
DASO	Divisional Artillery Survey Officer.
Data Display Unit	Located at the Gun Position, the DDU displays information and firing data transmitted from the Command Post.
Datum Point	Now known as a Registration Point, the Datum Point is a point that the co-ordinates of which are known and which can be ranged upon by observation. It was used to establish the correction of the moment (qv) for nearby targets, for which meteorological information was not available.
DAU	Delay Arming Unit.
David High Velocity	See *Ordnance QF 2-pounder.*
Davit	In Coast Artillery this was an iron post fitted with a pulley which was used to hoist ammunition to a higher level. Similar in appearance to an ordinary ship's davit it was

8 feet 6 inches high and made of 3½ inch bar iron with an eye and ring. Davits were capable of lifting 8 cwt. See *Muzzle Davit*.

Day Diary — Used in Counter Battery/Bombardment offices from the Second World War through 1972 to collate all reports received for the day. Replaced by the Hostile Battery Collation Sheet.

Daylight Signalling Lamp — Also known as the Lucas Lamp, the Daylight Signalling Lamp was used for communication between the Observation Post and the Battery Command Post. Its use ceased in Europe in about 1935.

Daylight Signalling Short Range — See *Daylight Signalling Lamp*.

DC — (i) Detachment Commander.
(ii) Disappearing Carriage.

DC A — Detonator Composition A.

DCBO — Divisional Counter-Bombardment Officer.

DCC — Displacement Correction Calculator. Coast artillery Second World War and later.

DCCT — Dismounted Close Combat Trainer. See *Invertron, PIFT* and *Puff Range*.

DCCU — Direct Current Charging Unit.

DCMU — Digital Colour Map Unit.

DCOS — Deputy Chief of Staff.

DCPO — Divisional Command Post Officer. (Royal Canadian Artillery).

DCSR — Daily Combat Supply Rate.

DD — Danger Distance.

DDL — Digital Data Link.

DDRA — Deputy Director Royal Artillery.

DDU — Data Display Unit.

DE — (i) Direct Entry.
(ii) District Establishment.
(iii) Difference Eastings. See *DN*.

DE & S — Defence Equipment and Support.

Deacon — During the Second World War a self-propelled 6-pdr anti-tank gun was introduced based on the medium artillery tractor (Matador) chassis, with an armoured minimal body and cab and a fully rotating armoured turret mounted on what would have been the centre of the cargo platform. It equipped a battery in each anti-tank regiment.

Dead Ground — Ground which cannot be seen from the observer's position.

Dead Ground Trace — A tracing prepared by the Command Post Officer to show areas which cannot be engaged by the battery owing to intervening crests.

Dead Space — Area within the maximum range of a weapon which cannot be covered by fire from a particular position because of:
(i) intervening obstacles;
(ii) nature of the ground;
(iii) characteristics of the trajectory; or
(iv) the mechanical limitations of the weapon.

Decam — To remove camouflage material.

DED — Data Entry Device.

Def — Defence.

Defence Electric Light — The early name for a searchlight used to illuminate targets for coast artillery. The name was introduced in the 1880s. The name was changed in 1940 to Coast Artillery Searchlight. See *Coast Artillery Search Light*.

Defence Equipment and Support — The organisation created by merger of the Defence Procurement Agency and Defence Labour Organisation in 2007.

Defence Ordnance Safety Group	The title by which the Ordnance Board is now known.
Defence Procurement Agency	The organisation which replaced MoD(PE) during the 1990s until 2007. See *MoD(PE)*.
Defence Surveyors' Assocation Prize	Known prior to 1997 as the Field Survey Association Prize, the Defence Surveyors' Association Prize is awarded for the practical application of survey techniques. See *Field Survey Association Prize*.
Defensive Fire	Fire put down in order to prevent the enemy exploitation of an attack. Such fire is usually registered when a position is occupied, with the mission being fired when called for by the defending commander. See *DF(SOS), Final Protective Fire, Priority Defensive Fire* and *Registration*.
Defensively Equipped Merchant Ships	Merchant ships in the Second World War provided with light AA guns manned by Army detachments (initially, not necessarily RA). This role was taken over by the RA in Feb 1942. Eventually 5 Maritime Regts RA were formed (1, 3, 4, 5 and 6 Maritime RA). They manned both AA (Bofors, oerlikons and rockets) and also low angle armaments (6-inch, 4.7-inch, 3-inch and 12-Pdr) for use against surface targets. Their greatest strength was in August 1944 with a figure of 14,500 all ranks.
Defilade	(i) Protection which can be gained from an obstacle such as a hill, ridge, or bank against hostile ground observation and fire. (ii) A vertical distance by which a position is concealed from enemy observation. (iii) To shield from enemy fire or observation by using natural or artificial objects.
Deflection	The modification from the apparent direct line of sight from gun to target which must be applied to compensate for meteorological conditions and/or the movement of the target.
deg	Degree.
Degree	Used to describe angles of bearing or elevation.
De Havilland Dh82 Queen Bee	The DH82B Queen Bee was a remotely controlled drone developed from the DH82 Tiger Moth. A total of 420 were produced. The Queen Bee was used as a target drone for Anti-Aircraft practice. Powerplant: 130 hp de Havilland Gipsy Major. Wingspan: 29 feet 4 in Length: 23 foot 11 in Weight: Loaded 1770 lb Maximum speed: 109 mph Ceiling: 13 600 feet Range: 300 miles at 94 mph Armament: None
DEL	Defence Electric Light. See *Coast Artillery Search Light*.
Delay Fuze	A High Explosive shell fitted with a delay fuze will penetrate the target to some extent before detonating. This produces a significant cratering effect and a good destructive effect on buildings and similar types of cover.
Delay...(Minutes)	A Naval Gunfire Support report indicating that a ship is not ready to fire, and that firing will be delayed by the amount of minutes indicated. (Royal Canadian Artillery.)
Deliberate Fire Plan	See *Fire Plan*.
Demented Lawnmower	Nickname given to the Phoenix UAV, due to the sound made by its engine.

DEMS	Defensively Equipped Merchant Ships.
Dep	Depot.
Depression	The angle below the horizontal plane along which a gun is fired. See *Elevation*.
Depression Carriage	A variety of garrison carriage, fitted with rear chocks that could be depressed below the horizontal to 32°. It was developed by Lieutenant G. F. Koehler RA during the late Eighteenth Century during the siege of Gibraltar.
Depression Position Finder	The name ultimately applied to a Position Finder where it depends on the Angle of Depression to establish the position of the target. A coast artillery instrument. See also *Position Finder* and *Horizontal Position Finder.*
Depression Range Finder	Part of the equipment of a coast artillery battery, the Depression Range Finder determines the range of a target from its angle of depression. As with the Depression Position Finder this instrument was invented by Captain H. S. S. Watkins RA.
Depth Line	A line in a barrage between the final line and the final depth line. See *Barrage, Final Depth Line, Final Line, Linear Concentration* and *Standard Barrage.*
Depth of the Barrage	In a barrage the distance between the final line and the final depth line. See *Barrage, Final Depth Line, Final Line, Linear Concentration* and *Standard Barrage.*
Depth of Rifling	Measured from the top of a land to the bottom of a groove.
Deputy Dog Hat	Slang for the ECW Hat.
Desbrisay's Troop	Together with Lucknow Troop and Wood's Troop, one of the three troops in 76 (Maude's) Battery Royal Artillery.
Description of Target	An element in the call for fire in which the observer describes the installation, personnel, equipment or activity to be taken under fire.
Desert Budgie	Nickname for the Desert Hawk mini unmanned aerial vehicle. See *Desert Hawk.*
Desert Hawk UAV	A portable unmanned aerial vehicle (UAV) surveillance system employed by the Royal Artillery. Weight: 3.5 kg Length: 13 cm Wing Span: 21 cm Power: electric motor Desert Hawk has a wingspan of approximately 4 ft and, using its on-board rechargeable batteries, has a mission endurance of 75 minutes. Flying at speeds of between 40 and 80 kilometres per hour, the UAV follows a flight path that is plotted on a laptop computer using GPS co-ordinates. Desert Hawk, Nicknamed Desert Budgie by its operators, is intended to provide discreet, localized aerial video reconnaissance utilizing its low profile low noise electric propulsion system. Mission profile updates can be made and implemented 'on the fly' giving Desert Hawk tremendous flexibility and adaptability in dynamic situations. Designed principally for covert, real time video monitoring and recording, Desert Hawk combines versatility, simplicity, and reliability into a highly effective, survivable system. See *Phoenix.*
DESO	Defence Export Services Organisation
Destruction	See *Pin-Point Target.*
Destruction Fire	Fire delivered for the sole purpose of destroying material objects.
Det	Detachment. See *Gun Detachment.*
Detachment	See *Gun Detachment.*
Detachment Commander	The NCO in charge of a gun detachment. Also referred to as the Number 1. See *Gun Number.*

Detachments Front	On this order being given, the detachments fall in in front of their equipment.
Detachments Rear	On this order being given, the detachments fall in at the rear of their equipment.
Detonator Composition A	An igniferous initiator used in fuzes. See *Igniferous Initiator.*
Development of Rifling	The rifling in a barrel develops within the shot seating in a protion known as the Development of Rifling. See *Shot Seating.*
Devil's Carriage	See *Sling Wagon.*
DF	(i) Defensive Fire. (ii) Depth Fire. (iii) Direction Finding.
DFC	Depth Fire Cell.
DFDC	Depth Fire Direction Cell / Centre. Sometimes irreverently known as 'Don't Fire Guns, Don't Care.'
DFNS	Direct Fire Night Sight.
DFS	Direct Fire Sight.
DFSCC	Deep (Depth) Fire Support Coordination Centre.
DF(SOS)	Defensive Fire delivered on receipt of an emergency call. Became Final Protective Fire with change to QSTAG 225 fire discipline. See *Defensive Fire, Final Protective Fire* and *QSTAG.*
DFWES	Direct Fire Weapons Effect Simulation.
DGA	Director General of Artillery.
DGGWLS	Directorate General Guided Weapons and Electronic Systems. One of the directorates in the Land Systems Controllerate of the Procurement Executive. (Now replaced by DGWES.)
DGPS	Differential Global Positioning System.
DGWES	Directorate General Weapons and Electronic Systems (replaced DGGWLS).
DGZ	Desired Ground Zero.
DH	Desert Hawk, mini Unmanned Aerial Vehicle.
DH3	Desert Hawk Mark III. See *Desert Hawk.*
DI 3000	A time-pulse Electronic Optical Distance Measurer, mounted on the Electronic Total Station T1100. It is used in conjunction with a reflector, the distance being calculated by use of an infra-red pulse. A single pulse encompasses a number of measurements with the mean distance being displayed. Accuracy can be degraded by adverse weather conditions.
Dial Sight	A sight for measuring horizontal angles, thereby laying the gun for line. It consists of a fixed Main Scale, for laying the gun in the desired initial position (the centre of arc – given by a line from the director), and a Slipping Scale upon which the bearings to fire-on are set. It is a removable sight that fits into the gun's sight bracket.
Dial Sight Carrier	The mounting for both the Reciprocating and Calibrating Sights, sight clinometer and drift scale. It also provided the mount for a direct fire telescope and open sight if these were provided. See *Calibrating Sights* and *Reciprocating Sights.*
DIBUA	Defending in Built Up Areas. (Sometimes quoted as meaning Dying in Built Up Areas.)
Dickson Troop	One of the Troops in 2 Baker Bty Junior Leaders Regiment RA. See *Mercer Troop, Milne Troop* and *Stirling Troop.*
Dickybow	Divisional Counter Bombardment Officer.
Difference Altitude	The difference in altitude between two points usually sent during a polar mission and understood to be in mils unless metres is specified. (Royal Canadian Artillery.)

Differential Global Positioning System — Software for the Specialist Personal Global Positioning System Receiver (SPGR) which enable orientation and increased fixation accuracy. See *SPGR*.

Digitisation Stage — Normally followed by a number denoting the stage, i.e. DS1 for Digitisation Stage one.

Digri — The name given in some Indian Mountain Artillery Batteries to the Field Clinometer. See *Field Clinometer*.

dir — Direction.

Direct Action Fuze — This type of fuze functions instantaneously as a result of the mechanical action of the ground compressing the fuze nose. However, they do not function at very low angles of descent (approximately 2°), depending on the shape of the shell and the hardness of the ground. It was not unknown for a shell hitting hard ground to ricochet without the fuze nose making contact and activating. See *Graze Fuze*.

Direct Fire — Fire delivered on a target, using the target itself as a point of aim.

Direct Laying — Laying by looking over or through the sights at a visible target. Until the latter part of the nineteenth century all artillery fire was by direct laying. The development of high powered infantry rifles led to the development of Indirect Laying which enabled the guns to deploy in covered positions.

Direct Support — Units giving Direct Support to a battle group will give priority to that battle group's requirements for fire support. This fire support is normally guaranteed. Direct Support units provide forward observers, communications, liaison and advice to the battle group. Direct Support units have responsibility for fire planning and the coordination of all offensive support at every level of command from sub-units upwards. See *Close Support, General Support* and *General Support Reinforcing*.

Direction — The line between the observer and the target, upon which the observer makes his fall of shot corrections. Replaced OT with the change to QSTAG 225 fire discipline.

Direction GT — The line between the gun position and the target. See *OT* and *QSTAG*.

Director — An optical instrument used for measuring angles in both azimuth and magnetic bearing. See *Director L1A1*.

Director General of Artillery — The title of the officer in the War Office who held responsibility for artillery and other war-like stores.

Director L1A1 — The Director L1A1 is used to measure horizontal and vertical angles and to originate a compass bearing. It is used by the Royal Artillery for general survey work. AS90 Regiments use the director to establish INS update points. The director can also be used to transfer angles to guns to ensure correct orientation with the centre of arc, it can provide orientation for mortar locating and meteorological radars and measure radar mask angles. The director L1A1 has a magnification of 4.5 and a field of view of 200 mils. Its compass accuracy is given as +/- 20 mils. See *Centre of Arc*, Director, *INS* and *Mils*.

Director of Artillery — A position in the Master-General of the Ordnance's organisation and later the Ministry of Supply. See *Master-General of the Ordnance*.

Director Royal Artillery — The professional head of the Royal Regiment of Artillery. The DRA's Headquarters are located at the Artillery Centre, Larkhill, near Salisbury in Wiltshire. See *Appendix 5 Directors Royal Artillery*.

Direct Support See *In Direct Support*.

Dirty Thirty Nickname of 30 (Rogers's Coy) Battery RA.

Direx A UK One Time Pad numeric code using non-carrying arithmetic and used in nuclear artillery units for grid references and coordinates of actual or planned positions.

Disappearing Gun Developed by Colonel Moncrieff, the gun disappeared below the level of its parapet using the force of its recoil. The two types developed by Colonel Moncrieff were the Counterweight Carriage and the Hydro-pneumatic Mounting. See *Counterweight Carriage, Hydro-pneumatic Mounting* and *Moncrieff Carriage*.

Discarding Sabot Anti-tank round which discards an outer sabot in flight leaving a sub-calibre solid shot to travel to the target at an increased velocity. The light sabot and the not-so-light base-plate fell off after leaving the round, while the barrel and the tungsten-carbide core with its hardened cap and ballistic cap carried on towards the target at a tremendous velocity. See *APDS* and *APFSDS*.

Dismounted Branch From 1 July 1899 until 1924 the Royal Artillery was divided into three distinct branches, the Royal Horse Artillery, the Royal Field Artillery and the Royal Garrison Artillery. The term Dismounted Branch was used to describe the Royal Garrison Artillery during this period. See *Mounted Branch*.

Dismounted Close Combat Trainer Electronic, classroom based training system which allows two OP parties (or one OP party split in two) to operate over the same simulated target area from separate positions. The system can also be use as a training package for all artillery disciplines. See *Invertron, PIFT* and *Puff Range*.

Disp Displacement.

Displacement Calculator Introduced as the 'Calculator, Displacement, Field Branch Artillery' in 1956 as a replacement for the Sands Graph, the Displacement Calculator made it possible for command posts to plot the position of each gun relative to troop centre, by both bearing and distance. It was then possible to read off changes to line and range for each gun to a target anywhere within a full circular arc of fire. This enabled the fire of the guns to be concentrated onto the same aim point or for individual guns to be directed at their own aiming points on a linear of any orientation. Another use for the Displacement Calculator was finding the angle of sight, and although this function was rarely used it was possibly the most complicated instrument ever introduced into the Royal Artillery. See *Aiming Point, Linear, Sands Graph* and *Troop Centre*.

Dispersion A scattered pattern of hits by projectiles fired by the same weapon or group of weapons with the same firing data. The term applies to both accuracy and consistency. Thus we can have dispersion of rounds about the Mean Points of Impact (consistency) and dispersion of rounds or Mean Points of Impacts about the target (accuracy). See *Accuracy* and *Consistency*.

Dist Distribution.

Distance Transmitter Unit Part of the LINAPS system, it fits completely within the wheel hub of the gun. See *LINAPS*.

District Establishment Part of the Headquarters and District Establishment Royal Artillery, the formation which commanded the heavy batteries and provided both the District Officers and Master Gunners who held the actual armament on charge.

District Officer Prior to the Second World War District Officers were drawn from the Coast Artillery Establishment, the District

Officer was responsible for the equipment held in a particular coast artillery district. District Officers who were Commissioned Master Gunners themselves, were assisted in their work by the Master Gunners. Following the Second World War they were redesignated as Technical Instructors-in-Gunnery and were drawn from all branches of the Regiment. See *District Officer (HAA), District Officer (TIG)* and *Master Gunner.*

District Officer (HAA) — See *District Officer (Heavy Anti-Aircraft).*

District Officer (Heavy Anti-Aircraft) — A commissioned Warrant Officer who was responsible for care, maintenance and accounting of, equipments, including radar instruments, vehicles and ammunition of heavy anti-aircraft regiments. One DO (HAA) was appointed to each heavy anti-aircraft regiment. See *District Officer* and *District Officer (Technical Instructor-in-Gunnery).*

District Officer (Technical Instructor-in-Gunnery) — Existing in field, anti-aircraft and coast artillery branches, the DO (TIG) was a commissioned Warrant Officer, who had previously served as an Assistant Instructor-in-Gunnery. The DO (TIG) was involved in the drawing up and supervision of gunnery training programmes, including the teaching of detailed procedures, particularly in the Territorial Army. Selection for the post was by War Office Standing Committee. See *District Officer* and *District Officer (Heavy Anti-Aircraft).*

District Officer (TIG) — See *District Officer (Technical Instructor-in-Gunnery).*

Div — Division.

Div Arty HQ — Divisional Artillery Headquarters.

Divisional Ammunition Column — Operated by the Royal Field Artillery, the Divisional Ammunition Column was responsible for transporting all the ammunition, both artillery and small arms, for the Division. The DAC HQ was small – the 1915 standard comprised:

Lt Col
Adjutant
Sergeant-Major
Artillery Clerk
Battery Quatertermaster Sergeant
Clerk
Gunner
2 Medical Orderlies
6 Drivers for vehicles
1 Driver for spare horses
1 spare Driver
6 Batmen
A total of 23 personnel

The Divisional Ammunition Column collected ammunition from the Army Service Corps Divisional Ammunition Park for onward transportation to a re-filling point where it could be transferred to a Brigade Ammunition Column. When during 1916 Brigade Ammunition Columns were dispensed with the Divisional Ammunition Column became responsible for transporting the ammunition to a re-filling point where it could be collected by ammunition wagons belonging to the individual batteries. At any one time, a Divisonal Ammunition Column, together with the tactical units of the Division held one scale (the designated allocation of ammunition for the division). A second scale of ammunition was stored in the Ordnance Depot. A Divisional Ammunition Column comprised 4 Sections, namely, No's 1, 2 and 3 Sections which handled 18-pounder and small-arms ammunition, and No 4 Section which had a 'Howitzer Portion' for 4.5-inch and a 'Heavy Portion' for the 60-pounder ammunition. The latter portion was removed from the establishment in early 1915 when the 60-pdr guns were withdrawn from divisions. See *Brigade Ammunition Column* and *Divisional Ammunition Park*.

Divisional Ammunition Park — Operated during The First World War by the Army Service Corps, the Divisional Ammunition Park transported ammunition forward to a re-filling point where it was transferred to a Divisional Ammunition Column. See *Divisional Ammunition Column*.

Divisional Artillery Intelligence Officer — Position which during the 1960s and 1970s replaced the Divisional Counter-Bombardment Officer and was itself replaced by SO2 Arty (Int).

Divisional Counter-Bombardment Officer — A Major commanding a Locating Battery used post Second World War and through to the 1960s, when the post was replaced by the Divisional Artillery Intelligence Officer. Pronounced 'dickey-bow'. See *Locating Battery*.

Divisional Task Table — See *Monster*.

Divl — Divisional.

DKP — Decontamination Kit, Personal.

DL — Directed Logistics.

DLO — Defence Logistics Organisation.

DLSA — Directorate of Land Service Ammunition.

DM — A First World War British gas shell filling. Diphenylamine Chlorarsine.

DMO — Director of Military Operations.

Dmr — Drummer.

DMS — Direct Moulded Sole. A type of Army boot.

DMU(D) — Digital Master Unit (Data).

Dn — Direction.

DN — Difference Northings. See *DE*.

DN 181 — Target Tracking Radar (Part of the Rapier FSB2 AD system), also known as Blindfire and Radar Tracker.

Dn GT — Direction Gun Target.

DO — District Officer (Coast Artillery.)

DOAE — Defence Operational Analysis Establishment.

DOAST — Desired Order of Arrival Staff Table.

DOBG — Deep Operations Battlegroup.

D of A — Director of Artillery.

DO(HAA) — District Officer (Heavy Anti-Aircraft).

DO (TIG) — District Officer (Technical Instructor-in-Gunnery).

Dolphins — On muzzle-loading artillery pieces, dolphins were metal projections on the upper surface of the piece, midway between the breech and the muzzle. They could be used to lift the barrel. The name derived from the fact that early examples were very ornate and moulded in the form of dolphins.

Don 10 — Two wire communications cable for use with field telephones.

Donkey Walloper — Slang term used by members of the Royal Artillery to describe a member of the Royal Horse Artillery.

Don R — Dispatch Rider.

DOP — (i) Director of Practice.
(ii) Drop Off Point.

Dorrell Troop — One of the three troops in L (Nery) Battery RA. See *Bradbury Troop* and *Nelson Troop*.

DOSG — Defence Ordnance Safety Group.

DO(TIG) — District Officer (Technical-Instructor-in-Gunnery).

Doubleates — Nickname given to 88 Battery RFA during the First World War.

Double Duck — Nickname of 22 (Gibraltar 1779-83) Battery RA. See *Down Hill Gunners*.

Double Ducks — Nickname of 55 (The Residency) Headquarters Battery RA.

Double Plus — If a battery is augmented to Double Plus, it had almost a complete battery attached as additional personnel.

Dover Troop — One of the three troops in 22 (Gibraltar 1779-1783) Battery RA. Named after Captain Dovers, the first Battery Commander. See *Koehler's Troop* and *Sortie Troop*.

Down — (i) Part of a Fire Order which is used to indicate that the target is lower in altitude than the point which has been used as a reference point for the target's location.
(ii) A correction used by an observer to indicate that a decrease in height of burst is desired.
(iii) The practice whereby Gun Line Section Commanders, Detachment Nos 1 and Safety raise their hand to show the Command Post they are ready. For example, Down 1, Down Left Section or Down Safety meant that the Command Post had visually seen the raised hand and it could now be lowered, and that the Command Post were going to carry on with the Fire Mission. See *Down Safety*.

Down Hill Gunners — An alternative nickname of 22 (Gibraltar 1779-183) Battery RA. See *Double Duck*.

Downman's Troop — Named after Lieutenant General Sir Thomas Downman KCB KCH, it is the senior troop in B Battery Royal Horse Artillery. The other three troops being Sahagun Troop, El Tamar Troop and Corunna Troop. See *Downman KCB KCH, Lieutenant General Sir Thomas.*

Down Safety — When firing in peace time on any artillery range, it is essential that the rounds land in the designated safe impact area. This is achieved by a safety party carrying out a number of checks before the guns fire, i.e. checking that the data given to the guns will land in the impact area (map check), and physically checking the guns by eye (sights and compass check). Once the safety officer is happy for the guns to fire, he will tell the command post officer 'down safety' and raise his hand in the air. The command post officer is then clear to fire the guns. See *Down*.

DP — (i) Decision Point.
(ii) Distribution Point.
(iii) Design Pressure.
(iv) Delivery Point.

DPA — (i) Defence Procurement Agency.
(ii) Defended Ports Abroad.

DPEE — Director of Proof and Experimental Establishments.

DPF — Depression Position Finder. See *Position Finder.*

DPGS — Differential Global Positioning System.

DPICM — Dual Purpose Improved Conventional Munition. A second generation bomblet round that was both anti-personal and armour penetrating, introduced in 1970s.

DPM — Disruptive Pattern Material.

DPO — Driving Permit Officer.

DPS — Day's Pay Scheme.

Dr — Driver.

DR — Dispatch Rider.

DRA	Director Royal Artillery.
Dragon	(i) Various marks of tracked artillery tractor used during the 1920s. The name is said to derive from the function of the tractor, as a drag-gun. (ii) Battery Honour Title of 111 (Dragon) Battery RA which was granted on 18 October 1926 under authority of 20/ARTY/4544/AG6a. Battery currently in suspended animation. See *Battery Honour Titles.* (iii) Battery Honour Title of 127 (Dragon) Battery RA which was granted on 18 October 1926 under authority of 20/ARTY/4544/AG6a. See *Battery Honour Titles.* (iv) Battery Honour Title of 129 (Dragon) Battery RA which was granted on 18 October 1926 under authority of 20/ARTY/4544/AG6a. See *Battery Honour Titles.*
Dragon Day	Battery day of P Battery (The Dragon Troop) Royal Artillery.
Dragons	(i) Nickname of 127 (Dragon) Battery RA. (ii) Nickname of 129 (Dragon) Battery RA.
Dragon Troop, The	(i) Battery Honour Title of P Battery (The Dragon Troop) RA which was granted on 18 October 1926 under authority of 20/ARTY/4544/AG6a. See *Battery Honour Titles.* (ii) B Battery RHA was unofficially known as 'The Dragon Troop' during the early years of the twentieth century. The title originated from the part played by the Battery in the Boxer Rebellion of 1900. It was during this campaign that the Battery was presented The Military Order of the Dragon. B Battery is the only Battery in the RHA to posses this medal.
Draught Parade	Training with the guns on Wormwood Scrubs (The King's Troop RHA).
Drawers – Jungle Fruity	Slang term used in the Junior Leaders Regiment RA to describe the green underpants with rubber buttons at the front and drawstrings at the side.
DRF	Depression Range Finder.
Drift	The lateral movement of a spin-stabilised shell which is generated by the spin imparted by the rifling of the gun. This will cause the shell to drift in the direction of the spin. This is counteracted either by a correction device on the sights or by calculating a corrected line, which is passed to the guns before firing.
Drill Order	A light scale of equipment used for mounted parades, or for a drill or procedural exercise to test technical ability.
Drive on Angle	The angle on which the MLRS Launcher is aligned following receipt of a fire mission. Having received the fire mission, the MLRS detachment will drive the launcher out of its hide to its firing point, (usually moving less than 100 m) and align the launcher with the specified drive on angle. Using the on-board navigation equipment, the launcher's location is fed into the ballistic computer which has already had the full fire mission details entered. The launcher is then elevated and fired. This process can take as little as a few minutes to complete. See *Multiple Launch Rocket System.*
Driver Internal Combustion	The title given to a Driver of a motorised vehicle in the Royal Artillery (pre-Second World War) to differentiate from a driver of a horsed team. This was the basic grade of driver in the Royal Artillery. See *Driver Mechanic, Driver Operator and Driver RA.*
Driver Mechanic	A higher grade of driver than a Driver Internal Combustion. See *Driver Internal Combustion, Driver Operator* and *Driver RA.*

Driver Operator — A driver who was also responsible for operating the vehicles wireless set. See *Driver Internal Combustion, Driver Mechanic* and *Driver RA*.

Driver RA
Driver Royal Artillery — Driver Royal Artillery. See *Dvr IC, Dvr Mech* and *Dvr Op*. As with the Driver IC, the introduction of motor transport into the British Army made it necessary to distinguish between drivers of horse drawn vehicles and those of motor vehicles. This distinction was made by the addition of suffixes to the title Driver. A Driver RA, was one trained to drive a horse drawn vehicle, including gun teams and ammunition wagons. See *Driver Internal Combustion, Driver Mechanic* and *Driver Operator*.

Drivers' Day — I Parachute Battery (Bull's Troop) RHA Battery Day – 5 May. Drivers' Day celebrates the action at Fuentes D'onoro during the Peninsula War.

Driving Band — An important part of any artillery projectile. Made from copper and designed to engage with the rifling in the barrel to such an extent that an impression of the rifling is pressed into the copper. There are three main reasons for having a driving band: (i) to impart spin from the rifling to the projectile; (ii) to form a seal between the barrel and the projectile thus preventing propellant gases escaping (windage); (iii) to engage the rifling as the projectile is loaded and thus stop it slipping back. See *Bad Ram* and *Windage*.

Drone — See *Midge*.

Dronies — Nickname given to members of Drone Troops in Locating Batteries.

Droop — The sagging effect on the muzzle of a long barrel on its trunnions.

Drop — A correction used by an observer to indicate that a decrease in range along the observer target line is desired.

Dropping into Action — The act of unlimbering the gun and placing it 'in action'. The term derives from the act of unhooking and lowering the trail to the ground.

DROPS — The Demountable Rack Offload and Pickup System (DROPS) vehicles form the logistic backbone of the British Army. The type used by the Royal Artillery is the Improved Medium Mobility Load Carrier (IMMLC) produced by Foden. These trucks are 8 x 6 load carriers with a 15 tonne flatrack payload which allows the rapid transfer of flatracks or containers. The IMMLC is used primarily as an ammunition carrier in support of AS90.
Length: 9.11 m
Height: 3.18 m
Weight (Kerb): 14.04 tons
Weight (Loaded): 32.96 tons (IMMLC)
Engine: Perkins Eagle 350 Diesel

Drop Shots — Derogatory nickname used by other arms to refer to the artillery. See *Drop Shorts*.

Drop Shorts — Derogatory slang term used by other arms to refer to the artillery. See *Drop Shots*.

DRPC — Dummy Rocket Pod Container.

DR RA — Dress Regulations Royal Artillery. Generally followed by the year of issue.

DRS — Daily Range Summary.

DRT — Direct Recruiting Team.

DRU — Dynamic Reference Unit.

DS — (i) Directing Staff.
(ii) Direct Support; for example 7 Para RHA were DS to the Royal Scots Dragoon Guards Battle Group. See *Direct Support*.

	(iii) Digitisation Stage. (iv) Dressing Station. (v) Discarding Sabot. See *APDS* and *APFSDS.*
DSA	(i) Divisional Supply Area. (ii) Defence Surveyors' Association.
DSAP	Distributed Situational Awareness Picture.
DSD	Director of Staff Duties.
DSG	Divisional Support Group.
DSL	Depression Sight Line. Coast artillery Second World War and later.
DSO	Decision Support Overlay.
DSP	Driver Switch Panel.
DSSR	Daylight Signalling Short Range.
DST	Defence School of Transport.
DSTG	Deep Strike Task Group.
DSV	Detachment Support Vehicle (Rapier Units).
DTA & C	Director Territorial Army and Cadets.
DTED	Digital Terrain Elevation Database.
DTG	Date Time Group.
DTIO	Directorate of Targeting and Information Operations.
DTL	Deep Trench Latrine.
DTMO	Divisional Trench Mortar Officer (First World War).
DTTR	Detachment Tactical Training Range (Part of RARH).
DTU	(i) Distance Transmitter Unit. Part of the LINAPS system. See *LINAPS.* (ii) Data Transmission Unit.
DU	Depleted Uranium.
DUAI	Directions for the Use of Artillery Instruments.
Duke of Richmond's Flying Artillery	The name by which the first two troops of Royal Horse Artillery were sometimes known at the time of their formation in 1793. At that time the Duke of Richmond was the Master-General of the Ordnance.
Dumbell Copse	One of the Triangulation Exercise Stations on the now defunct RA Survey Course.
Dumping	The act of putting on the ground, generally at gun positions, stocks of ammunition over and above the reserves normally carried by the mobile echelons.
Duncan Essay	Annual competition for the best essay on a given artillery subject.
Duplex	The name given to twin barrelled gun equipments.
Dustbin	Nickname for the Rapier Field Standard B launcher. See *Dusty Bin.*
Dusty Bin	Nickname given to Towed Rapier, derived from the similarity to a wheeled dustbin. See *Dustbin.*
Dvr	Driver.
Dvr IC	Driver Internal Combustion. See *Dvr Mech, Dvr Op and Dvr RA.*
Dvr Mech	Driver Mechanic. See *Dvr IC* and *Dvr Op.*
Dvr Op	Driver Operator. See *Dvr IC, Dvr Mech* and *Dvr RA.*
Dvr RA	Driver RA.
Dwarf platform	In fortifications and coast batteries this was a traversing platform, which was higher than the casemate variety, thereby permitting the gun to fire over a parapet. See *Traversing Platform.*
Dwell at…(time)	Order used when the engagement of a particular target, for example, a line in a barrage, is to continue at the planned rate of fire until further orders, instead of proceeding to the next line as indicated in the original fire plan. 'Dwell at…' is cancelled by the order 'Re-start'.
DZ	Drop Zone.
DZSO	Drop Zone Safety Officer.

E – Edward – 1927
Easy – 1943
Echo – 1956

EAA	East African Artillery, part of the 11th East African Division during the Second World War.
EAG	Experimental Assistant in Gunnery.
Eager Beaver	An all terrain fork lift truck, used for ammunition handling.
Eagle Troop, The	Battery Honour Title of N (The Eagle Troop) Battery RHA which was granted on 18 October 1926 under authority of 20/ARTY/4544/AG6a. See *Battery Honour Titles.*
Eagle Troop Day	24 March. Battery Day of N Battery (The Eagle Troop) RA.
Eagles	Nickname given to members of N Battery (The Eagle Troop) RA and 49 (Inkerman) Headquarter Battery RA.
EAM	Equipment Ammunition Magazine. See *Anti-Aircraft Ordnance Depot* and *Intermediate Ammunition Depot.*
Earl Roberts Memorial Prize	Instituted in 1928 in memory of Field Marshal The Earl Roberts VC KG KP GCB OM GCSI GCIE VD late Bengal Artillery and RA, 1832–1914. Awarded to the Young Officer most deserving on the grounds of general efficiency and character during his cadetship at the Royal Military Academy and the course for newly-commissioned artillery officers at the Royal School of Artillery.
Early Warning	A phrase used during the Second World War to describe the system used to give warning of the approach of enemy aircraft by radar and sound location to anti-aircraft positions and sites.
EB	Electronics Box.
EBO	Effects Based Operations.
EBP	Effects Based Planning.
EBSM	Experimental Battery Sergeant-Major.
ECA	Elevation Crab Angle. (MLRS).
ECAS	Emergency Close Air Support.
ECBA	Enhanced Combat Body Armour.
ECCM	Electronic Counter Counter Measures.
ECEF	Earth-Centred, Earth-Fixed (mapping systems).
Echelon	There are three levels of echelon, F, A and B. *Artillery Training Volume II, Pamphlet 1 1949* describes them as follows: F Echelon: Contained the essential personnel and vehicles for fighting. In a field regiment, the F Echelon consisted of the reconnaissance parties, the regimental headquarters group and the gun groups. The ammunition vehicles were often also grouped within this echelon. A Echelon: Contained the personnel and vehicles required by the unit at short notice to maintain its fighting efficiency. A Echelon was normally located at the Wagon Lines. B Echelon: Contained the personnel and vehicles necessary to collect, breakdown and distribute stores and supplies for the regiment. Vehicles that could conveniently be left out of battle were also located with this echelon. In modern usage however, F Echelon is not used in relation to artillery organisation, whilst the A Echelon is split into A1 and A2 Echelons.
ECIFS	Emergency Close-in Fire Support. See *CIFS.*
ECM	Electronic Counter Measures.

ECP	Equipment Collection Point.
ECW	(i) Extreme Cold Weather. (ii) Equivalent Constant Wind.
ED	(i) Extra Duty. (ii) Emergency Destruction. (iii) Extra Drill.
EDB	Extruded Double Base.
EDM	Electronic Distance Measuring Equipments. For example, the Tellurometer. See *Tellurometer*.
EDR	Effective Downwind Report. A meteorological message.
EEPROM	Electronically Erasable Programmable Read Only Memory.
EF	Elevation Finding. Sometimes written as E/F. See *Effie* and *GL*.
EFC	Equivalent Full Charge.
eff	Effective.
Effie	The nickname given to the Elevating and Finding attachment associated with the GL1 anti-aircraft radar, which enabled the angle of elevation to the target to be shown with a reasonable degree of accuracy, thereby permitting the calculation of the height of the target. GL radar so fitted were known as GL 1 (E/F).
E-Fires	Emergency Fires.
EFP	(i) Explosively Formed Projectile. (ii) Education For Promotion (now replaced by CLM).
EFR	Equipment Failure Report.
EGSA	Elevated Ground Spike Antenna.
EI	Equitation Instructor, a SSgt or WOII.
Ein Feer Funf	Nickname for 145 (Maiwand) Commando Battery RA.
Ejector Projectile	This tool is used to unload a rammed shell. It is a long rod, with a conical cup at the end, which is inserted into the bore from the muzzle to fit over the nose of the projectile. The rod is then hammered to free the driving band from the lands, and the shell drops out through the open breech. A task much disliked by the detachment, especially if the barrel is hot after prolonged firing.
El	Elevation.
El Alamein Troop	One of the Troops in 2nd Squadron Honourable Artillery Company. See *Cassino Troop, El Hamma Troop* and *Honourable Artillery Company* .
ELD	Electric Light Director.
Electric Light Director	The officer or NCO who was responsible for regulating the movement of an electric light (searchlight) under the orders of either a fire commander or a battery commander of a coast battery. (Royal Garrison Artillery). The position is now defunct.
Electronic Angulation Head	Part of the OTIS equipment. See *OTIS*.
Electronic Time	A setting on the Multi-Role Fuze. See *PH, PL* and *PN*.
Electronic Total Station	See *Leica TC1100*.
Elephant	(i) Type of sectional steel shelter with a curved top used in the First World War. (ii) Nickname of 10 (Assaye) Battery RA.
Elephant Battery	See *Bail Battery*.
Elev	Elevation.
Elevating Arc	The toothed arc which is used to elevate the gun, it is operated by the elevating hand wheel.
Elevating Mass	The ordnance and recoil system in the cradle that elevate together on the saddle.
Elevation	The angle above the horizontal plane along which a gun is fired. See *Depression*.
Elevation Finding	This was used to describe a GL Radar that had the facility to establish an elevation. See *GL*.

Elevation-Indicator	Used for indirect laying in coast artillery, the Elevation-Indicator consisted of a circular plate graduated in yards, carried on a horizontal shaft which was revolved by an arc attached to the cradle. Using the Elevation-Indicator the Quadrant Elevation could be given to the gun without the use of the sights.
El Hamma Troop	One of the Troops in 2nd Squadron Honourable Artillery Company. See *Cassino Troop, El Alamein Troop* and *Honourable Artillery Company*.
ELINT	Electronic Intelligence.
Elongated Shell	A projectile, the length of which was greater than that of its diameter or calibre. It replaced round shot.
Elongated Shot	See *Elongated Shell*.
Elsie	(i) Nickname given to the Searchlight Control Radar (Second World War), presumably derived from Light Control. (ii) A small anti-personnel mine in service between 1960 and the 1990s.
El Tamar Troop	Named after an action during the Second World War, it is together with Downman's Troop, Sahagun Troop and Corunna Troop, one of the four troops in B Battery Royal Horse Artillery.
ELXLE	Aide memoire for gun laying, standing for Elevation, roughly for Line, Cross Level, accurate for Line and finally accurate for Elevation.
EM	(i) Electromagnetic. (ii) End of Mission.
EMCDB	Elastomer Modified Cast Double Base.
EMCON	Emission Control.
EMER	Electrical and Mechanical Engineer Regulations.
EMERA	Electrical and Mechanical Engineers Officer Royal Artillery.
Emergency Battery	Constructed around the coast of Britain at the start of the Second World War as an anti-invasion measure. The guns necessary to arm these batteries were found from every available source, large numbers came from warships scrapped by the Royal Navy in the 1920s. Installations were kept simple, mainly consisting of a quick-setting slab of concrete to take the shipboard pedestal mounting of the naval guns. Other sites used either baulks of timber, or the prefabricated Arrol-Withers platform. See *Arrol-Withers*.
Emergency Destruction	Procedures to destroy a nuclear weapon in an emergency.
Emergency Fires	An enhanced form of Artillery Target Indication, whereby, in extreme situations, non-specialist observers are able to call in all types of fire.
EMP	Electromagnetic Pulse.
Empty Guns	This order is sent by the officer giving the final order for the guns to move. The order is given in the form 'Empty guns at…' It must be accompanied by a safe grid reference, safe target grid correction or safe target number and is in its own right an order to fire. As soon as all guns have reported empty to the gun position officer he/she will in turn report 'Guns empty'. See *Cease Firing, Cease Loading* and *Check Firing*.
EMR	Early Morning Rehearsal (The King's Troop RHA).
EMS	Engine Management System.
EMU	Engine Management Unit.
en	Enemy.
End of Mission	A command given to terminate firing on a specific target.
Engage at…	A fire discipline phrase indicating the time at which artillery shells from the firing battery should arrive at the

	target. The phrase has now been replaced by Time on Target. See *TOT*.
Eng. Sub O	Engagement Subsequent Order. A BATES fire mission engagement sequence. See *BATES*.
Eng. Sub O P	Engagement Subsequent Order Polar. A BATES fire mission engagement sequence. See *BATES*.
ENOHD	Extended Nominal Ocular Hazard Distance.
EO	Electro-Optical.
EOC	Elswick Ordnance Company.
EOCM	Electro-Optical Counter Measures.
EOD	Explosive Ordnance Disposal.
EODM	Electronic Optical Distance Measurer. An eye safe laser. See *DI 3000*.
EOM	End of Mission.
EOP	Emergency Observation Post. Coast artillery. (Second World War and later.)
EOT	Electro-Optical Tracker. Part of the Rapier FSB2 AD system.
EPC	(i) Electronic Plane Converter. (ii) Education for Promotion Certificate.
EPIAFS	Enhanced Portable Inductive Artillery Fuze Setter. Entered service with the Royal Canadian Artillery in 2007.
EPIP	European Personnel, Indian Pattern, (a type of tent).
EPM	Electronic Protection Measures.
EPPU	Electronic Pack Processor Unit.
EPRDU	Electronics Pack Remote Display Unit. Part of the SPHVM system. See *SPHVM*.
Eqpt	Equipment.
Equipment(s)	All guns, howitzers, mortars and missile launders with which the Royal Artillery is armed are known as Equipments.
Equipment Ammunition Magazine	During the Second World War these were supplied from Intermediate Ammunition Depots, and they in turn supplied ammunition to the gun sites. See *Anti-Aircraft Ordnance Depot* and *Intermediate Ammunition Depot*.
Equivalent Full Charge	Each propellant charge causes a different amount of wear. Very little is caused by the lowest charge used, whilst rather more is caused by the highest charge. 1 EFC usually represents one round from the highest normal charge used by a particular type of gun, lower charges are 'worth' less than one, super charges more than one. In some cases EFC values vary with the propellant type. The number of rounds fired at each charge was recorded in a gun's Memoranda of Examination. In 1949 the Memorandum of Examination was replaced by the *Gun History Book*. This gives the total EFCs fired, which in turn indicates when a full examination is needed and enables a revised muzzle velocity to be calculated. See *Memorandum of Examination* and Gun History Book.
ERA	Explosive Reactive Armour.
ERBS	Extended Range Bomblet Shell.
ERE	Extra-Regimentally Employed (working away from your parent Regt).
ERFB	Extended Range Full Bore.
ERFB-BB	Extended Range Full Bore with Base Bleed.
ERO	Extended Range Ordnance.
ERS	Early Release Scheme.
ERV	Emergency Rendezvous.
ES	(i) Electro Static Recordings which are used to assess the state of Rapier FSB2 prior to firing.

	(ii) Equipment Support (REME).
ESC	Extreme Service Conditions.
ESCP	Extreme Service Conditions Pressure.
ESM	(i) Electronic Support Measures. (ii) Elevation Servo Motor. (iii) Experimental Sergeant-Major.
ESR	Electro Slag Refined.
ESS	Eastern Shuttle Service (Maritime RA).
Essex Gunners, The	Regimental title of 36 Regiment RA. Now in suspended animation the title identifies the Regiment's former recruiting area.
Estab	Establishment.
Estb	Establishment.
ESTRA	Export Support Team Royal Artillery.
ESV	Elevation Servo Valve.
ESW	Emergency Smoke Withdrawal.
ET	(i) Electronic Time. A setting on the Multi-Role Fuze. See *PH, PL* and *PN*. (ii) Equipment Table.
ET	(iii) Electrothermal.
ETA	Estimated Time of Arrival.
ET-C	Electrothermal-Chemical.
ETF	Electronic Time Fuze.
ETH	Entrenching Tool Hand.
ETI	Elapsed Time Indicator.
ETS	(i) Electronic Total Station. An item of artillery survey equipment. See *EODM* and *Leica TC1100.* (ii) Equipment Table Scale.
EU	Electronic Unit.
Eurasian and Native Christian Company of Artillery	Raised in Bengal immediately following the Indian Mutiny, the Battery served in the Khasia and Jaintra Hills in 1862–3. Re-organised as a Mountain Battery in 1865, its title was changed to The Eurasian Battery of Artillery. Following service in the Bhutan campaign the battery was disbanded.
Eurasian Battery of Artillery	See *Eurasian and Native Christian Company of Artillery.*
European Mule Battery	Title by which No. 5 Mountain Battery RGA was known during its service in the Third Burmese War (1885–91). The name was first used by the CRA, Colonel W. Carey in his account of the war. See *Mountain Artillery, British.*
EVA	Electronic Velocity Analyser.
Everest Carrier	A lightweight metal frame, worn on the back and designed to facilitate the carrying of heavy weights such as radio sets when operating on a manpack basis. Everest Frames were first introduced during the Second World War.
EVM	Elevation Valve Module.
EW	(i) Electronic Warfare. (ii) Early Warning (Second Wrold War).
Exact Observation	The practice, used by siege artillery in the early twentieth century, of conducting indirect fire by utilising two observation posts sufficiently far apart to form a good triangle with the target and another with the gun position. By carrying out a series of trigonometrical calculations it was possible to obtain line and range, whilst being unable to see the target from the gun position.
Examination Battery	A coast artillery battery whose role included supporting the naval examination service who were in turn responsible for stopping shipping to establish identity and cargo carried. The battery facilitated this by firing 'bring to' rounds should the ship fail to obey the examination

service stop signals. If necessary, and if directed to do so by the examination service, the battery would then engage the offending ship directly.

EXCON — Exercise Control.

Executing Commander — The officer commanding forces possessing a nuclear delivery capability and is specifically designated in an approved plan to execute a nuclear strike. (NATO Definition). See *Releasing Commander.*

Expense Magazine — A small magazine in fortifications and coast artillery batteries in which ammunition for the immediate use of the guns is stored. Expense Magazines are generally found on the terreplein.

Experimental Assistant in Gunnery — A member of the ATS/WRAC staff based at Shoeburyness See *ATS* and *WRAC*.

Experimental Battery Sergeant-Major — An Assistant Instructor in Gunnery posted permanently to experimental work under the auspices of the Master-General of the Ordnance department of the War Office. This rank/position is now defunct. See *Experimental Sergeant-Major*.

Experimental Sergeant-Major — An Assistant Instructor in Gunnery posted permanently to experimental work under the auspices of the Master-General of the Ordnance department of the War Office. This rank/position is now defunct. See *Experimental Battery Sergeant-Major*.

Exptl — Experimental.

External Ballistics — The sequence of events which occur between the moment the projectile leaves the muzzle of the gun and the moment of impact or burst of the projectile. See *Ballistics* and *Internal Ballistics*.

Extree — A 17th century alternative name for axletree.

Eye Bolt — In muzzle-loading artillery this was a long bolt which passed through the top of the cheek and terminated below the side of the gun carriage. Its function was to secure the cheek pieces together.

Eyre's — Battery Honour Title of 58 (Eyre's) Battery RA which was granted on 5 October 1934 under authority of 20/ARTY/6824/AG6a. See *Battery Honour Titles.*

F – Freddie – 1927
Fox – 1943
Foxtrot – 1956

F — Artillery code used during the First World War meaning 'Far'.

F&FS — Fuze and Fuze Setter.

F&M — Fire and Movement.

FA — Field Artillery.

FAB — Field Artillery Brigade. (First World War, Royal Australian Artillery.)

Fabulous Fifth — Nickname for 5 Gibraltar (1779–83) Field Battery RA, now 19/5 Gibraltar (1779–83) Battery RA.

FAC — (i) Forward Air Control.
(ii) Forward Air Controller.

FACE — Field Artillery Computer Equipment.

FAD — *Field Artillery Drill*, training manual, abbreviation is normally followed by the year of publication.

FADC — Formation Air Defence Cell. See *CADC* and *DADC*.

Falconet	Aerial target system used for ground based air defence firings.
FAM	Forward Air Marker. See *FAC, LTMO, Op-Ack* and *Tac Group.*
FAME	Field Artillery Manual Equipment.
Familiarisation Visit	A 3-day visit to the Royal Artillery aimed at undergraduate and graduate potential officers, although those who intend to enter RMAS as non-graduates, or those interested in pursuing a Gap Year Commission are also encouraged to attend. The visit is designed to give a detailed insight into life as a Royal Artillery Officer. See *RAIV.*
Fan, Protractor, No 4	See *Tetley Fan.*
FAOR	Fighter Areas of Responsibility.
FAP	Forward Ammunition Point.
FARELF	Far East Land Forces. Established after the Second World War, with its Headquarters in Singapore, FARELF ceased to exist in about 1970 when UK forces withdrew from 'East of Suez'.
FARP	Forward Arming and Refuelling Point. (Army Air Corps.)
Farr	Farrier.
Farr QMS	Farrier Quartermaster Sergeant. (Rank no longer in use.)
FAS	Future Army Structure.
FASIPT	Field Artillery Systems Integrated Project Team.
FASS	(i) Future Artillery Systems Support. (ii) Field Artillery Systems Support.
FASS (IPT)	Field Artillery System Support (Integrated Project Team).
FAST	Forward Area Supply Team. Rapier.
Fast Air	Air Force Jet Attack Aircraft.
FAT	(i) Field Artillery Trainer. (ii) Field Artillery Training. Training pamphlet series used before the First World War. (iii) Field Artillery Tractor.
FAWG of SCARF	Field Artillery Working Group of the Standing Committee on the Accuracy of Artillery Fire.
FAWS	Future Artillery Weapons Systems (pronounced 'fours').
FAX	Fuel Air Explosive.
FB	Firing Battery.
FBA	Field Branch Artillery.
FBI	Fuze Bar Indicator.
FBO	Fire By Order. See *AMC.*
FBTU	Field Battery Training Unit.
FC	(i) Fire Command. (ii) Fire Commander. (iii) Fire Control.
FCA	Fire Control Application.
FC BISA	Fire Control Battlefield Information System Application (pronounced 'FC beeza').
FCC	(i) Fire Coordination Centre. (ii) Flight Control Computer. Part of the Phoenix UAV system. See *Phoenix.* (iii) Fire Control Centre.
FCE	Fire Control Equipment.
FCE Mk 7	See *Yellow Fever.*
FCE No 7	See *Yellow Fever.*
FCL	Fire Coordination Line.
FCO	Fire Control Orders.
FCP	(i) Fire Control Panel. Part of the MLRS system. See *Multiple Launch Rocket System.* (ii) Fire Control Point.
FCPT	Fire Control Panel Trainer (MLRS training equipment).
FCS	(i) Fire Control System. (Part of the MLRS system.) See *Multiple Launch Rocket System.*

	(ii) Flight Control System. Part of the Phoenix UAV system. See *Phoenix*.
FCU	Fire Control Unit. Part of the MLRS system. See *Multiple Launch Rocket System.*
Fd	Field.
FD	Fixed Defences.
FDC	Fire Direction Centre.
FDL	Forward Defended Locality or Line (Second World War), replaced by FEBA
FDT	Fire Direction Table. A coast artillery instrument used from the Second World War until the abolition of coast artillery.
FEBA	Forward Edge of Battle Area.
F Echelon	See *Echelon*.
Feed Tin	The nickname given to the Austin 7 cars when issued to D/3 RHA during the 1930s.
FEMW	Field Engineering and Mine Warfare. Generally followed by the number of the relevant pamphlet.
FEO	Fire Effects Officer. (Royal Canadian Artillery.)
FESC	Fire and Effects Synchronisation Centre. Formally known as the Fire Support Coordination Centre (FSCC). (Royal Canadian Artillery.)
FESTA	Introduced in early 1945, this was a scheme involving multiple shooting with air observation posts. Two AOPs worked with each battery, with each AOP conducting two shoots simultaneously. This meant that each battery would be engaging four targets at once. This meant that each gun in a heavy battery engaged a different target. To ensure that this worked, OP and signal drills needed to be perfect.
FEZ	Fighter Engagement Zone.
FFA	(i) Fighting the Fixed Armament. (ii) Free Fire Area.
FFB	Fitted For BATES.
FFCS	Future Fire Control System.
FFD	Fit For Deployment.
FFE	(i) Fire For Effect. (ii) Free From Explosives. See *Army Form G904*.
FFMA	Forward Force Maintenance Area.
FFR	(i) Fitness for Role. (ii) Fitted For Radio. Applied to vehicles configured to carry Radio equipment. (iii) Free Flight Rocket.
FF RR	The Second World War Artillery Code for Rapid Fire for Effect; definitely used by COBU in the Mediterranean theatre.
FFW	Fitted For Wireless. (Now known as FFR.)
FG	Fire Group.
FGA	(i) Fighter Ground Attack. (ii) Frontier Garrison Artillery (Pre-1948 Indian Army.)
FG Call	Call for fire from Arty/R aircraft, Immediate Neutralisation target, one battery ranging with groups of rounds. See *Arty/R* and *Immediate Neutralisation.*
FG Comd	Fire Group Commander.
FH70	A towed howitzer capable of independent movement achieved via an auxiliary power unit. FH70 entered service with the British Army during 1978. It was normally towed into action, but if the situation warranted it a small petrol engine mounted on the gun could be used to move short distances on the battlefield. Detachment: 8

Height: 2.56 m
Length: 9.8 m (in the travelling configuration); 12,400 mm (in the firing configuration)
Barrel Length: 6, 022 mm
Maximum Weight: approximately 9,600kg; 8,800kg (in firing position)
Auxiliary Engine: Volkswagen 1,795cc petrol
Shell Loading System: Automatic
Calibre: 155mm
Ammunition: HE, Smoke, Illuminating
Maximum Range: Unassisted Projectile: 24 km
Rocket Assisted Projectile: 30 km
Shell Weight: (HE) 43.5 kg
Rate of Fire: 6 rounds per minute
Engine: Volkswagen 1,795cc petrol

FHC Field Handling Container.

FIBUA Fighting in Built Up Areas.

Fid In muzzle-loading artillery this was either a small piece of twine or sometimes a wooden peg which was placed in the vent when the gun was not in use. Also known as a Vent Plug.

Fidus Et Audax Fidelity and Audacity. Motto of the Gloucestershire Volunteer Artillery and currently used by 266 (Gloucestershire) Parachute Battery RA.

Field Artillery Computer Equipment Based on an Elliott 920B stored programme computer and a control console, together with a teleprinter for the passage of data between CPs. Capable of producing gun data, carrying out survey computations and storing target records. FACE was installed in either tracked (FV432) or wheeled (FV 610) armoured command posts or alternatively in Mk 9 Land Rovers.

Field Artillery Manual Equipment A manual backup system for the Field Artillery Computer Equipment (FACE).

Field Artillery Tractor The wheeled vehicle used to draw the 25-pdr field gun and certain anti-tank guns in the Second World War, commonly known as a Quad.

Field Battery Linear Target Artillery Staff Duties (Field Branch) 1954 defined a Field Battery Linear Target as being fired by one battery and being 250 yards in length. See *Concentration, Linear, Medium Battery Linear Target* and *Heavy Battery Linear Target.*

Field Branch Artillery The term applied, certainly shortly after the Second World War, to all natures of artillery designed primarily for the engagement of ground targets by indirect fire.

Field Clino See *Clinometer.*

Field Clinometer See *Clinometer.*

Field Day An eighteenth and nineteenth century term for training exercises, the usage may have extended into the early twentieth century.

Field Handling Container The fibreglass 'winebottle' that Javelin/HVM missiles are carried in.

Field Manual The US equivalent of a UK training pamphlet. They have occasionally been used by the Royal Artillery. Field artillery Field Manuals are in the FM 6 series.

Field Plotter An instrument that was employed by the battery commander, prior to 1938, when he was the battery's sole observer, to solve the triangle between target, observer and battery. It appears to have been taken out of service prior to the Second World War.

Field Punishment Number One This punishment, which is no longer employed within the Royal Artillery, or indeed anywhere within the British Army involved tying a Defaulter to the wheel of a gun for a number of hours per day.

Field Radar Instructors Course This course was in two parts, part one being held at either the School of Coast Artillery or the School of Anti-Aircraft Artillery dealt with basic electricity and wireless as a preliminary to the proper understanding of radar. The second part of the course was held at the School of Artillery at Larkhill and dealt with the field radars in use and their practical application. Successful officer candidates were usually appointed as an instructor in field radar at the School of Artillery, Larkhill. The course is no longer run. See *School of Anti-Aircraft Artillery* and *School of Coast Artillery.*

Field Rocket Machine Name given to the land service rocket tubes employed between 1817 and 1867. The launcher consisted of a folding iron tripod supporting a nine foot long cast iron tube. The centre leg of the tripod, was aligned with the tube and was fitted with a bracket and wrench to which could be attached the elevating lever. Rope was bound around the tube in two or three places to facilitate handling when hot. The tube was aimed using a tangent scale and an elevating bar. Initially issued in 3-, 6- and 12-pdr versions, the 3-pdr version was withdrawn soon after issue. The 6-pdr weighed 63 pounds and the 12-pdr 73 pounds.

Field Service Marching Order Fighting order and large pack, used during the first half twentieth century.

Field Service Regulations The top level army doctrine during the first half of the twentieth century.

Field Storage Site The location where nuclear capable artillery units held their PNL whilst in the field. See *PNL.*

Field Survey Association Prize See *Defence Surveyors' Association Prize.*

FIFSO Forward Indirect Fire Safety Officer.

Fighting Lamp Used to illuminate the breech of a gun so that it could be manned at night. The Royal Artillery adopted the Tremlett pattern for use in coastal forts up until the 1890s. The brackets for these lamps can still be seen in the remaining coast fortifications around the United Kingdom. Also known as a Fighting Lantern or a Fighting Light.

Fighting Lantern See *Fighting Lamp.*

Fighting Lights Electric Searchlights, manned by the Royal Engineers, which were used in conjunction with coast artillery to illuminate targets. Unlike fixed lights they were used to follow a moving target to enable the guns to engage it. In 1907 it was agreed that the fighting lights would come under the command of the RGA battery commander whose battery they supported. See *Fixed Light* and *Fighting Lamp.*

Fighting Map A map used by the battery commander at the gun position to record targets and tactical information and to produce a bearing and distance from his battery to a target. Employed during the First World War it was gradually merged with artillery board. See *Artillery Board.*

Fighting Mercers Nickname of G Parachute Battery (Mercer's Troop) RHA.

Fighting the Fixed Armament The common name by which a confidential manual issued in 1911 was known, Its official title was 'The Organisation and Fighting of the Fixed Armament of a Coast Fortress or Defended Port.'

File Out Time to lead horses out of lines ready to be on parade (The King's Troop RHA).

Fill Gun An electronic device used to load crypto settings into BID 250.

Final Depth Line The line farthest from the opening line on which a barrage finishes. See *Barrage, Linear Concentration* and *Standard Barrage.*

Final Line The line nearest to the opening line on which a barrage finishes. See *Barrage, Final Line, Lines, Linear Concentration, Opening Line,* and *Standard Barrage.*

Final Protective Fire A close defensive fire mission where the target is usually located on the approach route most likely to be used by the enemy. The Final Protective Fire forms the final barrier of fire assigned to protect the defended location. Usually one is selected per battery in close consultation with the commander of the supported arm. When not engaged on other tasks, they are laid onto, and loaded in preparation to engage the Final Protective Fire target. Replaced DF(SOS) with change to QSTAG 225 fire discipline. See *Defensive Fire, DF(SOS), Priority Defensive Fire* and *QSTAG.*

FIP Fault Insertion Panel.

Fire by Order Fire by Order meant that the guns could not fire until given the executive order to 'Fire' originating from the person who initiated 'Fire by Order'. The observer had to initiate 'Fire by Order' for divisional and larger concentrations and the GPO always ordered it when working with air observers. When fire by order was in force the guns reported 'Ready' to the person who initiated it. It remained in force until a new sequence of initial orders or 'Cancel Fire by Order' was given. Now replaced by At My Command. See *AMC.*

Fire Command In coast artillery, a Fire Command was a sub-division of a fortress or section established for the purpose of fighting the fixed armament. It was the highest unit of executive artillery command in coast artillery. See *Fire Commander.*

Fire Commander The Royal Garrison Artillery officer responsible for the efficiency, as a fighting unit of a fire command. See *Fire Command.*

Fire Control Application A small laptop computer weighing 2.7 kg (including battery) with an operating system based on Windows XP. The FCA uses the NATO Armaments Ballistic Kernel software.

Fire Control Battlefield Information System Application Replacement for BATES when the Bowman communications system is fielded, the Fire Control Battlefield Information System Application is a Command and Control system for Indirect Fire Support. It provides the Royal Artillery with a fire control capability which facilitates the most effective management of current and emerging Indirect Fire Support weapons and ammunition.

Fire Coordination Area An area with which specified firing restraints have been applied and into which fire in excess of those restraints will not be delivered without the approval of the authority establishing the firing restraints. (Royal Canadian Artillery).

Fire Coordination Line A line established in order to coordinate fire support between airborne, helicopter-borne, or seaborne forces and link-up forces, or between any two converging friendly forces.

Fire Discipline The language of fire control. It consists of words, phrases, rules and conventions which have specific meanings and which result in some definite action at the guns. The aim of fire discipline is to ensure that the appropriate action is taken in the FDC, DFDC, FPC, CP and at the guns/MLRS strictly in accordance with the intentions of the originator and with the minimum of delay.

Fire Direction Centre An American term adopted for Regimental Main Headquarters in the 1970s, although in the US Army is has a somewhat different use. See *Main HQ.*

Fire Direction Table An instrument used in coast artillery to convert information received from observation posts into gun data.

Fire Effects Officer The Royal Canadian Artillery equivalent of a forward observation officer. See *Forward Observation Officer.*

Fire For Effect Number of rounds specified (i.e. 5 Rounds Fire For Effect) are fired by each gun as quickly as possible. This may be qualified in two ways. (i) 5 Rounds Fire For Effect two zero seconds – first and second rounds fired immediately the remaining rounds will be fired at 20 second intervals. (Interval may vary) (ii) 5 Rounds Fire For Effect Scale 2 – similar to (i), the first two rounds are fired immediately and the remaining rounds are fired at the interval specified. Scale 2: one round every 30 seconds, Scale 4: one round every 15 seconds etc.
(ii) Fire order indicating that Fire For Effect is desired.

Fire Group Commander A WO2 post in HVM equipped units.

Fire Mission (i) Specific assignment given to a fire unit as part of a definite plan.
(ii) Fire Order used to alert the battery and to indicate that the message following is a call for fire.

Fire Mission Grid A fire mission where the target location is given by a grid reference.

Fire Mission Polar A fire mission where the target location is given by Polar Coordinate, derived by Laser Range Finder from an accurately known position. See *Polar Coordinates.*

Fire Piquet During hostilities, the Fire Piquet is used to fight fires in camp or barracks. During peacetime, they can be employed as a secondary guard force.

Fire Plan The more or less precise ascertaining of the position and type of target and as a consequence, how it is to be engaged. There are three types of artillery fire plan, namely the quick fire plan, the deliberate fire plan and the nuclear fire plan.
(i) The quick fire plan originates at brigade or lower level and may consist of a simple plan utilising a single battery or a more complicated one involving an entire regiment or more. Quick fire plans are usually the responsibility of the commander of the battery in direct support of the armoured regiment or infantry battalion conducting the operation. If more than one battery is involved in the planning, the regimental commander will conduct the final coordination of the plan. The quick fire plan is made directly with the commander of the supported arm.
(ii) The deliberate fire plan normally originates at brigade or higher level and usually involves more than one artillery regiment. Planning by commanders and their artillery advisers takes place at the various levels of command. The detailed plan is made by the armoured

or infantry unit commanders and their direct support battery commanders. Their plans are coordinated by the regimental commander or the CRA and firm orders for the fire plan are then issued by the artillery headquarters at the level at which the operation is initiated.
(iii) The nuclear fire plan usually originated at brigade or higher level, however, battery commanders were required to advise their supported arms commanders during the initial planning stage on the selection of desired ground zero and also on troop safety considerations.

The barrage, is a more complicated and extensive version of the Fire Plan. See *CRA* and *Barrage*.

Fire Planning Cell — An entity introduced with BATES as part of the BC's party in a direct support battery. Responsible for coordinating the indirect fire support provided by artillery, aviation and mortars.

Fire Support — The collective and coordinated use of indirect fire weapons, armed aircraft and other lethal and non-lethal means in support of a battle plan. As such, fire support can be delivered by Mortars, Field Artillery, Naval Gunfire Support, Attack Helicopters, Close Air Support and any other air delivered weapons. Non-lethal means of Fire Support is comprised of electronic warfare, illumination and smoke. Fire support is used to destroy, neutralize and suppress enemy weapons, enemy formations or facilities. Fire support coordination is achieved by establishing a Fire Support Coordination Centre at the supported unit or formation Command Post. See *Fire Support Coordination Centre.*

Fire Support Control Cell — Part of the BATES system. See *BATES.*

Fire Support Coordination Centre — A US term introduced in the 1970s having various UK meanings. Now part of a formation HQ responsible for planning and coordinating of all forms of fire support and created around an artillery staff nucleus.

Fire Support Coordination Exercise — An exercise which can include artillery, infantry mortars, NGS and fast air.

Fire Support Coordination Line — A line established by the appropriate ground commander to ensure coordination of fire not under his control but which may effect current tactical operations. The Fire Support Coordination Line is used to coordinate fires of air, ground or sea weapons systems using any type of ammunition against surface targets. The Fire Support Coordination Line normally follows well defined terrain features. The establishment of the fire support coordination line is coordinated with the appropriate tactical air commander and any other supporting elements. These supporting elements may attack targets forward of the fire support coordination line, without prior consultation with the ground force commander, provided the attack will not produce adverse surface effects on, or to the rear of the line. Attacks against surface targets behind this line must be coordinated with the appropriate ground force commander. Known as the Bomb Line during the Second World War.

Fire Support Coordination Measure — Any one of a number of measures employed by commanders to facilitate the rapid engagement of targets while ensuring suitable safeguards for friendly forces are in place.

Fire Support Team	These teams which form part of the Regimental Tac Groups, are resourced and qualified to provide control of artillery support, mortar fire, close air support and close combat attack. They are used in place of the more usual FOO party. Fire Support Teams were originally known as Joint Effects Teams by 7 Para RHA who were amongst the first to trial the concept. See *Close Combat Attack, Close Air Support, Joint Effects Team, Joint Offensive Support Team* and *Forward Observation Officer.*
Fire Support Team Commander	The current term for what used to be known as a Forward Observation Officer. See *Fire Support Team* and *Forward Observation Officer.*
Fire Unit	The term applied to the smallest artillery organization, consisting of one or more weapon systems, capable of being employed to execute a fire mission. Mainly used in the air defence fraternity.
Firing Battery	Defined in *Field Artillery Training 1914* as being six guns and six ammunition wagons. However, four gun batteries with four ammunition wagons also existed. In mountain artillery, the firing battery consisted of the mules carrying the various portions of the gun and carriage, two ammunition mules for each subsection, one pioneer mule per section, one mule for telephone equipment and relief mules for the gun and carriage complete for one subsection.
Firing Tables	As with Range Tables these provide data to set up the correction of the moment graph and make other corrections for use when employing predicted fire. See *Range Tables.*
Firing under Precautions	The piece is fired whilst the detachment are under cover, usually applies when testing new ordnance.
First Captain	The rank of Major was abolished in the Royal Artillery in 1827 and was replaced with that of First Captain. The Second in Command of the troop, company or battery was known as the Second Captain. The rank of Major was reinstated in 1872, with the consequential demise of the rank of First Captain. See *Second Captain.*
First Degree Safety Line	The minimum safe distance from a nuclear strike for warned exposed troops. See *Second Degree Safety Line* and *Troop Safety Line.*
First Line Ammunition	Operational ammunition which is held and carried by a unit for each equipment and weapon used by that unit. The quantity of First Line Ammunition held by a unit depends on the type and intensity of conflict and theatre of operations in which it is involved, although five days 'Daily Ammunition Expenditure Rate' is generally used as a planning figure. See *Second Line Ammunition, Reserve Ammunition* and *With Weapons Scales.*
First Line Wagons	The name given to those battery ammunition wagons which were not included in the firing battery. See *Firing Battery.*
First Reinforcements	During the Second World War those men in an Artillery Regiment who would provide Royal Artillery battle casualty replacements.
First Salvo at ...	A portion of a naval gunfire support message to the observer from the ship providing the support, to indicate that due to proximity of troops, the ship will not fire at the target but will offset the first salvo a specific distance and direction from the target. (Royal Canadian Artillery.)
FIS	Fuze Interface System.
FISH	Fighting In Someone's House (tongue in cheek variant of FIBUA).

Firelight	See *AD10.*
FIT	First Impact Trace.
Fixation	The locating of a given a point on the earth's surface by map (grid) reference or coordinates (and height) with sufficient accuracy for gunnery purposes. Fixation was determined by survey processes. See *Battery Grid, Regimental Grid* and *Theatre Grid.*
Fixed Ammunition	See *QF Ammunition.*
Fixed Azimuth Barrage	See *Fixed Azimuth System.*
Fixed Azimuth System	Employed around London this anti-aircraft measure involved the establishing of fourteen fixed ground base-lines within the Inner Artillery Zone covering the approaches to London from the north-east. Each line had sound locators located at either end. When a target, or targets, crossed a base-line the data from the sound locators was passed to a computing instrument in the operations room at Brompton. Once the raid track and height had been established, the gun control officer selected a sub-division of a gridded map of London and passed this information to the command posts of the heavy anti-aircraft positions, which already had relevant gun data prepared for each grid. A barrage could then be fired into the appropriate grid.
Fixed Bearing	(i) The bearing read from the sight at datum point ranging. (ii) Used when recording fired data for reduction of date. See *Bearing.*
Fixed Defences	Non-mobile coast defence batteries.
Fixed Lights	Electric searchlights, manned by the Royal Engineers, which illuminated a target area for coast artillery. They were known as Fixed Lights due to the fact they would only illuminate that area and would not follow a target moving out of it. In 1907 it was agreed that they would come under the command of the fortress commander, an RGA Officer. See also *Fighting Lights.*
FIZ	First Impact Zone.
FLA	Four Letter Abbreviation.
Flag-Basher	Slang name for a signaller during the 1920s and 30s. It derived from the practice of signalling with flags both in Morse and Semaphore. See *Flag-Wagger.*
Flaggie	Nickname for a signaller.
Flag Gun	During the eighteenth century the flag gun carried the Royal Standard on the line of march and indicated the headquarters of the army when in camp. The gun being fitted with a socket on the trail to take the standard.
Flag-Wagger	Slang name for a signaller, certainly used during the Second World War and probably before. As with Flag-Basher, it derived from the original practice of signalling with flags in both Morse and Semaphore. See *Flag-Basher.*
Flashless Propellants	These were introduced during the Second World War. However, 'Flashless' is a relative term, the definition being that it 'was unlikely to attract the attention of the naked eye at 4000 yards'. Muzzle flash in fact comprises three different types of flash, namely, primary, intermediate and secondary. Most of the flash derives from the last, this being caused by hot combustible gases, mainly hydrogen and carbon dioxide, mixing with air and burning.
Flashlight Battery	A colloquial name used during the Second World War to refer to searchlight batteries.
Flash Spotting	A method of locating hostile artillery by cross observation of the flash generated by the propellant charges on firing, originally developed by the Royal Engineers in the First

	World War, but subsequently developed by the Royal Artillery. Positions were located by cross-referencing from two or more flash spotting locations.
Flash to Bang time	Slang for the length of time available/taken to complete an operation. Derived from Flash Spotting, where the distance for the firer is computed by counting the seconds between seeing the flash and hearing the bang.
Flaties	Nickname given to non-RHA personnel by RHA personnel. The term refers to the flat buttons worn by RA units, as opposed to the ball buttons of the RHA.
FLSC	Flexible Linear Shaped Charge.
FLET	Forward Line Enemy Troops.
Flight Premature	See *Premature.*
FLOC	(i) Future Land Operational Concept. (ii) Future Land Operating Concept.
FLOCARK	Features, Lanes, Obstacles, Canalizing Ground, Routes, Key Terrain. (Royal Canadian Artillery.)
Floppy (Plural Floppies)	Jungle hat.
FLOT	Forward Line of Own Troops.
Flowerpot	See *Jhansi Flower Pot.*
FLTS	First Line Test Set. Test set for Javelin S15.
Flying Gunners	The name given to the Royal Artillery Motorcycle Display Troop.
Fly the footprint	A type of mode of operation employed where an unmanned aerial vehicle, such as a Phoenix has no precise manoeuvre planned, but where the sensor field of view is controlled by the UAV operator moving his/her joystick to the left or right. When employed by the Image Analyst, the required parameters for this type of mission can be preset.
FM	(i) Fire Mission. (ii) Filter Module. (iii) Field Manual.
FM1G	Fire Mission, One Gun.
FM2 Bty	Fire Mission, Two Batteries.
FM2(etc)G	Fire Mission, Two (etc) Guns.
FMA	(i) Force Maintenance Area. See *FFMA.* (ii) Forward Maintenance Area.
FM all avail.	Fire Mission, All Available.
FM Bty	Fire Mission, Battery.
FM CFF	Fire Mission Call For Fire. A BATES fire mission engagement sequence. See *BATES.*
FM CFF P	Fire Mission Call For Fire Polar. A BATES fire mission engagement sequence. See *BATES.*
FMD	Firm Map Detail.
FM Div	Fire Mission, Division.
FMF	Forward Maintenance Facility.
FM Grid	Fire Mission Grid.
FML	Far Mortar Line. See *NML.*
FMO	Fire Mission Order.
FM Polar	Fire Mission Polar. See *Polar Coordinates.*
FM Regt	Fire Mission Regiment.
FMV	Fitter, Motor Vehicle. (Second World War.)
FO	(i) Forward Observation. (ii) Forward Observer.
FOB	(i) Forward Observer Bombardment. See *Bombardment Troop* for an explanation of the role. (ii) Forward Operating Base.
FO Bty	Forward Observation Battery.
FOBU	Forward Observation and Bombardment Unit. No 1 FOBU formed on 26 April 1942, changing its name to No 1 Bombardment Unit in July 1942.

FOBEX Forward Operating Base Exercise.

F of I Figure of Insensitiveness.

Fogg Memorial Trophy An A Battery (The Chestnut Troop) RHA trophy awarded to the winning team of an inter-troop football competition.

FOGS Fibre Optic Gyroscope System.

Followed by... Part of a fire order message used to indicate a change in the rate of fire. See *Rate*.

FOM Fibre Optically guided Missile.

FONG Forward Observer Naval Gunnery. See *NGSFO*.

FOO Forward Observation Officer. See *OPO*.

FOO Tech Forward Observation Officer Technician. (Royal Canadian Artillery.) See *OP Ack*.

FOP (i) Forward Observation Party (1950s).
(ii) Forward Observation Post. (First World War.)
(iii) Fortress Observation Post. See *Fortress Plotting Room*.

Forage Horses Feed; a mixture of hay, nuts, mix, barley and oats. (The King's Troop RHA).

Fortress Commander The Royal Garrison Artillery officer commanding either a coast fortress or a defended port.

Fortress Observation In coast artillery, this was a centralised system of collection information on targets and for disseminating it to the guns in a form which enabled them to engage the enemy ships accurately.

Fortress Observation Post A small protected location which housed the personnel and instruments of the observation posts of the coast artillery of a fortress. Observation data was passed to the Fortress Plotting Room. See *Fortress Plotting Room*.

Fortress Plotting Room The room where observations from fortress observation posts were plotted so that continuous target location information could be passed to the relevant gun batteries. See *Fortress Observation Post*.

Fortune Radio appointment title used to identify a Forward Air Controller. See *Appointment Titles*.

Forty-niners Nickname given to members of 49 Fd Regt RA.

Forward Air Controller A member of a TAC Group or an OP Party who is trained to request, plan, brief and control Close Air Support operations both for Low Level and Medium/High Level operations. All Bombardiers in 148 (Meiktila) Commando Forward Observation Battery RA are qualified FACs. See *FAM, LTMO, Observation Post Part* and *TAC Group*.

Forward Air Marker A soldier who had qualified on the FAM course, the predecessor of the now defunct LTMO course, the FAM would generally be an Op-Ack who was trained to designate a target with a laser for attack by an aircraft. The aircraft was not however, controlled by the FAM, but would remain under someone else's control. Each Tac group would have a FAC qualified person, and a number of FAM/LTMO qualified personnel. See *FAC, LTMO, Op-Ack* and *Tac Group*.

Forward Observation Officer A Royal Artillery Officer attached to an 'other arm' unit, responsible for calling in the fire of the guns. The first reference to the Forward Observation Officer appeared at the Practice of 1909, although the post was not formally recognised in the Artillery hierarchy until its inclusion in *Field Artillery Training 1914*. In the First World War referred to any battery officer sent forward to observe from an OP. See *Observation Post Officer*.

Forward Observation Officer Technician The Canadian term for the OP Ack. The FOO Tech's role is to either agree or disagree with the Forward Observation

Officer's data. The FOO Tech provides a double check. Technically, both know OP fire discipline, theory of indirect fire, and can shoot the guns. The FOO has greater depth of knowledge on the support and coordination role and is the fire support adviser and coordinator to his arms commander. The FOO tech is capable of conducting shoots on their own, particularly during fire plans, with the signaller providing the double check. (Royal Canadian Artillery.) See *OP Ack*.

Forward Observation Party — A Naval Gunfire Support party consisting of a Captain, PA, 2 Driver/Operators an RO2 from the Navy (1950s).

Forward Observation Post — This term was used at the start of the First World War, but was later changed simply to Observation Post, as by definition, it is almost always 'forward'.

Forward Observer Naval Gunnery — The title used prior to the introduction of the title NGSFO. See *NGSFO*.

Four Wheeled Hussars — Nickname given to the RHA owing to their dress uniform being similar to that worn by the Hussar Regiments.

Forward Observation Officer — A Royal Artillery Officer attached to an 'other arm' unit, responsible for calling in the fire of the guns. The first reference to the Forward Observation Officer appeared at the Practice of 1909, although the post was not formally recognised in the Artillery hierarchy until its inclusion in *Field Artillery Training 1914*. In the First World War the name was used to refer to any battery officer sent forward to observe from an OP. See *OPO*.

Forward Observer Unit RA (Airborne) — A unit formed to provide observation post parties for Air-borne artillery. Eventually three Regular Army FOU RA (Airborne) were formed, together with one Territorial Army FOU RA (Airborne). See *Airborne Support Net*.

1st FOU RA (Airborne) was formed in June 1944 as part of 1st Airborne Division. The unit consisted of twenty Officers (1 Major (Maj. D. R. Wight Boycott), eighteen Captains and one Subaltern) and sixty other ranks. This unit served at Arnhem.

2nd FOU RA (Airborne) was formed in August 1944 as part of 6th Airborne Division, it was composed of both Royal Artillery and Royal Canadian Artillery personnel and served in the airborne assault on the Rhine, later moving to the Far East, although not seeing any active service in that theatre. 2 FOU RA (Airborne) eventually served in Palestine, before being renamed 334 Forward Observation Battery RA (Airborne) in 1947.

3rd FOU RA (Airborne) was formed at Eboli in June 1944, like 2 FOU RA (Airborne) it was formed of a mix of RA and RCA personnel, the unit served in southern France, Italy and Greece.

880 Forward Observer Battery RA (Airborne) TA was formed in 1947, and served through to 1961 when following amalgamation with 289 Parachute Light Regiment RA TA it was renamed S Battery, 289 Parachute Regiment RHA TA.

Forward Storage Site(s) — Permanent ammunition storage facilities established in 1 (BR) Corps area during the 1980s.

FOS — Fall of Shot.

FOsB — Forward Observers Bombardment.

FOU — Forward Observation Unit.

FOU(AB) — Forward Observation Unit (Airborne).

FOU RA (Airborne) — Forward Observer Unit RA (Airborne).

Foundation Day — 1 February, anniversary of the founding of the first two troops of RHA. Celebrated by A Battery (The Chestnut Troop) RHA, to commemorate the foundation of the Troop on 1 February 1793.

FOV — Field of View.

FP — (i) Front Pivot.
(ii) Firing Point.
(iii) Firing Platform.
(iv) Fire Plan.

FPC — (i) Fire Planning Cell.
(ii) Fire Planning Computer.

FPF — Final Protective Fire. See *PDF*.

FPO — Firing Point Officer.

FPOL — Forward Passage of Lines. See *RPOL*.

FPR — Fortress Plotting Room.

FQMS — Farrier Quartermaster Sergeant.

FR — Formation Reconnaissance.

Fraggles — Nickname given to members of 4/73 (Sphinx) Special Observation Post Battery RA. The name is taken from a children's television programme, 'Fraggle Rock' and derives from the fact that members of the Battery spend a lot of their time underground.

FRAGO — Fragmented Order.

FRES — Future Rapid Effect System.

Fresh Target — A naval gunfire support message sent by the observer to the firing ship to indicate the fire will be shifted from the original target to a new target by spots (corrections) applied to the computer solution being generated. (Royal Canadian Artillery.)

FRFS — Fortress Range Finding System. This used the HPF.

FRG — (i) Federal Riot Gun.
(ii) Forward Repair Group (REME), deployed by forward workshops or battalions to support forward troops.

Friction Tube — A device that functioned not unlike the striking of a match to initiate the propellant in late nineteenth century artillery equipments.

Friendly — A report that indicates the potential target has been identified as friendly according to laid down friendly act criteria.

Friendly Fire — Firing on, or being fired on by friendly forces. It is a common axiom amongst all branches of the armed services that 'Friendly Fire, isn't'.

Frontier Garrison Artillery — A part of the pre-1948 Indian Army. The Frontier Garrison Artillery was a branch of the Indian Mountain Artillery, which consisted of older soldiers, who were no longer as active as they used to be. They manned the stationary post guns which were located in a number of the frontier forts. Members of the Frontier Garrison Artillery were often derisively referred to as 'The Blokes'. See *Post Gun*.

Front Pivot — A gun mounting which was traversed using a pivot at the front of the platform.

FRRD — Fin Restraint and Release Drive.

FRS — Fin Restraint Strap.

FRT — Forward Repair Team.

FRTV — Forward Repair and Test Vehicle. (Part of the Rapier AD system.)

FRV — Final Rendezvous.

fs — Feet per Second.

FS — (i) Flash Spotting.
(ii) Free Standing.

FS2010 — Force Structure 2010.

FSA	(i) Forward Support Area. (ii) Field Survey Association. (iii) Financial Systems Administrator.
FSB	Fire Support Base.
FSB1	Rapier Field Standard B1.
FSB2	Rapier Field Standard B2.
FSC	(i) Ferret Scout Car. (ii) Rapier Field Standard C. (iii) Full Service Charge.
FSCC	(i) Fire Support Coordination Centre. (ii) Fire Support Control Cell.
FSCEX	Fire Support Coordination Exercise.
FSCL	Fire Support Coordination Line.
FSCM	Fire Support Coordination Measure.
FSCOCU	Field Standard C Operational Conversion Unit. (Since renamed SAWOCU.)
FSE	Fuze Setter Electronic.
Fsg	Flash Spotting.
FSG	Forward Support Group.
FSH	Fuze Setter Head.
FSMO	Field Service Marching Order.
FSOP	Flash Spotting Observation Post.
FSP	(i) Flash-Spotting Post. (ii) Full Standard Pack.
FSPB	Fire Support Patrol Base. (Royal Australian Artillery – Vietnam Conflict.)
FSR	Field Service Regulations.
FSS	Field Storage Site. See *PNL.*
FSSL	Fire Support Safety Line. See *NFL.*
FST	Fire Support Team.
FST Comd	Fire Support Team Commander.
FSU	Frame Store Unit. Part of the Phoenix UAV system. See *Phoenix*.
FT	Firing Table. *See GFT* and *TFT.*
FTF	Fly the Footprint.
FTMV	Firing Table Muzzle Velocity.
FTRS	Full Time Reserve Service.
Ftr/QMS	Fitter Quartermaster Sergeant. (Rank no longer in use.)
Ftr/S/Sgt	Fitter Staff Sergeant. (Rank no longer in use.)
FTRT	False Target Range Template.
FTS	Field Test Set.
FTX	Field Training Exercise.
FTZWMV	Firing Table Zero Wear Muzzle Velocity. Used in Calibration.
FU	Fire Unit; refers to individual Rapier Fire Units.
Full Colonel	A Colonel as opposed to a Lieutenant Colonel, who is referred to as a Half Colonel.
FULL COMD	Full Command.
Full Screw	Nickname for a Bombardier. See *Bomb, Bombardier* and *Lance Jack.*
Full Standard Pack	A pack used to hold air defence missiles which are themselves contained in field handling containers.
Fundys	Fundamentals.
FUP	Forming Up Point.
FUT	Fire Unit Truck.
Futchell	This normally consisted of three strong pieces of wood forming the bottom base of the limber, and connecting the axletree bed with the splinter bar.
Future Army Structure	Restructuring of the Army during the period 2005–2007 which saw a 50% reduction in close air defence manpower and a reduction in general support batteries.
Fuze	The fuze causes the shell to detonate and/or burst at

the correct point in its trajectory. Dependant on the type, fuzes can be set to cause the shell to burst in the air, immediately on striking the ground/target, or to delay the burst to permit greater penetration and thereby cause enhanced structural damage.

Fuze Bar Indicator — See *Fuze Indicator*.

Fuze Event — The point in the trajectory of a carrier shell when the fuze activates. In the case of a Bomblet round, the fuze event causes the sub-munitions to be dispensed from the carrier shell. See *Bomblet*.

Fuze Indicator — An instrument used to converted range to fuze length, taking account of muzzle velocity and corrector settings. Each charge and gun combination had a separate instrument. The Fuze Indicator should not be confused with the Fuze Setter which set the fuze length onto the fuze. Due to its shape it was sometimes referred to as a 'fuze bar indicator'. See *Fuze Key* and *Fuze Setter*.

Fuze Key — Used to set the required fuze length on the fuze. Fuze keys could also be used to insert and remove fuzes. See *Fuze Indicator* and *Fuze Setter*.

Fuze Length — The length of time taken for a fuze to burn prior to exploding its projectile.

Fuze Setter — Introduced during the Second World War as a replacement for the Fuze Key, this instrument was used to set the fuze length. The required length was first set on the fuze setter which was then placed over the fuze nose so that lugs inside the setter engaged notches in the rotating part of fuze nose (which were also used with fuze keys) and the non-rotating part. The setter was then turned until it reached 'stops', which meant that the correct fuze length had been set. The advantage of the setter was that once it was set correctly all the fuzes would be set to the same setting, even in bad light. It should not confused with the Fuze Indicator. See *Fuze Indicator* and *Fuze Key*.

FV — (i) Fighting Vehicle.
(ii) Familiarisation Visit. See *RAIV*.

FV610 — Artillery Command Vehicle version of the Saracen Armoured Personnel Carrier. The FV610 was fitted with a higher roof over the rear compartment. Space was provided for a map table and an awning could be fitted to the rear. It was possible to use the awning to attach two or more Command Vehicles together. A normal vehicle detachment consisted of the driver, a radio operator (sometimes combined with the driver as a driver/operator), either the Gun Position Officer or a TARA Sergeant, and two TARAs. An example of the FV610 can be seen in Firepower, The Royal Artillery Museum. See *Gun Position Officer* and *TARA*.

FV623 — The Alvis Stalwart Mk II Limber vehicle. Used by the Royal Artillery as an ammunition supply vehicle. The FV623 was fitted with an extra seat in the cab for the crane operator together with four extra seats for ammunition handlers. An ATLAS 3001/66 hydraulic crane was fitted in the cargo area. See *Alvis Stalwart*.

F/W — Fireworker. Eighteenth century rank.

FW — Fixed Wing.

FWA — Fixed Wheel Axle.

FWD — Four Wheel Drive. More powerful than the usual lorry, used to tow 6-inch Hows. (First World War.)

FwdSS — Forward Storage Site.

FWR — Fire When Ready.

Fze — Fuze.

G – George – 1927/1943
Golf – 1956

G	(i) Gunnery (Field) professional qualification designation. (ii) Artillery Code used during the First World War meaning 'Fire'.
G Vehicle	See *George Truck*.
G1098	The Army Form which authorises the complete scale of equipment and stores for a unit in the British army.
G1	Personnel.
G2	Intelligence and Security.
G3	Operations, O&D and Training.
G4	Service Support.
G5	Civil Affairs and Public Relations.
G6	Communications and MIS.
G7	Future Development.
G8	Plans, Resources and Finance.
G9	Civilian Management and Budgets.
G904	See *Army Form G904*.
GA	General Alert.
GAC	(i) Gun Area Commander. (ii) Gun Angle Control. (Coast artillery Second World War and later.)
Gaine	For safety reasons, shell fillings must be hard to detonate, it is therefore sometimes necessary to provide extra initiation power to achieve this. The Gaine is a device which causes the high explosive to detonate as a result of the action of the fuze. See *Fuze*.
Galloper Gun	Introduced during the eighteenth century and sometimes referred to as 'Gallopers', galloper guns were 1½-pdr guns mounted on light carriages which had a split trail and were drawn by one horse. They were designed to keep up with cavalry and provided a source of highly mobile fire. Their use was discontinued in 1746.
Gallopers	See *Galloper Gun*.
Galloping Gunners	Nickname given to the Royal Horse Artillery.
Gambardier	Nickname given to members of the Royal Garrison Artillery during the First World War. The origin of the term is unknown.
G and A	Guns and Ammunition.
GAP	Gun Aiming Point.
Gap	One of the Triangulation Exercise Stations on the now defunct RA Survey Course.
Gap Year Commission	Formerly known as the Short-Service Limited Commission. See *SSLC*.
Gar	Garrison.
Gardiner's Troop	With Salamanca Troop, one of the two troops forming E Battery RHA.
Garrington Gun	An 88 mm towed gun developed after the Second World War. It had a novel carriage design and fired 25-pdr ammunition with a longer barrel. The intent was to adopt a new ammunition with a 22 lb shell capable of reaching 17,100 yards. Cancelled mainly due to NATO's adoption of 105 mm.
Garrison Gunner	Any member of the Royal Garrison Artillery.
Garrison RML	When introduced into service, this nature of equipment consisted of the following calibres: 64-pdr weighing 64 cwt; 7-inch weighing 4½, 6½ & 7 tons; 8-inch weighing 9 tons; 9-inch weighing 12 tons; 10-inch weighing 18 tons; 10.4-inch weighing 28 tons; 11-inch weighing 25 tons;

12-inch weighing 35 tons; 12.5-inch weighing 38 tons 17.72-inch weighing 100 tons. RMLs remained in service until 1908, the last being 10-inch and 12.5-inch which were used with special case shot against torpedo boats.

Garrison Standing Carriage A type of carriage for guns not intended to be placed on the front faces of a fort, but possibly to be employed for curved fire. A ground platform of wood, stone or concrete with a slope of 1 in 24 was required. It had four wheels, known as trucks, and was generally copied from naval carriages. Some Garrison Standing Carriages had the rear trucks removed and replaced with blocks, these were then known as a Carriage, Garrison and Rear Chock.

Garr Sergt-Major Garrison Sergeant-Major. This abbreviation has now been replaced by GSM.

Gas-Check A flat plate of metal used to impart spin to a projectile in a rifled gun and to seal the bore. It was placed behind the projectile on loading the gun and fell away when the projectile left the muzzle. It was first used in order to overcome erosion of the bore caused by windage. The precursor of the driving band on BL shells. The Gas-Check removed the need for studs on the projectile. Also known as an 'Automatic Gas-Check'.

GAT Garrison Artillery Training manual, abbreviation is normally followed by the year of publication. i.e. GAT 1910.

Gaza Troop One of the Troops in 3rd Squadron Honourable Artillery Company. See *Aden Troop, Honourable Artillery Company* and *Rhine Troop.*

Gazala Troop Together with Aden Troop, Hook Troop and Martinique Troop, one of the four troops in 74 Battery (The Battle Axe Company) Royal Artillery.

Gazelle A French designed helicopter, built under licence by Westland Helicopters. The Gazelle is used by the Army Air Corps as a general purpose helicopter, capable of carrying out a variety of battlefield roles. It is equipped with a Ferranti AF 532 stabilised, magnifying observation aid which can be used by the observer when carrying out the Air Observation Post role. See *Air Observation Post.*

GB Gun Bearing.

GBAD Ground Based Air Defence; sometimes corrupted by gunners to Garage Based Air Defence.

GBAD BMA GBAD Battle Management Application – a replacement for ADCIS.

GBAD BriC GBAD Bridging Capability.

GBAD Bridging Capability Designed to ensure the rapid circulation of Air Space Control measures from the highest levels of Air Defence command down to the Fire Units.

GBAD SC Ground Based Air Defence Siting Computer.

G/Burst Ground Burst.

GC Gun Captain. (Royal Garrison Artillery.)

GCC Gunnery Career Course.

GCC Fd Gunnery Careers Course Field.

GCC (Tgt) Gunnery Careers Course (Targeting). A course run at the Royal School of Artillery.

GCI Graphical Control Instrument.

G Class See *Green Class.*

GCS (i) Ground Control Station. See *Ground Data Terminal* and *Phoenix.*
(ii) Gunner Command Systems.

GD Gun Drill.

GDA	Gun Defended Area (AA – Second World War).
Gd Room	Guardroom.
GDT	(i) Ground Data Terminal. See *BATES, FC BISA, Ground Control Station,* and *Phoenix.* (ii) Gun Density Trace.
GDU	Gun Display Unit. See *BATES.*
General Alert	The highest level in NATO's non-emergency Alert State Hierarchy. See *Military Vigilance* and *Simple Alert.*
General Secretary	The General Secretary is responsible for Regimental Welfare and Comradeship. He manages the day-to-day running of the Royal Artillery Charitable Fund, the Royal Artillery Association and the Kelly Holdsworth Trust.
General Service Corps	From 1942 until the end of the Second World War most men started their military service in the General Service Corps as direct enlistment into a regiment or corps was suspended in order to enable better manpower allocation.
General Staff Officer	There were three grades, 1, 2 and 3. These were filled, respectively, by officers of the following ranks; Lieutenant Colonel, Major and Captain.
General Support	General Support Regiments are currently equipped with multi-launch rocket systems. They normally deploy to attack targets by utilising the maximum range of MLRS, which is in excess of 25 km. General Support Regiments can be used to support close support regiments in the General Support Reinforcing role. General Support tasks include, fire support to a supported force as a whole, not to particular sub-units. It is often used to influence the corps or divisional battle and is not generally available to support subordinate brigades or other units. See *Close Support, Direct Support General Support Reinforcing* and *MLRS.*
General Support Reinforcing	A General Support Reinforcing Regiment provides fire support to the force as a whole, with a secondary role of providing fire for another artillery unit. It does not provide guaranteed fire and will only respond if its has no higher priority task of its own to perform. It is usually accompanied by controls on times when fire is available and/or the amount of ammunition which is available for the reinforcing task. See *Close Support, Direct Support* and *General Support.*
GENFOR	Generic Enemy Forces.
GEO	Geographic Coordinates.
Geographic Coordinates	The latitude and longitude of a location.
Geordie Gunners	Regimental title of 101 (Northumbrian) Regt RA (V). Identifies the regimental recruiting area.
George	The mascot of 94 (New Zealand) Battery RA. George is a stuffed Kiwi, which was presented to the Battery in 1968 by the Right Honourable K. J. Holyoake, Prime Minister of New Zealand. During his time with the Battery, George has been awarded six operational medals and has qualified twice over for the Long Service and Good Conduct Medal.
George Truck	Battery Reconnaissance vehicle, now known as a Golf Vehicle. Named after its vehicle Tac Sign 'G', or 'GA', 'GB' or 'GC' before the reintroduction of 6 Gun Batterty in the late 1950s. GC would only be applicable to George and not Golf since 3 Troop Field Battery only existed during the period 1938–40. See *Monkey Truck* and *Tac Sign.*
Get onto data	Expression used to describe when two or more BATES units are 'talking' to each other.

GF	(i) Gunfire – A specified number of rounds fired on a target by a Troop, Battery or Regiment. See *GF Target*. (ii) Artillery Code used during the First World War meaning 'gunfire for fleeting target'.
GFE	Government Furnished Equipment.
gfr	After an officer's name in the Army List, this signified attendance on the Field Radar Instructors Course.
GFT	Graphical Firing Table.
GF Target	Gunfire Target. See *GF*.
GGC	Gun Group Commander. (Royal Garrison Artillery.)
G(gw)	Gunnery (Guided Weapons); professional qualification designation.
GH	Guidance Head; used with Blowpipe, Javelin and HVM.
Gibraltar 1779–1783	(i) Battery Honour Title of 5 (Gibraltar 1779–1783) Battery RA which was granted on 13 Nov 1934 under authority of 20/ARTY/4968/AG6a. Battery personnel wear the French 1914 *Croix de Guerre* medal ribbon under their beret badges and on dress uniforms in recognition of the action at Pontavert on 26–27 May 1918. See *Battery Honour Titles*. (ii) Battery Honour Title of 19 (Gibraltar 1779–1783) Battery RA which was granted on 13 November 1934 under authority of 20/ARTY/4968/AG6a. See *Battery Honour Titles*. (iii) Battery Honour Title of 21 (Gibraltar 1779–1783) Battery RA which was granted on 13 November 1934 under authority of 20/ARTY/4968/AG6a. See *Battery Honour Titles*. (iv) Battery Honour Title of 22 (Gibraltar 1779–1783) Battery RA which was granted on 13 November 1934 under authority of 20/ARTY/4968/AG6a. See *Battery Honour Titles*. (v) Battery Honour Title of 23 (Gibraltar 1779–1783) Commando Headquarters Battery RA which was granted on 13 November 1934 under authority of 20/ARTY/4968/AG6a. See *Battery Honour Titles*.
GIC	Gunnery Instructors Course. Abbreviation generally followed by the relevant abbreviation denoting type of course. For example: GIC (AD) – Gunnery Instructors Course (Air Defence).
GID	Ground Impact Detector. Part of the Phoenix UAV system. See *Phoenix*.
Girdles	See *Ped-Rails*.
GL	Gun Laying (Radar).
GLO	Ground Liaison Officer (often referred to as Glow-worm).
Glorious 12th	Nickname given to 12 Regiment RA.
Glow-worm	See *GLO*.
GLPS	Gun Laying and Positioning System.
GLS	Gun Laying System. See *SPGR* and *HALO*.
GLSC	Gun Line Section Commander.
GLSO	Gun Line Safety Officer.
GM	Ground Manoeuvre.
GMA	Grid Magnetic Angle.
GMAT	Guided Missile Ammunition Technician.
GMLRS	Guided Multiple Launch Rocket System.
GN2	Gaseous Nitrogen.
GNF	Guns Now Firing. See *NF*.
Gnr	Gunner.
Gnr Comms	Gunner Communications. See *Arty Comms*.
Gny	Gunnery.
GO	(i) General Order. Generally followed by the number identifying the relevant order.

	(ii) Artillery Code used during the First World War meaning 'Continue firing in your own time'.
GOCRA	General Officer Commanding Royal Artillery
Go Down	Sergeant's Office in Sub Section (The King's Troop RHA).
Gobblers	Nickname given to P Battery Coast Defence (later 21 Hy Battery) in the 1930s.
Gods Venerable Artillery	Nickname used during the 1970s for 266 (Gloucestershire) Battery RA, one of the three Territorial Army Observation Post Batteries. See *Golf Five Alpha*.
Golandauz	A Indian private soldier of the Bengal, Bombay or Madras Regiments of Artillery.
Golf	Gun Position Officer/Battery Reconnaissance Officer Tactical Sign. The Tactical Sign denotes both the Gun Position Officer/Battery Reconnaissance Officer and his /her TARA Sergeant. They are responsible for conducting a reconnaissance of the gun position, the laying of gun markers within the gun position and the reconnaissance of command post positions. Golf should not be confused with the G Party which existed as party of Battery HQ during the Second World War. See *G Party, Gun Position Officer, Battery Reconnaissance Officer, Reconnaissance Party, Tactical Sign* and *Technical Assistant Royal Artillery*.
Golf bag principle	During the Second World War regiments used different equipment for particular operations. For example, anti-aircraft regiments manned 7.2-inch Howitzers in Burma (two guns being held by ordnance parks in each corps) and multiple rocket launchers in the final months in north-west Europe. Similarly, field regiments used mountain guns in Italy, 5.5-inch in Burma and 105 mm SP during the run-in fire plan on the Normandy beaches. Anti-tank batteries were double equipped with mortars in Burma (3-inch) and sometimes operated them in Italy (4.2-inch). See also *Jungle Field Regiment*.
Golf Five Alpha	Nickname of 266 (Gloucestershire) Parachute Battery RA, derived from the initials of the former title of the battery, the Gloucestershire Volunteer Artillery, the GVA. See *Gods Venerable Artillery*.
Golf Party	See *G Party*.
Golf Truck	See *George Truck*.
Golf Vehicle	See *George Truck*.
Goniometric Sight	An early form of Dial Sight. See *Dial Sight*.
Go On	Order to the guns to continue a previously suspended action.
GOP	Gun Observation Post. Coast artillery, Second World War and later.
GOR	(i) Gun Operations Room. (ii) Gurkha Other Rank.
Gordon Gunners	Two anti-tank regiments formed during the Second World War from the Gordon Highlanders, and known as Gordon Gunners. The units concerned were 92 ATk Regt, which had been 4 Gordons, a corps machine gun battalion in the BEF and 100 ATk Regt which had been 9 Gordons, a standard infantry battalion.
Gorham's Mixture	A form of case shot designed by Major C. A. Gorham, the Deputy Judge-Advocate General and an old gunner. Used during the Second Afghan War. Its name was an allusion to 'Gregory's Mixture', which was a domestic medicine widely used in Victorian nurseries.
Goschen Medal	Awarded each year, by the Master Gunner's Committee, to a serving non-commissioned officer of the Royal Artillery (Regular or Territorial Army) for noteworthy

service. Noteworthy service is defined in this instance, as service that provides some tangible benefit or brings credit to the Royal Regiment. Service to a single unit may be considered if there has been benefit to a substantial number of soldiers. The service may be rendered in the year of the award or over a period of years culminating in the year in question. See *Napier Medal*.

Goschen Parade — A Parade held to mark the end of training at the Junior Leaders Regiment Royal Artillery. Due to the disbandment of the Junior Leaders Regiment this parade has now passed into history.

Gp — Group.

GP — Gun Position.

GP 31 — Gun Position 31.

G Party — Comprising the Battery Captain (BK), the Command Post Officer and the Gun Position Officers, the G Party formed part of the Battery HQ group during the Second World War. See *Golf* and *O Party*.

GPEOD — General Purpose Electro-Optical Device.

GPMG — General Purpose Machine Gun.

GPMG (SF) — General Purpose Machine Gun (Sustained Fire).

GPO — Gun Position Officer. See *Command Post Officer, Section Commander* and *Subaltern*.

GPOA — Gun Position Officer's Assistant. (Second World War).

GPO's Check Map — Introduced during the 1950s for use in conjunction with the Plotter FC, FBA, the GPO's Check Map comprised a clear plastic circular GPO's Protractor measuring 12 inches in diameter with range arms that could be clipped to its central pivot. This protractor was mounted over a 1:50,000 or similar scale map and marked with any information related to troop safety. In order to establish firing data against a target it was necessary for the the plotter and check map to agree to within 1 degree and 100 yards. See *GPO* and *Plotter FC, FBA*.

GPPNVG — General Purpose Passive Night Vision Goggles.

GPS — Global Positioning System.

GPS Denial — The term applied to the process by which units are prevented from using the Global Positioning System, and under which conditions they have to revert to standard manual survey methods. See *Meaconing*.

GPSO — Gun Position Safety Officer.

GR — (i) Grid Reference.
(ii) Grid.

Grandma — See *Granny*.

Granny — Nickname given to the 15-inch howitzer introduced towards the end of the First World War. This was effectively a scaled up version of the 9.2-inch howitzer, the original version of which was known as 'Mother'.

GRAP — Ground Recognised Air Picture.

Grape Shot — As with Case Shot, Grape shot was a type of anti-personnel weapon. It consisted of a number of lead balls, fitted around an iron shaft and encased in a canvas bag. A length of strong twine was then tied around the bag and between the balls, giving an appearance, similar to a bunch of grapes, hence the name. Manufacture ceased after 1868. See *Caffin's Grape Shot*.

GRAP IOC — Ground Recognised Air Picture Interim Operating Capability.

Graze Fuze — These fuzes function, unlike the Direct Action Fuze, at all angles of descent but with a delay of about 0.01 second, although some Graze Fuzes are designed to employ a longer delay. They do not rely on the fuze nose

	being compressed but rather on the slight but sudden retardation of the shell on contact with the target. See *Direct Action Fuze.*
Green Archer	Radar FA No 8 Mortar location radar capable of detecting a 3-inch mortar bomb at 4.5 miles (7.3 km). An X-band radar, built by EMI, the prototype was mounted on a FV436 APC, but the service version was towed. Green Archer was replaced by Cymbeline.
Greenbacks	Nickname given to 97 (Lawson's) Battery RA.
Green Class	Tear Gas filled munitions. Second World War and later.
Green Ginger	Development name given to the AD11 and AD12 radar systems. See *AD11* and *AD12.*
Green Mace	RARDE developed rapid-firing 4-inch (10.1 cm) heavy AA gun. It was intended to be used in conjunction with Red Sea predictor. The ammunition used consisted of a fin-stabilised dart and discarding sabot. Ammunition was carried in two large cylindrical magazines. Capable of firing 75 rounds per minute. The project was cancelled in 1956. Only one example exists, and this can be seen at Firepower, The Royal Artillery Museum.
Green Maggot	Army issue sleeping bag.
Greens	See *JGs.*
Green Star	A First World War gas shell filling consisting of 35 per cent Sulphuretted Hydrogen and 65 per cent Chloropicrin. A cloud gas, Green Star was never used in anger.
Greys Troop	One of the Troops in 159 (Colenso) Bty RA. See *Longdens Troop* and *Nurses Troop.*
Grid	See *Battery Grid, Fixation, Orientation, Regimental Grid* and *Theatre Grid.*
Grid Bearing	The angle at a point measured clockwise between the direction of grid north and the specified direction.
Grid Convergence	The angle between grid north and true north.
Grid Magnetic Angle	The angle at a point measured the shortest way between the direction of grid north and magnetic north.
Grid North	The northerly or zero direction indicated by the grid datum of directional reference.
Grid Smasher	Unofficial nickname for MLRS. See *Grid Square Removal System, Grid Square Remover* and *MLRS.*
Grid Square Removal System	Unofficial nickname for MLRS. See *Grid Smasher, Grid Square Remover* and *MLRS.*
Grid Square Remover	Nickname applied to the Multiple Launch Rocket System, due to the large area covered by a single salvo from a battery of launchers. See *Grid Smasher, Grid Square Removal System* and *MLRS.*
GRO	(i) General Regimental Order. (19th century.) (ii) Garrison Routine Order.
Grot	A slang term for a dirty soldier.
Ground Control Station	A part of the Phoenix UAV system. Operated by a detachment of three: Mission Controller, Air Vehicle Controller and Image Analyst. The shelter contains three workstations equipped with high resolution colour displays. The operator is able to select a thermal image view of the battlefield or a map displaying the positions of the target and the UAV. Two UAVs can be controlled at the same time by one ground control station. See *Phoenix.*
Ground Data Terminal	A part of the Phoenix UAV system. Image data is transmitted by a steered, 360° video data link to the ground data terminal and then by cable to the control station which can be up to 1 km away. Target data is then transmitted to the forward artillery units via BATES (or its replacement the FC BISA) directly to the guns. The

UAV determines the fall of shot onto the target area and the control station generates correction data which is again downloaded to BATES or the FC BISA and to the guns. The guns can then re-engage the target using the corrected data and the UAV provides images for target damage assessment. See *BATES, FC BISA, Ground Control Station,* and *Phoenix.*

Ground Impact Detector A part of the Phoenix UAV system. See *Phoenix.*

Ground Light Ball An illuminating shell, which developed from the Carcass. There was very little difference between the two types of projectile. See *Carcass* and *Parachute Light Ball.*

Ground Scouts According to *Field Artillery Training 1914* these were mounted men whose duty was to precede the brigade (the term then in use for a regiment) and ascertain whether the ground was suitable for its movement. They were also to point out obstacles and to look for and indicate the best points for passage. Mountain artillery units employed dismounted men in this role, often filling it with the gunners detailed as pioneers.

Ground Zero The point on the surface at, below or above the point of burst of a nuclear weapon.

Group Difference In coastal artillery, the difference between the range from the group to the target and the range from the range-finder.

Group of Targets Two or more targets on which fire is desired simultaneously. A group of targets may be designated by a letter and number combination or a nickname.

Grouping The allocation of resources for command.

Grove's Troop The name given to one of the Troops in 5 (Gibraltar 1779–1783) Battery RA. It commemorates the time when as Grove's Company, 5 (Gibraltar 1779–1783) Battery RA forebear, was one of five artillery units stationed in the garrison at Gibraltar during the great siege of 1779–1783.

Grummets Material fixed around the driving band of some shells to protect them from damage in transit.

Grunt Nickname given to a member of a gun detachment. See *Gun Bunny, Muzzle Maggot* and *Trail Ape.*

Grupp The name given during the first half of the twentieth century to case shot by some Indian mountain batteries. The name derive from a corruption of grape shot, which had not been used for many years. See *Case Shot* and *Grape Shot.*

GS (i) General Support.
(ii) General Service.
(iii) Gunnery Staff.

GSA (i) Ground Spike Antenna.
(ii) Gun System Automated.

GSC (i) General Service Corps.
(ii) Gunnery Staff Course. See *GSC(N)* and *GSC(O).*

GSC(N) Gunnery Staff Course (NCOs).

GSC(O) Gunnery Staff Course (Officers).

GSDE Generator Set Diesel Engine. (Part of the Rapier AD system.)

G(SD)(Tech) General Staff Duties (Technical).

GSG General Support Group.

GSM Garrison Sergeant-Major.

GSO General Staff Officer.

GSR (i) General Support Reinforcing. GS Rft is also used as an abbreviation for this title.
(ii) General Staff Requirement. A term used until the 1980s when it was replaced by the Service Requirement (Land).

GS Rft — General Support Reinforcing. GSR is also used as an abbreviation for this title.

GST — General Staff Target. Replaced by the Service Target (Land).

GT — (i) Gun Target line.
(ii) Gun to Target.

GTI — General Training Index.

GTL — Gun Target Line.

G Tp — 7th troop of many field regiments, in HQ Battery, equipped with Green Archer then Cymbeline and providing brigade artillery intelligence section, 1960s–80s.

G Truck — See *George Truck.*

GTT — Gunnery Training Team.

GTT(V) — Gunnery Training Team (Volunteer).

GTV — Gun Towing Vehicle.

Guided MLRS — See *Guided Multiple Launch Rocket System.*

Guided Multiple Launch Rocket System — A missile equipped with a unitary 90 kg High Explosive warhead (roughly ten times the high explosive content of a 155 mm artillery shell), having a range of 70 kilometres, complete with GPS guidance giving a accuracy of approximately 2 m. See *Multiple Launch Rocket System* and *Unitary Warhead.*

Gun, 105 mm, Field, L118 — See *L118 Light Gun* .

Gun — (i) A general term used to indicate a complete equipment, consisting of an 'ordnance' on its associated carriage or mounting. See *Ordnance.*
(ii) A comparatively long ranged, high muzzle velocity equipment using a low trajectory and firing a relatively small shell. Guns usually use fixed charges. See *Gun/Howitzer* and *Howitzer.*

Gun Aiming Point — Formally known as an Auxiliary Aiming Point. A GAP could be a topographical feature or an 'artificial' one, such as the gun's own aiming posts. See *Aiming Point.*

Gun Angles — Angles which are directly or indirectly set on the gun or are associated with the gun. They may be vertical or horizontal. Vertical Gun Angles include: Quadrant Elevation, Tangent Elevation, Angle of Sight and Jump. Horizontal Gun Angles include: Bearing, Switch and Lead.

Gun Arc — An early twentieth century form of indirect laying, utilising a board fixed to the foresight. The board was approximately 1 yard long and graduated in 1/2 degrees, with a hole at each graduation which would accept an acorn-shaped foresight. Corrections to line, for example, 'right two degrees' would be given by the observer, the layer would then move the acorn-shaped foresight four holes to the left and re-align the gun on the aiming point. The gun would then have been moved two degrees to the right. Also known as the Gunner's Arc.

Gun Area — An area which contains one or more gun positions. A Gun Area may be either Battery or Regimental in size. A Battery Gun Area is commanded by the Battery Captain, whilst a Regimental Gun Area is commanded by the Regimental Second in Command. See *Battery Area, Gun Platform* and *Gun Position.*

Gun Area Commander — Within a Battery Gun Area, this role is performed by the Battery Captain, whilst at Regimental level it is performed by the Regimental Second in Command. See *Battery Captain* and *Gun Area.*

Gun Auto-Sight — An instrument which applies continuously accurate deflections to the sights of a gun when being used against fast moving targets. See *Autosight.*

Gun-Buckers Gunners involved in Gun-Bucking.

Gun-Bucking Nickname for repository work.

Gun-Bunny A gunner serving with a regiment equipped with guns, as opposed to missiles. See *Cloudpuncher, Grunt, Muzzle Maggot* and *Trail Ape.*

Gun-Busters Gunners involved in Gun-Busting.

Gun-Busting Nickname for repository work.

Gun Captain In the Royal Garrison Artillery, the NCO commanding a single gun complete with its detachment and stores. See *Gun Group Commander.*

Gun Carrier Mark I Probably the first piece of self-propelled artillery ever to be produced, the Gun Carrier Mark I was developed during 1916 with the intention of supporting British tanks should a breakthrough occur.

Major Gregg, proposed that special mechanised artillery should be built using parts of the Mark I tank. The first prototype participated in the Tank Trials Day at Oldbury on 3 March 1917. As a result of the trials an order of fifty vehicles was given to Kitson & Co. in Leeds, with deliveries to the army commencing in June and ended in July of that year.

Despite its parentage, the Gun Carrier Mark I bore little resemblance to the Mark I tank. The tracks were low, almost flat, unlike those of the tank which were the full height of the superstructure. A rectangular superstructure, located at the rear of the carrier covered the Daimler 105 hp engine and the transmission. Also located in the superstructure were the vehicle commander, a mechanic and two gearsmen. The double tail wheel of the Mark I tank which was intended to aid steering and attached to the rear of the vehicle, was retained, but photographic evidence suggests that they were often disposed of as being useless. The front comprised an open area which was capable of holding either a 60-pdr medium gun or a 6-inch howitzer. In order to transport a gun, the wheels had to be removed from the gun carriage and attached to the side of the carrier until required. It was possible to fire the 60-pdr from the vehicle, however in reality only the howitzer could be so fired. The guns could, where necessary, be unloaded via a pivoting cradle assisted by two winding drums driven by the engine. An armoured cab was located above front of the track frame on each side, the driver occupied the one on the left and the brakesman the one on the right. Communications between the driver and brakeman and the vehicle commander in the superstructure at the rear were extremely difficult. This resulted in difficulties when moving as in the Mark I, four men (including the two gearsmen in the superstructure) had to cooperate in order to steer the carrier.

Two Gun Carrier Companies were formed in July 1917. Each Company consisted of twenty-four vehicles. It is possible that none of them ever fired a shot in anger. As none of the expected breakthroughs materialised the vehicles were relegated to the role of supply tanks. One carrier being able to transport the equivalent carrying capacity of 291 human porters.

Two of the carriers were finished as Gun Carrier Cranes, these would perform the role of salvage tanks and as such had a hand-operated crane mounted at the front. In these versions the forward cabs were absent.

A Gun Carrier Mark II was partly developed in 1917 however this never moved beyond the prototype stage

and the sole outcome was that the original Gun Carrier became known as the Gun Carrier Mark I.
Designed: July 1916
Manufacturer: Kitson & Co
Produced: Between June and July, 1917
Number built: 48
Crew: 4 plus gun detachment
Primary Armament: 60-pounder field gun or 6-inch howitzer
Engine: Daimler petrol engine, 105 hp
Suspension: Unsprung.

Gun Control When at Gun Control, the NCO in charge of the gun takes independent control of his/her gun and selects his/her own target and engages it as appropriate. Gun Control is particularly used when engaging tanks.

Gun Cosies Irregular shaped screens that were usually made of painted and garnished hessian, sometimes fitted to gun shields during the Second World War as a form of camouflage.

Gun Data This consists of the information passed to and displayed on the sights or dials of a gun. It includes, bearing, elevation, angle of sight and fuze length.

Gun Density Trace Used from the Second World War until the 1960s, the Gun Density Trace showed coverage (arcs and ranges) of enemy artillery. It was replaced by Weapon Density Trace.

Gun Detachment The personnel required to serve a gun. The term derives from the time when guns were drawn from the arsenal or were in fixed positions (e.g. siege guns, coast artillery etc.) and detachments were formed from a pool of gunners to man them. The detachment for a 25-pdr consisted of: No. 1 Sgt, No. 2 Bdr or L/Bdr rammer, No. 3 layer, Nos. 4–6 ammunition, No. 7 driver. Detachments always 'Take Post' at the double and 'Stand Easy' at a marching pace, a tradition from battles of old when the guns were deployed in front of the infantry and the sight of gunners apparently running away from their guns could lead to panic in the ranks.

Gun Difference In coastal artillery, the difference, at any moment, between the range from the gun to the target and the range from the range-finder.

Gun Display Unit. Part of the BATES system, the GDU has a numeric keypad, with additional acknowledgement keys which enable the number one to transmit fire discipline acknowledgements and digital information, i.e. ammunition states and charge temperatures, to the command post. See *BATES*.

Gunfire (i) Now known as 'fire for effect'. Gunfire was fired as rapidly as possible, without concern for the other guns in the battery. An interval (a specified number of seconds) could be ordered by the originator. During the 1950s it was used synonymously with 'Fire for Effect' but the term is no longer in use.
(ii) Tea laced with rum served to the troops in their billets by the Officers and Warrant Officers on the morning of Christmas Day.

Gunfire Target Any shoot in which the risk of failure to hit the target had to be taken, as failure was certain if either speed or surprise was not achieved. GF Targets aimed to cause casualties and not to neutralise a target. Typical GF Targets were moving targets or those which were stationary but were liable to move or take cover. See *GF*.

Gun Group (i) The modern definition of a Gun Group is that Close Support gun groups deploy into either Artillery Reserved

Areas or Artillery Manoeuvre Areas, dependant on the type of deployment. Gun Groups are controlled as a central resource and are allocated according to availability or operational priorities. This central control allows maximum flexibility and concentration of force onto targets requested by Tac Groups. They are also controlled centrally for movement, this ensures they remain in range for tasking when operating in support of a fluid and fast-moving situation. See *AMA, ARA* and *Tac Gp.*
(ii) Prior to the introduction of the modern definition for a Gun Group, the definition was the guns of the regiment together with their troop leaders, this version remained in use until the introduction of six gun batteries in the 1950s.
(iii) In the Royal Garrison Artillery this term was used to describe one or more adjacent guns of the same nature under the command of an officer or NCO.

Gun Group Commander In the Royal Garrison Artillery the title given to a Section Commander in charge of a Gun Group. The Gun Group Commander could be either an officer or an NCO. See *Gun Captain* and *Gun Group.*

Gun Guide A member of a gun detachment sent forward with the Gun Position Officer and Battery Guide to be briefed on the track plan and lead his gun into position later.

Gun History Book Maintained for every gun, the *Gun History Book* provides a record of wear measurements, repairs and modifications, maintenance and rounds fired by the barrel as 'Equivalent Full Charge. Formerly known as the 'Memorandum of Examination.' See *Memorandum of Examination.*

Gun/Howitzer A field artillery equipment which combines advantages of both the gun and the howitzer. Gun/Howitzers are more versatile than either guns or howitzers alone. See *Gun* and *Howitzer.*

Gun Lascar See *Lascar.*

Gun Laying System A variant of the Specialist Personal Global Positioning System Receiver (SPGR), which is issued to sound ranging units for Hostile Artillery Locator (HALO) orientation. See *SPGR* and *HALO.*

Gun Line Section Commander A Staff Sergeant in charge of three guns within a battery. Thus there are two Gun Line Section Commanders in a six gun battery. See *Section Commander.*

Gun Marker Marker used by the Gun Position Officer to indicate the position and direction to locate each gun.

Gunner, The Monthly magazine of the Royal Regiment of Artillery, first published in 1919.

Gunner's Arc See *Gun Arc.*

Gunner's Calipers These took many different forms during the muzzle-loading period, they were used to measure the width of the gun bore or the shot and useful mathematical tables were engraved into them.

Gunners Gold Rust deposits on your personal weapon, or bayonet. A heinous crime in any military unit and rarely if ever found on a personal weapon carried by a member of the Royal Artillery.

Gunners' Quadrant An alternative name for a Field Clinometer. See *Field Clinometer.*

Gunner's Stiletto During the 17th century, the gunner's stiletto was a symbol of office, in addition to being a useful tool. Examples exist where the blade is marked off in a scale that would, when measured at the bore of the gun, give the weight of the shot required for that gun.

Gunnery	The practical application of the science of ballistics.
Gunnery Career Course	A course eleven months in duration for Senior NCOs in the Royal Artillery. The course was introduced in 1984 with the aim of providing a pool of trained and highly graded SNCOs and WOs who may be employed both at Gunnery Staff and Regimental Duty.
Gunnery Careers Course Air Defence	A forty-nine week course at the Royal School of Artillery which is designed to instruct experienced Air Defence senior non-commissioned officers in the employment and deployment of Ground-Based Air Defence (GBAD) Systems.
Gunnery Careers Course Field	A forty-nine week course run by the Royal School of Artillery designed to extensively develop the professional knowledge and skills of senior non-commissioned officers in the operation and employment of Close Support Field Artillery systems. Subjects covered by the course include: the engagement of targets by the observer, the deployment and tactical handling of Close Support and General Support Artillery and command and control. Also included on the course is instruction on ballistic computation, Range Safety, Survey and Meteorology.
Gunnery Instructors' Course (Field)	A thirty-three week course run by the Royal School of Artillery designed to train officers in the technical operation and tactical handling of Field Artillery systems up to Divisional Level. Included in the course is training in the deployment of Field Artillery systems, including MLRS and STA, and the technical supervision, planning and conduct of fire missions and fire plans for both live firing and dry training. Officers who successfully pass the course may subsequently be employed as Gunnery Instructors of Artillery Staff or within technical Gunnery Staff appointments.
Gunnery Training Team (Volunteer)	Part of CVHQ RA the GTT(V) comprises IG/TIG (Field x 3; Depth Fire x 2; Air Defence x 3) and MG/SMIG (Field x 2; Depth Fire x 1; Air defence x 2). Part of CVHQ RA. See *CVHQ RA, IG, MG, SMIG* and *TIG*.
Gun Number	A member of a gun detachment. Derived from the practice of numbering members of a gun detachment during drills to facilitate training. See *Gun Detachment* and *Number 1.*
Gunn Troop	One of the Troops in 33 Campbell Bty Junior Leaders Regiment RA. See *Borgard Troop, Shrapnel Troop* and *Wingate Troop*.
Gun Operations Room	The operations centre of an anti-aircraft formation or area.
Gun Platform	(i) In fortifications and coast artillery batteries this was originally a horizontal plane made of stone, masonry or wood on which the gun would be placed. Later gun platforms were laid at different angles of inclination in order to check the recoil of the gun on firing. Special platforms were gradually introduced such as the traversing, siege, ground and garrison. See *Dwarf platform, Mortar Platform, New Pattern Traversing Platform, Siege Platform* and *Traversing Platform*. (ii) In current usage this is the ground on which the gun is deployed and on which it is brought into action. See *Battery Area, Gun Area* and *Gun Position*.
Gun Position	The area containing the gun lines of a section, troop or battery and the associated ammunition detachment it may

include a command post. See *Battery Area, Gun Area* and *Gun Platform*.

Gun Position 31 Located within the Bergen-Hohne/Munsterlager Range Complex. Gun Position 31 was used almost constantly by the Meteorological Troop from 94 Regiment RA, and was usually a good place to call into on exercise for a brew.

Gun Position Officer The title first appeared towards the end of the First World War, and prior to 1938 was applied to one of the section commanders in a battery with responsibilities for the whole battery. It was during the Second World War that the term came to mean the subaltern officer responsible for a troop gun position. This subaltern was responsible for orienting and maintaining the troops' parallelism and for the production of firing data in the troop command post. With the reversion in the late 1950s to six gun batteries the gun position officer once again became responsible for the entire battery and in particular the reconnaissance and preparation of battery positions. See *Command Post Officer, Gun Position Officer's Party, Section Commander* and *Subaltern*.

Gun Position Officer's Party During the late 1940s each troop provided one Gun Position Officer's party, responsible for the reconnaissance and preparation of the troop position. The party included the Gun Position Officer, a Gun Position Officers Assistant, the Troop Sergeant-Major and the necessary personnel to establish and maintain communications. See *Gun Position Officer.*

Gunpowder *See Black Powder.*

Gunpowder Tie The name given to the Royal Artillery Historical Society Tie by Neil Robertson of the National Army Museum. The RAHS have since accepted the title as the official name of the tie. The name derives from the fact that the colours, sky blue, black and yellow, represent the constituent parts, in their correct proportions, of gunpowder.

Gun Programme A copy is issued to each gun in the battery. The gun programme contains the necessary details, taken directly from the AB 545 and the Programme Shoot Form, for the gun concerned to fire in the relevant concentration or barrage. See *Army Book 545* and *Programme Shoot Form.*

Gun-rule An instrument similar to a slide rule which forms part of the sights on British designed guns, which is used to convert ranges to angular elevations that are corrected for the different muzzle velocities of the gun. The scale on the gun-rule has cursors for each charge that are set to the gun's current muzzle velocities. The cursor for the ordered charge is then aligned with the ordered range marked on another scale. Usually fitted to British guns as an integral part of the sights for one-man laying. This is achieved by a bubble in an arm aligned to the range scale which is levelled by physically elevating the gun barrel to the required elevation.

Separate 'bar' form gun-rules were used with guns where they could not be integrated with the sights, for example on the 105 mm Priest SP, and for intermediate charges, such as the 2½, etc for the 25-pdr. See *Muzzle Velocity* and *Tangent Elevation.*

Guns and Ammunition A section of Strike Branch Royal School of Artillery, responsible for providing full technical instruction on all artillery natures.

Guns of Manoeuvre Late eighteenth and early nineteenth century term for guns manned by field batteries. See *Guns of Position.*

Guns of Position — See *Position Battery* and *Guns of Manoeuvre.*

Gun Target line — A term introduced with ABCA procedures in 1965, which replaced the BT line. Also known as the Line GT. See *ABCA* and *BT*.

Gun Team — The horses pulling a gun and limber. Often incorrectly used to refer to the detachment. See *Detachment.*

Gun Tractor — A vehicle for towing guns, it also carries the detachment, the gun stores and ammunition. (Royal Australian Artillery.)

Gunzen — A hand-held fire control computer. Measuring 6-inches by 4-inches, the Gunzen initially backed up FACE and finally replaced it in Territorial Batteries when FACE was withdrawn in the mid-1990s. When fitted with the chip appropriate to the guns of the battery gunzen was capable of carrying out all the firing calculations necessary for up to eight guns and was capable of storing a substantial number of target records. See *FACE.*

GVA — Gloucestershire Volunteer Artillery.

GW — Guided Weapon.

GYC — Gap Year Commission. See *SSLC.*

Gyde Award — Originally awarded to the most efficient Junior Leader commissioned from the Royal Military Academy Sandhurst, the award was changed to the Royal Artillery officer who has proved to be the most deserving on grounds of general efficiency and character during any course for Young Officers at the Royal School of Artillery and in conjunction with the Ambrose Pratt Memorial Award. See *Ambrose Pratt Memorial Award.*

Gyn — A gyn was used for installing extremely heavy guns. It was used with large timber blocks known as 'scotches' which were placed under the gun in stages as it was gradually raised by the gyn. When high enough, the carriage could be moved into or out of the space below the barrel. This procedure, which was known officially as repository exercises and more informally as scotch up, gun-busting or gun-bucking, could only be carried out by a well trained and disciplined team of gunners.

GZ — Ground Zero.

H – Harry – 1927
How – 1943
Hotel – 1956

(H) — (i) Howitzer. Used in this form as part of a unit title for a RFA battery equipped with howitzers.
(ii) A Second World War Royal Canadian Artillery anti-aircraft battery designation. A type H battery was a Heavy battery manning either 4 x 3.7-inch or 4 x 4-inch anti-aircraft guns. A numerical prefix indicated that the standard compliment had been increased by the multiple of the prefix. This (2H) indicated a heavy anti-aircraft battery equipped with eight guns. See *(L)*, *(LS)* and *(M).*

H — Hydrogen.

H1 — See *Hotel 1.*

H2 — See *Hotel 2.*

H/A — High Angle, replaced Upper Register.

HA — High Angle, replaced Upper Register.

HAA — Heavy Anti-Aircraft.

HAC — Honourable Artillery Company.

HAD — Heavy Air Defence.

HAF	High Angle Fire.
HAG	Heavy Artillery Group. (First World War.) Formally known as HAR.
HAHQ	Heavy Artillery Headquarters. (First World War).
Half Colonel	A Lieutenant Colonel, as opposed to a Colonel who is referred to as a Full Colonel.
Half Concentrate	Converging the guns to shift the barrels from a parallel lie towards the centre, to engage a target half the width of the gun position.
Half-Moon Copse	One of the Triangulation Exercise Stations on the now defunct RA Survey Course.
Half-pint	Early artillery rocket, which was intended to replace gun artillery, but never entered service.
HALO	(i) Hostile Artillery Location. The original developmental name for the Advanced Sound Ranging Programme, ASP. See *Advanced Sound Ranging Programme.* (ii) High Altitude Low Opening. A form of parachute insertion.
Hamel Gun	The name by which the L118/L119 Light Gun is manufactured under licence in Australia for the Royal Australian Artillery and the Royal New Zealand Artillery. See *L118 Light Gun* and *L119 Light Gun.*
Hampshire & Sussex Gunners	Regimental title of 47 Regiment RA. Identifies the regimental recruiting area.
HAN	Hydroxyl Ammonium Nitrate.
Hand Horse	The off-side unridden horse in each pair of a gun team. See *Gun Team.*
Handspike	A wooden lever which was used to assist with moving a gun or its carriage. A Roller Handspike had a roller on its heel to make moving a gun easier.
H & TD	Heating and Tie-down. Honest John.
Hanson Cup	A silver cup, awarded annually to the best senior non-commissioned officer in the Royal Artillery. The award is made to the SNCO who has been seen to uphold the traditions of the Warrant Officers' and Sergeants' Mess; a gunner who has worked the hardest to promote the values, standards and ethos which are pivotal to any successful Mess; a sergeant or staff sergeant who has sacrificed their time for the benefit of others and thus brought honour to the rank and to the Mess. The name derives from BSM Hanson who was originally presented the cup in 1910, after winning a regimental shooting competition twice. Following his death, the cup passed to his wife and on her death to their grandson, Mr Philip Rhodes, who in turn presented it to the Regiment in 2003.
H&I	Harassing and Interdiction fire.
HAR	Heavy Artillery Reserve. (First World War.) Precursor of the HAG.
Harassing fire	A fire mission designed to hamper movement to the front, hinder the conduct of operations and reduce enemy morale.
Har Pty	Harbour Party.
Harry Battery	Derogatory nickname for members of 4/73 (Sphinx) Special Observation Post Battery RA.
Harry Larkers	Nickname for the Royal School of Artillery, Larkhill.
Hathi	Name given to a type of heavy artillery tractor used in the First World War. The name is derived from the Hindustani word for elephant.
Haybox	An early form of insulated food container, made of metal and packed with hay, it was designed to keep smaller

containers of food and tea hot whilst being transported to battery positions from the cookhouse.

Hay Up Secure Hay nets in horses stall after feeding.

Hazara Mountain Train The first of the Indian mountain batteries to be formed. The mountain train was formed in September 1850, with six 3-pounder smooth-bore guns. The establishment at the time of organisation was: two native officers, three havildars (sergeants), three naiks (corporals), fifty-four gunners and two buglers. In addition there was one darogah (responsible for purchasing rations) and thirty-three syces (responsible for looking after the mules). The gun, trail, wheels and two pairs of ammunition boxes per gun were carried on battery mules. Hired mules were used to carry additional ammunition. Each ammunition box contained sixteen round shot and four case shot. At the time of formation there were also two elephants on strength, however, in 1856 these were replaced with a further twenty-five battery baggage mules. See *Case Shot, Mountain Train* and *Round Shot*.

HB (i) Hostile Battery.
(ii) Heavy Battery.

HB Chart Hostile Battery Chart.

HBCS Hostile Battery Collation Sheet. Replaced Day Diary.

HBHC Hostile Battery History Card. In use from the 1940s until 1972.

HBHS Hostile Battery History Sheet. In use from the Second World War until 1972.

HBRS Hostile Battery Record Sheet. In use from 1972 it replaced both the Hostile Battery History Card and Hostile Battery History Sheet.

HCDR High Capacity Data Radio. See *Bowman*.

HCI Human Computer Interface.

HD (i) Designation for Heavy Draught horses such as Shires and Clydesdales. These were used to draw medium artillery pieces. A Heavy Draught horse could draw 1 ton (including weight of transport).
(ii) Heavy Duty (vehicles).

HDG Heading.

HE (i) High Explosive.
(ii) Higher Establishment.

Head Mounted Night Vision System The HMNVS gives the wearer the ability to operate effectively at night, whilst being able to engage a target as soon as it is identified. The HMNVS system includes a laser aimer which is attached to the weapon stock. This aimer has four modes: visible torch, infra-red torch, infra-red laser and visible red dot.

Headquarters and District Establishment The formation which commanded the heavy batteries and provided both the District Officers and Master Gunners who held the actual armament on charge.

HEAT High Explosive Anti-Tank.

Hebs Abbreviated title given to the Royal Artillery Range, Hebrides.

HECA Hoist Electrical Control Assembly.

HE Common Shell circa 1880s this term referred to a hollow shell filled with a bursting charge of lyddite as opposed to black powder. See also *Common Shell*.

Hedgehog (i) A form of defence used in the Napoleonic wars when the guns were threatened with capture by cavalry or infantry. The officer in charge would give the command 'Hedgehog'. Two gunners armed with muskets would

commence firing at the enemy. The remainder of the detachment would run up the Ammunition Wagon to the rear of the gun and take shelter between the gun and the wagon.
(ii) A heavily protected position, particulary used during the 'Cracker' operations in Oman. See *Cracker Battery*.

Height and Range Finder Used in preference to DPF systems when gun range became long enough to require the increased long range accuracy this system provided. They comprised a range of combined height and range finders and was introduced into the anti-aircraft branch of the Royal Artillery prior to the Second World War. The were capable of providing, as their name implies both height and range information. Thus removing the requirement for two separate instruments on the gun position. Three variants existed, the Number 8 manufactured by Goerz, the Number 9 manufactured by Levallois and the Number 10 manufactured by Barr and Stroud. See *DPF*.

Height of Burst The vertical distance from the ground or target to the point of burst.

Helex Heliborne Exercise.

Heli-Bedford Nickname given to the Bedford lorry used in place of a helicopter on exercise, when the helicopter is unavailable. See *Bedicopter.*

Helicopter Handling Instructor An Officer or SNCO who has been trained by JATE and is qualified to select, lay and man day and night landing sites subject to certain limitations. See *JATE*.

Helicopter Handling Team The team consists of a Helicopter Handling Instructor, a Landing Point Commander and a number of Riggers/ Marshallers.

Helidaf As with the Heli-Bedford, but with the substitution of a DAF lorry for the Bedford. See *Heli-Bedford*.

Helmieh Hussars Nickname given to B and M Batteries RHA, part of 1st Brigade RHA (latter 1st Regiment RHA), when they were converted to RHA Mounted Rifles in 1921 whilst awaiting embarkation at Helmieh, Palestine. It was anticipated at the time that they would be deployed to Ireland as RHA Mounted Rifles.

Helquest Helicopter Request.

HEP High Explosive Plastic. The American name for the HESH round. See *HESH*.

Herbies Slang term used to refer to Canadian gunners. The non-artillery personnel in Canadian gunner units have been known to call themselves 'Herbies' Helpers.' (Royal Canadian Artillery.)

Hermes 450 A tactical UAV, using the same airframe as the Watchkeeper UAV which became operational with 32 Regt RA in mid-2007.

HES High Explosive Spotting.

Hesco Concertainer Bastion Emplacement A type of temporary, quickly assembled gun emplacements. Made up from fibre-lined mesh boxes, delivered as flat packs, which are pulled open and filled with local aggregate to create fortification walls.

HESH High Explosive Squash Head.

Heavy Battery Linear Target *Artillery Staff Duties (Field Branch) 1954* defined a Heavy Battery Linear Target as being fired by one heavy battery and being 180 yards in length. See *Concentration, Field Battery Linear Target, Linear* and *Medium Battery Linear Target*.

Hexagon Barrage	See *Chevron Barrage*.
HF	(i) Harassing Fire. (ii) Height Finder. (iii) High Frequency (Radio).
HFI	Height and Fuze Indicator.
HG	Hostile Gun.
HGB	Hostile Gun Board. Used in 1950s in counter-bombardment offices to plan counter-bombardment fire against hostile batteries.
H-Hour	The time at which an operation commences and attacking troops cross their start line. See *Zero Hour*.
HHI	Helicopter Handling Instructor. See *JATE*.
HHS	High Hardness Steel.
HHT	Helicopter Handling Team.
HIDACZ	High Density Air Control Zone. An Airspace Control Measure / Air Defence term.
Hide	A location in which a force conceals itself before operations or before moving into battle position.
High Angle	A command contained in fire orders to obtain high angle fire. See *High Angle Fire*.
High Angle Fire	Fire delivered at elevations greater than the elevation of maximum range which is usually given as 800 m / elevation. Formally known as Upper Register fire. See *Upper Register*.
High Capacity Data Radio	The UHF subsystem of the Bowman communications system. See *Bowman*.
High Explosive Anti-Tank	A type of artillery round used against armoured vehicles.
High Explosive Plastic	An anti-tank ammunition which detaches a scab at high temperatures from the inner side of the armour plate to neutralise the tank crew.
Highland Gunners	Regimental title of 19 Regiment RA. Identifies the regimental recruiting area.
Highland Gunners March, The	The Barren Rocks of Aden – regimental march of 19 Regt RA.
High Pay-off Target list	A list of high value targets that on being located can be engaged without recourse to confirmation.
High to Gauge	A term used to describe a round of ammunition which is in fact too large to fit the barrel. This would cause the round to jam on engaging the rifling and the sudden check could cause the round to detonate with catastrophic effects on the gun and its detachment.
High Value Target	A target whose loss would significantly damage the enem's ability to carry through his intentions.
High Velocity Armour Piercing	A type of artillery round used against armoured vehicles.
High Velocity Charge	A charge which gives the maximum velocity obtainable with the service projectile.
High Velocity Missile	See *Starstreak*.
Hills Troop	One of the two gun troops in 28/143 Battery (Tomb's Troop) RA. See *Cassino Troop* and *Skeddys Troop*.
HIMAD	High to Medium Air Defence (above 1000 feet).
HIPPASS	High Pressure Pure Air Supply System.
Hislop's Troop	One of the Troops in 97 (Lawson's) Battery RA. See *Lawson's Troop*.
Hittile	A missile, generally an air defence variety, which achieves its aim by hitting the target, and contains only a small explosive charge. As opposed to a missile which relies on a proximity fuze which detonates near the target and destroys it with the resulting fragmentation effect.
HJ	(i) Honest John. A nuclear tipped missile. See *Honest John*.

(ii) Herbert Johnson. (Regimental Tailor, used when describing various items of uniform.)

HKSRGA Hong Kong and Singapore Royal Garrison Artillery.

HKSRA Hong Kong and Singapore Royal Artillery, part of the Royal Artillery, recruited in India, mostly Punjabi.

HKVDC Hong Kong Volunteer Defence Corps.

HLS Helicopter Landing Site.

HLT High Level Tripod; part of the OTIS system. See *OTIS*.

HM Hostile Mortar.

HMEX High Molecular Weight Explosive.

HMLC High Mobility Load Carrier.

HMNVS Head Mounted Night Vision System.

HNA Host Nation Assistance.

HNS Host Nation Support.

HOB Height Of Burst.

Hollow Charge A shaped charge producing a deep cylindrical hole of relatively small diameter in the direction of its axis or rotation to pierce armour plate.

Hondeghem Battery Honour Title of K (Hondeghem) Battery RA which was granted on 24 January 1951 under authority of 20/ARTY/6271/AG6a. See *Battery Honour Titles*.

Hondeghem Day Battery day of K (Hondeghem) Battery RA. Celebrated on 27 May each year.

Honest John Honest John was a long-range free flight artillery rocket capable of carrying either a nuclear or high explosive warhead. The rocket was officially described as being 762 mm in diameter, although the warhead, motor and fins were all of different diameters. With a weight of 5,800 pounds it used a solid propellant giving a range of 12 miles. The Basic (M31) Honest John system was first deployed in 1954. The M31 was replaced by the M50 improved Honest John in 1961. The M50 had a reduced system weight, a shortened length, and increased range. During its service life the designation was changed to MGR-1. Between 1960 and 1965, a total of 7,089 improved Honest John rockets, less warheads, were produced and delivered. In July 1982, all Honest John rocket motors, launchers, and related ground equipment items were type classified obsolete when the system was replaced by the Lance. The Royal Artillery Nuclear Regiments (24, 39 and 50 Missile Regiments) were equipped with two Honest John Rocket batteries and two towed 8-inch M1 Howitzer batteries. See *Lance*.

Honourable Artillery Company Formed by Henry VIII under Royal Charter in 1537, the HAC is the oldest regiment in the British Army. Based at Armoury House, London, the HAC was originally an infantry unit, although its formation pre-dates the introduction of the word 'infantry' into the English language. At the time of its formation, 'artillery' was used to refer to any weapon which projected a missile. Between 1781 and 1973 the unit comprised both infantry and artillery sub-units. Members of the regiment fought as infantry, cavalry and artillery in the Boer War and the First and Second World Wars. The HAC was also the first regiment to be given the privilege of marching through the city of London with 'drums beating, colours flying and bayonets fixed'. During the 17th century, the Regiment was charged with the responsibility for maintaining law and order within the London. Although strictly speaking not part of the Royal Artillery, the HAC do maintain many Royal Artillery traditions and functions.

The Honourable Artillery Company provides target information and intelligence for the deep strike systems (such as the Multiple Launch Rocket System and strike aircraft) of the British Army and NATO. The Regiment is organised into three patrol squadrons, a signal squadron, a headquarters squadron, a liaison troop and a regimental band and corps of drums. The HAC is the only territorial army surveillance and target acquisition regiment. The Regiment has a regular army sister organisation, 4/73 Special OP Battery, which in war would form a fourth surveillance and target acquisition patrol squadron.

In addition to its operational role the Regiment is privileged to be the unit chosen to carry out state and ceremonial functions within the City walls. This includes firing Royal Salutes at Her Majesty's Tower of London on the occasions of royal birthdays, state visits and the state opening of Parliament. The HAC also provides the Guards of Honour in the Guildhall Yard for State visits when it exercises its right to march through the City.

Full details of the History of the Honourable Artillery Company can be found in the following books: G. Goold Walker, *The HAC;* and *The HAC in the Great War;* G. A. Raikes, *The History of the HAC,* 2 volumes and R. F. Johnson, *Regimental Fire. Honourable Artillery Company in World War II 1939–1945.*

Honorary Colonels — All Territorial Army gunner units have Honorary Colonels appointed by Her Majesty The Queen on the recommendation of the Military Secretary, the Master Gunner and the Director Royal Artillery. They are recognised army appointments. See *Honorary Regimental Colonels.*

Honorary Colonels Commandant — Up to three gentlemen of distinction with Gunner connections may be appointed as Honorary Colonels Commandant. See *Colonels Commandant* and *Representative Colonel Commandant.*

Honorary Regimental Colonels — Every regular gunner unit has an Honorary Regimental Colonel appointed by the Master Gunner in consultation with the DRA. See *Honorary Colonels.*

Honour Title — See *Battery Honour Titles.*

Hook Troop — Together with Aden Troop, Gazala Troop and Martinique Troop, one of the four troops in 74 Battery (The Battle Axe Company) Royal Artillery.

Hooking In — The act of harnessing the gun team to the limber.

Horizontal Ballistic Angle — See *Ballistic Angles.*

Horizontal Gun Angles — See *Gun Angles.*

Horizontal Position Finder — The name ultimately applied to a Position Finder where it does not depend on the angle of depression to establish the position of the target. These were used where no suitable elevated site could be found for the Position Finder. See also *Position Finder* and *Depression Position Finder.*

Hornby Troop — (i) With Lodge Troop, one of the two troops in Q (Sanna's Post) Headquarter Battery.
(ii) One of the Troops in 40 Wardrop Bty Junior Leaders Regiment RA. See *Mansergh Troop, Nicholson Troop* and *Park Troop.*

Horse Field Battery — A designation used in India up until the time of the Mutiny to distinguish horse drawn field batteries from those drawn by bullocks. They were armed with four smooth-bore 9-pounder guns and two smooth-bore 24-pounder howitzers. They also had an additional 3-pounder smooth-bore gun and a mountain howitzer which were carried on pack mules for operations in mountainous terrain. See *Bullock Field Battery.*

Horse length — According to *Field Artillery Training 1914* this was a measurement of 6 feet. A horse width was given as 3 feet, which included 3 inches outside the riders knee on either side. See also *Mule Length.*

Hostile — A report indicating that a potential target has been positively identified as hostile according to defined hostile act criteria.

Hostile Battery — Any number of enemy weapons that appear to be controlled by one command post.

Hostile Battery Chart — The working map of the artillery intelligence office which replaced the Counter Bombardment Chart during the 1960s. On it are recorded all hostile batteries and the artillery intelligence office's major sources of information (such as locating units and observation posts). The chart is also used to provide the background over which the Bearing Report Trace, and the Shelling Connection and Activity Trace, may be superimposed. See *Bearing Report Trace, Counter Bombardment Chart, Hostile Battery* and *Shelling Connection and Activity Trace.*

Hostile Battery Collation Sheet — This replaced the Day Diary in the Counter Bombardment organisation. See *Day Diary.*

Hostile Batteries List — A list of located hostile batteries with their allocated numbers, coordinates and other information. First used in the First World War and sometimes issued as a map trace.

Hostile Gun Board — Used during the 1950s in counter battery offices to plan counter battery fire against hostile batteries. See *Hostile Battery.*

Hotel 1 — Tactical sign for Command Post Main. Also referred to as How 1. See *Hotel 2, How Truck* and *Tactical Sign.*

Hotel 2 — Tactical Sign for the Step-up Command Post. Also referred to as How 2. See *Hotel 1, How Truck* and *Tactical Sign.*

Hot Shot — Heated iron shot used particularly by coast artillery against wooden ships. Some were later filled with molten iron prior to firing. The furnaces for heating hot shot were still in place in the batteries on Gibraltar in the 1870s and drills using hot shot were still being carried out at that time.

Housewife — Colloquial name for the needle and thread kit issued to soldiers.

How — (i) Howitzer.
(ii) Phonetic letter H.

How 1 — See *Hotel 1.*

How 2 — See *Hotel 2.*

How Truck — The battery command post vehicle which was named after its tactical sign 'H'. In the late 1950s, with the introduction of two battery command posts in the 6 gun battery, (and following the introduction of the new phonetic alphabet) the two BCPs became known as Hotel 1 and Hotel 2, but are still more usually referred to as 'How 1' and 'How 2'.

Howitzer — A general term describing a comparatively short ranged, low muzzle velocity equipment which uses a high trajectory and fires a relatively heavy shell. Howitzers usually use variable charges. See *Gun* and *Gun/Howitzer.*

Howitzer 155 mm L8A1 — See *M44.*

Hoxters — Extra drills allotted to cadets at the RMA Woolwich. Even for such minor offences as having a boot lace tag showing below your puttee.

HP — (i) Horizontal Plane.
(ii) Hose Power.

HPF	Horizontal Position Finder.
HP Mounting	Hydro-Pneumatic Mounting.
HPP	Hydraulic Power Pack.
HPSS	Hydraulic Power Supply System.
HPT	High Payoff Target.
HPTL	High Payoff Target List.
HQ & DE	Headquarters and District Establishment.
HQCEAA	Headquarters Commander East African Artillery.
HQCMA	Headquarter Corps Medium Artillery. Early Second World War and before.
HQDRA	Headquarters Director Royal Artillery.
HQLO	Headquarters Liaison Officer.
HQRA	Headquarters Royal Artillery.
HQWS	Headquarters Woolwich Station.
HRF	Height and Range Finder.
HS	(i) A First World War British gas shell filling, Mustard Gas. The abbreviation derives from the fact that the gas was known colloquially as Hun Stuff. (ii) Hydraulic Swivel.
Ht	Height.
HTM	Heavy Trench Mortar (First World War). Manned by the Heavy Artillery. See *LTM* and *MTM.*
HTPB	Hydroxyl Terminated Poly Butadiene.
HUMINT	Human Intelligence (sources).
HV	(i) High Velocity. Used during the First World War to refer to a High Velocity gun. (ii) High Velocity. See *High Velocity Charge.*
HVAP	High Velocity Armour Piercing.
HVFC	High Velocity Full Charge.
H Vic	High Velocity (First World War).
HVM	High Velocity Missile. See *Starstreak.*
HVM (SP)	See *SPHVM.*
HVT	High Value Target.
HVTL	High Value Target List.
Hy	Heavy.
Hyderabad Contingent	A force maintained during the late nineteenth century under treaty with the Nizam of Hyderabad. It included four field batteries officered from the Royal Artillery in much the same way as the Indian mountain batteries. They had done fine service in the Central Indian Campaign during the Indian Mutiny.
Hyderabad Day	Battery day for N Battery (The Eagle Troop) RHA.
Hydro-Pneumatic	A form of recoil system, where hydraulics are used to control the gun recoil, and gas compression is used to return the gun to the firing position after discharge.
Hydro-Pneumatic Mounting	A 'disappearing gun mounting'. The gun is loaded under cover, and then raised by hydro-pneumatic pressure to the firing position. The recoil generated by firing the gun caused it to depress back into its protective emplacement. Whilst this form of mounting offered protection to the detachment, there were objections to the complexity of the mounting and the slow rate of fire possible with this design. This form of mounting superseded Moncrieff's counterweight system. Both the 6-inch breech-loader and 10-inch breech-loader were mounted in this fashion. See *Disappearing Gun, Counterweight Carriage, Hydro-pneumatic Siege Dissapearing Carriage* and *Moncrieff Carriage.*
Hydro-pneumatic Siege Disappearing Carriage	This mounting was developed for the wrought iron 64 pr. R.M.L. to enable it to be mounted in permanent emplacements in forts. However, difficulties with the design

resulted in its being only approved for the 6.6-inch howitzer. An 8-inch howitzer was fired off it successfully, but this was not proceeded with. It required an anchorage capable of absorbing a firing strain of 19 tons. Due to this requirement guns using this mounting were allotted to the siege train owing to the difficulties associated with making this anchorage where parapets were already formed. See *Hydro-pneumatic Mounting.*

I – Ink – 1927
Item – 1943
India – 1956

IA	(i) Inspectorate of Armaments. (ii) Improved Ammunition. (iii) Image Analyst.
IAD	Intermediate Ammunition Depot. See *AAOD* and *EAM.*
IARRCIS	Interim Allied Rapid Reaction Corps Information System.
IAV	Infantry Armoured Vehicle.
IAZ	Inner Artillery Zone. Second World War and later anti-aircraft.
IBA	In-Bore Adapter.
IBMS	Intelligent Battery Management System.
ICC	Information Coordination Centre.
ICCL	Inter-Component Coordination and Liaison.
ICE	Individual Compass Error.
ICM	Improved Conventional Munitions.
ICP	Intelligence Collection Plan.
ICSC(L)	Intermediate Command and Staff Course (Land).
ICV	Individual Compass Variation.
ID	Identification.
Identification Friend or Foe	An electronic method of identifying aircraft as hostile or friendly. See *SIFF.*
IDG	Imagery Downlink Group. Part of the UAV Battery organisation.
IDT	Interactive Display Terminal.
IED	Improvised Explosive Device.
IEDS	Interactive Electronic Training Delivery System.
IETP	Interactive Electronic Technical Publications.
IEU	Improved Electronics Unit. Part of the MLRS system. See *Multiple Launch Rocket System.*
IF	Intermediate Frequency.
IFC	Instructor in Fire Control. See *IG.*
IFCCS	Indirect Fire Control Computer System. (Royal Canadian Artillery.)
IFF	Identification Friend or Foe. See *SIFF.*
IFPA	Indirect Fire Precision Attack.
IFU	Interface Unit.
IFWES	Indirect Fire Weapons Effect Simulator.
IG	Instructor in Gunnery. See *IFC.*
Igniferous Initiator	A composition used to initiate burning, as opposed to detonation, in the caps of primers and in the detonators of igniferous fuzes, graze fuzes and some direct action fuzes. All igniferous fuzes are essentially sensitive to the heat or friction produced by a blow.
IGTTFE	Instruction of Gunnery Training Team Far East.
II	(i) Image Intensification. (ii) Image Intensifier.
IIR	Impact Indicator Round.

Illum	Illuminating. See *Illumination.*
Illumination	An artillery round designed to give night time illumination over a target area. Formerly known as a star shell. See *Star Shell* and *Illum.*
Illumination Fire	Fire delivered with the intention of illuminating an area. See *Illumination.*
ILRRPS	International Long Range Reconnaissance Patrol School (based in Bavaria, Germany).
IM	Insensitive Munitions.
IMA	Indian Mountain Artillery.
IMAP	Insensitive Munitions Assessment Panel.
IMATT	International Military Advisory and Training Team.
IMATT (SL)	International Military Advisory and Training Team (Sierra Leone).
IMB	Indian Mountain Battery.
IMINT	Imagery Intelligence.
Imjin	Battery Honour Title of 170 (Imjin) Battery RA which was granted on 26 April 1954 under authority of 20/ARTY/6824/AG6a. Battery is now amalgamated with 25 Battery to form 25/170 (Imjin) Battery RA. Members of the battery are authorised to wear the emblem of the United States Presidential Citation. See *Battery Honour Titles.*
Imjin Day	Celebrated each year by 25/170 (Imjin) Battery RA in commemoration of the battle at Imjin on 22–25 April 1951.
Imjinite	Nickname given to a member of 170 (Imjin) Battery RA.
Immediate Neutralisation	A type of Fire Mission. The IN Mission, is the most common type of fire used by the observation post (OP). It could involve anything from three guns to a whole regiment or division. It is one of those missions that when an OP sees an opportunist target, they will just call down fire using High Explosive (HE) to stop the target doing whatever it is they are doing, i.e. a recce party, line laying party or a mass of tanks etc. Most other target types were given other identifying names such as harassment, counter bombardment, smoke, interdiction, destruction, danger close etc.
IMMLC	Improved Medium Mobility Load Carrier. See *DROPS.*
Impact Angles	The following angles are associated with impact: (i) Angle of Impact. The angle between the line of arrival and the surface of impact at the point of impact. (ii) Angle of Incidence. The angle between the line of arrival and the line drawn at right angles to the surface of impact (i.e., the 'normal') at the point of impact.
Improved Stabilisation Reference Package	Computer package which allows the FCS on MLRS to set the launcher for Azimuth and Elevation. See *FCS* and *MLRS.*
IN	Immediate Neutralisation.
In-Bore Adapter	A 14.5 mm sub-calibre adapter for use with Abbot, AS90 and the Light Gun.
Incendiary Composition	See *Composition.*
INCREP	Incident Report.
Ind	Independent.
Indian Other Rank	A definition used to differentiate between Indian and British Other Ranks in mixed units, prior to Independence in 1948. See *BOR.*
Indigo Corkscrew	The development name of the AMES Type 86 radar used on the Thunderbird II SAGW systems. See *AD11.*
Indirect Fire	Artillery fire delivered when the target cannot be seen through the gun's sights. It can be either observed or predicted.

Indirect Laying	The gun is laid onto a target which is not visible from the gun position. This is the most common form of gun laying in use. A forward observer is required to spot targets, observe the fall of shot and correct onto the target if necessary. Indirect laying is achieved through the use of aiming points or aiming posts which are clearly visible to all the guns. The azimuth from the centre of the battery to the aiming point is then calculated, together with the azimuth to the target. The angle from the target to the aiming point is then determined, this angle is then set on the sight. The gun is then moved until the sight points at the aiming point at which time the gun barrel will be pointing at the target. The range is applied by reference to a table of ranges and elevations, from which the required elevation is selected and applied to the gun barrel via the clinometer.
In Direct Support	Artillery units in direct support of a unit or formation place give priority to requests for fire from that unit or formation. Artillery units in direct support provide liaison officers, communications and observation posts to the unit or formation concerned. See *Priority Call.*
Individual Angle Method	Introduced prior to the First World War, the Individual Angle Method was introduced, which eventually became the only method of orienting the guns. When no suitable Aiming Point was available and the Battery Commander was close to the guns he would point his director, which was set to 180°, at the target and then measured the angle to each gun. These angles were then ordered to the guns. The guns, in turn, aimed their dial sights at the director using the angle ordered, ensuring their barrels were parallel to the line between the director and the target.
Individual Protection Kit	Introduced in the 1970s and later, this is a lightweight kit which enables quick assembly of overhead protection.
Individual Weapons Sight	A rifle or GPMG mounted night vision sight, sometimes used by OP parties for observation purposes (1980s).
In ef	In Effect.
Infantillery	See *Artillery Mounted Rifles.*
Info Ops	Information Operations.
Inkerman	(i) Battery Honour Title of 49 (Inkerman) Headquarters Battery RA which was granted on 22 June 1955 under authority of 20/ARTY/6721/AG6a. See *Battery Honour Titles.* (ii) Battery Honour Title of 152 (Inkerman) Battery RA which was granted on 22 June 1955 under authority of 20/ARTY/6824/AG6a. Battery is currently in suspended animation. See *Battery Honour Titles.* (iii) Battery Honour Title of 156 (Inkerman) Battery RA which was granted on 12 July 1955 under authority of 20/ARTY/6271/AG6a. Battery is currently in suspended animation. See *Battery Honour Titles.*
Inkerman Day	Battery day of 49 (Inkerman) Headquarters Battery RA (40 Regiment RA). Held to commemorate the Battery's participation in the Battle of Inkerman during the Crimean War.
INLOC	In Location.
In Location	A Command Status referring to units or elements thereof which are located within the area of responsibility of another formation or unit but without that unit or formation having any responsibility towards them, other than those specified in orders.
INOP	Inoperative. (MLRS).
INS	Inertial Navigation System.

INS/GPS — Inertial Navigation System/Global Positioning System.

Insensitive Munitions — Munitions technology which increases the safe handling and transport characteristics of ammunition.

Inspectorate of Armaments — A department of the Ministry of Supply. Now defunct.

Instantaneous Fuze — A fuze designed to cause a shell to function immediately on impact.

Instructor in Fire Control — An artillery officer whose duties consisted of the administration and maintenance of fire control instruments and the training of personnel in their use. Eventually these duties were combined with those of the Instructor in Gunnery. See *Instructor in Gunnery*.

Instructor in Gunnery — An artillery officer whose duties consist of the technical training of personnel in all aspects of gunnery. See *Instructor in Fire Control*.

Instructor Operating Station — The instructor's console in the Warrior OPV Trainer.

ISUM — Intelligence Summary.

In Support — Artillery will provide support to the unit detailed, but will also be used to support other formations. See *In Direct Support*.

Int — Intelligence.

Interactive Electronic Training Delivery System — A system for providing limited training in the Bowman system, prior to the introduction of the full system.

Intercommunication Set Gun Control — A device used by the command post of the Royal Australian Artillery to verbally pass orders to the guns (the guns also use it to acknowledge said orders). See *Gun Display Unit*.

Interdiction Fire — Fire delivered to an area or point in order to prevent the enemy from using the area or point.

Intermediate Ammunition Depot — During the Second World War these were stocked from Central Ammunition Depots, and they in turn supplied ammunition to Equipment Ammunition Magazines. See *Anti-Aircraft Ordnance Depot* and *Equipment Ammunition Magazine*.

Intermediate Command and Staff Course (Land) — A course held at the Joint Services Command and Staff College.

Internal Ballistics — The sequence of events which occurs between the moment that charge is ignited and the moment the projectile leaves the muzzle of the gun. See *Ballistics* and *External Ballistics*.

Interval — Successive rounds of gunfire or battery fire can be separated by a stated interval, given in seconds. This interval is given, at gunfire/fire for effect, between rounds from any one gun, and at battery fire as the interval between each successive gun in the battery. An example would be '6 rounds gunfire, 40 seconds.' See *Battery Fire*, *Fire For Effect* and *Gunfire*.

Intrep — Intelligence Report.

Intsum — Intelligence Summary.

INU — Inertial Navigation Unit.

Invalids — During the 18th and early to mid-19th centuries these were soldiers who had been pensioned off from active service as unfit due to age or wounds. They served in Invalid Companies/Battalions and performed nominal garrison duties only. Postings were normally within the United Kingdom, although some Invalids served in foreign postings, such as the detachment of who garrisoned the island of Heligoland from 1808 through to 1822.

Invalid Company	See *Invalids*.
Invalid Battalion	See *Invalids*.
Invertron	Replacing the Puff Range, the Invertron was a classroom based training system consisting of a screen, a set of slides, multiple projectors, a number of speakers and many small monitors and radios. The Invertron was used as an aid to training artillery TAC and observation post parties. Every type of battlefield fire support was available from the 81 mm mortar through to Naval Gunfire Support and MLRS. An area landscape was displayed whilst OP parties called in simulated fire missions. All ammunition types in service were available, graphical interpretations of their effects being displayed on the screen. The Invertron has now been replaced by the Invertron AFCT in which the slides and projectors have been replaced with computer generated imagery projected via a telejector, See *DCCT, PIFT* and *Puff Range*.
Invertron AFCT	See *Invertron*.
IO	Intelligence Officer.
IOM	Inspector of Ordnance Machinery.
IOR	Indian Other Rank. See *BOR*.
IORA	Intelligence Officer Royal Artillery.
IOS	Instructor Operating Station.
IP	(i) Identification Point. (ii) Initial Point.
IPB	Intelligence Preparation of the Battlefield.
IPE	Individual Protection Equipment.
IPK	Individual Protection Kit.
IPT	(i) Integrated Project Team. (ii) Interest Recognition Trainer.
IR	Infra-red.
IRB	Incremental Reinforcement Battalion.
IRC	Inflatable Raiding Craft. As used by 148 (Meiktila) Commando Forward Observation Battery RA.
IRG	Immediate Replenishment Group.
Irish	Battery Honour Title of 24 (Irish) Battery RA which was granted on 18 October 1926 under authority of 20/ARTY/4544/AG6a. See *Battery Honour Titles*.
Ironside Troop	One of the Troops in 39 Roberts Bty Junior Leaders Regiment RA. See *Alanbrooke Troop, Porteous Troop* and *Ramsay Troop*.
IS	Internal Security.
ISA	Inertial Sensor Assembly.
ISAU	Ignition, Safety and Arming Unit; part of the Javelin AD missile system.
ISAWES	Individual Small Arms Weapons Effect Simulation.
ISC	Isolator Series Container.
ISD	In Service Date.
ISGC	Intercommunication Set Gun Control. The Royal Australian Artillery equivalent to the ALS. See *ALS*.
ISPL	Illustrated Spare Parts List.
ISRD	In Service Reliability Demonstration.
ISRP	Improved Stabilisation Reference Package. Part of the MLRS System. See *Multiple Launch Rocket System*.
ISRP/PDS	Improved Stabilisation Reference Package and Position Determining System. Part of the MLRS system. See *ISRP* and *MLRS*.
ISTAR	Intelligence, Surveillance, Target Acquisition and Reconnaissance.
ITE	Individual Training Establishment.
IWS	Individual Weapons Sight.

J – Johnnie – 1927
Jig – 1943
Juliet – 1956

J	Artillery Code used during the First World War meaning 'Just'.
J, The	The Jungle.
JAA	Jungle Aural Adjustment.
JAAT	Joint Air Attack Team.
JACC	Joint Airspace Control Centre.
Jacket	An officer posted to a RHA Regiment is said to get his 'jacket'.
JADOCS	Joint Automated Deep Operations Coordination System.
JALO	Joint Air Land Organisation. Formerly known as JASO.
JAMC	Joint Air Mounting Centre.
JAMES	Joint Asset Management and Engineering Solutions.
Jamrep	Jamming Report.
JAOC	Joint Air Operations Centre.
JAOP	Joint Air Operations Plan.
JATO	Jet Assisted take-off.
Java	Battery Honour Title of 137 (Java) Battery RA which was granted on 17 October 1935 under authority of 20/ARTY/5043/AG6a. See *Battery Honour Titles.*
Java Troop	One of two troops in M (Headquarters) Battery 3 RHA, Java Troop is the support troop of the Battery comprising the Quartermaster Department, Quartermasters (Technical) Department, Battery Quartermaster Sergeant, Motor Transport and BMETS section. See *BMETS* and *Madras Troop*.
Javelin	Introduced as a replacement for the Blowpipe short range air defence missile. Javelin is a short-range, shoulder launched, close air defence guided weapon system. Its primary role is the protection of combat units and static locations against low level air attack. The system and its detachment were carried in a Land Rover and trailer or a Spartan APC, and was manportable over short distances. Javelin has been replaced by Starstreak HVM. Length: 1.4 m Missile Diameter: 76 cm Missile Weight: 11.1 kgs Max Range: 4.5 kms Warhead Weight: 2.72 kgs Max Altitude: 3,000 feet Max Speed: Mach 1.7 + Fuse Proximity or Impact Guidance: Semi Automatic Command to Line of Sight (SACLOS) Mount: Man Portable.
JBF	Junction Box (Front).
JBMOU	Joint Ballistics Memorandum of Understanding.
JBR	(i) A First World War British gas shell filling. Arseniuos Chloride mixture. (ii) Junction Box (Rear).
JE	Joint Effects.
JEC	Joint Effects Cell.
JEI	Joint Effects Integration.
Jellite	A First World War British gas shell filling of unknown composition.
JERNAS	Export version of Rapier FSC. See *Rapier FSC*.
Jerrycan Battery	Derogatory nickname given to 88 (Arracan) Battery RA.
JET	Joint Effects Team. See *CCA, CAS, FST* and *FOO*.

JETTS	Joint Effects Tactical Targeting System.
JEWT	Jungle Exercise Without Trees. Description of jungle training in UK.
JF	Joint Fires.
JFACC	Joint Force Air Component Commander.
JFACTSU	Joint Forward Air Control Training and Standards Unit. See *FAC* and *SupFAC*
JFC	Joint Fires Cell.
JFHQ	Joint Forces Headquarters.
JFI	Joint Fires Integration.
JFLCC	Joint Force Land Component Commander.
JFMCC	Joint Force Maritime Component Commander.
JFSOC	Joint Fires Staff Officers Course.
JGs	Jungle Greens.
JGAT	Joint Guidance and Allocation of Targeting.
J/Gnr	Junior Gunner (in the Junior Leaders Regiment Royal Artillery).
JGTO	Joint GBAD Training Organisation. See *GBAD*.
JGWTU	Joint Guided Weapons Trials Unit.
Jhansi Flower Pot	Nickname given to a type of 5-inch BL Howitzer issued to some batteries in India.
JHSU	Joint Helicopter Support Unit.
JHQ	Joint Headquarters.
Jig 1	Tactical Sign for a battery sergeant-major. See *Jig 2* and *Tactical Sign*.
Jig 2	Tactical Sign for a battery guide. See *Battery Guide, Jig 1, Reconnaissance Party* and *Tactical Sign*.
JIMSG	Joint Insensitive Munitions Steering Group.
JLRRA	Junior Leaders Regiment Royal Artillery (now disbanded).
JLV	JTIDS Link Vehicle. See *JTIDS*.
JMC	Joint Maritime Convention.
JNCO	Junior Non-Commissioned Officer.
JOA	Joint Operations Area.
Jock Column	A Second World War formation, used during the desert war. A jock column consisted of one squadron of tanks, six 25-pdr field guns, a troop of 2-pdr anti-tank guns, one company of infantry and a number of anti-aircraft pieces. Jock Columns were used to harass the enemy, where with experience, it became obvious that the most valuable component of the column was the field guns. In effect, the other components of the column supported the field guns. The mobility of the Jock Column meant that they could be employed to make up for the lack of mass artillery, although their dispersed tactics meant they had little chance of inflicting major damage on the enemy. Jock Columns derived their name from the officer who originally conceived the idea, General Jock Campbell VC.
Joint	Activities, etc, in which elements of more than one service of the same nation participate.
Joint Air Attack Team	An offensive team concept using air and aviation assets, the JAAT is normally supported by artillery fire, naval gunfire support may be provided if in range. Electronic Warfare assets may also be used to support the team. See *Air, Aviation* and *Naval Gunfire Support*.
Joint Asset Management and Engineering Solutions	A computer software management programme for a Regiment's vehicles and equipment.
Joint Ballistics Memorandum of Understanding	An agreement between France, Germany, Italy, the United Kingdom and the United States for the characteristics of

a 155 mm ordnance of 52 calibre length. See *Ballistic Memorandum of Understanding.*

Joint Forward Air Control Training and Standards Unit — Based at RAF Leeming. The Royal Artillery's Forward Air Controllers undergo training, both as Forward Air Controllers and as Supervisory Forward Air Controllers, at this unit. See *FAC* and *SupFAC.*

Joint Effects Tactical — The second of the Fire Control Battlefield Information System Application programs. It is designed to support the Land Component Commanders Battlespace exploitation by the coordination, integration and synchronization of Joint Find and Delivery Assets to deliver Joint Indirect Effects. See *Fire Control Battlefield Information System Application.*

Joint Effects Team — The original name given to the fire support team by 7 Para RHA who were one of the first regiments to trial the concept. See *Close Combat Attack, Close Air Support, Fire Support Team* and *Forward Observation Officer.*

Joint Fires — The simultaneous and complimentary employment of artillery, mortars, attack helicopters and aviation assets. Joint Fires may include combinations of any or all of the aforementioned elements.

Joint GBAD Training Organisation — Formed in 2006, the Joint GBAD Training Organisation is responsible, under the Chief Instructor of Strike Branch at the Royal School of Artillery, Larkhill for providing rapier, HVM and ACS training at a variety of locations. See *GBAD.*

Joint Offensive Support Team — This Royal Australian Artillery team is made up of a forward observation officer (usually a captain), his assistant (usually a bombardier) and two artillery signallers (gunners). As well as being trained in calling in artillery fire missions, they are also trained to call in naval gunfire and CAS missions. See *Fire Support Team* and *Joint Offensive Support Coordination Centre.*

Joint Offensive Support Coordination Centre — This Royal Australian Artillery group is responsible for directing fire missions and liaising with other support agencies. See *Joint Offensive Support Team.*

Joint Rapier Training Unit — Formed on 1 April 1999, the JRTU was responsible for the delivery of all syllabus-based training on Rapier FSC to Army personnel and on ground based air defence to RAF personnel. The JRTU also supported equipment trials and provided Rapier demonstrations to UK and Foreign visitors. The JRTU was replaced in 2006 by the Joint GBAD Training Organisation. See *JGTO* and *Rapier FSC.*

Joint Services Defence Committee — A study group, made up of members from all three armed services, the civil emergency services and other organisations.

Joint Service Warrant Officers Course — Run at the Joint Services Command and Staff College at Shrivenham, this is a ten day course for warrant officers of all three services. The aim of the course is to provide the warrant officers with an awareness of joint, multinational and multi-agency operations, including the application of operational-level planning, in order to improve operational capability.

Junior Tactical Targeting Course — Run by the targeting section of the Royal School of Artillery, the course is for lance bombardiers through to sergeants.

Jury Axle	A local modification to the Ordnance QF 25-pounder carriage which was produced in Burma. It had a narrower wheelbase (by about 20-inches) than the normal 25-pounder and as such was suitable for towing by Jeep and could also transported by air in a Dakota aircraft. It was subsequently adopted officially following further minor modifications and together with a new platform for use with the narrow wheelbase as the Carriage 25-pdr Mark II. See *Ordnance QF 25 Pounder.*
JOST	Joint Offensive Support Team. (Royal Australian Artillery.)
JOSTCC	Joint Offensive Support Co-ordination Centre. (Royal Australian Artillery.) See *Joint Offensive Support Team.*
JOTES	Junior Officers' Training and Education Scheme.
Journal, The	*The Journal of the Royal Artillery.*
JPA	Joint Personnel Administration.
JPR	Joint Personnel Recovery.
J/RSM	Junior Regimental Sergeant-Major (in the JLRRA).
JRTU	Joint Rapier Training Unit. See *JGTO* and *Rapier FSC.*
JSC&SC	Joint Services Command and Staff College.
JSDC	Joint Services Defence Committee.
JSEODOC	Joint Service Explosive Ordnance Disposal Operations Centre.
JSP	Joint Service Publication.
JSTU	Joint Service Trials Unit (16 JSTU (Thunderbird) and 21 JSTU (Rapier).
JSWOC	Joint Service Warrant Officers Course.
Jt	Joint.
JTAC	Joint Terminal Attack Controller. See *Forward Air Controller.*
Jt AD	Joint Air Defence.
JTF	Joint Task Force.
JTFC	Joint Task Force Commander.
JTFHQ	Joint Task Force Headquarters.
JTIDS	Joint Tactical Information Distribution System.
JTTC	Junior Tactical Targeting Course.
JUEP	Joint UAV Experimental Program.
Jumbos	Nickname of 137 (Java) Battery RA.
Jump	A vertical angular movement of the gun on firing. Jump affects the direction of the line of departure. See *Line of Departure.*
Jumpers	Nickname given in the early twentieth century to appearing/disappearing targets which were used for target practice.
Jungle Aural Adjustment	A method of adjusting fire by the sound of the rounds impacting.
Jungle Field Regt RA	Formed in the Second World War in Burma, Jungle Fd Regts were equipped as follows: Two batteries, each of two troops of four jeep-drawn 3.7-inch howitzers and one battery of eight 3-inch mortars which were transported in jeeps and trailers. OP Parties and command posts were equipped with jeeps whilst the signallers were provided with a small number of 15-cwt and 3-ton trucks to carry supplies.
Jungle Exercise Without Trees	Simulated jungle training conducted in the UK prior to deployment to a jungle area.
Jungle Greens	Dress introduced in about 1943 and worn until introduction of tropical combat dress in the 1970s. See *Battle Dress* and *Khaki Drill.*
Jungle Warfare School	Located at Kota Tinngi in Malaya, the school was established by FARELF in the early 1950s and closed around 1970. It had a world wide reputation for excellence.

	Other Jungle Warfare schools had existed in India during the Second World War.
JWH	Jersey Wool, Heavy.
JWI	Jungle Warfare Instructor.
JWIC	Jungle Warfare Instructors Course.
JWS	Jungle Warfare School.
JWT	Jungle Warfare Trained.
JWW	Jungle Warfare Wing.

K – King – 1927/1943
Kilo – 1956

K	Kelvin.
Kabul 1842	Battery Honour Title of 51 (Kabul 1842) Battery RA which was granted on 23 July 1930 under authority of 20/ARTY/4735/AG6a. Battery currently in suspended animation. See *Battery Honour Titles*.
Kairouan Troop	One of the Troops in 88 (Arracan) Battery RA. See *Borneo Troop*.
KB	Artillery Code used during the First World War meaning 'Continue firing with balloon observation'.
KC	Krupp Cemented.
KD	Khaki Drill.
KE	Kinetic Energy.
Kelly Holdsworth Trust	Administered by the Royal Artillery Charitable Fund, the Trust exists to assist gunner officers who served in the regular army, their widows/widowers and their children if under 21 years of age, who are in need, hardship or distress. Additionally, the Trust can help with the education or advancement of children who qualify to receive benefit.
Kemmel Day	Battery day of 84 Field Battery RA, later 166 Heavy Anti-Aircraft Battery RA. Celebrated on 25 April each year. The Battery is now in suspended animation.
KEP	Kinetic Energy Penetrator.
Kerrison Predictor	One of the first fully-automated anti-aircraft predictors, the Kerrison Predictor was used to attempt to predict the correct point of aim at an aircraft. The Predictor, also known as the No. 3 Predictor, mounted on a large tripod, was the first of its kind to be fast enough to be used in the demanding high-speed low-altitude role. It was also the first to be used with the 40 mm Bofors Light Anti-Aircraft gun. Previous predictors having been employed with the 3.7-inch Heavy Anti-Aircraft gun. Inputs to the Predictor included wind speed, gravity, ballistics of the gun and the rounds it fired, angle to the target in both azimuth and altitude, and a user-input estimated speed. The Predictor drove motors attached to the traversal and elevation gears of the otherwise unmodified Bofors gun. The three-man detachment for the predictor were required to input the various calculations and to ensure that the predictor pointed at the target whilst the gun detachment itself was simply required to keep the gun loaded. It proved capable of being able to hit practically anything that flew in a straight line, being particularly effective against dive bombers. However, due to its weight (over 500 pounds) and its complexity the Army was unable to produce it in any numbers. A major disadvantage to the system was that it required a large electrical generator to drive the gun. This resulted

in an increase in the logistical load. Due to its complexity, the system took some time to set up and therefore its use was largely restricted to static emplacements, whilst field units continued to rely on either the integral sights of individual guns or the stiffkey sights introduced in late 1943. See *Bofors*, *Predictor* and *Stiffkey Sight*.

KFS — Knife, Fork and Spoon.

KGV Cup — King George 5th Cup. The annual inter-TA Gunnery Competition.

KGVI Cup — King George 6th Cup. This is the annual Inter-UOTC Gunnery Competition, it is one of the oldest competitions in the history of the Territorial Army and is normally held at Warcop. See *UOTC*.

Khaki Drill — Hot climate dress introduced in the late nineteenth century and worn in various styles until the 1960s. See *Battle Dress* and *Jungle Greens*.

Kiang Troop — One of the troops, together with Chin Troop, of 127 (Dragon) Battery RA.

Kicking Mule — Nickname given to the Battery Badge of 176 (Abu Klea) Battery RA. Approval from HQ DRA on 22 June 1993 allowed the return to the old style Battery Badge, dating from 1931. The adoption of the Kicking Mule commemorates the unique part played by this animal in the annuls of the Royal Artillery and particularly 176 (Abu Klea) Battery RA.

Kih — Kilometres in the Hour.

Kinetic Energy Penetrator — An armour piercing solid shot projectile.

Kinetic Operations — Military operations that rely on continual movement to achieve the desired effects.

King George 5th Cup. — See *KGV Cup*.

King George 6th Cup — See *KGVI Cup*.

King's Gunner — See *Queen's Gunner*.

King's Shot, The — See *Boche-Buster*.

King's Troop RHA, The — The title of The King's Troop RHA was granted under authority of Army Order 134 of 1947. Based at St John's Wood Barrack, The King's Troop RHA forms part of the Household Troops. The Troop carries out ceremonial duties as ordered by general officer commanding the Household Division, in particular the firing of salutes on state occasions. Originally known as the Riding House Troop RHA, it was renamed at the request of King George VI on his first official visit to the Troop after its reformation following the Second World War.

Kinies — Nickname given to Kinetheodolite Operators in the ATS.

Kinky Kirkee — Derogatory nickname for 79 (Kirkee) Commando Battery RA.

KIP — Kit Individual Protection.

Kirkee — Battery Honour Title of 79 (Kirkee) Commando Battery RA which was granted on 18 October 1926 under authority of 20/ARTY/4544/AG6a. See *Battery Honour Titles*.

Kirkee Boys — Nickname for members of 79 (Kirkee) Commando Battery (1980s).

Kit Check — Slang term used in the Junior Leaders Regiment meaning to report sick.

Kiwis, The — Nickname for 94 (New Zealand) Battery RA.

KJ — Stannic Chloride. A First World War British gas shell filling.

KNC — Krupp Non-Cemented.

Koehler's Troop — One of the three troops in 22 (Gibraltar 1779–1783) Battery RA. Named after Lt Koehler, the inventor of the Koehler Gun. See *Dover's Troop* and *Sortie Troop*.

KQ — Artillery Code used during the FIrst World War meaning 'Are you ready to fire?'

L – London – 1927
Love – 1943
Lima – 1956

L (i) Left.
(ii) Artillery Code used during the First World War meaning 'High Explosive'.

(L) A Second World War Royal Canadian Artillery Ant-Aircraft battery designation. A type L battery was a light battery manning 4 x 40mm Bofors Guns. A numerical prefix indicated that the standard compliment had been increased by the multiple of the prefix. This (2L) indicated a Light Anti-Aircraft battery equipped with eight guns. See *Bofors, (H), (LS)* and *(M)*.

L1 Tactical Sign for a Battery Light Aid Detachment. See *L2, L3* and *Tactical Sign.*

L2 Tactical Sign for a Battery Light Aid Detachment. See *L1, L3* and *Tactical Sign.*

L3 Tactical Sign for a Battery Light Aid Detachment. See *L1, L2* and *Tactical Sign.*

L118 Light Gun The 105 mm Light Gun is towed by a medium-weight vehicle or carried around the battlefield underslung by a Puma or Chinook helicopter. In service since 1975, it replaced the 105 mm Pack Howitzer. Robust and reliable, the gun proved its worth in the Falklands, firing up to 400 rounds per day. Royal Artillery L118 Light Guns are fitted with the LINAPS system, which enables the gun to be unhooked and in action in 30 seconds. New Light Gun ammunition is in development, with an increasingly lethal round and an extended range. The L118 uses the L19 ordnance to fire the range of ammunition previously used by the Abbot self-propelled gun.
Detachment: 6
Weight: 1,858 kg
Length: 8.8 m
Width: 1.78 m
Height: 2.13 m
Ammunition: HE, Smoke, Illuminating, Target Marker
Maximum Range: (HE) 17.2 km. Shell.
Anti Tank Range: 800 m
Shell Weight HE 15.1 kg
Rate of Fire: 6 rpm
See also *LINAPS* and *L119 Light Gun.*

L119 Light Gun Basically the same as the L118, but using the L20 ordnance to fire American M1 ammunition. Only a limited number are in service with the Royal Artillery, mainly in training units. See *L118 Light Gun.*

L4 Light Machine Gun See *Bren Light Machine Gun.*

L5 Pack How See *105 mm Pack Howitzer (L5).*

L85 Individual Weapon Calibre: 5.56 mm
Weight: 4.98 kg (with loaded magazine and optical sight)
Length: 785 mm
Barrel Length: 518 mm
Muzzle Velocity: 940 m/s
Feed: 30 round magazine
Effective Range: 400 m
Cyclic Rate of Fire: 610–775 rounds per minute
An under slung grenade launcher can be fitted to the L85 Individual Weapon. See *CWS, L86 Light Support Weapon, SUSAT* and *UGL.*

L86 Light Support Weapon	Calibre: 5.56 mm Weight: 6.58 kg (with loaded magazine and optical sight) Length: 900 mm Barrel Length: 646 mm Muzzle Velocity: 970 m/s Feed: 30 round magazine Effective Range: 1000 m Cyclic Rate of Fire: 610–775 rounds per minute See *CWS, L85 Individual Weapon* and *SUSAT.*
L/A	Low Angle, replaced lower register.
LA	Low Angle, replaced lower register.
LAA	Light Anti-Aircraft.
LAACC	Light Anti-Aircraft Control Centre.
LAAD	Limited Area Air Defence.
LAA/SL Regt RA	Light Anti-aircraft/Searchlight Regiment Royal Artillery.
Laboratory	A room or building where gunpowder was mixed and/or made into charges prior to being stored in magazines. Laboratory work also involved the filling of shells.
LACS	Lightweight Artillery Computer System. See *BATES* and *BMETS.*
LAD	Light Aid Detachment (REME).
LADA	London Air Defence Area.
Ladle	During the muzzle-loading period, this copper-headed ladle was used for placing the propellant charge in the bore of the gun.
LADs	Launcher Azimuth Drive system. Part of the MLRS system. See *Multiple Launch Rocket System.*
LAGERS	Lightweight Artillery GPS Enhanced Receiver System.
LAIT	Land Accident Prevention and Investigation Team.
Lamp-swinging	Story telling amongst groups of soldiers, usually of the 'I remember when …' variety.
Lancashire and Cumbrian Gunners	Regimental title of 12 Regiment RA. Identifies the regimental recruiting area.
Lancashire Artillery Volunteers	Regimental title of 103 Regiment RA (V). Identifies the regimental recruiting area.
Lancaster Gun	Developed by Charles Lancaster, the Lancaster Gun fired an elongated shell. The elliptical bore gave a rotary motion to the shell. The 68 pdr of 95 cwt. fired an 86 lbs shell to a range of 5,600 yards using a charge of 12 lbs and an elevation of 18 degrees.
Lancastrite	A First World War British gas shell filling of unknown composition.
Lance	Liquid-fuelled surface to surface missile that replaced the Honest John. Missile Range: 10 to 110 kilometres Missile Weight: 1294 kg (approximately) Detachment: 6 (driver plus 5) Warhead: Nuclear (various yields were available) Propulsion: Pre-packaged bi-propellant, liquid rocket system. Guidance: Simple inertial Launchers: M752 Self-propelled, tracked. M740 Towwed lightweight launcher. See *M688 Lance Loader Transporter* and *M752 Lance Launcher.*
Lance Jack	A term used in general conversation when referring to a Lance Bombardier. Similar in usage to Sarge or Bomb. See *Bomb* and *Full Screw.*
Lance Sergeant	It was introduced as a rank in the Royal Artillery in 1920 and abolished in 1946. Lance Sergeants were identified by

wearing three stripes, whereas full sergeants wore three stripes with a gun above the stripes.

Land Command Staff Pool (Volunteer) — One of the three component pools of CVHQ RA. However, recruitment of personnel for LCSP (V) is controlled by HQ LAND Command and not by CVHQ RA. See *CVHQ RA, All Arms Staff Officers Liaison & Watchkeepers Group* and *RA Specialist Pool (V).*

Land Environment Air Picture Provision — A system designed to provide the land environment with enhanced air situational awareness.

Land Front Armament — See *Movable Armament*.

Land Service — Ordnance is designated Land Service or Sea Service according to the use to which it was to be put.

Land Service Number — Numbers assigned to military weapons, equipment and ammunition. All such numbers are prefixed by the letter L. This system of designation was introduced in the mid 1950s. See *Service Designation.*

Land Service Operational Requirements Branch 6 — The Branch, responsible for artillery operational requirements from the 1960s to the 1990s.

Landing Point — A location within a landing site where a helicopter may land. See *Landing Site* and *Landing Zone.*

Landing Point Commander — A substantive bombardier who has been trained by a helicopter handling instructor to lay a single landing point by day but may operate the landing point by day and night. See *Helicopter Handling Instructor* and *Landing Point.*

Landing Site — A site within a landing zone containing one or more landing points. See *Landing Point* and *Landing Zone.*

Landing Zone — A specified zone within an objective used for the landing of aircraft which contains both landing sites and landing points. See *Landing Points* and *Landing Sites.*

Land Mattress — A Second World War rocket launcher, which initially consisted of a crude trailer carrying 40 rocket launching tubes. The rockets consisted of a 29-pound Naval bombardment warhead fixed to an RAF 3-inch rocket motor and using a standard Army artillery fuze. The rockets only had one charge, range being adjusted by way of an elevation setting and a special braking ring or spoiler fixed to the nose of the rocket. The spoiler was fixed in order to slow the rocket down and thus reduce its range. The title 'Land Mattress' derives from Land (Army) and Mattress was the launcher's Naval cover name. The first version was tested in 1944, after which a battery comprising 10 fire units equipped with 32-round launchers was established with 10,000 rockets. The battery's baptism of fire (approximately 960 rockets) took place on 31 October 1944. In 1945 a standard production model 30-round launcher was issued. This launcher could fire its rockets over a fairly broad series of ranges, governed by spoilers (large ring, small ring or no ring). The time required to fire a complete salvo was slightly under 8 seconds.
Calibre: 76.2 mm
Number produced: 100 plus
Detachment: 5
Weight (in action): 1118 kg
Elevation: 65 degrees to 35 degrees
Traverse: 20 degrees
Ammunition: High explosive rocket
Ammunition Weight: 30.53 kg
Muzzle Velocity: 353 metres per second
Range: 7230 metres

Rate of Fire: 30 rounds per minute
The Standard production model was also known as the Projector, Rocket, Three Inch, Number 8 Mark 1 or the Tillings-Stephens Projector after the manufacturers.

Lands The raised portions of rifling within the bore of the barrel.

Landy An abbreviated form of name given in general conversation referring to a Land Rover.

Lane A longitudinal section of a barrage, within which the fire of a battery or regiment moves forward. See *Barrage, Linear Concentration* and *Standard Barrage.*

Langridge Before the introduction of canister, this term referred to the collection of junk that was loaded loose into the barrel of a gun as an anti-personnel weapon.

Lanyard (i) A light rope or cord which was attached to a friction tube and pulled in order to fire the gun.
(ii) See Appendix B for the story of the Royal Artillery white lanyard.
(iii) During the Late 1940s early 1950s 245 Armament Battery wore a red lanyard in place of the usual white RA lanyard. See *Armament Battery.*

LAO Launching Area Officer.

LAP Local Air Picture.

Large Spread In Naval gunfire support a report by an observer to the ship to indicate that the distances between the bursts of a salvo are excessive. (Royal Canadian Artillery.)

Larkers Nickname for the Royal School of Artillery, Larkhill. See *Harry Larkers.*

LARNMISS Sequence of initial orders to the guns for fire for effect; Line (Switch from Zero Line), Angle of Sight, Range, Number of Rounds, Method of Fire (Troop Fire, Gun Fire or Salvo), Interval, Sweep, Search. See *TALAMEF* and *TALAPFRIRF.*

Larkspur A family of military radios which replaced the Wireless Set No. 19 etc. Larkspur radios were identified by a letter and two figure identifier. The letter indicated the type of use the radio was designed for, namely, A: Manpack, i.e., A42, B: Manportable, i.e., B48 and C: Vehicle borne, i.e., C45. The Larkspur family was in turn replaced by the Clansman family of radios. See *Station Radio A41, Station Radio A42, Station Radio A43R, Station Radio B43/R220, Station Radio B44, Station Radio B48, Station Radio C11/R210, Station Radio C42, Station Radio C45HP* and *Station Radio BCC 46U*

Lascar An Indian enlisted man employed by the Royal Artillery in India to clean guns, carriages etc.

LASER Light Amplification by Stimulated Emission of Radiation.

Laser Inertial Automatic Pointing System This navigation and pointing system is used with the L118 and L119 light guns, it is based on an inertial navigation system which enables the gun to be unhooked and into action in 30 seconds. It replaces the traditional dial sight and takes into account trunnion tilt, without the need to level any spirit level bubbles as with traditional dial sights. It is an autonomous gun-mounted system which comprises the FIN3110L integrated inertial/GPS navigation system, a large screen layers display and control unit, a wheel hub mounted odometer, and a power management system. A navigation display unit is also installed in the cab of the gun-towing vehicle. By mounting the INS/GPS directly above the gun barrel the direct measurement of elevation and azimuth is achieved which allows quick and accurate laying. Using its GPS capability LINAPS also provides the precise location of the gun platform together with a route navigation capability.

A touch-screen display tells the gun controller when his gun is laid onto the correct target data provided by the CP. Thus improving the accuracy of the fall of shot to a greater degree than was possible with the conventional dial sight. See *L118 Light Gun* and *L119 Light Gun*.

Laser Point Using polar coordinates from an unsurveyed position to compare the aimpoint with the mean point of impact and derive a correction that is applicable to the firing battery.

Laser Point Registration Adjustment of the mean point of impact on a polar mission from a surveyed location to derive a registration.

Laser Range Finder Used for measuring distances to visible objects accurately. See *Laser Target Marker*.

Laser Target Marker Used for illuminating targets for engagement by laser guided weapon systems. The Laser Target Marker is also capable of measuring distances to visible objects accurately. See *Laser Range Finder*.

Laser Target Marker Operator A soldier who had qualified on the now defunct LTMO course, the successor to the FAM course. The LTMO would generally be an Op-Ack who was trained to designate a target with a laser for attack by an aircraft. The aircraft was not however, controlled by the LTMO, but would remain under someone else's control. Each Tac group would have a FAC qualified person, and a number of LTMO qualified personnel. See *FAC, FAM, Op-Ack* and *Tac Group*.

Laser Telemetry Monitoring Facility The LTMF round gives information on how consistent the operator is with tracking the target, and how close the missile would have been to the target. Part of the HVM AD System. See *HVM*.

LASO Launch Area Safety Officer.

Last Safe Moment This involves firing rounds onto the target as close as possible to your own assaulting troops. The three rounds fire for effect last safe moment drill involves firing three rounds (per gun) fire for effect as close to your own troops as possible, as they advance onto the objective. Rounds have to be fired, and the report of rounds complete made to the forward observation officer within twenty seconds. See *Fire For Effect*.

LATEO 'Unseen' the motto of 4/73 (Sphinx) Special Observation Post RA Battery RA.

Late Feed Duty to clean lines, feed and make the horses comfortable (The King's Troop RHA).

Lateral Plane of Sight The plane which is at right angles to the vertical plane of sight and which also contains the line of sight. When the line of sight is horizontal, the lateral plane of sight is the horizontal plane. See *Line of Sight* and *Vertical Plane of Sight*.

Lateral Spread A technique which is used to distribute fire on a line perpendicular to the gun-target line. See *Range Spread*.

Launcher Position Officer A position within a surface to surface missile regiment, similar to a gun position officer. See *Gun Position Officer*.

Launching Area Officer In corporal missile regiments, the LAO received the missile from the servicing battery or troop, he was then responsible for preparing the missile for firing. Following fuelling of the missile, and after it had been raised to the firing position, the LAO could make last minute adjustments by way of a platform mounted on a cherry-picker type vehicle. The LAO would then retire to a trench approximately 100 yards from the missile to await the order to fire.

LAV — Lancashire Artillery Volunteers.

LAW — Light Anti-Tank Weapon.

Lawson's Company — Battery Honour Title of 97 Battery (Lawson's Company) RA which was granted on 18 October 1926 under authority of 20/ARTY/4544/AG6a. See *Battery Honour Titles.*

Lawson's Troop — One of the Troops in 97 (Lawson's) Battery RA. See *Hislop's Troop.*

Layer — The gun number responsible for laying the gun. See *Laying.*

Layers Display and Control Unit — Used with the Light gun the LDCU combines an 8.1-inch touch sensitive electro-luminescent display, powerful processing user friendly, menu-driven display of gun laying and navigation information, communicating with other LINAPS sub-systems via a bi-directional serial interface. See *LINAPS.*

Laying — The process whereby the gun is aimed by using its sights. It may be direct, when the target is visible from the gun position, or indirect, when the target cannot be seen from the gun position and suitable aiming points have to be employed. See *Aiming Posts, Direct Laying* and *Indirect Laying.*

Laying by Line of Metal — In order to lay by line of metal, the layer of a smoothbore artillery piece would aim straight across the groove in the breech to the foresight. Due to the breech being broader than the muzzle, this would result in the piece being fired at a slight elevation. Trained gunners knew what range 'line of metal' represented for each nature of artillery piece in service. See *Line of Metal.*

Laying Cords — Introduced in 1901, these were used by a battery to mark lines of indirect fire, by utilising the following procedure. The layers would mark off equal distances from the aiming posts previously planted by the battery commander. The procedure was really only suitable on open ground, and remained in force until the introduction of directors.

LBdr — Lance Bombardier (rank).

L/Bdr — Lance Bombardier (rank).

LBM — Lever Breech Mechanism.

L Bty — Light Battery. Used during the 1930s. See *Light Battery.*

LCC — Land Component Commander.

LCHR/Lchr — Launcher.

LCMR — Lightweight Counter Mortar Radar.

LCSP (V) — Land Command Staff Pool (Volunteer). See *CVHQ RA, All Arms Staff Officers Liaison & Watchkeepers Group* and *RA Specialist Pool (V).*

LCU — Loaders Control Unit.

LCV — (i) Lorried Command Vehicle.
(ii) Light Command Vehicle.

LD — Line of Departure.

LD1 — Designation for light draught horses used to draw field artillery pieces (6 horses per gun team). See *HD* and *LD2.*

LD2 — Designation for light draught horses used to draw transport vehicles, for example, GS wagons and limbers using 6 horse teams. LD2 horses were heavier than LD1 horses. See *HD* and *LD1.*

LDA — Launch Danger Area.

LDCU — Layers Display and Control Unit. See *LINAPS.*

LDF — Local Deployment Facility (JTIDS).

LDP	Launcher Data Processor. Part of the Rapier FSB2 air defence system.
LDS	Launcher Drive System. Part of the MLRS system. See *Multiple Launch Rocket System.*
LDU	Layers Display Unit.
LDV	Laser Doppler Velocimeter.
LE	(i) Low Explosive, a propellant. (Ordnance.) (ii) Late Entry, officer first commissioned at over the age of 30.
LE	(iii) Lower Establishment. (iv) Locally Employed.
Leaders	The front pair of horses in a gun team.
LEAPP	Land Environment Air Picture Provision.
LEC	Locally Employed Civilian.
Le Cateau	Battery Honour Title of 93 (Le Cateau) Battery RA which was granted on 3 August 1954 under authority of 20/ARTY/6271/AG6a. Battery currently in suspended animation. See *Battery Honour Titles.*
LEDs	Launcher Elevation Drive system. Part of the MLRS system. See *Multiple Launch Rocket System.*
Lefroy Gold Medal	Awarded every second year to the Royal Artillery officer (Regular or Territorial Army) who is adjudged to have made an outstanding contribution to the science and application of artillery. The award consists of a gold medal and a honorarium of £75.
Left	(i) A directional deviation used by an observer in adjusting ground or naval gunfire. See *Right*. (ii) Fire correction used by an observer to indicate that a lateral shift to the mean point of impact perpendicular to the observer-target line is required. See *Right*.
Leg iron	A leather legging, reinforced with a steel strip worn by wheel drivers on the right leg to protect it from the pole of the limber.
Leg Over	The hind leg of a gun team horse gets over the top of a slack trace, where it will gall the horse unless quickly corrected.
Leica TC1100	Known as the Electronic Total Station, this is a combined angular and distance measuring instument. It is a full transit theodolite, capable of a full 6400 mil transit in the vertical plane. An electronic optical distance measurer is incorporated in the telescope. See *DI 3000.*
Length of Ram	When a shell is rammed, the driving band engages in the shot seating and is deformed to fit the rifled portion. The length of ram is the distance from the breech face to the base of the projectile. See *Shot Travel.*
LEOC	Late Entry Officers Course.
Leslie's Troop	One of the two troops in N Battery (The Eagle Troop) RA. Named after the Battery Commander at the Battle of Hyderabad. Not currently in use (2007) due to N Battery (The Eagle Troop) RA being reduced to troop size. See *Brooke's Troop.*
LEU	Launch Effect Unit.
LEWT	Light Electronic Warfare Team.
LF	Landing Force.
LG	Large Grain. A type of gunpowder.
LGB	Laser Guided Bomb.
LGSC	Long Gunnery Staff Course.
LH40C TLE Laser Range Finder	A Laser Range Finder which is used to measure range, azimuth and elevation of a selected target, both accurately and instantly. It can be interfaced with the Specialist Global Positioning System Receiver (SPGR) to form a target locat-

ing system. It can be hand-held or tripod mounted. See *SPGR* and *TLE.*

LHS Load Handling System (DROPS).

Leipzig Day Battery day of O Battery (The Rocket Troop) RA.

Lieutenant Fireworker The most junior officer rank in the Royal Artillery during the eighteenth century. The Lieutenant Fireworker commanded a team of mattrosses and had expertise and responsibility for ammunition. See *Mattross.*

Lieutenant-General of the Ordnance A member of the Board of Ordnance and the deputy to the Master-General of the Ordnance. The holder was appointed by the crown under letters patent. Having been established in 1544, it was abolished in 1855 on the abolition of the Board of Ordnance. See *Board of Ordnance* and *Master General of the Ordnance.*

Life of a Gun This is defined by the number of rounds that can be fired through a barrel accurately and safely. Once the rifling is so worn as to render it inaccurate, the gun will be returned for relining.

Lift The movement of fire from one line to the next in a barrage. See *Barrage, Linear Concentration* and *Standard Barrage.*

Lifting Barrage The lifting barrage was intended to have shells hit an enemy trench until just prior to the attacking troops arriving at that trench, the barrage would then lift to the next trench line. Whilst being economical in ammunition, it required fairly complicated calculations to ensure that all guns would hit their assigned target, and failed in its mission if the enemy had troops located between trench lines. See *Barrage* and *Creeping Barrage.*

Light Aid Detachment Most artillery regiments have a Light Aid Detachment, whilst some have a Workshop. Initially this was provided by the Royal Army Ordnance Corps, and following its formation, by the Royal Electrical and Mechanical Engineers. The LAD is tasked with providing 1st line repair and recovery support for virtually every Artillery Field Regiment gun and associated equipment. Some LAD are capable of providing limited 2nd line support. See *REME* and *Workshop.*

Light Anti-Aircraft/Searchlight Regiment RA First formed in 1943, these regiments had the benefit of having both 40 mm Bofors LAA guns and searchlights in one unit. By 1951, there were nine searchlights to every twelve guns in a battery.

Light Balls Used during the smooth-bore period a Light Ball was a canvas case, stretched over an oblong frame work of wrought iron and bound with cord. The framework was filled with a composition which burned with an intense flame for a long period of time. Light Balls were to be used at night to illuminate an enemy's working parties, very much as illumination rounds are used today. See *Illumination.*

Light Command Vehicle Used at brigade and higher level formations as a command post vehicle, the LCV was normally equipped with two wireless sets. (Second World War.)

Light Electronic Warfare Team A small, two personnel team, who, by using various items of electronic equipment permit friendly callsigns to identify and engage enemy locations. See *Fire Support Team.*

Light Gun See *L118 Light Gun* and *L119 Light Gun.*

Light Mountain Battery Unlike a mountain battery, these batteries moved in draught, rather than using pack mules, although a minimum number of ordnance mules were available so that they could move in pack if necessary. The establishment was 4 british officers, 3 viceroy commissioned officers, 221 Indian Other Ranks and 6 followers. The battery had 110 mules and 23 ponies. Only 72 rounds of ammunition were carried per gun, as opposed to the 120 carried by a mountain battery. See *Mountain Battery, British.*

Light Regiment (Mortar) RA — During the 1950s a Light Regiment Royal Artillery, equipped with mortars consisted of an RHQ and three batteries, each of three troops of four 4.2-inch mortars. Each light battery was in direct support of an infantry brigade whilst each light troop was in direct support of an infantry battalion.

Lightweight Artillery Computer System — LACS was a rugged laptop (RLT) which used existing BATES processor cell software and therefore had the same capability as the BATES processor cell. Based on laptop technology, many of the components of BATES were incorporated in the system. Increased memory enabled the setting up data for both an allotment cell and a command post to be stored. Transported in their own carrying cases, both the RLT and the thermal dot matrix printer were man portable. LACS was used with both light gun battery groups and the Battlefield Meteorological System. See *BATES* and *BMETS*

Lightweight Counter Mortar Radar — A lightweight radar designed to automatically locate mortar weapons through 6400 mils whilst remaining sufficiently lightweight to support insertion by airborne troops. Capable of detecting and tracking mortar rounds at ranges out of the effective range of most mortar weapons, the Lightweight Counter Mortar Radar has the ability to locate the firing weapon with a target location error sufficient to neutralize the hostile weapon utilising any of the available counterfire assets. Operated by a two person crew, it is fully capable of deployment by helicopter and most types of vehicle. See *Counterfire.*

Light Weight Launcher M740 — The alternative Lance missile firing platform to the M752 Lance Launcher. See *Lance, M752 Lance Launcher* and *Zero Length Launcher.*

Lightweight Multiple Launcher — A firing stand holding three air defence missiles, two versions exist one for Javelin and one for HVM. See *HVM* and *Javelin.*

LIM — Length in Metres. A essential statistic when planning air and sea movement of unit.

Lima 1 — See *L1.*

Lima 2 — See *L2.*

Lima 3 — See *L3.*

LIMAWS — Light Medium Artillery Weapons System.

LIMAWS (G) — Lightweight Mobile Artillery Weapons System (155 mm Gun).

LIMAWS (R) — Lightweight Mobile Artillery Weapon System (Rocket). Based on the six-wheeled, four-wheeled drive Supacat High Mobility Transporter, LIMAWS(R) will be capable for firing ATACMS and GMLRS munitions. It will carry an RPC of 6 GMLRS rockets.

Limber — Originally a limber was a wheeled and detachable part of a gun carriage that enabled it to be horse drawn by supporting the gun trail and providing the means for hitching the gun team to the gun carriage. It carried ammunition, tools and often members of the gun detachment. It ceased to be essential when vehicles replaced horses, but was retained with some guns, notably 25-pdr, and renamed as an 'ammunition trailer'. During the seventeenth century the limber was also known as a lymore. See *Lymore.*

Limber Gunner One gunner in each gun detachment is usually appointed 'limber gunner' and is responsible for the routine care and maintenance of the gun.

Limber Supply Ammunition is supplied to the guns directly from the gun limber, as opposed to the standard procedure of using ammunition from one of the ammunition wagons. Under war establishment, a mounted sub-section would consist of the gun and two ammunition wagons. See *Wagon Supply.*

LINAPS Laser Inertial Automatic Pointing System. See *L118 Light Gun* and *L119 Light Gun.*

Lincolnshire & Humberside Regimental title of 50 Missile Regiment RA. The Regiment is now in suspended Gunners animation. The title identified the Regiment's recruiting area.

Line (i) Communications via laid line, as opposed to radio.
(ii) When associated with the target, this is the direction of the line of sight in a horizontal plane. It is the angle which the vertical plane of sight makes with a horizontal reference line (the Zero Line or Centre of Arc). It is measured clockwise from the horizontal reference line, with a magnitude of from 0 mils to 6400 mils. It is sometimes referred to as the Map Line or the Line to Target. When Line is obtained by shooting, it is known as Corrected Line.

Linear A linear target is one which falls along a straight line, with guns aimed along the target at equal distances from one another. The line is oriented on a bearing. See *Linear Concentration.*

Linear Concentration A linear concentration produces a line of fire on a target which is strictly linear in shape, for example a road or railway line. See *Barrage, Field Battery Linear Target, Heavy Battery Linear Target, Linear Target, Medium Battery Linear Target, Simple Concentration* and *Standard Barrage.*

Line BT The line joining the battery to the target. See *Line OT.*

Line Correction of the Moment Corrections which are common to all guns of a battery and which hold good for a definite period of time. They consist of corrections to counteract variations associated with cross-component of equivalent constant wind, a portion of drift for the standard projectile not automatically applied by the sight and for very long range guns, the rotation of the earth.

Line GT The grid bearing from the gun line to the target. See *Gun Target Line* and *GT.*

Line of Departure (i) The direction of motion of the projectile at the moment of leaving the gun. It is the tangent to the trajectory of the muzzle.
(ii) Formerly called the Start Line, it is the line that attacking troops cross at H-Hour.

Line of Metal In the days of smooth bore artillery, the Line of Metal extended from the a groove located at the top of the guns breech along the top of the barrel to the foresight. See *Laying by Line of Metal.*

Line of Sight A straight line between the sights and the target. Also known as the line GT. See *GT* and *Line GT.*

Line Of Sight Beam Rider A form of missile guidance, used with semi-automatic command to line of sight systems.

Line OT The line joining the observer to the target. See *Line BT*.

Liner The inner, rifled, tube of a piece of ordnance.

Lines (i) Location where the horses are kept.
(ii) The successive lines on which a barrage moves forward. See *Barrage, Linear Concentration, Opening Line* and *Standard Barrage*.

Lines Horses The gun team horses (The King's Troop RHA).

Line Telegraphy Communications via laid line, as opposed to radio. See *Line*.

Line To Shoot Down To The nearest range that the commander of the battle wishes to achieve. The gun position officer needs to know the location of the Line To Shoot Down To when choosing his gun position. He has the Line To Shoot Down To marked on his map and must then work out his crest clearance for any obstacles (mountains, trees etc.) that fall between his arcs of fire, his gun position and his Line To Shoot Down To. He can then establish whether he can achieve his Line To Shoot Down To by using a simple equation.

Line to Target See *Line*.

Lining-Plane An early form of dial sight. Originally of a German design. See *Dial Sight*.

Link 11 A secure half-duplex tactical data information link (TADIL) used by NATO that can receive or transmit, but not both simultaneously, a sequential data exchange digital link. It exchanges digital information among airborne, land-based and ship-board tactical data systems. It is the primary means to exchange data such as radar tracking information beyond line of sight. Link 11 can be used on either high frequency (HF) or ultrahigh frequency (UHF). Used as part of the Recognised Air Picture Command and Control system. See *ALES* and *Link 16*.

Link 16 A jam-resistant high-speed digital data link which operates over-the-air in the L band portion (969–1206 MHz) of the UHF spectrum. Selected by the US and NATO as the main tactical data link for Theatre Missile Defence. It has been developed to meet the information exchange requirements of all tactical units, supporting the exchange of surveillance data, EW data, mission tasking, weapons assignments and control data. Using Link 16, military aircraft as well as ships, Army and Marine units can exchange their tactical picture in near real time. Link 16 also supports the exchange of text messages, imagery data and provides two channels of digital voice (2.4Kbit/s and/or 16 Kbit/s in any combination). As with Link 11, Link 16 is used as part of the Recognised Air Picture Command and Control system. See *ALES* and *Link 11*.

Link Shoot A method used during the Second World War whereby the fire of two or three troops could be concentrated onto one target.

Link-Sign Three letter call-signs adopted in 1942, that were changed on a daily basis. Within regiments and sub-units using a single call-sign the various stations used link-signs comprised of the call-sign and a numeric suffix, known as an affix. In practice, the three letter link-sign and affix on a battery net would be abbreviated to the first letter of the link-sign and the affix. See *Affix*.

Linstock During the muzzle-loading period, the Linstock was used to light the powder train, or portfire. It was customary for the slow match to be lit on the order 'Prepare for action'. It was kept burning continuously on the gun position. It was possible for it to be carried lighted on the march. The head of the Linstock, which held the slow match was often highly decorated. Linstocks were normally issued on a scale of one for every two guns. At one time they were carried by the officers. See *Portfire*.

Listening Post — A small party deployed forward of mortar locating radars with the task of telling the radar operators when and where to transmit.

Lister Twister — The nickname given to the member of the Auxiliary Territorial Service, who in the Second World War Searchlight units was responsible for hand cranking the Lister generator which powered the unit searchlight.

Littlejohn Adaptor — A conical attachment, named after its Czechoslovakian inventor, Jamecek, which when fitted to the muzzle of an anti-tank gun caused the special tungsten cored ammunition to be squeezed down as it travelled through the attachment in order to increase muzzle velocity.

Liverpool & Manchester Gunners — Regimental title of 3 RHA. Identifies the regimental recruiting area.

LIVEX — Live Firing Exercise.

LJFSOC — Land Joint Fires Staff Officers Course.

LL — See *LL Call*.

LLAD — Low Level Air Defence.

LL Call — During the First World War this call was used to denote 'all available batteries to open fire for attack of a very favourable target'. In a similar vein, during the Second World War the same call was used as a call for fire from Arty/R aircraft, requiring a concentration of batteries against a priority target. See *Arty/R*.

LLIU — Local Link Interface Unit. Part of the Phoenix UAV system. See *Phoenix*.

LLM — Launcher Loader Module. See *Multiple Launch Rocket System*.

Lloyd's Company — Battery Honour Title of 43 Battery (Lloyd's Company) RA which was granted on 18 October 1926 under authority of 20/ARTY/4544/AG6a. See *Battery Honour Titles*.

Lloyd's Legends — Nickname given by 43 Battery (Lloyd's Company) RA to ex-members of the Battery.

LLRR — Large Long Range Rocket.

LLT — Low Level Tripod. Part of the OTIS system. See *OTIS*.

LLTR — Low Level Transit Route.

LLTU — Local Link Termination Unit. Part of the Phoenix UAV system. See *Phoenix*.

LLTV — Low-Light Television.

LLW — Low Level Wind.

LM — (i) Line of Metal.
(ii) Loitering Munitions.

LMA — Launcher Manoeuvre Area. (MLRS). See *Artillery Manoeuvre Area*.

LMD — Light Mobile Digger.

LML — Lightweight Multiple Launcher. See *HVM* and *Javelin*.

LMTF — Lead Mechanised Task Force.

Lnchr — Launcher.

LNV — Limit of Night Visibility.

LO — Liaison Officer.

LOAC — Law of Armed Conflict.

Loading Bar — In coast artillery, this was a short, strong iron bar fixed just over and just in front of the point where the muzzle on the gun came when recoiling. The tackle which was used in raising the shot to the muzzle was attached to the loading bar.

LOB	Left Out of Battle
Lob	The traditional way of cooking composite rations in some detachments, as in 'lob it all in'.
Loc	Locating.
LOC	Lines of Communication.
Locating	The post Second World War term for target acquisition, survey and meteorology. After 1952 used as part of a regiment or battery designation. For example 94 Locating Regt RA. See *Observation.*
Locating Battery	A small divisional unit, which incorporated the divisional counter-bombardment staff, together with various means of locating enemy weapons, in particular, mortars. Each battery was commanded by the divisional counter-bombardment officer. See *DCBO.*
Location Report	Introduced in during the late 1960s the Location Report is used, usually by target acquisition elements, to report the location of hostile guns, mortars or rocket launchers.
Location Statement	Reported by a sub-unit to its higher headquarters and to other sub-units in accordance with standard operating procedures or on request.
Loc Def	Local Defence.
Locrep	Location Report.
Locstat	Location Statement.
Lodge Troop	With Hornby Troop, one of the two troops in Q (Sanna's Post) Headquarter Battery.
Loitering Munition	A Precision Munition which will be capable of being fired into a predetermined orbit. The munition will be capable of maintaining the orbit for a significant period of time and either of attacking a predetermined target when required, or where there is a Man-In-The-Loop, attacking a target selected whilst the munition is in flight. See *Precision Munition.*
London Air Defence Area	Commanded by Brigadier General E. B. Ashmore, LADA was established in 1917 as a direct response to Zeppelin raids on London.
London and Invicta Gunners	Regimental title of 16 Regiment RA. Identifies the Regiment's recruiting area.
Long Base	A base of sound ranging microphones (usually six) involving miles of Don8 cable and in front, an advanced observation post with remote control and line to sound ranging headquarters. Used for long range gun location and counter-battery work. All microphones were/are carefully surveyed in and in pits with camouflage covers. See *Short Base.*
Long Cecil	Name given to a gun designed and built by Mr Labram, the Chief Engineer of De Beers workshop in Kimberley South Africa in 1899. Whilst not quite up to Royal Arsenal standards, considering the tools required had to be made first it was quickly finished. Its statistics were: Breech Loading; Calibre 4.1 inch; Range 8000 yards; Firing a 28 lb shell. The gun was first fired on 19th January 1900 and fired a total of 255 rounds. The gun was used in the defence of Kimberley from the Boers.
Longdens Troop	One of the Troops in 159 (Colenso) Bty RA. See *Greys Troop* and *Nurses Troop.*
Long Observation Course	The course was designed to train instructors in Royal Artillery survey methods and either the sound-ranging or flash-spotting fields. The course was mixed with half officers and half other ranks. Successful candidates were appointed as instructors in the three subjects at the School of Artillery. The course is no longer run.

Long Range Snipers, The	Nickname for the Royal Regiment of Artillery.
Look Out Men	According to *Field Artillery Training 1914*, these were men specially detailed to assist the battery commander in watching the movements of both enemy and friendly troops and discovering new objectives.
Loose Barrel	A Loose Barrel is a homogeneous barrel encased in a jacket. The jacket extends from the breech end to part way up the barrel and has a sealing ring at the front end to keep out moisture and dirt. The barrel is prevented from rotating inside the jacket by screws or dowels. The breech ring is attached to the jacket and is tightened to hold the barrel firmly. In some heavier ordnance a removable breech bush is used to secure the barrel to the ring and jacket. The jacket gives the barrel girder strength but does not take any of the firing stresses. See *Monobloc Barrel* and *Built-up Barrel*.
Loose Liner	(i) The liner is the inner tube of a barrel, which carries the rifling on its inside face. When it becomes excessively worn, the liner may be removed and replaced with a new one without completely dismantling of the barrel. (ii) Loose liners were a feature of Second World War guns and were fitted in a jacket (full or part length) but were also used to line down a larger calibre. Liners had feathering (or similar) to stop them rotating.
LOS	Line of Sight.
LOSBR	Line Of Sight Beam Rider.
Lost	A report from a forward observer to indicate that rounds fired by a gun were not observed and that therefore the fire cannot be controlled or adjusted on the basis of observation.
Louisburg	Battery Honour Title of 53 (Louisburg) Battery RA which was granted on 3 May 1937 under authority of 20/ARTY/5023/AG6a. See *Battery Honour Titles*.
Low Angle Fire	Fire delivered at angles of elevation at or below the elevation that corresponds to the maximum range, generally below 45°. See *Lower Register*.
Lower Register	Firing at an elevation angle of less than 45°.
Lowland Gunners	Regimental title of 40 Regiment RA. Identifies the regimental recruiting area.
Low Level Wind	Correction applied before firing Honest John missiles, it was measured either by wind set or meteor theodolite at the launcher position.
LP	(i) Listening Post. (ii) Landing Point. See *LS* and *LZ*. (iii) Liquid Propellant.
LPBG	Lead Parachute Battle Group.
LP/C	Launcher Pod/Container (MLRS).
LPC	Landing Point Commander. See *HHI* and *LP*.
LPO	Launcher Position Officer.
L Pr	Line Printer. Used with the FACE system.
LR	Left Ranging. See *RR*.
LRATGW	Long Range Anti-Tank Guided Weapon.
LRD	Launch and Recovery Detachment. See *Phoenix*.
LRF	Laser Range Finder. See *LTM*.
LRF/NOD	Laser Rangefinder/Night Observation Device.
LRU	Line Replaceable Unit.
LRU BIT	Line Replaceable Unit Built in Test.
LS	(i) Land Service. (ii) Landing Site. See *LP* and *LZ*.
(LS)	A Second World War Royal Canadian Artillery anti-aircraft battery designation. A type LS battery was a light battery manning 6 x 40 mm Bofors guns. A numerical prefix indicated that the standard compliment had been

increased by the multiple of the prefix. This (2L) indicated a light anti-aircraft battery equipped with eight guns. See *Bofors (H), (L)* and *(M)*.

LSA — Land Service Ammunition.
LSC — Left Section Commander (The King's Troop RHA).
LS&GC — Long Service and Good Conduct Medal.
LSH — Light Support Helicopter.
LSIC — Low Speed Interface Controller.
LSL — Long Service List.
LSM — Last Safe Moment.
LSO — (i) Laser Safety Officer.
(ii) Launcher Safety Officer.
LS OR 6 — Land Service Operational Requirements Branch 6.
LST — (i) Launcher Status (MLRS).
(ii) Loudspeaker T-Box.
LSV — (i) Launch Support Vehicle. Part of the Phoenix UAV system. See *Phoenix*.
(ii) Logistic Support Vehicle.
LSW — Light Support Weapon. See *L86 Light Support Weapon.*
Lt — (i) Light.
(ii) Lieutenant.
LT — Loader Transporter, also written as L/T
L/T — (i) See *LT*
(ii) Line Telegraphy. (Term now obsolete.)
LtAD — Light Air Defence.
LTD — Laser Target Designator.
LTM — (i) Laser Target Marker. See *LRF*.
(ii) Light Trench Mortar (First World War). See *HTM* and *MTM.*
LTMF — Laser Telemetry Monitoring Facility (HVM AD System).
LTMO — Laser Target Marker Operator. See *FAC, FAM, Op-Ack* and *Tac Group.*
L Toc — Line Telegraphy.
LTOS — Length based Terms of Service.
LTSDT — Line To Shoot Down To. See *LTSOT.*
LTSOT — Line To Shoot Out To. See *LTSDT.*
LTU — Lines Test Unit.
LTV — Launcher Towing Vehicle. Part of the Rapier Air Defence system. See *Rapier.*
LU — Launcher Unit.
Lucas Lamp — See *Daylight Signalling Lamp*.
Lucknow Troop — Together with Desbrisay's Troop, and Wood's Troop, one of the three troops in 76 (Maude's) Battery Royal Artillery.
LUMAT — Limitations in the Use of Missiles and Ammunition in Training.
Lurk — To drop off a patrol with the intention of gaining intelligence, for example by eavesdropping on conversations. The patrol will be fully camouflaged and may be dropped from a moving vehicle. Also applies to a temporary position where digging in etc. is not carried out, but defence relies on stealth.
LV — Launch Vehicle, part of the Phoenix UAV system.
LW — (i) Limited War.
(ii) Local Warning. As afforded by Radar. See *EW.*
LWB — Long Wheel Base (Land Rover).
LWB FFR — Long Wheel Base Fitted For Radio. See *LWB.*
LWL — Lightweight Launcher. See *Lance, M752 Lance Launcher* and *Zero Length Launcher.*
LWR — Line of Weapon Release.
LWTCTG(G) — Land Warfare Collective Training Group (Germany).
LX — Left Section. (First World War.)

Lydd	Heavy artillery and land front armament range on the Kent coast.
Lyddite	High Explosive shell filling made from picric acid in its fused form. Lyddite was introduced in 1896. It was named after the testing ground at Lydd in Kent.
Lyddite Common	See *Common Lyddite.*
Lymore	A seventeenth century alternative name for a limber. See *Limber.*
Lynch Pin	The iron pin which passed through the axletree and was used to secure the truck on to the axle.
Lynx	Prior to the introduction of the WAH-64 Apache, the Lynx helicopter was employed by the army air corps to counter the threat posed by enemy armoured formations. In order to achieve this, the Lynx was armed with 8 x TOW missiles. During hostilities, it is likely that Lynx would have operated in a two or three ship formation under the direction of a section commander, possibly flying in a Gazelle. This type of formation was typically known as an Aviation Reconnaissance Patrol. In addition to its anti-tank helicopter role, the Lynx was used to provide fire support using machine guns, or to conduct troop lifts and casualty evacuations. See *Aviation Reconnaissance Patrol, Gazelle* and *TOW.*
LZ	Landing Zone. See *LP* and *LS.*

M – Emma – 1904
Monkey – 1927
Mike – 1943/1956

M1	US origin 155 mm Gun (towed) that equipped two batteries in each heavy regt from late 1943.
M10 Self-Propelled 3-inch Anti-Tank gun	See *Wolverine.*
M107	The M107 175 mm Self-Propelled gun is identical to the M110A2 except for the barrel and mounting. Armament: 1 x 175 mm M113 Gun. See *M110A2.*
M109	Widely used US origin 155 mm SP How introduced into UK service in mid 1960s.
M109A1	M109 fitted with a barrel 39 calibres long.
M109A2	The full title of the M109A2 is the M109A2 155 mm Self-Propelled Howitzer. A later model of the M109A1. Armament: 1 x 155 mm Howitzer. Ammunition: 36 rounds carried on the equipment, further supplies carried by battery ammunition vehicles. (i) HE (ii) Smoke (iii) Illuminating (iv) Minelet (v) Bomblet (vi) Rocket Assisted (vii) Nuclear Secondary Gun Armament: 1 x 12.7 mm anti-aircraft machine-gun Detachment: 8 (5 plus driver on the equipment, 2 on the ammunition vehicles) Combat weight: 23,786 kg Empty weight: 19,730 kg Length: 6.256 m Length: (gun forward): 6.612 m

Height: 3.289 m with AA gun
Width: 3.295 m
Range (Road): 390 km
Speed: 56 Kph
Engine: Model 8V71T Detroit 9.3 litre Diesel, 8-cylinder; 405 bhp at 2,300 rpm

M109A3 — M109A1 upgraded to M109A2 standard.

M110 — 203 mm ordnance taken from towed 8-inch Howitzers and fitted to the same SP carriage as 175 mm M107. Entered UK service in about 1970.

M110A1 — M110 fitted with long barrel, entered UK service in 1981 when 76 (Maude's) Heavy Battery was converted.

M110A2 — The official title of the M110A2 is the 8-inch Self-Propelled Howitzer M110A2. It consisted of a M110A1 fitted with a muzzle brake.
Armament 1 x 8-inch (203 mm) M201 Howitzer.
Ammunition: Maximum of 3 rounds carried on the equipment, with the remainder being carried by battery ammunition vehicles.
(i) HE
(ii) Rocket Assisted
(iii) Nuclear
Detachmenet: 11 (6 plus driver on the equipment, 4 on the limber vehicle). Two additional detachment members were provided for nuclear duties.
Weight in action: 28,350 kg
Length (gun forward): 10.7 m
Length (hull only): 5.72 m
Height (top of mounting (0°): 2.809 m
Height (top of barrel, travelling): 2.93 m
Width: 3.149 m
Track width: 0.457 m
Maximum road speed: 56 km/h
Range (roads): 725 km
Engine type: GMC Model 8V71T Detroit Diesel
Engine power: 405 bhp
Engine capacity: 9.3 litres
Fuel capacity: 1,137 litres
Ammunition capacity: 2 x 8-inch rounds
Main armament elevation: -2° to +65°
Main armament traverse: 60°
Apart from the barrel and mounting the M110A2 is almost identical to the M107 175 mm Self-Propelled gun. See *M107*.

M27 Warhead — Nuclear weapon used with the Honest John Rocket. See *M47 Warhead* and *M48 Warhead.*

M289 — First model of Honest John launcher.

M386 — Later model of Honest John launcher replacing M289 in about 1963.

M31 — Original designation of Honest John rocket.

M40 — US origin 155 mm Gun SP that equipped two batteries in 369 Hy Regt TA during the 1950s. It was an open top casemate configuration designated Royal Artillery service as the 155 mm SP, M40.
Weight: 36.3 tonnes
Length: 9.1 m
Width: 3.15 m
Height: 2.7 m
Detachment: 8 (Number 1, driver, 6 man gun detachment.)
Armour: 12 mm
Main armament: 155 mm M2 gun

Ammunition: 20 rounds
Engine: Wright (Continental) R975 EC2 developing 340 hp
Operational range: 170 km
Road Speed: 38 km/h
Off-Road Speed: 23 km/h

M44 — US origin 155 mm How SP that equipped two regiments in BAOR from the mid-1950s until it was replaced by Abbot in the mid-1960s. It was an open top casemate configuration. Uniquely UK assigned UK designations to this US equipment – 'Howitzer 155mm L8A1 on Mounting Howitzer 155 mm L4A1'.

M47 Warhead — Nuclear weapon used with the Honest John Rocket. See *M27 Warhead* and *M48 Warhead.*

M48 Warhead — Nuclear weapon used with the Honest John Rocket. See *M27 Warhead* and *M47 Warhead.*

M422 Shell — 203 mm Nuclear shell employing the W33 nuclear weapon. See *M424 HES Shell.*

M424 HES Shell — A high explosive spotting shell which was ballistically matched to the M422 shell, and used for live firing training. See *M422 Shell.*

M454 shell — 155 mm nuclear shell employing the W48 nuclear weapon.

M50 — Later model of Honest John rocket. See *Honest John.*

M688 Lance Loader Transporter — Adapted from the M113 series of armoured personnel carrier the M688 Lance Loader Transporter was capable of carrying two mated missiles or two main missile assemblies, it was fitted with an integral crane with an operational lift capacity of 1909 kg. See *Lance* and *M752 Lance Launcher.*

M7 — See *Priest.*

M752 Lance Launcher — Adapted from the M113 series of armoured personnel carriers the M752 Lance Launcher proved to be a popular and reliable vehicle. It was both easy to drive and maintain. The two-man detachment, consisting of a driver and a commander had a small compartment in the front left of the vehicle. When in action the cab could be folded flat to protect the inside from the blast generated when the missile was fired. The rest of the vehicle was open and the rear wall consisted of a door that folded down to form a ramp to permit easy access. Each M752 Lance Launcher was commanded by a lieutenant with a sergeant as second in command. There was a detachment of from 8–10. The detachment manned the radio, deployed the launcher and provided local defence. Launchers could be deployed with or without a missile and would move independently to their surveyed location and hide up, deploying at the last possible minute to fire the missile at the required time. Once fired the launcher would 'scoot' to its next location, resupply point or hide area. See *Lance.*

m — Metres.

M — (i) Militia.
(ii) Artillery Code used during the First World War meaning 'mostly'. As in mostly grouped from a mean point of impact.

(M) — (i) Mixed. See *ATS.*
(ii) Mortar. Used as part of a unit title.
(iii) A Second World War Royal Canadian Artillery anti-aircraft battery designation. A type M battery was a medium battery manning 4.3-inch guns. A numerical prefix indicated that the standard compliment had been increased by the multiple of the prefix. This (2M) indicated

	a medium anti-aircraft battery equipped with eight guns. See *(H)*, *(L)* and *(LS)*.
M Vehicle	See *Monkey Truck*.
MA	(i) Military Analysis. (ii) Military Assistant. (iii) Mountain Artillery.
MAA	Medium Anti-Aircraft.
MAAD	Manual of Anti-Aircraft Defence. Generally followed by the relevant volume and pamphlet number.
MAC	Minor Access Cell, Part of the ADCIS and BATES systems. See *ADCIS* and *BATES*.
MACA	Military Aid to the Civil Authority.
Machine Fuze Setter	See *MFS* and *MFS11*.
Machine Fuze Setter No. 11	See *MFS* and *MFS11*.
MacIlwaine Cup	Gunner rugby trophy instituted by a Gunner Officer Herbert MacIlwaine whilst stationed at Larkhill in 1926. The cup is competed for annually.
Madras Day	Battery day of M (Headquarters) Battery 3 RHA celebrated each year on 23 January.
Madras Troop	One of two Troops in M (Headquarters) Battery 3 RHA, Madras Troop is the command troop of the Battery, it is tasked with running the Fire Direction Centre and the Fire Support Coordination Centre. See *Java Troop*.
MAF	Manual Acquisition Facility.
Magazine	Building or buildings with passages leading thereto, in which powder in bulk (historically), filled cartridges, or shells are stored.
Magazine Store	In nineteenth century coast artillery a chamber within a magazine in which the hides, wadmiltilts and spare magazine clothing may be kept. See *Magazine* and *Wadmiltilts*.
Magslip	An electrical means of transmitting information from the predictor to the dials of one or more guns.
Mag to Grid	A slang term meaning to get rid of, or throw away. The term is derived from map reading, where it is used in connection with calculating the declination to north.
Maharajpore	Battery Honour Title of 54 (Maharajpore) Battery RA which was granted on 3 May 1937 under authority of 20/ARTY/5023/AG6a. Battery is currently in suspended animation. See *Battery Honour Titles*.
Main Headquarters	The Main element of a Headquarters at any level. The actual operating headquarters with current authority and most of the headquarters staff. The term was introduced into artillery when commanding officers took a Tac HQ out of regimental headquarters. Main HQ normally deployed in the vicinity of the guns and was traditionally run by the adjutant. The term was replaced by the US term FDC in the 1970s. See *Alternate Headquarters, Battery Headquarters, FDC, Rear Headquarters, Regimental Headquarters, Step-Up* and *Tactical Headquarters*.
Main Position	The position from which a regiment/battery fires the major fireplans or tasks of a battle. See *Alternative Position, Roving Position* and *Temporary Position*.
Main Repair Group	The main element of a REME deployed formation workshop.
Mains Troop	One of the Troops in O/Headquarters Battery 'The Rocket Troop' RHA. See *Bogues Troop*.
Maint	Maintenance.
Maiwand	Battery Honour Title of 145 (Maiwand) Battery RA which was granted on 16 August 1928 under authority of 20/ARTY/4544/AG6a. See *Battery Honour Titles*.
Maiwand Day	Battery day of 145 (Maiwand) Commando Light Battery RA (currently in suspended animation). Celebrated on 27 July.

Maj Major.

Major Subordinate Commander NATO term for Regional Commanders, e.g. those of AFNORTH, AFCENT and AFSOUTH.

Make Toast Slang term used by members of the Junior Leaders Regiment RA in place of Take Post. See *Take Post.*

Mallet's Mortar Robert Mallet, a civil engineer, designed a 36-inch mortar weighing 46 tones and capable of throwing a shell weighing between 21 and 26 cwts to a range of 2759 yards. Two prototypes were developed in 1857 for potential use in the Crimean War, but neither saw service. One example can be seen at Fort Nelson in Portsmouth and the other is displayed outside Woolwich Barracks.

MAMBA Mobile Artillery Monitoring Battlefield Radar. An air portable, small and accurate artillery locating system, it was developed by Ericsson under the name ARTHUR and aquired by the Royal Artillery whilst COBRA was being developed. MAMBA can locate enemy artillery positions, including howitzers, multiple rocket launchers and mortars. It achieves this by scanning the horizon for enemy projectiles and uses their trajectories to locate the enemy battery. It can also operate as a fire control system and can locate the 'splash'of ally artillery. Currently deployed by 5 Regt RA, the radar is mounted on Alvis Haggulunds BV 206 tracked vehicle.
Detachment: 8
Detection Range: 30 kilometres
Time in to Action: 5 minutes
Accuracy: Below 15 kilometres 50 circular error probable
15 to 20 kilometres 100 circular error probable
Above 20 kilometres 0.35% of range to target
Ability: Locate a maximum of 8 targets simultaneously
Target Capacity: 100 per minute
See *COBRA.*

Management of Artillery Resources and Tactical Information System A computerised tool being developed for use by the CRA and his staff. See *CRA.*

Man In The Loop A system which requires human intervention at some point and is therefore not fully automatic.

Manky Cats Nickname of P Battery (The Dragon Troop) RA.

Manorbier Artillery Air Defence Range near Tenby in Wales.

Man-pack A method of carrying equipment or supplies on a man's back. See *Animal Pack* and *Everest Carrier.*

MANPADS Man Portable Air Defence Systems.

Man-Portable Surveillance and Target Acquisition Radar See *MSTAR*

Mansergh Memorial Award Awarded by the Royal Artillery Association for outstanding acts of bravery not otherwise recognised or special achievement by individuals. The award was originally the Master Gunner's award.

Mansergh Troop One of the Troops in 40 Wardrop Bty Junior Leaders Regiment RA. See *Hornby Troop, Nicholson Troop* and *Park Troop.*

Mantlet A protective curtain of woven rope hung inside an embrasure of a fortification or coast artillery battery to protect the gun detachment. It was designed to prevent rivet heads and other matter flying into the casemate if the exterior was struck. Mantlets were made in a variety of shapes to suit different forms of shield. They were soaked

	in a solution of chloride of calcium to prevent their being ignited by the flash of the gun when firing. The portions of the Mantlet nearest the gun muzzle were hung on a bar so that they could be pulled close to the gun at any degree of training. They were used for guns of 10-inch calibre and upwards. See *Mantlet Bar.*
Mantlet Bar	An iron bar, fixed to the shield across the embrasure from which the mantlet was hung. See *Mantlet*.
Manual of Anti-Aircraft Defence	A series of instructional pamphlets issued prior to and during the Second World War which defined the air defence role and the necessary procedures to be adopted to counter the air threat.
Map Bearing	A bearing measured from the map, or obtained by computation the bearing. It can be used in relation to any specified point on the trajectory. In order to avoid confusion, it is referred to as either, the 'Bearing to the Target', or if another point is being considered, it is referred to as the 'Bearing to ...'. See *Bearing*.
Mapco	Standard low level numeric code for grid references from the Second World War until replaced by Batco in 1980s.
Map data	The bearing and distance from guns to target to which no corrections for non-standard conditions have been applied.
Mapex	Map Exercise.
Map Line	See *Line*.
Map Range	The horizontal distance from the gun to a point vertically above or below the target. When obtained by shooting, it is referred to as the 'Reduced Range'.
Map Shooting	See *Predicted fire.*
MAPS	Manual Artillery Plotting System. (Royal Canadian Artillery.)
Mapx	Map Exercise.
Maritime Regt RA	The Maritime Regt RA was was formed in Feb 1942, to take over the role of providing gun detachments on DEMS. Eventually five Maritime Regts RA were formed (being 1, 3, 4, 5 and 6 Maritime RA). They manned both AA (Bofors, oerlikons and rockets) and low angle armaments (6-inch, 4.7-inch, 3-inch and 12-pdr) for use against surface targets. Their greatest strength was in August 1944 with a figure of 14,500 all ranks.
Maritimer	Nickname by which members of the Maritime Regiment Royal Artillery were referred to, particularly by themselves.
Mark	(i) A call for fire on a specified location to orient the observer or to indicate targets. (ii) In naval gunfire support, a report made by the forward observer when firing illumination to indicate the instant of optimum light on the target. (Royal Canadian Artillery.)
Marking Fire	Fire used for the purpose of identification.
Martinique 1809	Battery Honour Title of 13 (Martinique 1809) Headquarters Battery RA which was granted on 13 November 1934 under authority of 20/ARTY/4984/AG6a. See *Battery Honour Titles.*
Martinique Troop	Together with Aden Troop, Gazala Troop and Hook Troop, one of the four troops in 74 Battery (The Battle Axe Company) Royal Artillery.
Martin's Liquid Iron Shell	See *Martin's Shell.*
Martin's Shell	This shell was designed by an employee of the Royal Laboratory at Woolwich in 1855. Consisting of a hollow spherical shell lined with a mixture of loam and cow-hair for insulation into which was poured molten iron which

had been heated to this state in an Anderson's Cupola. Then, it was used as a replacement for 'red hot shot'. It could not however, be used in RML guns and was declared obsolete in 1869. See *Anderson's Cupola*.

MARTIS — Management of Artillery Resources and Tactical Information System.

Master Driver Royal Artillery — A Warrant Officer Class 1 based at Bovington, the Master Driver RA is responsible for all driving policy within the Regiment.

Master-General of the Ordnance — Usually held by a serving General, the Master-General of the Ordnance was responsible for the British Artillery and following its formation in 1716, the Royal Artillery. The Master General was also responsible for all engineers, fortifications, military supplies, etc. The position was frequently a cabinet level one, especially during the late-18th and early-19th centuries. The Master General of the Ordnance was the head of the Board of Ordnance. Despite the fact that the Board of Ordnance was abolished in 1855, the position of Master-General of the Ordnance still exists as the Fourth Military Member of the Army Board, usually in the rank of lieutenant-general, with responsibilities for overseeing procurement and research and development. The Master-General of the Ordnance is currently the head of Land Systems procurement in MOD (PE). See *Board of Ordnance* and *Ordnance Board*.

Master Gunner — A title within the Royal Artillery with a number of meanings, often causing confusion to outsiders. The rank has existed since about 1540. At that time Master Gunners were employed, under the Master Gunner of England, to take charge of the guns, ammunition and stores in certain forts in England. They did not become members of the Royal Artillery until some time after 1815. After this date they can be found in the lists of the invalid battalions, and later, those of the coast brigade.

(i) In coast artillery, the Master Gunner was a warrant officer, whose duty it was to take charge of a sub-district of coast artillery under the supervision of a district officer. He was responsible for maintaining and accounting for coast defence and anti-aircraft stores until 1956, when these branches of the regiment were abolished.

(ii) The current Warrant Officer Class 1 (Master Gunner) is a senior instructor in gunnery, employed at the Royal School of Artillery where the rank replaced those of Warrant Officer Class 1 (Sergeant-Major Instructor in Gunnery). The rank also replaced the Warrant Officer Class 1 (Experimental Sergeant-Major) at the former Experimental Establishment. The rank is equivalent to a Regimental Sergeant-Major within a regiment. See *Invalids* and *Master Gunner St James's Park*.

Master Gunner Royal School of Artillery — The Senior WO1 (MG) at RSA Larkhill. See *Master Gunner*.

Master Gunner St James's Park — The Master Gunner St James's Park is the head of the regiment in all regimental matters and the channel of communication between the regiment and the captain general. The appointment was instituted in 1678 and was originally known as the Master Gunner of Whitehall & St

James's Park. The earlier Master Gunners were responsible for the artillery defence of Whitehall Palace and the Palace of Westminster. The appointment of Master Gunner St James's Park is held by a distinguished Royal Artillery Officer selected by the captain general on the advice of the colonels commandant and has honorary status over all Commonwealth Artilleries. The Master Gunner St James's Park, is known generally as 'The Master Gunner'. This position should not be confused with the rank of WO1 (Master Gunner). A list of Master Gunners Whitehall and St James's Park is given in Appendix 3. See *Master Gunner.*

Master Stitch — Colloquial title by which the Master Saddler is known within the RHA.

Massey's Troop — The name given to 5 (Gibraltar 1779–1783) Battery RA Observation Post Troop. It commemorates the bravery shown by Captain Massey and the Battery on 27th May 1918 when the Battery was overrun. The Battery fought hand to hand before destroying the dial sights, rendering the guns useless to the enemy. Only five members of the Battery escaped alive. Captain J. H. Massey RFA was awarded both the Military Cross and the *Croix de Guerre* posthumously as a result of his gallant acts in defence of the gun position. In addition, the French Government, owing to the extreme bravery and courage its soldiers and officers had displayed awarded 5 Battery RFA the highest category of *Croix de Guerre,* the *Palme en Bronze,* the Battery continues to wear this unique decoration today with immense pride.

Mat — Matross.

Matador — See *AEC Matador.*

MATC — Mountain Artillery Training Centre.

Matross — First appearing on the establishment in 1639. A Matross was a Gunner's Assistant. The name is said to come from the German *matrossen* meaning sailors owing to the tasks allotted them in action, (for example, traversing, loading, firing, sponging, manning dragropes, etc.), being deemed to be sailors' work. They were less highly trained technically than gunners. Armed with muskets and bayonets, their duties included guarding the guns and wagons on the march, and assisting when breakdowns occurred. Later they also took over from the fusiliers the job of preventing the drivers running away when the shooting started (until 1793 drivers were civilians). The rank of matross was abolished in 1783 and all serving matrosses being elevated to the rank of gunner.

MATS — Model Aircraft Target System.

Maude's — Battery Honour Title of 76 (Maude's) Battery RA which was granted on 24 January 1951 under authority of 20/ARTY/6271/AG6a. In 1933 an unofficial battery custom existed, whereby Indian motor drivers of the unit were trained in gun drill, so that they could take their place beside the British ranks manning the guns in the battery. This was unusual, as since the mutiny in 1857, only the Mountain Artillery and Frontier Garrison Artillery had Indian gunners. Indeed, it had not been customary to permit Indian drivers to drive gun teams or motorised gun towers. See *Battery Honour Titles.*

Maude's Day — Battery day of 76 (Maude's) Battery RA held on 25 September.

Martinique Troop — One of 3 Troops in 74 Battery (The Battleaxe Company) RA.

MAVD	MLRS Aim Verification Device.
MAW	Medium (Range) Anti-tank Weapon.
Maxim Nordenfeldt Powder	American Guncotton powder gelatinised with Ethyl Acetate (an explosive).
MB	Mountain Battery. See *PB.*
MBP	Mortar Base Plate.
MBSGD	Multi-Barrel Smoke Grenade Dischargers.
MBT	Main Battle Tank.
MC	(i) Mission Controller. See *Phoenix.* (ii) Motorcycle.
MCB	Main Circuit Breaker.
MCCL	Multi-Channel Command Link. Part of the Javelin air defence missile system. See *Javelin.*
MCIU	Meteorology Computer Interface Unit.
MCLOS	Manual Command to Line of Sight. The guidance system used with Blowpipe. See *Blowpipe.*
McNaughton Graph	Devised by General McNaughton of the Royal Canadian Artillery in 1941, this graph was employed as a simple alternative to the then current method of conducting airburst ranging. So impressed with this system was the Commander-in-Chief Home Forces, General Sir Alan Brooke (Later Field Marshal Sir Alanbrooke, Master Gunner Saint James's Park) that he immediately took steps to have this method of airburst ranging introduced into the Royal Artillery.
MCPA	Meteorology Command Post Area.
MCPV	Meteorology Command Post Vehicle. Part of the BMETS system.
MCS	Modular Charge System used with the AS90 with the 52 calibre barrel. See *AS90.*
MCV	Modified Carrier Vehicle. Part of the COBRA system. See *COBRA.*
md	Mean Deviation.
MD	(i) Modified Cordite. (ii) Mean Detonation. (iii) Master Driver. A WO1 appointment. See *Warrant Officer Class 1.*
MDA	Muzzle Danger Area.
MDM	Medium artillery, eg. 155 mm guns. (Royal Australian Artillery.)
MDP	Meteorological Datum Plane.
MDS	Main Dressing Station.
MDT	Modified Cordite of a Tubular construction (a propellant).
MDU	Mine Distribution Unit. Part of the MLRS system. See *Multiple Launch Rocket System.*
ME	(i) Main Effort. (ii) Military Engineering.
Meaconing	One of the methods by which an enemy may deny the use of the Global Positioning System to units in the field. Meaconing consists of the re-broadcast of genuine GPS signals (usually at a stronger strength than the satellite signal) in order to cause GPS Denial and generate inaccurate survey. See *GPS Denial.*
Mean Point of Burst	The point whose coordinates are the arithmetic average or mean of the coordinates of the separate point of burst of a finite number of projectiles fired or released at the same aiming point under a given set of conditions. See *Mean Point of Impact.*
Mean Point of Impact	The point whose coordinates are the arithmetic average or mean of the coordinates of the separate point of impact of

	a finite number of projectiles fired or released at the same aiming point under a given set of conditions. See *Mean Point of Burst*.
Mechanical Time Fuze	A fuze which operates by means of a clockwork mechanism, and is designed to cause the shell to function before impact.
Mechanised Howitzer	Name given to a type of howitzer used in Bail (or Elephant) Batteries during the 1890s. The name referred to the mechanism of the howitzer itself, and did not refer, as many suppose, to the method of traction. See *Bail Battery*.
Med	Medium.
Medium Battery Linear Target	Artillery Staff Duties (Field Branch) 1954 defined a Medium Battery Linear Target as being fired by one medium battery or two batteries of smaller calibre and being 400 yards in length. See *Concentration, Field Battery Linear Target, Linear* and *Heavy Battery Linear Target*.
Medium Range Unmanned Airborne Surveillance and Target Acquisition System	A proposed rotary wing UAV that did not work and was cancelled before development was completed. See *UAV*.
Medium Stressed Platform	Used for the carriage and airdrop of tactical loads of heavy equipment such as the Pinzgauer Gun Towing Vehicle and the L118 Light Gun. It is possible to use the Medium Stressed Platform to airdrop items of equipment upto a maximum weight of 8,182 kg (18,000 lb).
Meiktila	Battery Honour Title of 148 (Alam Hamza) Commando Forward Observation Battery RA which was granted on 29 July 1954 under authority of 20/ARTY/6271/AG6a. See *Battery Honour Titles*.
Mekometer	A late-19th, early-20th century two man range-finding instrument.
MEL	Main Events List.
MEM	Micro Electro Mechanical (Technology) See *MEMSAD*.
Memoranda of Examination	This provided a record of wear measurements, repairs and modifications, maintenance and rounds fired by the barrel as 'Equivalent Full Charge'. The Memorandum of Examination was replaced by the *Gun History Book* in about 1949. See also *EFC* and *Gun History Book*.
MEMSAD	Micro Electro-Mechanical Safety and Arm Device.
Mercer Troop	One of the Troops in 2 Baker Bty Junior Leaders Regiment RA. See *Dickson Troop, Milne Troop* and *Stirling Troop*.
Mercer's Day	18 June, celebrated as the Battery Day of G Parachute Battery (Mercer's Troop) RHA. Also known as Waterloo Day.
Mercer's Troop	Battery Honour Title of G Parachute Battery (Mercer's Troop) which was granted on 18 October 1926 under authority of 20/ARTY/4544/AG6a. See *Battery Honour Titles*.
MESA	Middle East School of Artillery (Almaza, Heliopolis on the outskirts of Cairo, Egypt); now defunct.
ME School of AA and CA	Middle East School of Anti-Aircraft and Coast Artillery.
Met/met	(i) Meteorological. (ii) Meteorologist. (iii) Meteorology.
Met.BM	Ballistic Meteorological Message.
Met.BWR	Ballistic Wind Report.
Met.CDR	Chemical Downwind Report.
Met CM	Meteorological Computer. (Computer Met Message).
Met.EDR	Effective Downwind Report.

Meteorological Data — This is essential for conducting predicted fire missions as it enables corrections to be made for the non-standard wind speed, wind direction and temperature. Command posts combine meteorological data with other data for non-standard conditions to produce the correction of the moment. Data was distributed to command posts during the Second World War by Meteor Telegram and now by way of the Met Message.

Meteorological Datum Plane — The MDP is comprised of the temperature, pressure, humidity, wind speed and wind direction at ground level.

Meteorology — The science of the properties and conditions of the atmosphere. Meteorology is very important to ballistics and field branch gunnery as the conditions of the atmosphere have a considerable effect on the flight of projectiles.

Meteor Telegram — Now known as a 'Met Message'. The Meteor Telegram gave air pressure, wind speed and direction for times of flight of 5, 10, 20, 30, 40 and 50 seconds. See *Meteorological Data.*

Meteorology Troop — Comprised of the artillery surveyors who provide the meteorology data to the guns via the command post.

METFP — MET Firing Point Low Level.

Method A — See *Murder.*

Method B — Developed by the artillery of the 2nd New Zealand Division during the Second World War. This type of fire mission was possibly not widely adopted at regimental level but eventually became the basis of the rumpus fire mission. In Method B a regimental concentration of rectangular shape with a battery frontage (of for example 200 yards) was used against small company localities. The batteries' tasks were echeloned along an axis 100 yards apart. If batteries were ordered to fire more than one round they searched an area 50 yards by 25 yards. See *Rumpus* and *Search.*

Method R — See *Method B* and *Rumpus.*

Met Message — See *Meteor Telegram* and *Meteorological Data.*

Met TA — MET Target Area Low Level.

Met.TM — Temporary Mobile Message.

Met Tp — Meteorology Troop.

MEZ — Missile Engagement Zone.

MFC — Mortar Fire Controller.

MFDC — (i) Mortar Fire Direction Computer.
(ii) Missile Fire Direction Centre, 1980s lance regiment.

MFPS — Mobile Field Photo Section. 1950s.

MFS — (i) Machine Fuze Setting. Usually followed by the mark number, for example the MFS11, also known as the Machine Fuze Setter No. 11.
(ii) Mechanical Fuze Setter. Used in Coast Artillery units from the Second World War onwards.

MFS11 — The automatic fuze setter used with the static 3.7-inch anti-aircraft gun. A round would be placed in the rocking tray, which would then convey it to the fuze setter, withdraw it after the fuze had been set, swing it into line with the breech and then ram the round home. The tray would then swing clear as the breech closed and the gun would be fired automatically. All the loaders had to do was keep the rocking tray supplied.

MFSRA — Manual of Field Service Royal Artillery.

MG — (i) Master Gunner.
(ii) Mustering Gunners.

MGM-5 — See *Corporal.*

MGM-52 — See *Lance.*

MGO	Master General of the Ordnance.
MGR-1	See *Honest John*.
MGRA	Major General Royal Artillery.
MGRSA	Master Gunner Royal School of Artillery. See *Master Gunner*.
MI	Medical Inspection.
Mi2h	Miles in two hours. The speed of a convoy expressed in terms of the distance to be covered in two hours.
MICA	MLRS Interactive Computer Aid.
MICV	Mechanised Infantry Combat Vehicle.
Middleton's Company	Battery Honour Title of 160 Battery (Middleton's Company) RA which was granted on 16 August 1928 under authority of 20/ARTY/4544/AG6a. Battery is currently in suspended animation. See *Battery Honour Titles.*
Midge	AN/USD 501, CL89 Drone, UAV that flew a programmed course, 1970s–90s.
MIF	Missile in Flight.
Mighty D	Nickname of D Battery RHA. See *Shiny D.*
Mike Target	Quick concentration by all guns of one regiment onto one target.
Mike Truck	Named after its vehicle Tac Sign. See *Monkey Truck* and *Tac Sign.*
Mike Vehicle	Named after its vehicle Tac Sign. See *Monkey Truck* and *Tac Sign.*
Military Assistant	The personal staff officer a very senior officer.
Military Training Qualification	These are training qualifications for members of the University Officer Training Corps. There are three levels of qualifications which are referred to as MTQ1, MTQ2 and MTQ3.
Military Vigilance	The lowest rung in NATO's non-emergency alert state hierarchy. See *General Alert* and *Simple Alert.*
Militia Artillery	Part of the Auxiliary Artillery of longstanding and under control of Lords Lieutenant of countries, came under War Office control in 1871 and became part of the Special Reserve in 1907.
Millimetre Gun	The Vickers 75 mm gun – actually a howitzer – firing a 12½ lb shell and an 18 lb double shell. It gained popularity with the West African Frontier Force due to its power in dealing with stockades and in jungle fighting. It was less effective than the 10-pdr mountain gun and was unsuited to mountain work. It was however, brought into service as the 2.95-inch QF as a movable armament for some coaling stations. It was the first pack equipment to be fitted with a buffer, although this was to eliminate strain on the carriage and not to reduce recoil.
Mills Grenade	See *No 36 Grenade.*
Milne Troop	One of the Troops in 2 Baker Bty Junior Leaders Regiment RA. See *Dickson Troop, Mercer Troop* and *Stirling Troop.*
Mils	There are 6400 mils in a circle, 6400 is north, 1600 is East, 3200 is South and 4800 is West. There are 17.77 recurring mils in a degree. One mil equates to one metre at 1000 metres from the observer. Anything under 1000 mils is referred to in the following form: for example, 340 mils will be expressed as three forty mils. Bearings over 1000 are expressed in the following way, 3200 mils being referred to as three, two hundred mils. To add confusion the Russian system uses a circle of 6000 mils.
Minden	(i) Battery Honour Title of 12 (Minden) Battery RA which was granted on 18 October 1926 under authority of 20/ARTY/4544/AG6a. See *Battery Honour Titles.*

	(ii) Battery Honour Title of 32 (Minden) Battery RA which was granted on 18 October 1926 under authority of 20/ARTY/4544/AG6a. See *Battery Honour Titles.*
Minden Day	Battery day celebrated by both 12 (Minden) and 32 (Minden) Btys.
Ministry of Defence (Procurement Executive)	The organisation responsible for equipment acquisition from the 1960s until the 1990s.
MIS	Management Information System.
Miscellaneous Target	Harassing Fire targets engaged by Royal Canadian Artillery during the Second World War. Such targets were listed as 'ML Targets' and numbered consecutively across the entire corps front. Regiments fired at scale 1 onto each group of targets using a Time on Target procedure. See *Harassing Fire, Scale* and *Time on Target.*
Misfire	(i) Failure to fire or explode properly. (ii) The failure of a primer or of the propelling charge of a round to function, wholly or in part.
MITL	Man In The Loop.
MITRA	Methods of Instruction Team Royal Artillery.
MIU	MLRS Interface Unit. (Part of the BATES system).
Mixed	A designation added to the title of an anti-aircraft regiment containing a proportion of women from the Auxiliary Territorial Service. See *ATS.*
Mixed Bullets	See *Shrapnel.*
Mixed Pack Brigade	During the 1920s Mixed Pack Brigades comprised one British Pack Battery and two Indian Pack Batteries. At this period, the title Brigade was used to denote what later became known as a Regiment.
MK1	Military Knowledge 1.
MKRS	Markers.
MLC	Military Load Classification.
MLRS	Multiple Launch Rocket System.
MLRSDC	Multiple Launch Rocket System Detachment Commander.
ML Section	Mortar Location Section. (Royal Canadian Artillery.)
ML Target	Miscellaneous Target. (Royal Canadian Artillery.)
MM	Artillery Code used during the First World War meaning 'Trench Mortar'.
MMA	Missile Main Assembly. Part of the lance missile. See *Lance.*
MMI	Man Machine Interface.
MMLC	Medium Mobility Load Class (DROPS).
MMW	Mean Measured Wear.
MN	See *Maxim Nordenfeldt Powder.*
MNC	(i) Major NATO Commander. (ii) Multi-National Commander.
MND(C)	Multi-National Division (Central).
MND(N)	Multi-National Division (North).
MND(SE)	Multi-National Division (South-East).
MND(SW)	Multi-National Division (South-West).
MN Powder	Maxim Nordenfeldt Powder.
MNT	Mono Nitro Toluene (Explosive).
MOBAT	Mobile Battalion Anti-Tank Gun. See *BAT* and *WOMBAT.*
Mob Stores	Mobilisation Stores.
MOC	Methods Of Control.
MOD90	Military Identification Card.
MODACS	Ministry of Defence Accountable Controlled Stores. See *WOCS.*
Model Number	This comprises a series of letters and figures which indicate the model and modifications. An example would be L1A1 B4. This would indicate the following: L1 – Land Service Model 1. L is always used, except when

X is used to distinguish developmental models. The number refers directly to the basic name it follows and is only changed when either a modification changes the role of the item or a different major component is fitted.
A1 – The number advances when a change in design or an important alteration is made, which is not significant enough to warrant a change to the L number. They are used to qualify the L number only by identifying modified items. A numbers are replaced by E numbers when referring to developmental models with the designation X.
B4 – This number is used to indicate changes in either the material used or the method of manufacture. They are advanced in the same way as A number.
See *Service Designation*.

Modified Cordite — A form of cordite which contained less Nitro-Glycerine than ordinary cordite. This resulted in less erosion to the rifling owing to the lower temperatures generated (a propellant).

Modified on Call — Fire plan that may be varied by the subordinated infantry commander by direct order to the artillery OP (First World War).

MoD(PE) — Ministry of Defence (Procurement Executive).

Modular Net Interface Equipment — The portable Net Interface Equipment to the radio set in the BATES system. See *BATES, NIE* and *SANIE.*

Molar — Radio appointment title. This title was used army-wide by AQ staff officer, however, in the Royal Artillery the following officers used the title. At HQRA level by the deputy assistant adjutant & quartermaster general. At a regimental headquarters level by the quartermaster. At battery level by the battery captain.
See *Appointment Titles*.

MOLO — Military Observer Liaison Officer.

Moncrieff Carriage — A disappearing counterweight carriage invented by Colonel Moncrieff. See *Counterweight Carriage*.

Moncrieff Pit — A concrete pit into which was fitted a disappearing carriage developed by Colonel Moncrieff. See *Disappearing Gun, Counterweight Carriage, Hydro-pneumatic Mounting, Moncrieff System* and *Moncrieff Carriage.*

Moncrieff System — Colonel Moncrieff's system of mounting guns on the disappearing principle in dispersed pits, protected from direct fire and well concealed from observation. See *Disappearing Gun, Counterweight Carriage, Hydro-pneumatic Mounting, Moncrieff Pit* and *Moncrieff Carriage.*

Mongs — Slang term standing for 'Men Of No Gunnery Skills'.

MONIE — Modular Net Interface Equipment. See *BATES, NIE* and *SANIE.*

Monkey Truck — Nickname given during the Second World War to signals trucks. There were several M trucks in a battery, all fitted for line laying. After the Seond World War, with the introduction of the Larkspur Radio system and due to the shorter range of the VHF sets compared to the previous HF sets, M trucks were frequently used in the Rebroadcast role. Batteries retained a line laying vehicle into the 1970s. Normally found at FDC/Brigade level. See *FDC, George Truck* and *Rebro.*

Monobloc Barrel — A simple homogeneous barrel which has no liner and no jacket. The breech ring is fitted directly to the barrel. See *Built-up Barrel* and *Loose Barrel.*

Monster — The Divisional Task Table. This table was known as the Monster to differentiate from the AB 545 (Tiddler). It was used to allot tasks to units. Tactical information was shown at the top, so that adjutants did not have to copy the information from the divisional RA operation order. Allotted tasks were listed in a similar manner to that employed with the AB 545. Units not under command that were firing in the programme were not named. Each task, whether it was the same target with different timings and treatment or a different target entirely would be given a separate serial. An asterisk in the remarks column was used to denote superimposed artillery. See *Tiddler*.

MOR — Malay Other Ranks. See *BOR* and *IOR*.

Morning Prayers — Nickname for Morning Briefing for Officers.

Morse Taper — Fitting into a tapered funnel, this finely machined tapered spigot ensures a tight fit.

Mortar — Prior to the First World War mortars were large calibre pieces of ordnance firing a heavy shell at high angles of elevation (from 15 to 50 degrees). During the 1860s, the British Armed Forces used 8-, 10- and 13-inch iron mortars and Coehorn and Royal mortars made of brass. The 13-inch land service mortar had a range of 2900 yards using a charge of 9 lbs. The bursting charge used in the 13-inch shell was 10 lbs 15 ozs. Some rifled mortars, using the Palliser system of rifling, were tested in 1879 but the design was abandoned. See *Bomb Vessel* and *Trench Mortar*.

Mortar Battery — In fortifications and siege operations this was a casemated position used for concealing mortars from return fire.

Mortar Fire Controller — A non-Royal Artillery soldier trained to direct his/her units mortar fire. The Mortar Fire Controller undertakes a role similar to a forward observation officer in the Royal Artillery. See *Forward Observation Officer*.

Mortar Location Section — A Royal Canadian Artillery unit which corresponded with the Counter Bombardment units in the Royal Artillery. (Second Wolrd War.)

Mortar Platform — Similar to those used for guns, but without a slope. A 13-inch mortar platform was 12 feet square. See *Dwarf platform, Gun Platform, New Pattern Traversing Platform, Siege Platform* and *Traversing Platform*.

Mortrep — Hostile mortar report.

Most Consistent Charge — The charge which at the selected range, produced the smallest probable error for range.

Mostly — A generalised observation of the fall of shot of a group of rounds, being expressed as 'mostly left', 'mostly right', 'mostly long' or 'mostly short'.

Mother — Nickname originally given to the first 9.2-inch howitzer which entered service in 1914. Its first saw service at Neuve Chapelle. Used as the inspiration for the Royal Artillery Monument at Hyde Park Corner, the actual howitzer is now on display at the Imperial War Museum, London. During the First World War, the title Mother was eventually used colloquially to describe all 9.2-inch howitzers.

MOU — Memorandum of Understanding.

Mountain Artillery, British — Whilst most mountain artillery was manned by Indian personnel, there were, prior to 1881, two British mountain batteries comprising two garrison companies of the Royal Artillery who manned, on a temporary basis, the equipment held by the mountain trains. However, Regimental Order 13 of 1881 specified that six garrison companies of the Royal Artillery were to be permanently armed as mountain batteries, companies fulfilling this role were distinguished by the addition of the word 'Mountain' after their battery number. From 1889, ten garrison companies

	of Royal Artillery were converted permanently to mountain artillery, these batteries being numbered from one to ten. It was from this date that British mountain artillery batteries were constituted as a separate branch of the regiment. The gunner establishment of British mountain batteries consisted of Royal Artillery personnel, whilst the driver establishment was made up of Indian personnel. See *Mountain Train*.
Mountain Train	The original name for a mountain battery, but later used to denote the equipment, native establishment and the animals which were attached to a garrison company of the Royal Artillery when it became a mountain battery for a time.
Mountain Train Battery	A title used briefly during the mid-1860s for Indian mountain trains. The word train was dropped from the title in 1865. See *Hazara Mountain Train* and *Mountain Train*.
Mounted Branch	From 1 July 1899 until 1924 the Royal Artillery was divided into three distinct branches, the Royal Horse Artillery, the Royal Field Artillery and the Royal Garrison Artillery. The term Mounted Branch was used to describe the Royal Horse Artillery and the Royal Field Artillery during this period. See *Dismounted Branch*.
Mounting	The structure of a gun that supports the ordnance and has no wheels in contact with the ground when firing (contrast this with the carriage).
Movable Armament	At the beginning of the twentieth century these were the more or less mobile guns and howitzers provided in all coast defences, for use against land attacks. At later dates movable armaments were known as Armament of General Defence, the Armament for the Protection of Land Fronts and finally the Land Front Armament. Despite the changes of name, movable armament remained the term used in common parlance, whilst the title remained in use abroad.
Movement Light	Illumination provided by searchlights to facilitate all types of movement in a theatre of operations. The scheme originated in the Second World War when it was known as Artificial Moonlight. See *Movement Light Battery*.
Movement Light Battery	An independent self-contained unit, consisting in 1952 of a battery headquarters and three troops. Each troop comprised two sections, with each section having two detachments equipped with 90 cm searchlights. Movement Light Batteries were GHQ troops, and were provided on a scale of one per corps. Batteries were normally controlled by the Corps Commander Royal Artillery. For highly mobile operations the battery could be placed under divisional command. The smallest unit assigned to a divisional task would be a troop. Movement Light Batteries were always retained under the control of the appropriate artillery commander. See *Movement Light*.
Mov Lt Bty	Movement Light Battery.
MP	Microphone Position.
MPa	Mega Pascal.
mpb	Mean Point of Burst.
MPC	(i) Missile Practice Camp. (ii) Main Processing Cell. Part of the BATES System.
mpi	Mean Point of Impact.
MPL	Manual Primer Loader.
MPP	Military Proof Party.
MPRT	Misfire Primer Removal Tool.
mpsb	Mean Points of Burst. See *mpb*.
mpsi	Mean Points of Impact. See *mpi*.

MQ — Artillery Code used during the First World War meaning 'Stop firing or wait'.

MQM-57 — An early form of unmanned aerial vehicle, the MQM-57, known at the time as a 'drone', had the following characteristics:
Maximum speed at mean sea level: 160 knots (184 mph)
Normal operational height: 1000 feet
Radius of action: 30 miles.

It carried an airborne control system, a transponder to improve the performance of the tracking radar, a recovery parachute, and photographic equipment (see below). A MQM-57 system consisted of twelve drone aircraft and the relevant ground support equipment. Eight of the drones were equipped with the daytime Triple Array Vinton Camera whilst the remaining four had the KS 53A camera system and flares for night use.

Ground equipment consisted of a tracking radar, the Radar FA No. 13 Mk. I, two sets of radio control equipment, (one at the launch/recovery site and one located at the tracking radar), launching and recovery equipment, photographic processing and interpretation equipment and test and repair facilities.

Only one drone could be flown at a time, and a minimum of three hours was required to service the drone before it could be flown again. See *Phoenix*.

MR — Map Reference.

MRA — See *Tellurometer*.

MRATGW — Medium Range Anti-tank Guided Weapon.

MRF — Multi-Role Fuze. See *ET, PH, PL* and *PN* for details of the various settings available.

Mr Gnr — Master Gunner (abbreviation in use at least until the 1950s).

MRG — Main Repair Group.

MRL — Multiple Rocket Launcher. A generic term for multi-barrelled rocket launchers such as MLRS.

MRR — Minimum Risk Route.

MRSI — Multiple Round Simultaneous Impact.

MRTI — Multi-Role Thermal Imager.

MRUASTAS — Medium Range Unmanned Airborne Surveillance and Target Acquisition System.

MSAM — Medium Surface-to-Air Missile.

MSC — Major Subordinate Commander.

MSD — Minimum Safe Distance.

MSFS — Minimum Safe Fuze Setting.

Msg — Message.

MSH — Medium Support Helicopter.

MSI — Military Ski Instructor.

Msl — Missile.

MSL — Mean Sea Level.

Msn — (i) Musician.
(ii) Mission.

MSP — Medium Stressed Platform.

MSR — Main Supply Route.

MSSS — Multi Spectral Screening Smoke.

MST — Missile Supply Trailer.

MSTAR — MSTAR is a lightweight Pulse Doppler J Band all weather radar that has replaced the ZB 298 in the detection of helicopters, vehicles and infantry. Powered by a standard army field battery, MSTAR uses movement to detect targets, varying from an individual person to a main battle tank. A 'Fall of Shot' mode enables the adjustment of artillery or mortar fire onto targets up to a range of 30

km. The electro luminescent display which shows dead ground relief and target track history, also has the ability to superimpose a map grid at 1:50,000 scale, to ease transfer to military maps. The full day and night capability of MSTAR allows 24 hour surveillance of the battlefield by the OP party. MSTAR can be vehicle borne being fitted onto an hydraulic mast across the rear of the Warrior allowing observation to be carried out without exposing the vehicle. It can also be broken down into four easily man-packed loads.
Detection Range: 100 m to 30 km
Surveillance Sector: 196 to 6400 mils
Acquisition Sector: 196 to 710 mils
Weight Unpacked: 35.5 kg
Weight Bagged: 55.5 kg
Weight Boxed: 97.7 kg

MSV — Meteorology Support Vehicle. Part of the BMETS system.

Mt — Mount.

MT — (i) Mechanical Transport.
(ii) Motor Transport.
(iii) Mechanical Time. A fuze.
(iv) Artillery Code used during First World War meaning 'Mechanical Transport'.

MTF — Mechanical Time Fuze.

MTM — Medium Trench Mortar (First World War). Manned by the field artillery. See *HTM* and *LTM.*

Mtn — Mountain.

MTO — (i) Mechanical Transport Officer.
(ii) Motor Transport Officer.
(iii) Message to Observer. BATES message reporting shot, ToF, and angle T.

MTQ — Military Training Qualification.

M Truck — See *Monkey Truck.*

MTWO — Motor Transport Warrant Officer.

MUAV — Mini Unmanned Aerial Vehicle. See *TUAV* and *UAV.*

Mud Gunners — Slang for Canadian field artillery. (Royal Canadian Artillery).

Mule Length — A unit of measure, laid down by *Field Artillery Training 1914* as six feet, but by *Artillery Training Volume 1 Drill 1934* as eight feet. The reason for the increase in length is not explained. This measure was used in training manuals when referring to the various formations and manoeuvres adopted by mountain artillery. The width of an ammunition mule is given in both manuals as four feet. See *Horse Length.*

Multiple Launch Rocket System — The 227 mm Multiple Launch Rocket System was introduced into the Royal Artillery to replace the M107 gun deployed with corps artillery heavy regiments. The MLRS is self loaded with two rocket pod containers, each containing six rockets. Loading is power assisted and single round 'Fire for Effect' (12 rockets) delivers 7728 bomblets or 336 scatterable anti-tank mines. Operated from hides, usually as a battery of nine launchers, MLRS requires frequent relocation to reload and avoid counter attack.
Detachment: 3
Weight loaded: 24,756 kg
Weight Unloaded: 19,573 kg
Length: 7.167 m
Width: 2.97 m
Height (stowed): 2.57 m
Height (max elevation): 5.92 m

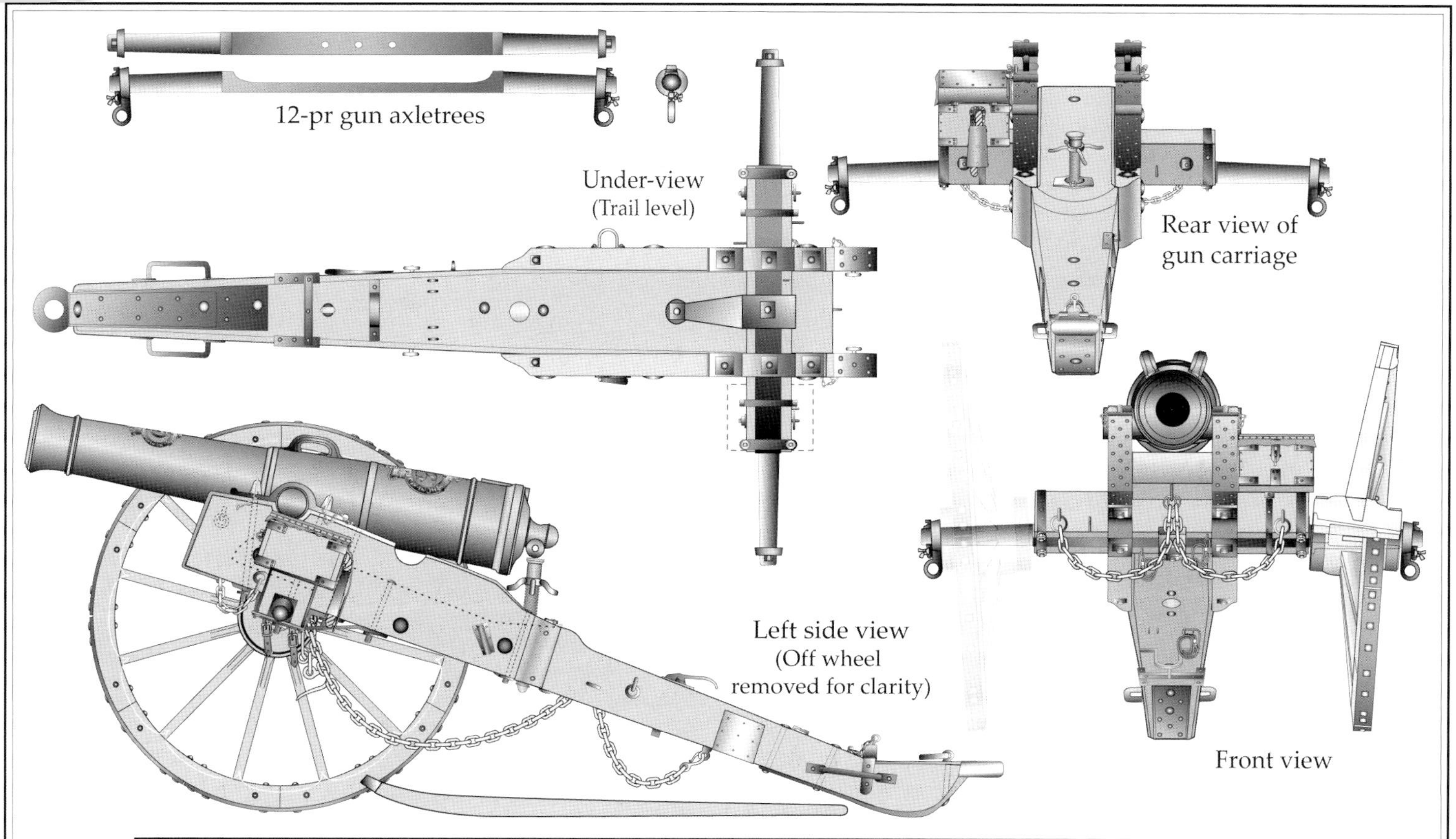

Medium 12-pr gun with block trail carriage and post 1813 wheels

Figure 11.6 | Part two of three

A group of F Battery, A Brigade Royal Horse Artillery in the Second Afghan War, 1878 – 1881.
(National Army Museum)

Elephant Battery.

Indian mountain battery in action.

Indian mountain battery on the march.

18-pounder battery in action during 1918.

6-inch howitzer fitted with ped-rails.

18-pounder field gun in camouflaged emplacement.

M Battery Royal Horse Artillery in action at Dakka during the Third Afghan War, 1919.
(Illustrated London News Picture Library)

Railway gun.

Kings Troop RHA firing 13-pounder guns of WW1 vintage at the Ceasefire at Woolwich 26 May 07.

17-pounder anti-tank gun.

3.7-inch heavy anti-aircraft gun on static mounting.

Pheasant – 17-pounder anti-tank gun on 25-pounder field gun carriage.

Self-propelled 40mm bofors gun.

6-pounder anti-tank gun.

Priest self-propelled 105mm gun.

7.2-inch bouncing howitzer.

Bofors 40 mm light anti-aircraft gun on static mounting.

25-pounder gun howitzer.

5.5-inch gun firing at night – showing the considerable amount of flash produced.

Sexton GPO

Green Mace.

39 Regt RA firing GMLRS on Op Herrick. (Courtesy *Gunner* Publications)

79 Cdo Bty, 29 Cdo regt RA on Op Herrick in Afghanistan (Courtesy *Gunner* Publications)

Lt Haughey guns firing - 1 RHA on Op Telic in Iraq (Courtesy *Gunner* Publications).

MLRS (Courtesy *Gunner* Publications)

Unrotated projectile multiple launcher.

Max Road Speed: 64 kph
Road Range: 480 km
Engine: turbocharged 8 cylinder diesel
Rocket Diameter: 227 mm
Rocket Length: 2.93 m
Rocket Weight: M77 Bomblet 302.5 kg; AT2 SCATMIN 254.46 kg
Range: M77 Bomblet 11.5-32 kms; AT2 SCATMIN 39 kms
Due to concerns over the persistency of the sub-munitions, these rounds were withdrawn from service in 2007 and replaced by GMLRS. See *Guided Multiple Launch Rocket System.*

Multiple Round Simultaneous Impact — A type of fire mission in which a gun fires several rounds at varying elevations resulting in all of the fired rounds impacting at the same time.

Murder — Developed by the artillery of the 2nd New Zealand Division during the Second World War and originally known as Method A, the Murder fire mission was a concentration of all the guns of a regiment or sometimes the entire divisional artillery on to a pin-point target.

Mushroom Head — The part of the breech of a BL type of ordnance that is mounted in the breech block and provides obturation, a chamber for the tube and is penetrated by the axial vent. See *Obturation.*

Mussolini's Revenge — Slang for the 105 mm pack howitzers in Canadian service, especially after cracks were discovered in a number of the barrels. See *Spaghetti Gun.*

Mustering Gunners — The title given to former junior gunners leaving the Junior Leaders Regiment RA, Bramcote on completion of their training as they were posted to their regiments.

Mut & Jeff — Slang term used in the Junior Leaders Regiment RA to describe the tins of mutton and peas found in ration packs.

Muzzle Brake — A Muzzle Brake reduces recoil stresses and thus increases the stability of the carriage on firing.

Muzzle Davit — A small jib crane made of 2-inch bar iron, 4-feet in height. It was used to lift a shell to the muzzle of an RML gun for loading.

Muzzle Derrick — See *Muzzle Davit.*

Muzzle Maggot — Nickname given to a member of a Gun Detachment. See *Gun Bunny, Grunt* and *Trail Ape.*

Muzzle Premature — See *Premature.*

Muzzle velocity — The velocity at which the shell leaves the muzzle. Muzzle velocity is different for each charge used. It decreases as the barrel wears so calibration firing is periodically undertaken to determine the current muzzle velocity. It is also affected by propellant temperature, variations between manufacturing batches of propellant, and other factors that are still not fully understood.

MV — (i) Muzzle Velocity.
(ii) Military Vigilance.

MVMD — Muzzle Velocity Measuring Device.

MVR — Muzzle Velocity Radar.

MVSU — Map Video Selection Unit.

MX — High Explosive Substance.

N – Nuts – 1927
Nan – 1943
November – 1956

N	(i) Nitrogen. (ii) No Flash. (iii) Artillery Code used during First World War meaning 'Guns in position at …'.
NAA	National Artillery Association.
NABK	NATO Armaments Ballistic Kernel.
NAI	Named Area of Interest.
NAIAD	Nerve Agent Immobilised Enzyme Alarm and Detector.
NAMFI	NATO Air Missile Firing Installation. Located in Crete, with a similar role to that of Manorbier.
Napier Medal	Awarded each year, by the Master Gunner's Committee, to a serving Royal Artillery captain or subaltern (Regular or Territorial Army) for noteworthy service. Noteworthy service is defined as service that provides some tangible benefit or brings credit to the Royal Regiment. Service to a single unit may be considered if there has been benefit to a substantial number of soldiers. The service may be rendered in the year of the award or over a period of years culminating in the year in question. See *Goschen Medal*.
NAPS	Nerve Agent Pretreatment Set. See *BATS*.
NASP	NATO Ammunition Supply Point.
National Artillery Association	Formed in 1863. Its aims are to advance and promote the science and practice of artillery in the Territorial Army through competitions. This they continue to support.
NATO	North Atlantic Treaty Organisation.
NATO Armaments Ballistic Kernel	A computer program architecture which defines interfaces and data definitions. Different companies (such as LogicaCMG) have their own software that implements the NABK. See *Fire Control Application*.
Nature	Type, generally used to denote ammunition, although occasionally applied to other equipment.
NAV	Navigation.
Naval Gunfire Staff Officer	Operating, together with his/her team in the supporting arms coordination cell in the command ship or the fire support coordination cell when the landing force is ashore, the NGSO is the naval gunfire support adviser to whichever commander he/she is serving. The NGSO is also responsible for the command and control of the naval gunfire support officers and the naval gunfire liaison officers. See *NGSFO, NGLO* and *NGSSO*.
Naval Gunfire Support Forward Officer	Pronounced 'Nigsfo'. In 1972 each NGSFO party consisted of an officer, a bombardier, a lance bombardier, a gunner and a Royal Navy radio operator. Every member of a NGSFO party must be both commando and parachute trained. Every officer is a qualified FAC. All soldiers must successfully pass the 12 week Naval Gunfire Assistants (Basic) Course, which introduces them to all aspects of naval gunnery including morse code.
NAVEX	Navigation Exercise.
Navigation Display Unit	The towing vehicle navigation display is a large flat panel, touch sensitive display which provides the in-cab display and control of navigation data. The NDU also provides a reversionary pointing capability in the event that the lay-

ers display and control unit is unavailable, or a primary display function in a less harsh vehicle environment. See *Layers Display and Control Unit* and *Laser Inertial Automatic Pointing System*.

Navigator See *Sperry Navigator* and *SPADE*.

NBC Nuclear, Biological and Chemical.

NBCC Nuclear, Bacteriological and Chemical Centre.

NBSD Normal Burst Safety Distance.

NC (i) A First World War British gas shell filling consisting of Chloropicrin plus 20% Stannic Chloride. The Stannic Chloride being added to give better penetration of gas masks.
(ii) Nitrocellulose.

NCS Net Control Station.

ND (i) Neutral Density.
(ii) Negligent Discharge. The accidental firing of a weapon. A chargeable offence in the armed forces.

NDU Navigation Display Unit. See *Layers Display and Control Unit* and *Laser Inertial Automatic Pointing System*.

Nearly All Lovely Canadian Cuties Are Praying For Men Feeling Frisky Every Damn Friday Fire Order Mnemonic standing for: Nature of Target, Ammunition, Line, Corrections to line, Clinometer laying, Angle of sight, Position corrections, Fire by order, Method of ranging, Fuse corrections, Fuse, Elevation, Description, Fire.

NEC Network Enabled Capability.

Neglect A report to the Forward Observer to indicate that the last round(s) was fired with incorrect data and that the round(s) will be fired again using correct data.

Nellies Nickname for 10 (Assaye) Battery Royal Artillery.

Nelson Troop (i) Nickname given to I Battery RHA, due to the battery cypher worn on their sun helmets. To overcome this nickname, members of the Battery wore a cypher on both sides of tropical head-dress, as opposed to all other batteries who only wore the badge/cypher on the left hand side.
(ii) One of the three troops in L (Nery) Battery RA. See *Bradbury Troop* and *Dorrell Troop*.

Nery Battery Honour Title of L (Nery) Battery which was granted on 18 October 1926 under authority of 20/ARTY/4544/AG6a. Battery now amalgamated with E (The Eagle Troop) Battery RHA as L/N (Nery) Battery (The Eagle Troop) RHA. See *Battery Honour Titles* and *Eagle Troop, The*.

NES No Enemy Seen (Second World War).

NET Not Earlier Than. See *NLT*.

Net See *Radio Net*.

Net Interface Equipment All cells in the BATES system are connected, for each radio net, by a Net Interface Equipment to the radio set. Two variants are available, the MONIE and the SANIE. A crypto device is incorporated in the NIE to ensure secure communications. See *BATES*, *MONIE* and *SANIE*.

Neutralization Fire Fire which is delivered in order to hamper or interrupt movement and/or the firing of weapons by the enemy.

Neville Walford Medal Awarded every three years to a serving Royal Artillery officer (Regular or Territorial Army) who during the period since it was last awarded produced the most valuable work in connection with foreign artillery. The award consists of a silver medal and an honorarium of £50.

NEWD	Night Exercise Without Darkness.
New Pattern Traversing Platform	These were slides that were substituted for the old 16 ft slides. There were two versions, the shortened 13 ft and the even shorter 11 ft See *Dwarf platform, Mortar Platform, New Pattern Traversing Platform, Siege Platform* and *Traversing Platform.*
New Zealand	Battery Honour Title of 94 (New Zealand) Headquarters Battery RA which was granted on 13 November 1934 under authority of 20/ARTY/6824/AG6a. See *Battery Honour Titles.*
New Zealand National Flag	94 (New Zealand) Battery RA has the unique distinction of being able to fly the New Zealand National Flag as its Battery flag.
NF	A zone call indicating that enemy guns were now firing. Used during the First World War. See *GNF* and *Zone Call.*
NFA	No Fire Area.
NFI	No Further Interest.
NFL	No Fire Line. (FSCM). See *FSSL.*
NFS	Naval Fire Support.
NFSO	Naval Fire Support Officer.
NG	(i) A First World War British gas shell filling consisting of Sulphuretted Hydrogen. (ii) Nitroglycerine.
NG^2	A First World War British gas shell filling consisting of 90% Sulphuretted Hydrogen and 10% Carbon Disulphide. NG^2 was used twice in 1916.
NGA	Naval Gunfire Assistant.
NGA(B)	Naval Gunfire Assistant (Basic).
NGF	Naval Gunfire.
NGFO	Naval Gunfire Forward Observer.
NGFS	(i) Naval Gunfire Support. (ii) Naval Gunfire Spotter.
NGLO	Naval Gunfire Liaison Officer. See *NGSLO.*
NGOC	Naval Gunfire Operations Cell.
NGS	Naval Gunfire Support.
NGSLO	Naval Gunfire Support Liaison Officer. See *NGSFO* and *NGLO.*
NGSFO	Naval Gunfire Support Forward Observer. Pronounced 'Nigsfo'.
NGSO	(i) Naval Gunfire Staff Officer. See *NGSFO, NGLO* and *NGSSO.* (ii) Naval Gunfire Staff Office.
NGSSO	Naval Gunfire Support Staff Officer. See *NGSO.*
N Hour	The time over target of the first warhead of a nuclear fireplan. Timings of subsequent nuclear strikes would be expressed as N plus *x* minutes. See *X-Hour.*
ni	Night.
NAIAD	Nerve Agent Immobilised Enzyme Alarm and Detector. In use with the British Army from the 1980s onwards.
Niagara	Battery Honour Title of 52 (Niagara) Battery RA which was granted on 16 August 1928 under authority of: 20/ARTY/4544/AG6a. See *Battery Honour Titles.*
Niagara Day	19 December. Battery day of 52 (Niagara) Battery RA.
NICD	North Irish Coast Defences. A Coast Artillery Command.
Nicholson Troop	One of the Troops in 40 Wardrop Bty Junior Leaders Regiment RA. See *Hornby Troop, Mansergh Troop* and *Park Troop.*
Nick Number	Part of a fire order, a Nick Number is used to group a number of targets together.

NIE	Net Interface Equipment. See *BATES, MONIE* and *SANIE*.
Nifty Fifty	Nickname of 50 Battery.
NIG	New In Germany
Night Picket	A light which is positioned a few hundred yards from the battery and visible to all guns within the battery which is used as an aiming point. See *Aiming Point*.
NIGs	New Intake Gunners.
Nigs Race	Run annually (at least during the 1980s) by 7 (Sphinx) Commando Battery this involved all members of the Battery who had not been to Norway before running 500 metres wearing nothing but a pair of DMS Boots. See *DMS*.
Nine Mile Sniper	Term used to describe the artillery by the other arms and services.
NIRTT	Northern Ireland Reinforcement Training Team.
NITAT	Northern Ireland Training and Advisory Team.
NKZ	Nuclear Killing Zone.
NLOS-LS	Non-Line Of Sight Launch System.
NLT	Not Later Than. See *NET*.
NMB	No Move Before (time).
NML	(i) No Movement Line. (ii) Near Mortar Line. See *FML*.
No 1 Dress	Blues.
No 2 Dress	Service Dress.
No 36 Grenade	Standard hand grenade used by the British Army until the 1970s.
NOD	Night Observation Device.
Noddy	See *AD12* and *FCE No. 7*.
Noddy Suit	NBC protective oversuit. See *NBC*.
NODLR	Night Observation Device Long Range. (Royal Canadian Artillery.)
No Duff	A radio proword used on exercise to indicate that the message contains real incident information and is not exercise related. For example: 'No Duff My vehicle is on fire.'
No Fire Area	An area into which artillery fire cannot be delivered unless expressly authorised as a temporary measure by the headquarters establishing the area.
No Fire Line	Artillery fire may not be delivered short of this line without the approval, or at the request of, the supported commander. Fire may be delivered beyond this line at any time without endangering friendly forces.
NOHD	Nominal Ocular Hazard Distance.
Nonne Bosschen Day	Battery day of 16 Field Battery RA (The Old Rooks), celebrated annually during the period between 1918 and 1939. The Battery later became 40 (The Old Rooks) Battery RA and eventually 40 (Wardrop) Battery RA (The Old Rooks) in the Junior Leaders Regiment RA.
Non Ridge	See *Non-Rigidity*.
Non-Rigidity	A value to be found in the firing tables to be used in the manual calculation of firing data. The figure produced was itself the combination of three values: slant range, density and horizontal component of velocity. See *Non-Rigidity Correction* and *Non-Rigidity Table*.
Non-Rigidity Correction	Applied to the predicted horizontal range when the angle of sight to the target is other than zero. It allows for the effects of uphill or downhill shooting. It is also known by the title correction to range for the non-rigidity of the trajectory.
Non-Rigidity Table	A table giving the corrections to range for targets above or below the height of the gun position.
Non-Standard Conditions	The firing data contained in range tables are for standard conditions of atmosphere, propellant temperature, muzzle

	velocity, projectile weight and trajectory with zero angle of sight. Range tables also include data to make corrections when conditions differ from the norm. As a consequence of non-standard conditions the maximum range of a gun varies and angular elevation gives different ranges under different conditions. During the Second World War British standard conditions were: temperature 60 degrees fahrenheit, 30 inches barometric pressure with no wind.
Non-Standard Projectile Correction	See *Abnormal Projectile Correction.*
North East Gunners	Regimental title of 4 Regiment RA. Identifies the regimental recruiting area.
North, East & West Yorkshire Gunners	Regimental title of 5 Regiment RA. Identifies the regimental recruiting area.
Not Recognized	A report indicating that the target type is unknown.
Not Seen	A report that the indicated target has not been seen.
Notty Ash Bizarre	Nickname of the South Nottinghamshire Hussars (307 Bty) with allusions to the comedian Ken Dodd.
NP Traversing Platform	See *New Pattern Traversing Platform.*
NR	Non-rigidity (of the trajectory).
NRA	Nuclear Reserved Area. An area of land reserved for nuclear delivery units.
NRD	Non-Regimental Duty.
NRF	NATO Response Force.
NRPS	Non-Regular Permanent Staff.
NSD	(i) Normal Safe Distance. (ii) Normal Safety Distance.
NSI	Nuclear Surety Inspection.
NSN	NATO Stock Number.
NSSC	Novice Ski and Survival Course.
NSWA	New South Wales Artillery.
NT	Artillery Code used during the First World War meaning 'Guns not firing at…'.
NTF	Notice To Fire.
NTM	Notice To Move. Usually accompanied by the time span involved, i.e. 72 Hrs NTM).
Nuc	Nuclear.
Nuclear Fire Plan	See *Fire Plan.*
Nuclear Surety Inspection	Conducted every 12–18 months on nuclear capable units by US Army inspector-general's branch to 'license' units and affiliated US Army custodial detachments as competent to handle nuclear weapons safely and securely.
Nuclear Weapons Release Procedure	Issued by the three Major NATO Commands. (Supreme Allied Commander, Europe (SACEUR), Supreme Allied Commander Atlantic (SACLANT), Commander in Chief Channel (CINCHAN).
Number 1	NCO in charge of a sub-section. During the horse drawn period, he would, in the RFA ride the near side leader of a gun team, whilst in the RHA he would be separately mounted like the rest of the detachment.
Number 3 Predictor	See *Kerrison Predictor.*
…(Number) Rounds	A fire order command used to indicate the number of projectiles per barrel to be fired on a specific target.
Number…In	The term used to indicate that gun/launcher number… is available for firing. See *Number…Out.*
Number…Out	The term used to indicate that gun/launcher number… is not available for firing. See *Number…In.*
NUOTC	Northumberland Universities Officer Training Corps.
Nurses Troop	One of the Troops in 159 (Colenso) Bty RA. See *Greys Troop* and *Longdens Troop.*

Nuts, The — Nickname given to A (The Chestnut Troop) Battery RHA.
NVAA — Northumberland Volunteer Artillery Association.
NVG — Night Vision Goggles.
NVRAM — Non Volatile Random Access Memory.
NWRP — Nuclear Weapons Release Procedure.
NZDA — New Zealand Divisional Artillery. (First World War.)
NZFA — New Zealand Field Artillery. (First World War.)

O – Orange – 1927
Oboe – 1943
Oscar – 1956

O — (i) Oxygen.
(ii) Artillery Code used during the First World War meaning 'Over'.
O&D — Organisation and Deployment, formerly Staff Duties. See *G3*.
OA — Operational Analysis.
OAS — Offensive Air Support.
OATS — Outside Air Temperature Sensor.
OB — Ordnance Board.
Oboe — See *Point Oboe*.
Oboe Tare — Observer/Target line. Currently known as the Oscar Tango Line this is an imaginary line drawn between the Target and the OP, used in target identification.
OB Proc — Ordnance Board Proceeding.
Observation — Title given to Survey Regiments after the Second World War, changed to Locating in 1952. Used as part of a unit title, i.e. 94 Observation Regiment RA. See *Locating*.
Observation Post Assistant — A non-commissioned officer trained to assist the observation post officer. See *Observation Post Officer*.
Observation Post Battery — During the 1970s three independent TA batteries were raised to provide formed and trained OP parties for regular batteries to bring these batteries to their WE of three OP parties. The regular batteries held vehicles and some other equipment for these parties. The TA batteries had a gun section, initially of 25-pdr, for training purposes. The TA batteries were 307 (SNH) Battery, 266 (GVA) Battery and 269 Battery. The TA batteries lost this role under Options for Change.
Observation Post Officer — An officer with a similar role to a forward observation officer, but operating directly with his or her battery and not attached to another unit. See *Forward Observation Officer*.
Observation Post Party — The role of the Observation Post Party is to seek out enemy targets and then direct artillery fire from guns, rockets and mortars on to them. The are also capable of directing fast jets and attack helicopters on to the same targets. The OP party works alongside infantry or armour, and is responsible for the constant surveillance of an area of the battlefield. To assist in this task the OP party is equipped with a variety of hi-tech night and thermal-sights and MSTAR capable of picking up movement of tanks and personnel.
Observation Post Tank — When working with armoured units during the Second World War, an OP tank was made available by the supported armoured regiment. The forward observation officer and his team could work from the tank, dismount and set up an observation post with a remote link to the Wireless Set No 19, or use the jeep or scout car which

were also party of the equipment of a forward observation party, according to the needs of the situation. Observation post tanks had the main armament removed, and replaced with a dummy gun in order to make more room for additional radio sets. See *Armoured Observation Post Carrier, Command Tank, Forward Observation Officer, Ram Observation Post*, and *Wireless Set No 19*.

Observation Regiment — A Royal Artillery regiment organised and equipped to undertake artillery survey, to locate hostile weapons and other targets, and to range the guns of other regiments by such methods as cross-observation of either ground or airbursts, by sound ranging or by radar.

Observed Fire — Fire for which the points of impact or burst can be seen by an observer. The fire can be controlled or adjusted on the basis of observation. See *Lost*.

Observer Identification — The first element of a fire order message to establish communication and to identify the observer. (Royal Canadian Artillery).

Observer's Thermal Imaging System — A multi-purpose thermal imaging and laser system used primarily as a target acquisition device by dismounted OP parties. The system enables the observer to produce an accurate bearing, distance and angle of sight to a target. When used in conjunction with the Specialist Personal Global Positioning System Receiver to produce the fixation of the observer, a target location can be produced to an accuracy of better than 50 metres for eastings and northings. The laser target marker range is from 300 to 10,000 metres whilst the laser range finder has a range of from 200 to 6000 metres. OTIS has a traverse of 6400 mils. See *Observation Post*.

Observer-Target Distance — The distance along an imaginary straight line from the observer to the target. See *Line OT*.

Observing Officer — Term used both during the First World War and earlier for the officer deployed forward from the gun position to direct a battery's fire. See *Forward Observer*.

Obturation — The sealing of the rear of the breech chamber to prevent propellant gases escaping. This is provided by the breech in breech loading ordnance and by the cartridge case in QF ordnance.

OBUA — Operations in Built Up Areas.

OC — (i) Officer Commanding.
(ii) Ordnance Committee.

OCA — Old Comrades Association.

OCdt — Officer Cadet.

OCF — Operators Confidence Facility. Part of the Rapier FSB2 Aid Defence system.

OCP — Operational Commitments Plot.

OCRA — Senior officer at regimental duty at a defended port.

OCTU — Officer Cadet Training Unit (Pronounced 'Ok-Too')

ODOPs — Operation, Deployment and Operating Procedures.

Oerlikon — During the Second World War British-manufactured Oerlikon 20 mm anti-aircraft guns with a ceiling of 10,000 feet (3,048 metres) used high explosive, high explosive-incendiary and semi-armour piercing rounds to defend merchant ships by the Maritime Royal Artillery.

OFC — (i) Operational Fire Controller (Second World War anti-aircraft).

OFC — (ii) Operator Fire Control. Coast artillery Second World War and later, also mortar locating radar operator 1950s.

Offensive Fire — Fire delivered by supporting units in order to assist and protect a unit engaged in an offensive action.

Offensive Support	The available fire assets for Offensive Support include battle group mortars and artillery through attack helicopters to ground attack aircraft. See *Offensive Support Group*.
Offensive Support Group	Made up of combat support units, namely artillery, air and aviation. The OSG is a headquarters in its own right, commanded by a brigadier and can be assigned its own battlespace, missions and tasks. See *Air* and *Aviation*.
Offr	Officer.
OFOF	Orders For Opening Fire. (Royal Australian Artillery.)
OFP	Ordnance Field Park.
OHC	Overhead Cover. See *OHP*.
OHP	Overhead Protection. See *OHC*.
OK	Artillery Code used during the First World War meaning 'Direct hit'.
Old Bustard Dinner	The local nickname for the Late Entry Officers Dinner, held annually at the Royal School of Artillery Larkhill. The dinner was formally known as the QM Dinner.
Olpherts's	Battery Honour Title of 56 (Olpherts's) Headquarters Battery RA which was granted on 18 October 1966 under authority 20/ARTY/6824/AG6a. See *Battery Honour Titles*.
OM	Oil Mineral.
OME	Ordnance Mechanical Engineer. Coast artillery. See *SOME*.
OMLT	Operational Mentoring and Liaison Team.
Omnibus Circuit	A line communications circuit which was reserved for fire orders and officer-to-officer conversations. The regimental omnibus circuit connected the adjutant's office with the battery command posts, whilst battery omnibus circuits connected the battery command post and the troop command posts.
On-Call Target	A planned target other than a scheduled target on which fire is delivered when requested.
On peg	In position.
One Time Pad	A very simple yet almost completely unbreakable cipher. Used only once, the same key is utilised for encryption as for decryption. During the Second World War messages classified above 'Confidential' were encrypted using this system. Special One Time Pads were used in nuclear artillery units for fire orders and data from the 1960s to the 1980s. See *Slidex*.
OOTW	Operations Other Than War.
Op	Operator.
OP	Observation Post.
OPA	Observation Post Assistant.
OPA(B)	Observation Post Assistant (Basic).
OPAck	Observation Post Assistant.
OpAMS	Operator Artillery Meteorology and Survey. (Royal Australian Artillery.)
O Party	Comprising the battery commander and the observation officers' parties, the O Party formed part of the battery HQ group during the Second World War. See *G Party*.
OP Bty	Observation Post Battery.
OPCOM	Operational Command. See *OPCON, TACOM* and *TACON*.
OPCON	Operational Control. See *OPCOM, TACOM* and *TACON*.
OPCP	Operator Command Post. (Royal Australian Artillery).
OPDEM	Operations Demand. (a request for parts, etc) (Royal Australian Artillery).
Open	A command or request used as part of a set of fire orders to indicate that the forward observer desires points of

	impact or burst to be separated by the maximum effective width of the burst of the shell fired.
Open Action	The engagement of a target which is visible from the gun position but not necessarily from the individual guns. (Royal Canadian Artillery).
Open Position	Open positions are used for direct fire, as such they are in direct view of enemy observers. Due to the risks involved, these positions tend only to be employed when direct fire is considered necessary for the accurate engagement of a pin-point target, for example, a pillbox or observation post. See *Covered Position* and *Semi-Covered Position.*
Opening Line	The line of a barrage on which fire is first brought down by guns not firing in depth. The opening line should not be confused with the Start Line, (now known as the Line of Departure) which is the line from which the foremost attacking troops advance at H-Hour. See *Barrage, Linear Concentration* and *Standard Barrage.*
Open Sights	When using open sights, the gun is aimed directly at the target, without the use of dial sights or other outside influences.
Operational Ammunition	Ammunition which is for operational use, as opposed to that used for training purposes, comprises: first line ammunition, with weapon scales, second line ammunition and reserve ammunition.
Operational Readiness Test	A NATO test of a unit's ability to evacuate its barracks to a local survival area. Known as Exercise Active Edge in 1 (BR) Corps, there may have been other exercise names at other times.
OP Fan	Prior too, or immediately on occupation of the observation post the officer marks his map with the OP Fan. This consists of a fan drawn from the OP and covering the zone of observation. It shows grid bearings at 100 or 200 mm intervals, together with distances from the OP. Distances should be marked with the number of metres subtended by 1 degrees, or a sub tension table should be attached. See *Observation Post Officer.*
OPFOR	Opposing Forces – the enemy forces in exercises.
OPO	Observation Post Officer.
OpO	Operation Order. Sometimes written as opO.
Op Orders	Operation Orders.
OP Party	See *Observation Post Party.*
OPS	Operational Performance Standard.
Ops	Operations.
OPSEC	Operational Security.
Op Sit	Operational Situation.
OPSO	Operations Officer.
OPSWO	Operations Warrant Officer.
OPTAG	Operational Training and Advisory Group.
OP Tech	Observation Post Technician. The Canadian term for an observation post assistant. (Royal Canadian Artillery).
OPV	Observation Post Vehicle.
OQ3	A small radio-controlled aircraft launched from a ramp and controlled by a joystick and used as a light anti-aircraft target. Length: 8 feet Propulsion: Two-stroke petrol engine Speed: 120 mph in level flight, 170 mph in a dive
OQF	Ordnance, Quick Firing.
Orbat	Order of Battle.
Ord	Ordnance.
Ordnance	The term used to describe any type or nature of gun. Examples of sub types are designated light or field, heavy

or siege. The term refers to the complete barrel assembly, this typically comprises the firing mechanism, breech, barrel and muzzle brake.

Ordnance BL 6-inch 26cwt Employed during both the First and Second World Wars the BL 6-inch 26cwt howitzer was developed as the follow on to the 6-inch 25 and 30cwt howitzers. The term '26cwt' refers to the combined weight of the barrel and breach, namely 26 hundredweight (cwt), or approximately 1.3 tonnes.

When the 6-inch 26cwt howitzer entered service in 1915 it was fitted with wooden wheels, however during the interwar period it was retrofitted tyres. Although it saw service during the Second World War its use was limited after 1942 by the introduction of the BL 5.5-inch medium gun. It did experience a limited revival in Burma as a result of a number of premature detonations experienced in 5.5-inch guns. The 6-inch 26cwt howitzer was declared obsolete at the conclusion of hostilities in 1945. In service between 1915 and 1945.

Weight: 4.2 tonnes
Length: 2.2 metres
Detachment: 10
Shell: HE, smoke and illumination
Calibre: 6 in (152 mm)
Breech: Welin screw
Recoil: hydro-pneumatic
Rate of fire: 1 round per minute
Effective range: Approximately 9,600 yd (8,784 metres)
See *BL 5.5-inch Medium Gun, Hydro-Pneumatic* and *Welin Thread.*

Ordnance QF 2-pounder A 40 mm anti-tank and vehicle-mounted gun, employed during the opening years of the Second World War. It was actively used in France and during the North African campaign. However, as the armour on tanks became sufficiently thick to withstand the 2-pound armour piercing round's impact, it was gradually replaced by the 6-pounder anti-tank gun during 1942, although some remained in service until the end of the war. The 2-pounder was initially developed as a tank weapon and made its debut as the main armament of the Vickers-designed cruiser tank Mk I. In October 1934, the Director of Artillery accepted it as an anti-tank gun in the interests of economy and standardization and contracts to design a carriage were given to both Vickers and Woolwich Arsenal.

Vickers submitted the first design, which was accepted as the ordnance QF 2-pounder Mark IX on carriage Mk I and a limited number of pieces were built during 1936. The carriage had an innovative three-legged construction. In the traveling position, one of the legs was used as a towing trail, and the other two were folded. When the gun was positioned for combat, the legs were placed on the ground and the wheels raised. On completion the Woolwich Arsenal carriage was found to be cheaper and easier to produce than the Vickers design and was adopted as the ordnance QF 2-pounder Mark IX on carriage Mark II. It generally followed the same lines as the Vickers carriage but when the gun was emplaced for combat the wheels had to be removed. This variant too was manufactured by Vickers.

The unusual construction of the carriage gave the gun good stability and a traverse of 360 degrees, allowing it to quickly engage moving vehicles irrespective of their

direction of approach. The gun could be fired from its wheels, though this seriously reduced the degree to which if could be traversed. One Canadian development late in the war was the David High Velocity, which allowed 2-pdr ammunition to be fired from the 6-pdr. The idea was to improve the muzzle velocity of the shot. The system was still being developed when the war ended, and the development programme ended with it.
Place of origin: UK
In service: 1936–1945
Designed: 1936
Manufacturer: Vickers
Produced: 1936–1944
Weight: 814 kg
Barrel length: 2,081.5 mm / 52 calibres
Bore: 2,000 mm / 50 calibres
Shell: 40x304R
Calibre: 40 mm
Breech: Semiautomatic vertical block
Recoil: Hydro Spring
Carriage: Three-leg platform
Elevation: -13° to +15°
Traverse: 360°
Rate of Fire: 22 Rounds Per Minute
Muzzle Velocity: 792 m/s (2,600 ft/s) with Armour Piercing shot
Effective Range: 1,000 yards
Sights: No.24b

Ordnance QF 17-pounder — A 76.2 mm or 3-inch anti-tank gun developed during the Second World War. The 17-pounder was initially mounted on a 25-pdr carriage, being known as the 25/17-pdr or more usually by its codename of 'Pheasant'. The 17-pounder was also mounted in the Archer self-propelled anti-tank gun and the Sherman tank where it was known as the 'Firefly'. Considered by many to be the best allied anti-tank gun of the war. When using APDS ammunition it was capable of defeating all German armour. AP and APC ammunition for the 17-pdr was available from its introduction with APCBC ammunition becoming available in the spring of 1944. The original HE ammunition had been found to be lacking in effect resulting in a reduced charge version being provided during the summer of 1944, with a high capacity version following latter in the same year. From mid-1944 an APDS round based on the 6-pdr APDS design was also available.
Carriage: Mk I
Weight: 4700 lb
Gun weight (Mk I): 1820 lb
Transverse: 60°, 30° left and 30° right.
Elevation: 16.5°
Depression: 6°
Height (over gunshield): 63.25 inches
Width: 88 inches
Length (tail to muzzle): 289.5 inches
Calibre: 3 inches (76. 2mm)
See *AP, APC, APCBC, APDS, Archer* and *Pheasant*.

Ordnance QF 25 Pounder — Possibly the most well known artillery piece ever to have served with the Royal Artillery. The Ordnance QF 25-pdr was introduced into service just prior to the Second World War as a replacement for both the 18-pdr field gun and the 4.5-inch howitzer. It was the British Army's primary artillery field piece from that time through to the 1960s.

Even then small numbers remained in service for training purposes in the United Kingdom until well into the 1980s. Indeed it remained as the principal saluting piece of the Regiment until finally replaced by the L118 light gun in that role in 2006. The last British military unit to fire the gun in its field role was the Gun Troop of the Honourable Artillery Company on Salisbury Plain in 1992.

The introduction of NATO standardization led to the replacement of the 25-pdr with the 105 mm pack howitzer and subsequently the L118 light gun.

Considered by many to be the best field artillery piece of the the Second World War, the 25-pdr combined high rates of fire and a reasonably lethal shell together with high mobility.

An important part of the 25-pdr system was the ammunition limber. The gun was hitched to this and in turn the trailer was hitched to the tractor when on tow. If necessary, the gun could be hooked directly to a tractor. The limber carried thirty-two rounds of ammunition. Additional ammunition was carried in the gun tractor together with the gun detachment and various gun stores. Certain items of gun stores, such as sights, were carried cased on the gun itself. Each section (comprising two guns) had a third tractor that towed two ammunition trailers.

The gun detachment comprised the following:

No 1 – detachment commander (a sergeant)

No 2 – operated the breech and rammed the shell

No 3 – layer

No 4 – loader

No 5 – ammunition

No 6 – ammunition, normally the 'coverer' – the second in command of the gun detachment and responsible for ammunition preparation.

There was an official 'reduced detachment' of four men.

Ammunition

The principal ammunition type used was the high explosive shell, however, smoke, star (illuminating), chemical, and carrier projectiles were also available. A limited number of 20 lb (9 kg) solid armour piercing rounds, later replaced with a more potent version fitted with a ballistic cap was provided for anti-tank work. A shaped charge version was under development in Canada, but the introduction of the 17-pdr dedicated anti-tank gun ended its development.

The 25-Pounder was produced on two Self-Propelled mounts (Bishop and Sexton) and in Australia in a shortened version. The main variants were:

Mark I

Known officially as the Ordnance, Quick Firing 25-pdr Mark I on Carriage 18-pr Mark IV, or Ordnance, Quick Firing 25-pdr Mark I on Carriage 18-pr Mark V and commonly referred to as the 18/25-pdr. The Mark IV carriage had a box trail, whilst the Mark V had a split trail. These conversions of the 18-pdr first entered service in the late 1930s. A few were lost in the Norwegian Campaign and 704 in the withdrawal from France, leaving an approximately equal number in the UK's global stocks. They saw service in North Africa (until about late 1941) and Malaya. This mark of 25-pdr was limited to charge 3 due to its 18-pdr carriage.

Mark II

The Mark II, fitted to the Mark I carriage was the standard gun employed during the Second World War. Built mainly in the UK but versions were also produced in Australia and Canada. Deliveries commenced at the beginning of 1940. No Ordnance 25-pdr Mk II on Carriage 25-pr Mark Is were lost in France. This gun fired all three charges plus charge super. At a later date a series of charge increments were made available. These were added to charge super for direct fire anti-tank and necessitated the adoption of a muzzle brake to reduce recoil. Guns with this modification were known as the Mark II/I. The distinctive muzzle brake is an easily recognized feature of this gun.

Mark III

The Mk III ordnance was a Mk II with a modified receiver designed to prevent the rounds from slipping back out when loading whilst firing in the Upper Register. Those fitted with the muzzle brake were known as the Mk III/I, while the Mark IV were identical new-build versions which all featured the brake.

Additionally, a local modification was produced in Burma and known as the jury axle. It was subsequently adopted officially with other minor modifications and a new platform for the narrow wheelbase as the carriage 25-pdr Mark II. The Mark III carriage, also narrow, included a hinge to make it easier to fire the gun in the upper register. High angle fire had been introduced in Italy and used the increments originally introduced for anti-tank fire, adding them to charges 2 and 3 to give 25-pdr a total of 7 charges.

Type: Gun-Howitzer
Place of Origin: UK
In Service: 1930s to 1967
Designed: 1930s
Variants: Marks I, II, III and Short
Weight: 1.8 tons
Length: 18 ft 2 in (5.53 m) from muzzle brake to tip of handspike
Barrel Length: 31 calibres
Width: 7 feet wheelbase (Mk I carriage)
Detachment: 6
Calibre: 3.45 in (87.6 mm)
Breech: Vertical Sliding Block
Recoil: Hydro-pneumatic
Carriage: Box Trail
Elevation: -5° to +45° (70° with modified sight mount and digging).
Traverse: 360° on platform, 4° left and right on carriage
Rate of Fire: 6–8 round/min at gunfire
Muzzle Velocity: 1700 f/s Charge Super
Maximum Range: 13,400 yards using Charge Super
Feed System: Separate Loading
Sights:
Indirect Fire – Calibrating and Reciprocating
Direct Fire – Telescope

See *Bishop, Coverer, Jury Axle, Sexton, Quick Firing Ammunition* and *Upper Register*.

Ordnance Board

Almost fifty years after the abolition of the Board of Ordnance, the Ordnance Board, a totally new department, was created. The Ordnance Board consisted of a board of munitions experts, whose role was to advise the Army Council on the safety and approval of weapons. The Ordnance Board, and its name, survived as part of the Ministry of Defence until the mid-1990s when it was

	renamed the Defence Ordnance Safety Group. See *Board of Ordnance* and *Master-General of the Ordnance.*
Ordnance Field Park	A Royal Army Ordnance Corps (now Royal Logistic Corps) unit.
Ord's Troop	The name given to BHQ within 53 (Louisburg) Battery Royal Artillery.
Organisation for Manoeuvre	Every Royal Artillery unit at least during the Second World War and possibly both before and after, had an Organisation for Manoeuvre which assigned a standard designation, role, radio fit and detachment for each vehicle.
Orientation	The alignment of the director and other horizontal angle instruments, by reference to grid north with sufficient accuracy for the purpose required. Initial orientation is determined within the battery by magnetic compass or map measurement, then subsequently improved by survey processes. The use of such systems as GPS and LINAPS has greatly improved the time into action of guns and batteries. See *Battery Grid, Fixation, GPS, LINAPS, Orientation, Regimental Grid* and *Theatre Grid.*
Orientor Gyroscopic	See *PIM.*
ORP	Operational Ration Pack.
ORT	Operational Readiness Test.
OS	Offensive Support.
Oscar Tango	Observer/Target line. An imaginary line drawn between the target and the OP, used in target identification. Previously known as the Oboe Tare Line.
OSD	(i) Operational Stand down Package. (ii) Out of Service Date.
OSF	Odometer Scale Factor.
OSG	Offensive Support Group.
OSGB	Ordnance Survey Great Britain.
Osprey	The combined day/thermal/laser system fitted to the Warrior OPV, manufactured by Pilkington Optronics. See *RRDU* and *Warrior OPV.*
OST	Overall System Test. Part of the rapier AD system.
OT	(i) Oscar Tango. (ii) Oboe Tare Line. (iii) Observer to Target.
OTA	Otterburn Training Area.
OTACS	Otterburn Training Area Computer System.
OTC	(i) Officer Training Corps. (ii) Officer in Tactical Command.
OTIS	Observer's Thermal Imaging System.
OTP	(i) Operational Tour Plot. (ii) One Time Pad.
OTX	Overseas Training Exercise.
OU	From the Artillery Code, 'unobserved round'.
OUVS	Operational Utility Vehicle System.
Over	A round which falls beyond the target, as seen from the Observation Post. See *Short* and *Target Grid Correction.*
Overbank Carriage	In fortifications and coast batteries, this was a carriage with an added bracket that enabled the gun to fire over a 5-feet 6-inches high parapet. It was designed for use with light rifled guns on the flanks of forts or in batteries thrown up between the forts. Mountings of this type were built for the 40-pdr RML, the 40-pdr RBL and the 25-pdr RML.
Overhead Cover	Protection from weather and observation.
Overseas School of Artillery	The school of artillery established at Chapperton Down in 1916 to train BCs and their captains from the BEF.
OWL	Operator, Wireless and Line.

P – Pip – 1927
Peter – 1943
Papa – 1956

P	(i) Designation for pack mules or horses, such as those used in mountain artillery units. (ii) Prism. (iii) Pebble. (iv) Artillery code used during the First World War meaning 'Percussion'.
P1	Tactical sign for a battery POL truck. See *P2, POL* and *Tactical Sign.*
P2	Tactical sign for a battery POL truck. See *P1, POL* and *Tactical Sign.*
P&EE	Proof & Experimental Establishment (a 'unit' that proves and trials guns and ammunition).
P/A	Paid Acting, See *U/A.*
PA	(i) Pack Artillery. See *MA.* (ii) Primary Arc. (iii) Position of Assembly.
Pace Stick	The Pace Stick, so well loved by RSMs is said to have originated in the Royal Artillery. It was used by gunners to ensure correct distances between guns on the battlefield, thus ensuring effective fire. The original stick was more like a walking stick, with a silver or ivory knob. It could not be manipulated like the modern pace stick, as it simply opened like a pair of callipers; the infantry then developed the stick to its present configuration, as an aid to drill.
Packet	In vehicle movement terms this relates to a group of vehicles; regimental movements are made up of a number of packets.
Pack Gun	A gun that can be dismantled and transported in sections, often by mule. See *Pack Howitzer* and *Screw Gun.*
Pack Howitzer	A howitzer that can be dismantled and transported in sections, often by mule. See *Pack Gun* and *Screw Gun.*
PAD	(i) Passive Air Defence. (ii) Nickname given to a soldier living in married quarters.
PADS	Position and Azimuth Determining System. See *GPS, PIM, Survey Control Point* and *TAS 10.*
Palliser Conversion.	Adopted in 1863 this was a system named after its inventor, Captain Palliser, whereby the bore of a smooth bore gun was lined with a rifled, wrought iron tube, so converting it to an RML. This rifling consisted of three grooves and was also known as Woolwich Pattern Rifling. The wrought iron tube was expanded to fit the bore by firing a heavy proof charge. The resultant gun was more powerful than the original smooth bore. The Palliser system was adopted in 1863. Guns converted to this system were 64-pdr of 58cwt; 64-pdr. of 71cwt and the 80-pdr of 5 tons. See *Woolwich Pattern Rifling.*
Palliser Shell	Adopted by the Royal Artillery at the end of the 1860s for use in most RML guns. The Palliser Shell was a pointed shell cast nose downwards with the body in a sand mould, whilst the tip was in a water cooled iron mould. This resulted in the nose being extremely hard, consequently it was very effective at penetrating heavily armoured targets. It remained in service as the standard piercing projectile for many years. Like the Palliser Conversion, this shell was designed by Captain Palliser of the 18th Hussars.

Pam — Pamphlet. Generally followed by the relevant Pamphlet number. For example; 'Pam 1 – The Tactical Handling of Artillery'.

Panorama — A sketch of the ground visible from the OP drawn by the observer.

Papa 1 — See *P1*.

Papa 2 — See *P2*.

Parachute Jump Instructor — An RAF instructor employed at PTS to train parachutists.

Parachute Light Ball — The direct antecedent of the present day illuminating round, the parachute light ball was introduced in 1850, designed by Colonel Boxer, it comprised two outer and two inner hemispheres made of tinned iron. The outer hemispheres were riveted together, whilst the inner hemispheres were linked together by a chain. Following ignition by a fuze, the bursting charge blew the outer and inner hemispheres away and ignited the illuminating composition which was contained in the lower hemisphere. A parachute, attached to the lower inner hemisphere but contained in the upper inner hemisphere, was deployed to slow the rate of descent. The last parachute light ball retained in service was the 10-inch version, which was finally declared obsolete in December 1920, however, it is unlikely that any had been manufactured or used for many years prior to this. See *Ground Light Ball* and *Illuminating Round.*

Parafoos — Name given to members of the Second World War COBU who were parachute trained and assigned to 1st Airborne Division in North Africa.

Parallelescope — First introduced in 1917 as an alternative to aiming posts with the added advantage that it was easily usable at night. The parallelescope was placed a few yards from each gun and the layer aimed his sight onto its reflection in the mirror.

The original Parallelescope Mk I was a 3.7 × 2.9 inch mirror fitted to a slide approximately 22 inches long, mounted on a stand designed to keep it horizontal and fixed in its position. Later marks consisted of a flat mirror approximately two feet long, however, during the mid-1950s these flat mirrors were replaced by prism parallelescopes, which was slightly wider with a more robust and stable mount. Using a prism parallelescope allowed for a greater height difference between the dial sight and the parallelescope and therefore eliminated the need to horizontally level the instrument. Sometimes referred to as a 'Pscope', particularly in the Royal Australian Artillery.

Park Hall Camp — Located in Oswestry, Shrophire. Park Hall Camp was the home of 64 Training Regiment Royal Artillery during the 1950s.

Park Troop — One of the troops in 40 Wardrop Battery Junior Leaders Regiment RA. See *Hornby Troop, Mansergh Troop* and *Nicholson Troop*.

Partridge — The Mark II version of the 17-pdr anti-tank gun which, unlike the Mark I had a specially designed carriage which was much more effective. See *Pheasant.*

Part-Task Trainer — Computerised training equipment for Rapier FSB and FSC used to instruct, practise and test engagement procedures.

Past and Present Members Associaton — The 3RHA Old Comrades Association.

PATC — Pack Artillery Training Centre. See *Mountain Artillery Training Centre.*

Patrol Selection Course — Candidates for the Honourable Artillery are required to complete the six month long course which is designed to teach the basic skills required of a surveillance and target acquisition patrol soldier and also to assess the suitability of candidates for service with the patrol squadrons. Among the subjects taught as part of the course are: advanced navigation, first aid, close quarter battle skills, foreign equipment recognition, observation post construction, operation and routine and long range communications.

The course includes a number of physical and skills tests that candidates must pass in order to proceed to a patrol squadron; these tests include swimming, navigation, long distance marches over arduous terrain carrying heavy loads, and a demanding ten day final exercise during which proficiency in all the skills taught is assessed. See *HAC*.

Pattern Target — Devised during the Second World War by the artillery of 56 Division in Italy, this shoot consisted of the combined fire of four field, two medium and one heavy regiment. It was normally employed in the following manner: pairs of adjacent stonks by the field and medium regiments with intervals of between 200 and 300 yards between the pairs, and a fourth line 500 yards beyond the third pair (fired by the mediums) which consisted of a 1,200 yard stonk fired by the heavy regiment. See *Stonk*.

Pause Line — During a barrage a line on which fire is directed to cover friendly forces halted on an objective. See *Barrage, Lines, Linear Concentration* and *Standard Barrage*.

Pax — Passengers.

PAYD — Pay As You Dine.

PB — (i) Pack Battery. See *MB*.
(ii) Polybutadiene (a synthetic rubber).

PBAR — Pan Balkan Artillery Regiment.

PBIT — Power-up Built-in Test.

PBOE — Portable Bowman Operating Environment. Part of the Bowman communications system. See *Bowman*.

PBU — Push Button Unit.

PBX — Polymer Bonded Explosives.

PC — Provisionally Condemned.

PCC — (i) Pre-Commando Training Course.
(ii) Photoelectric Counter Chronograph.

PD — Point Detonating; a type of fuze. See *PDF*.

PDAL — Prioritised Defended Assets List.

PDB — Power Distribution Box. Part of the MLRS system. See *Multiple Launch Rocket System*.

PDF — (i) Point Detonating Fuze.
(ii) Priority Defensive Fire. See *FPF*.

Pdr — Pounder. As in 25-pdr, can also be found with a lower case 'p'. The abbreviation 'pr' was also used. See *Pr*.

PDR — Personal Development Record.

PDRM — Personal Dose Rate Meter.

PDS — Position Determining System.

PDT — Priority Depth Target.

PE — (i) Physical Efficiency.
(ii) Probable Error.
(iii) Plastic Explosive.
(iv) Peace Establishment.
(v) Peace Enforcement.
(vi) Permissible Error.

PEA — Preferred Engagement Arc. Rapier.

PEC — (i) Panel Electronic Circuit.

	(ii) See *Photoelectric Counter Chronograph.*
PECC	Photoelectric Counter Chronograph.
PED	Probable Error Deflection.
Ped-Rails	A series of wooden blocks, 24-inches by 10-inches fitted to the wheels of field guns and wagons during the First World War in order to reduce ground pressure and thus ease progress across soft sand and mud. Documentary evidence would suggest that a similar system was used for heavier artillery pieces under the title 'Girdles'.
Peg	The popular name by which a bearing picket is known. See *Bearing Picket.*
Peg, On	In position.
Pegasus Troop	A sub unit of 7 Para RHA into which all new soldiers are posted in order to prepare them for all arms pre-parachute selection.
Pepperpot	Introduced in late 1944 the Pepperpot involved a concentration of weapons, including tank guns, mortars, anti-tank and light anti-aircraft guns firing into an area. It was employed as an element of major fireplans.
PER	Probable Error for Range.
Percussion Fuze	A fuze that causes a shell to operate on impact.
Percussion Shrapnel	As the Royal Artillery entered the First World War with shrapnel only, it was found that by setting the time fuze to safe, the shrapnel shell would function on impact, giving a similar effect to a high explosive shell. It was also employed when there was insufficient time to set the time fuze. The battery commander would order percussion shrapnel to indicate that the time fuze should be set to safe. It was employed for ranging, against troops in buildings or behind walls, or when out of time shrapnel range. See *Shrapnel* and *Time Shrapnel.*
Percy	The Percy Mark I trench mortar introduced during the First World War was a 6-inch cylinder upended and bored out to 4-inches, rifled with three grooves and mounted on a pivot on an oak bed with elevation being given by use of a wedge. It fired an 8½-inch shell containing high explosive detonated by an exploder and a No. 44 fuze. One of its drawbacks was that it used black powder as a propellant and the smoke generated on discharge gave away the position of the mortar to the enemy. Percy Mark II never proceeded past the development stage, but Percy Mark III, a combination of Percy Mark I and Reginald proved to be extremely accurate, its drawback being a lightweight shell. See *3-inch Stokes Trench Mortar, Cuthbert, Reginald* and *Toby.*
Per. Shrapnel	See *Percussion Shrapnel.*
Personal Role Radio	The UK/PRC-343 is a small lightweight (1.5 kg) transmitter-receiver with 256 channels and a battery life of 20 hours in continuous use. Every member of a patrol is issued with a PRR which allows soldiers to communicate over distances of up to 500 metres – even through thick cover or the walls of buildings – without the need for shouting, hand signals or relaying messages. It enables section commanders to react quickly, aggressively and efficiently to rapidly changing situations including contact with the enemy, greatly increasing the effectiveness of infantry fire teams.
Petard	A type of mine, which is said to have been invented by the Huguenots around 1589. It was a bell-shaped gunpowder-filled container of brass or iron fixed to a wooden base. It was designed to be exploded against the door of a fort or other work thereby demolishing it. In the event of

the door being too strong, the petard was liable to become projectile to the extreme discomfort of the Petardier who had not kept strictly to the drill and retired after igniting the fuze. Evidence that such occurrences did happen has come down to us in the present-day expression 'hoist with his own petard'. See *Petardier.*

Petardier — The Petardier first appeared on the artillery establishment in 1618. Little is known of the early history of this rank, however when the bombardier came into being in 1686, there appeared one chief petardier and four petardiers with the same pay and status as their bombardier cousins. The speciality of the petardier was the petard, a type of mine said to have been invented by the Huguenots around 1589. The firemaster was expected to train petardiers in its use. As use of the petard diminished the duties of the petardier and bombardier became interchangeable, so eventually one had to go. The bombardiers survived, whilst after 1728 the petardiers disappeared from the establishment. See *Bombardier* and *Petard.*

Pettman's LS Percussion Fuze — A type of metal fuze used with Common Shell during the mid-1800s. It was armed by the action of the projectile being fired and exploded by the setting forward of a ball within the fuze when the projectile impacted with the target. See *Common Shell.*

PF — Position Finder. See also *Depression Position Finder* and *Horizontal Position Finder.*

PFA — Permitted Fire Area.

PFC — Position Finding Cell.

PFD — Pre-Flight Data. See *Phoenix.*

PG — (i) A First World War British gas shell filling consisting of 75% PS and 25% CG. PG was used largely in 4-inch trench mortar shells. See Also *PS* and *CG.*
(ii) Pivot Gun.

Pgda — Propaganda Shell.

PGM — Precision Guided Munition.

PGS — Portable Generator Set.

PH — (i) Pack Howitzer. See *105 mm Pack Howitzer (L5).*
(ii) Proximity High. A setting used on the multi-role fuze. See *ET, PL* and *PN.*

Ph 2 — Phase two training.

Pheasant — A Second World War anti-tank gun consisting of a 17-pdr piece mounted on a 25-pdr carriage. This version of the 17-pdr was known as the Mark I. With a detachment of 7 men and weighing 4625 lbs in action the 17-pdr had a top-traverse of 30° left and right. See *Partridge.*

Phoenix — (i) An all weather, day or night, real time surveillance and target acquisition system. The Phoenix Unmanned Air Vehicle's surveillance suite is data linked to a ground station which, in turn, transmits the intelligence gathered directly to artillery command posts. Almost entirely made from Kevlar, glass fibre, carbon reinforced plastics and Nomex honeycomb, with power being provided by a 25hp two stroke flat twin engine. For landing, the tail cone is ejected to extract a drogue parachute and the engine stops with the propeller in the horizontal position. The UAV inverts during the decsent so the vehicle lands on its upper surface to protect the mission pod. The force of the landing is absorbed by an air bag and frangible fin tips.

Phoenix can be launched within an hour of reaching its launch site. Up to 2 UAVs can be controlled from the same ground control station.

UAV Wing Span: 5.5 m
Max Launch Weight: 177 kg
Flight Radius: 50 kms
Max Altitude: 2700 m (9000 ft)
See *Desert Hawk.*
(ii) The name of the study that considered options for depth target acquisition when MRUASTAS was cancelled. See *MRUASTAS.*

Phoenix Launcher — The Phoenix Launcher is a standard 14 ton army lorry, fitted with a pallet mounted lifting crane, hydraulically and pneumatically operated launch catapult and ramp. There is also a computer to download mission data into the UAV prior to launch. Within sixty minutes of reaching a launch site, the UAV can be assembled and launched. A second UAV can be launched within a further 8 minutes.

The launcher accelerates the UAV from 0–64 Knots in just 12.6 metres, this creates thrust on the UAV of approximately 8 Gs. The Launcher is manned by 2 soldiers, who are supported by 4 others. Put very simply the Phoenix Launcher is a large hydraulic catapult. See *Phoenix.*

Phoenix Recovery Vehicle — An old style Land Rover GS fitted out to carry Phoenix in its broken down state. The whole UAV will fit directly into the rear of the Land Rover and the UAV will be built back at the launch vehicle. The recovery crew will re-test and make the UAV ready for its next mission. See *Phoenix.*

Photoelectric Counter Chronograph — A device for determining and recording muzzle velocities, introduced during the 1930s. The PECC worked by the projectile from the gun being calibrated passing in succession over two photo-electric cells placed at distances of approximately 100 and 200 feet in front of the muzzle. The light reaching the cells was focussed by a lens system and slit from a narrow strip of the sky at projectile height. The round passing over the cells caused a momentary darkening of each cell and an electric pulse was amplified and transmitted by cable to an electric chronograph. This measured the time interval between the first and second cell, which in turn could be converted into muzzle velocity by use of a table.

PHR — Predicted Horizontal Range.

PIAT — Projector Infantry Anti-Tank.

PIC — Press Information Centre.

Picquet — Overnight Guard Duty.

PID — Post Impact Delay (a type of fuze).

PIE — Pen Index Error. Sound Ranging.

Piece — The Barrel and breech assembly of the gun.

Pierced Steel Plank — Planks locked together to form hard standing, used during the Second World War and later.

PIFT — Pocket Indirect Fire Trainer.

Pig's Ear — The plate struck with a fist to fire the 3.7-inch heavy anti-aircraft gun. This was a term which was forbidden within 1st Singapore Regiment, for the Malay Gunners (being Muslim) would have nothing to do with a porcine component.

PIM — (i) Precision Indicator Meridian. See *PADS.*
(ii) Payload Interface Module. Part of the MLRS system. See *Multiple Launch Rocket System.*

Pin-point target — Now known as Destruction. A fire mission involving a single gun which was used to destroy a point target such as a building. The field clinometer was used for laying and the charge with the smallest probable error was used.

Also referred to as a Precision Shoot. See *Field Clinometer* and *Probable Error.*

Pintle — The hook or spindle upon which the gun carriage rests and to which it is secured when travelling.

Pinzgauer — See *TUM(HD).*

PIO — Press Information Officer.

PIR — Priority Intelligence Requirement.

Piss Flaps — Nickname given to the shell retaining clamps on the FH70. See *FH70.*

Pistol Gun — A single gun deployed at a new gun position, to register targets in advance of the arrival of the other guns. Pistol guns may also be deployed to harass the enemy with less chance of detection, or to mislead or confuse the enemy as to the location of other guns.

Pivot — In fortifications and coast artillery batteries this was the real or imaginary point about which a gun was traversed. The pivot consisted of a cast iron block into which a steel plug three inches in diameter fitted passing through a plate on the underside of the slide. There were six types of pivot, A–F as described below:
A: An imaginary pivot located in front of the platform, in the embrasure which gave a field of fire of 70 degrees.
B: Similar to A.
C: A central pivot with a circular racer which gave a 360 degrees traverse.
D: Located nearer to the rear of the slide than to the front which gave either a 180 or 360 degrees traverse.
E. Similar to D but only gave a 180 degrees traverse.
F. Located behind both front and rear racers which gave a 180 degrees traverse.
Casemate slides were only used with A type pivot racers. However, dwarf slides were used with all types of pivots. Both E and F type pivots were designed for use on Martello towers and are not found in any other location. See *Pivot Block, Racers* and *Traversing Platform.*

Pivot Block — In fortifications and coast artillery batteries this is the block about which the slide rotates and to which the slide is connected. All natures of medium gun on type C, D, E or F pivot racers required actual pivots. See *Pivot.*

Pivot Gun — Normally the right hand gun of a troop, when using an artillery board in the CP, the Pivot Gun was represented by the pivot for the range arm. It was the basis for calculating firing data in a troop or battery until troop or battery centre was adopted in 1956. See *Artillery Board, Battery Centre* and *Troop Centre.*

PJHQ — Permanent Joint Headquarters.

PJI — Parachute Jump Instructor.

PL — (i) Phase Line.
(ii) Predicted Line.
(iii) Proximity Low. A setting used on the multi-role fuze. See *ET, PH* and *PN.*
(iv) Primer Loader.

Plane of Departure — The vertical plane containing the line of departure. See *Line of Departure.*

Planks — Nickname sometimes given to the gunners. The name is said to derive from the First World War when the muddy conditions in the gun positions were so bad that the bodies of dead gunners were put under the guns to stop them sinking.

Planks, Army — Skis.

Planned Target — A target on which fire is pre-arranged. (Royal Canadian Artillery).

Planning Ranges — Owing to the non-standard conditions likely to exist at any given time, the guns of a unit may not be able to achieve their maximum range as indicated in the firing tables. As a result, for rough planning purposes, such as assessing the depth of coverage of the artillery in support of a formation, planning ranges are used which equate to 90% (to the nearest 500 metres) of the maximum range shown in the firing tables for the highest charge of the weapons in question.

Plan Position Indicator — A type of radar display.

Plassey — Battery Honour Title of 9 (Plassey) Battery RA which was granted on 3 May 1937 under authority of 20/ARTY/5023/AG6a.

Plassey Day — Battery day of 9 (Plassey) Battery Royal Artillery, celebrated on 23 June each year.

Platform — The ground on which guns were placed. In fortresses it usually consisted of stone paving on the structure of which a gun carriage was placed if the whole was to be able to traverse, i.e. the traversing platform.

PLG — Plug.

PLGR — Precision Lightweight GPS Receiver.

PLONKS — Potential Leaders of No Knowledge

Plotter DW — A device introduced with the 12-gun battery in 1938 to enable the data of one troop in a battery to be converted for the others. Replaced in mid-1940 by the Tetley Fan. See *Tetley Fan*.

Plotter FC — Plotter fire control. Also referred to as the Plotter FC, FBA, this was an instrument that produced map range and bearing anywhere in a 6400 mil arc and enabled TGC to be quickly plotted. Replaced artillery board in the late 1950s and subsequently replaced by similar functioning plotter lightweight in early 1960s. See *Artillery Board, GPO's Check Map* and *Plotter, FC, FBA, Light, No 1, Mk 1.*

Plotter FC, FBA — Plotter, Fire Control, Field Branch Artillery.

Plotter, FC, FBA, Light, No 1, Mk 1 — Following the introduction of the 105 mm L5 Pack Howitzer in the 1960s and the conversion to mils and metres it was necessary to replace the existing Plotter, FC, FBA with a new version. This was the Plotter, FC, FBA, Light, No 1, Mk 1 which had identical functions but benefited from a simpler physical design and a considerable weight saving. The rolling fan in a sealed case of the Plotter, FC, FBA was replaced with a set of plastic fans which clipped to a baseboard. The disc carrier could move vertically as well as horizontally owing to a rack and pinion system located on the side of the baseboard. See *Plotter, FC, FBA*.

PLU — Program Loading Unit.

PMP — Permissible Maximum Pressure.

PMPS — Polygroove Modified Plain Section. A form of rifling.

PMS — Power Management System. See *LCDU* and *LINAPS.*

PN — Proximity Normal. A setting used on the Multi-Role Fuze. See *ET*, *PH* and *PL*.

PNA — Public Network Adapter.

PNL — Prescribed Nuclear Load.

PO — (i) Public Order.
(ii) Plotting Officer. Coast artillery Second World War and later.

POA — Point of Aim.

POC — Personnel Ordnance College.

Pocket Indirect Fire Trainer — A computer-based training system which takes the form of a series of varied scenarios, enabling the user to practise the multiple skills required to successfully engage targets using indirect fire systems. The skills practised include map-reading, observation of an area, target identification, fire discipline and call for fire procedures.

Pod — The name given to the payload of the Phoenix UAV which contains the sensor turret.

P of A — Position of Assembly.

Point — A trigonometrical height, usually measured above sea level. May be given in feet or now more commonly in metres.

Point K — Adjusting (ranging) point for a barrage if other barrage points are unsuitable.

Point Oboe — The name given to the initial point of origin of a smoke screen. All other points are calculated from this initial point of origin. Thus, whilst a smoke screen may comprise a number of points of origin, there will only be one Point Oboe. See *Point of Origin*.

Point of Burst — The point where the projectile bursts, if it does so prior to impact. See *Point of Impact.*

Point of Graze — The point at which the trajectory intersects the horizontal plane through the trunnions. It is sometimes referred to as the 'Ballistic Point of Graze'. See *Trajectory* and *Trunnions.*

Point of Impact — The point where the projectile hits an object which ends its flight. See *Point of Burst.*

Point of Origin — A smoke screen is produced by the simultaneous engagement of one or more points of origin. These are placed so that the smoke produced forms a continuous screen in the required area. They may be a considerable distance apart, and it is normal for each point of origin to be allocated to a different gun. The initial Point of Origin is referred to as Point Oboe, with subsequent points of origin being numbered sequentially from two. See *Point Oboe*.

Pointing Stick — Part of the Rapier AD System the pointing stick allows the detachment commander to select visually, and direct the tracker and launcher on to, a target which has not been identified by the system's own radar. Once the operator has identified the target, he/she takes command of the system and tracks the target in the normal way. See *Rapier Field Standard B1, Rapier Field Standard B2*, and *Rapier Field Standard C.*

POL — Petrol, Oils & Lubricants.

Polar Coordinates — These are produced by combining direction, distance and vertical angle. Polar coordinates are used in conjunction with the laser range finder.

Polar Plot — The method of locating a target or point on the map by means of polar coordinates. See *Polar Coordinates*.

Polymer Bonded Explosives — The explosive filling used in insensitive munitions. See *Insensitive Munitions.*

Pontavert Day — Battery Day of 19/5 (Gibraltar 1779–1783) Battery RA. Commemorates 5 Battery's defence of the guns at Bois des Bosches in 1918. This action saw all but five members of the Battery killed during bloody fighting, which ensued after an overwhelming attack by German infantry broke through the 2nd Battalion Devons and attacked the gun position. The Battery was awarded the *Croix de Guerre Avec Palme* for this gallant action. Battery personnel wear the French 1914 *Croix de Guerre* medal ribbon under their beret badges and on dress uniforms in recognition of this action. See *Croix de Guerre Day.*

Porpoise A sealed and floating steel 'sledge' containing extra ammunition which was towed by the Priest 105-mm SP guns on D-Day owing to their on-board load of 69 rounds being less than that of the Sexton 25-pdr SP guns. This reduced ammunition load was due to the length of the 105-mm M1 round. The Porpoise was 13 ft 6 ¼ in long, 1 ft high and came in two widths, 3 ft 3 inches and 4 ft 6 in. One of its most important features was that each porpoise could be stowed under the vehicle immediately behind the towing Priest whilst onboard the landing craft, thus saving valuable stowage space.

Portee The vehicle on which certain types of guns were transported, as opposed to being towed, and from which they could be fired if necessary. For example, during the Second World War the 2-pdr anti-tank gun was carried in this fashion. Not to be confused with a self-propelled gun. See *SP*.

Porteous Troop One of the Troops in 39 Roberts Bty Junior Leaders Regiment RA. See *Alanbrooke Troop, Ironside Troop* and *Ramsay Troop*.

Portfire A composition of gunpowder, sulphur and saltpetre in a paper case. The portfire had a known burning time and was used to ignite the powder in the vent of an artillery piece.

POSB Post Office Savings Bank. The abbreviation was used by members of the Junior Leaders Regiment RA.

Position and Azimuth Determining System PADS was introduced in 1980 as a replacement for PIM and consisted of an electromechanical inertial platform in a sealed box mounted in a vehicle. It 'carried' fixation from a survey control point to where it was needed. Subsequently, orientation could be taken from it using a director layed on a mirror that formed part of the PADS case and aligned with the axis of the gyro platform. See *GPS, PIM, Survey Control Point* and *TAS 10*.

Position Battery The nineteenth century name for heavy artillery. Such guns whilst mobile, were due to their weight not as mobile as the field artillery, although they were trained to trot into position. Many territorial artillery units were formed as position patteries, and a feature of their field days was often the guns being drawn by two heavy-draught horses, tandem fashion, with civilian carters dressed in smocks leading the horses and the Nos 1 marching at their head with drawn swords. Also to be found as guns of position. Subsequent to the First World War, guns of this calibre were retitled Medium Artillery.

Position Correction A correction given for line and range to each gun so that its fall of shot would be roughly in a straight line with the pivot gun at right angles to the line of fire.

Position Determining System A PADS type device integral to an MLRS SPLL providing accurate fix and orientation which allows the FCS in MLRS to show its grid location and make ballistic calculations from launcher position to target. See *FCS, MLRS, PADS* and *SPLL*.

Position Finder Invented by Major H. S. S. Watkins this instrument was used in conjunction with the DRF to establish the position of a target for coast artillery. It gave the range and training from the gun and therefore did not need to be in the immediate vicinity of the battery, but could be located in a concealed position out of the smoke and dust liable to be generated by the battery firing and from possible counter-fire from the target. See also *Depression Position Finder, Horizontal Position Finder* and *Trainings.*

Position Finding Cell — Usually found in a coast battery, the Position Finding Cell housed apparatus for determining the range and position of a target.

Post Gun — Post Guns were kept at various stations throughout India for use in emergencies, they were not attached to any particular artillery unit. They were usually only intended to be fired from the post and not to be used for deployment in the field. Post guns were generally manned by members of the Frontier Garrison Artillery. See *FGA.*

POTL — Post Operational Tour Leave.

Powder Passage — In Coast artillery a passage along which powder in bulk or in cartridges was transported. See *Shell Passage.*

Power Management System — Part of the LINAPS system. Based on Ni-Cad battery technology, the system will automatically switch to an external power source such as the towing vehicle or an external generator when one is available. A single, fully charged PMS is capable of providing power to LINAPS for seven hours, this can be increased by 40% if Power Save Mode is selected. See *Layers Display and Control Unit* and *Laser Inertial Automatic Pointing System.*

PP — (i) Practice Projectile.
(ii) Proof Pressure.
(iii) Present Position.

PPI — Plan Position Indicator.

PPM — Power Pack Module.

PPMA — Past and Present Members Association.

PPS — (i) Polygrove Plain Section.
(ii) Precise Position System.
(iii) Primary Power System.

PPSS — Platform Preparation Start Specification (Bowman). See *Bowman.*

PPU — (i) Prime Power Unit. Part of the COBRA system. See *COBRA.*

PPU — (ii) Peripheral Processing Unit.

Pr — Pounder. May also be found with a lower case 'p'. The abbreviation pdr was also used in this respect. See *Pdr.*

PR — Predicted Range.

PRAC — Practice HESH.

Practice Ammunition — See *Training Ammunition.*

Practice Camp — A live firing exercise period.

Practice HESH — A ballistically matched inert shell fitted with a tracer.

PRC — (i) Portable Radio Communicator. The abbreviation is followed by the number of the type of radio in question. For example PRC 365. See *VRC.*
(ii) Pseudo Random Code.

PRC-343 — The Personal Role Radio. See *Personal Role Radio.*

PRE — Periodic REME Inspection.

Precision Adjustment — An obsolete term for a single gun destruction fire mission. See *Destruction* and *Pin-Point Target.*

Precision Attack — The use of precision guided munitions to attack targets whilst reducing the level of collateral damage. See *Precision Munition.*

Precision Guided Munition — See *Precision Munition.*

Precision Indicator Meridian — Introduced in the mid 1960s this was a gyroscopic device which enabled accurate orientation to be found without external reference. PIM consisted of a theodolite head with a gyroscope device fitted below it. PIM required approximately fifteen minutes to settle before being capable of producing a result, which then had to be corrected for grid convergence by manual calculation. It was issued to every battery until 1980 when it was replaced by the Position and Azimuth Determining System. See *PADS*.

Precision Munition — A Laser or GPS guided munition which is capable of destroying an individual target, whilst reducing the level of collateral damage to a minimum.

Precision Shoot — This type of shoot is used when the destruction of a small target is required, for example, a bunker or building. As the target is usually fortified in some way, medium or heavy guns firing HE or special shell with delayed action fuzes are more effective than the lighter types of gun. The shoot is conducted by a single gun. Adjustment of the mpi being carried out with five round groups with corrections being ordered with reference to the line BT. A precision shoot is slow and laborious and often expensive in ammunition. It may be terminated without a successful conclusion, in which case the target may be recorded as a battery target in case neutralisation is required at a later date. Also referred to as a Pin-point Target. See *mpi* and *BT*.

Pre-Commando Course — A course run by the Commando Training Wing 29 Commando Regt, for those gunners about to undertake the All Arms Commando Course at the Commando Training Centre Royal Marines at Lympstone in Devon. The course is designed to give new entrants the chance to develop the level of fitness and skills required to pass the All Arms Commando Course.

Predict — The order to prepare predicted data. See *Predicted Data*.

Predicted Data — Data obtained by applying the corrections required to compensate for local prevailing non-standard conditions to map data. The process of determining and applying such corrections is called prediction. See *Predict, Predicted Fire* and *Prediction*.

Predicted fire — Using predicted fire enables a target to be attacked without being ranged. The target is normally indicated by an eight figure (10 yards or metres precision) map reference, and with correction of the moment data (obtained either by calculation or as the result of a datum shoot) applied. Predicted fire is often referred to as map shooting as it is used against targets selected from a map or air photograph.

Predicted Horizontal Range — The range found by adding the Projectile Correction to the Standard Predicted Horizontal Range, and is the range required to hit the target with the ammunition in use and under the prevailing conditions, providing that, the target is in the same horizontal plane as the firing gun and that it is of range table muzzle velocity. See *Projectile Correction* and *Standard Predicted Horizontal Range*.

Predicted Line — This bearing is the line required to hit the target with the projectile in use, under the prevailing conditions. It is found by adding corrections for drift to the standard predicted line. See *Standard Predicted Line*.

Predicted Range — This range is required to hit a target under the prevailing conditions, providing the gun is of range table muzzle velocity. It is found by adding the non-rigidity correction to the predicted horizontal range. If the target is on the same level as the gun, the predicted range will be the same as the predicted horizontal range and will always be referred to as such. See *Non-Rigidity Correction* and *Predicted Horizontal Range.*

Prediction — The working out of the future position of a target in order that both the target and the projectile meet.

Predictor — An anti-aircraft instrument which enabled guns to engage fast moving targets more efficiently. It was designed to work out mechanically the future position of the target and produce firing data which was then passed to the guns. See *Kerrison Predictor* and *Tachymetric Predictor*.

Predictor, No. 3 — See *Kerrison Predictor.*

Prem — Premature.

Premature — A round which detonates before reaching its target, it may or may not cause damage and/or casualties. There are three types of Premature. (i) Bore Premature, where the round detonates in the bore of the piece; (ii) Muzzle Premature, where the round detonates within 100 metres of the muzzle and (iii) Flight Premature, where the round detonates somewhere along its trajectory, but prior to arriving at the target.

Prepare for Tanks — Order to the guns, indicating that an attack by tanks is considered likely, but not necessarily imminent. The gun positions are prepared for tank action. See *Tank Action.*

Preparatory Fire — Intense prearranged fire delivered in accordance with a time schedule and in support of an attack, for the purpose of disrupting the enemy's communications, disorganizing his defences and neutralizing his fire support means. Preparation fire may start prior to, at, or after H-hour and continues until lifted either on a pre-arranged time schedule or on request from the assault elements. Preparation fire may include nuclear and non-nuclear fire and may be delivered by air, ground, or naval means. See *H-Hour*.

Prescribed Nuclear Load — The first line ammunition carried by nuclear delivery units. See *First Line Ammunition.*

PREV — Previous.

PRF — (i) Plug Representing Fuze.
(ii) Pulse Repetition Frequency.

PRI — President of the Regimental Institution.

Priest — 105 mm American self-propelled gun introduced into the Royal Artillery in 1942. An initial order for 500 was placed. The name Priest originated from the similarity of the machine-gun position to that of a church pulpit. Entered service in time for the Battle of Alamein in the Western Desert and served through to the Normandy campaign, where the Priest was replaced by the Canadian-designed and built Sexton 25-pdr self-propelled gun, although most had UK built ordnance and mounting shipped to Canada.
Detachment: 7
Weight: 22,997 kg
Length with gun: 6.02 m
Height: 2.54 m
Width: 2.9 m
Main Armament: 105 mm howitzer
Secondary Armament: .50 calibre machine-gun
Ammunition: 69 rounds of 105 mm. If a No. 19 wireless set was fitted only 45 rounds could be carried.
Traverse: 15° left, 30° right
Elevation: +35° to -5°
Maximum Speed: 40 kph
Road Radius: 201 km
See *Priest OP* and *Sexton*.

Priest OP An armoured observation post vehicle, based on the Priest 105 mm self-propelled gun chassis. The gun was removed and replaced by additional communications equipment. See *Priest*.

Primary Training Centre Establishments created in 1942 with the introduction of the general service corps to provide six weeks basic training to all new recruits before their allocation to a regiment or corps.

Primary Training Wing Formed during the Second World War, PTWs were attached to corps training centres to provide basic training to new recruits using a War Office common syllabus to achieve TOET standards.

Prime Mover The vehicle that transported an artillery equipment between positions, usually but not exclusively by towing.

Primer The normal means of initiating the propellant of a QF equipment. Screwed into the base of the cartridge case, it is made up of a detonating composition and a magazine filled with gunpowder. When the cap is struck by the firing pin, the flash from the detonating composition passes to the gunpowder which explodes, increasing the flash and igniting the propellant charge.

Priming Iron In muzzle-loading artillery this was a tool for clearing the vent and piercing the cartridge case. It was normally made in the form of a non-ferrous metal spike.

Priming Pocket In India during the nineteenth century, priming tubes were not used, instead, priming powder was carried loose in a leather pocket. It was fired by applying a portfire, ignited by a slow match which was carried by the field artillery lighted when action was expected, attached to one of the axle-tree boxes. See *Portfire*.

Principal AV A phoenix unmanned air vehicle to which a mission has been allocated. See *Subsidiary AV*.

Principal Storekeeper of the Ordnance Responsible for the care and maintenance of ordnance stores. Reporting to the master-general of the ordnance, he was a member of the board of ordnance from the time of its constitution in 1597 until the office was abolished in 1855. See *Board of Ordnance* and *Master-General of the Ordnance*.

Priority Call A formation or unit which has artillery at priority call has priority rights on the fire of that artillery. However, artillery units at priority call do not normally provide liaison and observation. The term is generally used to indicate a priority or reservation on fire allotted in support of more than one formation or unit. See *In Direct Support*.

Priority Defensive Fire A defensive fire mission, which is generally targeted at a location where enemy forces are likely to be first detected, irrespective of the time of day. As with the final protective fire mission, when guns assigned to the priority defensive fire mission are not engaged on other tasks, they are laid onto, and loaded in preparation to engage the PDF. See *Defensive Fire* and *Final Protective Fire*.

Prism Powder Propellant used in the largest natures of RML, it took the form of hexagonal prisms, 2-inches in height and 2½-inches in diameter, with axial perforation. The prisms were built up in layers within the cartridge.

Probable Error A statistical construct similar to a standard deviation. For the accuracy of predicted fire, 50% batteries' mean points of impact fell within 1 PE of where they were aimed, 100% fell within 4 PE. Therefore, if the PE of MPIs was 125 yards all MPIs fell in a circle 500 yards radius. Since PE for different types of error can partially counter-balance one another they are combined using the root mean square method.

Probert Scale Used on the 25-pdr field gun, the Probert Scale was named after the artillery officer who invented it. The scale acted like a mechanical computer and expressed tangent elevation as a range between 0–45° engraved on the base of the cone. Range scales measured in hundreds of yards were also engraved on the cone and a muzzle velocity reader arm could also be read off against it.

Procedure Word See *Proword*.

Proceedings, The Abbreviated title by which the Proceedings of the Royal Artillery Institute are commonly known. See *Proceedings of the Royal Artillery Institute.*

Program Loading Unit Part of the Field Artillery Computer Equipment, which had no data storage capability.

Programme of Targets A number of targets of a similar nature, e.g., a counter battery programme. Programme of targets may be designated using the nature of targets involved or nicknames. (Royal Canadian Artillery).

Programme Shoot Form One copy is used for each target engaged during a concentration or barrage. The form contains all the necessary details for the engagement of a target, including such items as target number, ammunition type, target height, battery height, and correction of the moment.

Projectile Correction This correction makes allowance for any differences between the projectile fired and the standard projectile for which a range table was compiled. The projectile correction includes corrections for the non-standard weight or nature of the shell and the fuze. See *Predicted Horizontal Range.*

Projector Infantry Anti-Tank

The PIAT was one of the earliest anti-tank weapons to use a HEAT shell. Developed in 1941 and entering service in 1943. The PIAT had a rated range of 100 metres, but was typically fired at much shorter ranges. The three pound (1.4 kg) HEAT warhead was capable of penetrating 100 mm of armour at a range of 100 metres. Although primarily an infantry weapon, a number of PIATs were issued to each artillery battery for the anti-tank defence of the gun position. The PIAT remained in service with the British Army until 1950.

Manufacturer: ICI Ltd together with various other companies.
Service: 1942–1950
Overall length: 39 in (990 mm)
Weight: 31.7 lb (14.4 kg)
Projectile weight: 3 lb (1.35 kg)
Muzzle velocity: 450 ft/s (137 m/s)
Effective range: 110 yd (100 m) against armour, or 350 yd (320 m) if used in the 'house-breaking' role
Penetration: 4 in (102 mm) armour at 115 yd (105 m)
Ammunition:
Bomb HE/AT; Infantry Projector, AT, Mk 3/L.
Weight: approx 2 3/4 lb (1.25 kg).
Length: 16.6 in (422 mm).
Colour: Brown, with red filling ring around forward portion of body, a blue band edged above and below with yellow and with 'TNT3' in black on the blue band.

Projector, Rocket, Three Inch, Number 8 Mark 1 See *Land Mattress.*

Prolong A short rope attachment from the trail eye to the limber hook that was used to allow a gun to be withdrawn without limbering up.

PROM Programmable Read Only Memory.

Pronto Radio appointment title. This title was used army-wide by the signals representative, however, in the Royal Artillery the following officers used the title:
At HQRA level by the Officer Commanding 2 Squadron; at a Regimental Headquarters level by the Officer Commanding Signals Troop; at Battery level by the Signaller Sergeant. See *Appointment Titles*.

Proof Proof is the testing by firing of items of equipment or samples of ammunition before they are accepted into service with the armed forces. It establishes whether they are safe to be fired under service conditions, and that they operate within service specifications. All barrels, breeches, buffer/recuperators and indeed complete weapons have to be proved at one of the P&EE before being taken into service. Shells, fuzes and cartridges are tested at various stages of manufacture to ensure that they are safe and function correctly. See *P&EE*.

Proof Butts An area where guns are experimented on and tested.

Proword A word or phrase used in radio telephone procedure to facilitate communication by conveying information in a condensed standard form. Sometimes referred to as a 'Procedure Word'.

Prox Proximity. A type of fuze.

Proximity Fuze (i) A fuze designed to cause a high explosive shell to detonate in the air.
(ii) A fuze designed to cause anti-aircraft ammunition to detonate when near the target aircraft. See *VT Fuze*.

PRR Personal Role Radio.

PRS Pressure.

PRS BRG Present Bearing.

PRS EL Present Elevation.

PRT Permanent Range Team.

PRV Pressure Relief Valve.

PS (i) Permanent Staff.
(ii) Chloropicrin, a First World War British gas shell filling, also known as Red Star, the name was derived from Port Sunlight, where Lever Brothers first investigated it in their laboratory located there.
(iii) Pointing Stick.

PS and SSU Power Supply and System Selector Unit.

PSAO Permanent Staff Administrative Officer, in a TA unit.

PSC (i) Principle Subordinate Commander.
(ii) Patrol Selection Course.

psc Passed Staff College. On completion of the course the letters are entered after an officer's name in the Army List and the Royal Artillery Blue List.

Pscope Parallelescope.

psi Pounds Per Square Inch.

PSI Permanent Staff Instructor. A Regular Soldier serving with a TA unit in an Instructional capacity.

PSJ Power Supply (Javelin).

PSM Power Save Mode.

PSO (i) Peace Support Operations.
(ii) Principal Staff Officer.

PSP Pierced Steel Plank.

PSU Power Supply Unit.

Pt Point.

Ptarmigan A mobile, secure battlefield communications system designed to improve reliability, capacity and interoperability. It consists of a network of electronic exchanges or trunk switches connected by satellite and multi-channel radio relay links. Providing voice, data, telegraph and fax communications. There is also facility for a mobile phone or single channel radio access which gives mobile users an entry point to the system.

PTC — Primary Training Centre.

PTI — Physical Training Instructor.

PTS — Parachute Training School.

PTT — Part-Task Trainer.

PTU — Pressure, Temperature, and Humidity.

PTW — Primary Training Wing.

PU — (i) Polyurethane.
(ii) Pick-Up. A light vehicle used by troop commanders during the Second World War.

PUDT — Portable User Data Terminal. Part of the Bowman communications system. See *Bowman*.

Puff Range — An obsolete artillery OP training aid used prior to the introduction of Invertron. The Puff Range consisted of something that looked like a model railway layout made of hessian, constructed to simulate an area of terrain from a map. The hessian was laid over a chicken wire frame about six feet off the ground, with grid squares marked on the floor underneath. The effect of a shell landing was created by a smoke generator which was moved under the model, to line up with the grids painted on the floor. The 'smoke' was generated by passing ammonia vapour through concentrated sulphuric acid or a similar hazardous substance. The Puff Range was replaced by the Invertron and subsequently the Invertron AFCT. See *Invertron*.

Punishment Fire — A type of fire mission devised by the CRA 42nd East Lancashire Division during the First World War which consisted of the maximum number of guns of all available calibres being employed and firing a concentration of shelling for a specified duration on to a particular area from which the enemy had been most active.

PUP — Pull-up Point.

Pussers Planks — Skis.

Puzzle Palace — Nickname given to any regimental headquarters or in the King's Troop RHA to its Troop HQ.

PWT — Personal Weapons Test.

PZ — Pick-up Zone.

Q – Queen – 1927/1943
Quebec – 1956

Q — (i) The title by which the BQMS is addressed.
(ii) Tactical sign for a quartermaster. See *Tactical Sign*.
(iii) Artillery code used during the First World War meaning 'Left'.

QAD(W) — Quality Assurance Directorate (Weapons).

QAP — Quadripartite Advisory Publications, issued by the American, British Canadian and Australian Standardisation Program.

QBO — Quick Battle Orders.

QE — Quadrant Elevation.

QF — Quick Firing. See *Breech Loading, Breech Loading Converted* and *Obturation*.

QF Ammunition — Quick Firing Ammunition. See *25-pdr, Breech Loading Ammunition, L118 Light Gun* and *Obturation*.

QFC — Quadrant Fire Control.

QF Cartridge — See *Quick Firing Ammunition*.

QF Composition	Quick Firing Composition.
QF Fixed	Quick Fire Fixed. See *Quick Firing Ammunition.*
QF Semi-Fixed	Quick Fire Semi-Fixed. See *Quick Firing Ammunition.*
QF Separate	Quick Fire Separate. See *Quick Firing Ammunition.*
QGI	Qualified Gunnery Instructor.
QM	(i) Quartermaster. (ii) Artillery code used during the First World War meaning 'Mostly Left'.
QM(M)	Quartermaster (Maintenance).
QM(Maint)	Quartermaster (Maintenance).
QMS(I)	Quartermaster Sergeant (Instructor). Also given as QMS(Instr).
QMS(Instr)	Quartermaster Sergeant (Instructor). Also given as QMS(I).
QM(T)	Quartermaster (Technical).
QQ	Artillery code used during the First World War meaning 'More Left'.
QRF	Quick Reaction Force.
Qr Mr	Quartermaster. This abbreviation was in use during the 1920s and possibly earlier. It has now been replaced by QM.
QSTAGS	Quadripartite Standing Agreements. Part of the American, British Canadian and Australian Standardisation Program. Important artillery QSTAGs are: QSTAG 182 Battlefield Illumination. QSTAG 217 Tactical tasks and responsibilities for the control of artillery fire. QSTAG 221 Target numbering system. QSTAG 225 Call for fire procedures. The first edition of this, in 1965, combined with the previous QSTAGs resulted in comprehensive changes to fire discipline and procedures replacing the system that had evolved during the first half of the twentieth century. QSTAG 269 Survey accuracy requirement for surface to surface artillery. QSTAG 503 Bombing, shelling, mortaring, rocketing and location reports. QSTAG 515 Proforma for artillery fire plan.
Quadrant Elevation.	The angle between the angle of the bore, when the gun is laid, and the horizontal.
Quadripartite Working Group	Part of the American, British Canadian and Australian Standardisation Program
Quarter	Abbreviated form of address for a battery quartermaster sergeant. Certainly in use during the 1920s. See *Battery Quartermaster Sergeant* and *Quarterbloke.*
Quarterbloke	Nickname used to refer to the Battery Quartermaster Sergeant. See *Battery Quatermaster Sergeant* and *Quarter.*
Quartermaster (Maintenance)	The senior Quartermaster in a Regiment, commanding the regimental B echelon. Colloquially know as 'boots and socks'.
Quarter to Ten Guns	Skoda 9.45-inch howitzers purchased for use in the South African War.
Quebec 1759	Battery Honour Title of 18 (Quebec 1759) Battery RA which was granted on 6 June 1935 under authority of 20/ARTY/5019/AG6a. See *Battery Honour Titles.*
Quebec Day	Battery Day of 18 (Quebec 1759) Battery RA. Celebrated each year on 13 September.
Queen Bee	See *De Havilland Dh82 Queen Bee.*
Queen's Gunner	The holder of this post used to reside in the Round Tower at Windsor Castle with the responsibility of raising and

	lowering the flag there. His rank insignia consisted of a crown over the Royal Cypher which was in turn over a gun in gold on his forearm. The post was last filled by Gunner Samuel Parsons, who held the post for over fifty years, until he was discharged in 1912. The exact date on which the post was abolished is unclear.
Quick Action	A drill where guns are quickly brought into action whilst en-route from one gun position to another. The first gun to report 'ready for line' is directed into the centre of arc by a prismatic compass; then that gun passes line to the remaining guns so as to have them all parallel. See *Action.*
Quick Fire Fixed	See *Quick Firing Ammunition.*
Quick Fire Plan	See *Fire Plan.*
Quick Fire Semi-Fixed	See *Quick Firing Ammunition.*
Quick Fire Separate	See *Quick Firing Ammunition.*
Quick Firing	A form of ordnance where the propellant charge bags are contained within a brass cartridge case which provided obturation. See *Breech Loading, Breech Loading Converted* and *Obturation.*
Quick Firing Ammunition	In Quick Firing ammunition, the charge is contained in a cartridge case, usually made of brass. The cartridge case provides obturation and carries both the charge and the means of ignition screwed into the base of the case. There are three types of QF Ammunition: Fixed: Where the projectile and cartridge case are permanently joined together. A change in charge can only be made by changing the complete round. Semi-Fixed: Where the projectile is a machine fit to the mouth of the cartridge case, but the two are separable. This allows the charge to be changed at will, however, the ammunition is stored as a complete round. Separate: The projectile and the cartridge case are stored and loaded separately. This makes the change of charge a simple matter, but entails ramming and a consequently lower rate of fire. The top of the cartridge is normally closed by an easily detachable cup. Examples of guns using Separate Ammunition are the 25-pdr and the L118 Light Gun. See *25-pdr, Breech Loading Ammunition, L118 Light Gun* and *Obturation.*
Quick Firing Cartridge	See *Quick Firing Ammunition.*
Quick Firing Composition	An igniferous initiator used in primer caps.
Quoin	In muzzle-loading artillery this was a triangular wedge of wood which was placed under the breech of a gun in order to elevate and depress it. See *Stool Bed.*
Quo Fas et Gloria Ducunt	'Where Right and Glory lead'.
QWG	Quadripartite Working Group.

R – Robert – 1927
Roger – 1943
Romeo – 1956

R	(i) Right. (ii) Artillery code used during the First World War meaning 'Right'.
R0	Readiness State 0. At this state a unit must be able to deploy immediately.
R1	(i) Readiness State 1. (ii) See *Romeo 1.*
R2	(i) Reports and Returns. (ii) Readiness State 2.

	(iii) See *Romeo 2.*
R3	(i) Readiness State 3.
	(ii) Reports, Returns and Requests.
	(iii) See *Romeo 3.*
R&A	Range and Accuracy.
RA	Royal Artillery.
RA & TC CD	Royal Artillery and Tank Corps Command Depot.
RAA	(a) Royal Artillery Association.
	(b) Royal Australian Artillery.
RAAC	Royal Artillery Alpine Club.
RAAHS	Royal Australian Artillery Historical Society.
RAAT	Royal Artillery Adventurous Training.
RAAUS	Royal Artillery Association Uniformed Staff.
RABA&JLA	Royal Artillery Boys, Artificers and Junior Leaders Association.
RABSM	Royal Artillery Battery Sergeant Major.
RAC	Regional Air Commander.
RACAC	Royal Artillery Course Allocation Cell.
RACC	(i) Royal Artillery Captains Course.
	(ii) Royal Artillery Cricket Club.
Racers	Racers were curved tracks set into the floor of a gun emplacement so that guns could be traversed more rapidly. The smaller natures of gun used wrought iron racers, whilst those of 10-inches and over used steel racers. Racers were fixed on iron chairs or set in granite blocks. The configuration varied according the type of platform and method of mounting and the position depended upon the pivot used.
Racer Track	See *Racers.*
RACISG	Royal Artillery Command Information Systems Group.
RACP	Regimental Ammunition Control Point. See *ACP* and *BACP.*
RACPD	Royal Artillery Centre for Personal Development.
RACST	Royal Artillery Combat Shooting Team.
Radar & S/L Bty	Radar and Searchlight Battery.
Radar AA No 3 Mk 2(F)	Used for Mortar Location, the AA No 3 Mk 2(F) was developed from Radar AA No. 3 Mk 3. It was trailer-mounted and weighed 9½ tons. Power was supplied by a separate trailer mounted 15 kVA generator. Using a 10 cm wavelength, it had a maximum range 8,000 yards when detecting medium mortar rounds. Operating to an accuracy ± 25 yards with Plotter 3-pen FA No. 1 or 100-150 yards without the plotter. It required four operators and was used by Divisional Counter Mortar batteries. See *Radar AA No 3 Mk 3.*
Radar AA No 3 Mk 3	These Radars were used for Mortar Location, in the same way that the Radar AA No 3 Mk 2(F) was used. They were at their most accurate when linked to a 3 pen Westex recorder which took bearings from 3 radars and plotted them. Bearings and ranges from a single radar were accurate to 150 yards. Together with their associated equipment they were used by the divisional counter mortar batteries. Their main drawback being the slow speed with which the information received could be disseminated to the guns. See *Radar AA No 3 Mk 2(F).*
Radar AD No 11 Mk 1	See *AD11.*
Radar AD No 12 Mk 1	See *AD12.*
Radar CA No 1 Mk 4 (F)	Used for the control of artillery fire and engagement of moving targets the Radar CA No 1 Mk 4 (F) was developed in 1944 from a coast artillery 'fall of shot' radar. It was trailer-mounted and weighed 7¾ tons. Power was supplied by a 15 kVA generator mounted in a separate

trailer. Using a 3 cm wavelength it could in good conditions observe shell bursts at 20,000 yards. It required three operators. It was deployed in North West Europe and Italy.

Radar FA No 1 Mk 1 Used for the control of artillery fire and engagement of moving targets the Radar FA No 1 Mk 1 was developed from the Radar CA No 1 Mk 4 (F). It was mounted on a Half Track and weighed 10 tons. Power was supplied by a 6.25 kVA Generator mounted in a separate trailer. Using a 3 cm wavelength it could in good conditions observe shell bursts at 20,000 yards. It required 3 operators.

Radar FA No 1 Mk 2 Used for the control of artillery fire and engagement of moving targets the Radar FA No 1 Mk 2 was a post Second World War development of the FA No 1 Mk 1. See *Radar FA No 1 Mk 1.*

Radar FA No 2 Mk 1 Doppler radar for moving target indication.

Radar FA No 3 Mk 1 Mortar location radar that did not progress beyond the development and trials stage.

Radar FA No 3 Mk 2 Mortar location radar. Developed from the United States AN/APS-3 airborne radar, the Radar FA No 3 Mk 2 was trailer mounted and weighed 600 lbs. Power was supplied by a 1.2 kVA generator mounted in a separate trailer. Using a 3 cm wavelength it had a maximum range of 5,500 yards when detecting medium mortar rounds. It required 3 operators, one of whom maintained the artillery board. It entered service after the Second World War. See *Artillery Board.*

Radar FA No 8 See *Green Archer.*

Radar FA No 15 See *Cymbeline.*

Radar FA No 19 See *WF3M.*

Radar GS No 9 See *Robert.*

Radar GS No 14 See *ZB298.*

Radar No 1 Mk 1 Developed at the end of the Second World War for mortar locating and movement direction. The radar was very advanced for its time, its vehicle movement detection capability at long range has never been matched. First deployed operationally during the Korean War the radar suffered from a design fault with the generator, which caused the engine to seize due to an almost dry sump. See *Cymbeline, Green Archer* and *Ringworm.*

Radar No 4 Mk 6 Air Defence surveillance radar.

Radar No 4 Mk 7 Air Defence surveillance radar.

Radar Nomenclature The War Office introduced a system of radar nomenclature at the beginning of the Second World War. This system used letters for role followed by numbers 1–4 for function and Mark number for different radars with the same function.

Roles:
AA: anti-aircraft
CA: coast artillery
CD: coast defence
FA: field artillery

Functions:
AA No 1: Warning and Fire Control (Long Wave)
AA No 2: Searchlight Control
AA No 3: Fire Control
AA No 4: Local Warning
CD No 1: Surveillance and Tracking
CA No 1: Fire Control
CA No 2: Fire Command
FA No 1: Fire Control
FA No 2: Movement Detection

FA No 3: Mortar Locating
After the Second World War a new system was introduced. This used role letters and then allocated a number in chronological order, it seems to have started at 8. Roles:
AD: air defence
FA: field artillery
GS: general service

Radar Repair Vehicle — Operated by REME, this vehicle was fitted with test and reference equipment for radar equipments, in particular the Green Archer and Cymbeline radars, but possibly others as well.

Radar Tracker — Target tracking radar (Part of the Rapier FSB2 AD system), also known as DN 181 and Blindfire.

Radio Net — A group of radio stations that are capable of direct communication on a common frequency. Examples of radio nets used by the Royal Artillery include the Regimental Net and Battery Net.

Radio Nomenclature — In the 1930s the War Office introduced a system of nomenclature wireless sets. Numbers 1–9, in the least significant position defined the sets' primary role. Each later set with the same role added 10 to this number. Hence No 9 was the first generation AFV set, No 19 the next. The role numbers were:
1: short range brigade sets and artillery.
2: short range divisional sets.
3: medium range sets.
4: intercommunication sets.
5: long range sets.
6 & 7: special purpose sets.
8: infantry & manpack sets.
9: AFV sets that could be used on the move. This system lasted until the 1940s when a new system was adopted and applied to Larkspur in the 1950s. It used a letter followed by two digits:
A: very low power, dry battery.
B: low power, secondary battery.
C: medium power.
D: high power.
E: very high power.
To these, a two digit number was added:
10–30: MF/HF band (3-30 MHz)
40–60: VHF/UHF band (30 – 300 MHz)
70–99: SHF/EHF band (above 300 MHz)
This system lasted until the 1970s when the US originated Joint Electronics Type Designation System (JETDS) was adopted with the form AN/aaa-nn but replaced the prefix 'AN' (Army Navy) with UK and used a three digit number. JETDS applies to various equipments including radars and other observation devices, UK only uses it for radios, Clansman used this system. The letters, relevant to radios, mean:
First letter: installation:
A: piloted aircraft
F: fixed ground
G: general ground use
M: mobile ground
P: human portable
S: surface ship
T: transportable (ground)
U: General utility (multi-use)
V: vehicle (ground)

	Second letter, type of equipment, for communications: F: fibre optic G: telegraph or teletype I: interphone and public address L: countermeasures R: radio T: telephone (wire) Third letter, purpose: C: communications (two way) D: direction finding R: receiving. T: transmitting UK radios adopted the 300 series with the second and third digits roughly following the earlier radios.
Radio Stag	Listening watch maintained on the radio net. The duty generally lasts for an hour or so, during which time the gunner on duty has to listen to the mind-numbing hum in the radio headset whilst endeavouring to stay awake.
Radio Theodolite 20	Part of the BMETS system, the Vaisala RT20 has four antennae arranged in a two by two square format. These are fully interchangeable and when assembled it does not matter which antenna is set up in which position within this arrangement. Three of the antennae track azimuth and elevation, whilst the fourth is used to collect the met data from the sonde attached to the weather balloon. The RT20 does not emit radar, it merely receives the signals from the sonde. Time into action is approximately fifteen minutes, once assembled, the RT20 is placed upwind of the balloon inflation and launching device to enable it to track the elevation and azimuth of the balloon during its flight to an altitude that is at least 20 km above the Met Datum Plane (MDP). See *BILD, BMETS* and *MDP*.
RAFA	Royal Australian Field Artillery.
RAGA	Royal Australian Garrison Artillery.
RAGTE	Royal Artillery Gunnery Training Establishment. Pronounced 'Ragter'.
RAGTLS	Royal Artillery Gunnery Training Levels Study.
RAGTT(AD)	Royal Artillery Gunnery Training Team (Air Defence).
RAGTT(Fd)	Royal Artillery Gunnery Training Team (Field) (Under command of CAFTG(G)).
RAGWR	Royal Artillery Guided Weapon Range (Original title given to the Royal Artillery Range Hebrides (RARH) on establishment in 1957).
RAHAC	Royal Artillery Historical Affairs Committee.
RAHS	Royal Artillery Historical Society.
RAHT	Royal Artillery Historical Trust.
RAHQ	Royal Artillery Headquarters.
RAI	Royal Artillery Institution.
RAIV	A one-day visit to the Royal Artillery designed to introduce potential officers to the Royal Artillery. It is primarily aimed at potential officers who are either in the 6th form or in a gap year prior to attending university. The visit is intended to highlight the variety of roles available to a gunner officer and includes an interview and lunch in the officers' mess. See *FV.*
RAK	Radio Adapter Kit.
RALONGS	Royal Artillery Liaison Officer Naval Gunfire Support.
Railway Gun	A large calibre gun mounted on a railway carriage. See *Boche-Buster* and *Scene-Shifter.*
Railway Truck Mounting	A railway mounting for large calibre artillery pieces. See *Boche-Buster* and *Scene-Shifter.*

RA MCM Div — Royal Artillery Manning and Career Management Division.

RA Medal — See *Royal Artillery Medal.*

Rammer — The wooden stave used by the No. 2 of a detachment to 'ram' home the projectile. Some modern systems, such as the AS90, have automatic powered rammers. In smooth-bore days, the rammer would also be used to ram home the charge. See *Bad Ram.*

Ram Observation Post — A Canadian-built ram tank converted for use as an observation post vehicle. When production of Ram II finished in 1943 it was decided that a batch of 84 command/observation post tanks would be produced. The same basic vehicle could be employed either in the command tank role or as an observation post. Externally the Ram OP was identical to the final production model. It had a hull mounted machine gun, no auxiliary turret, late pattern suspension with trailing return rollers, and no side escape doors. The gun and turret basket were deleted and a dummy mantlet and gun fitted. This turret could rotate 45° to either side, thus enabling the observer to use the observation port, which was fitted with a sliding cover, located beneath the dummy barrel. Internally, a detachment of six could be accommodated together with wireless sets and map boards. The actual number in a detachment varied according to the precise role of the vehicle. Two wireless sets No. 19 were carried, one in the rear of the turret and one on the left hand side of the hull. Fittings were also supplied for a stereoscopic periscope in the turret cupola. The cupola could be rotated and there was a graduated scale on the underside to enable bearings to be easily read. Externally, there was an extra wireless aerial on the left hand track guard and two cable reels on the engine deck. These made it possible for an observer to operate at some distance from the tank whilst still using the internal wireless sets by remote control. The observer, observation post assistant and a signaller could thus establish a dismounted observation post whilst leaving the OP tank concealed some distance away.

Later in the war, rams of all types were converted to the OP role by the simple expedient of removing their guns, turret basket and ammunition stowage and fitting observation ports, extra wireless and internal fittings as found on the purpose built versions. Other ram variants included prime movers for 17-pdr anti-tank guns, armoured resupply vehicles, flame throwers and armoured personnel carriers as well as the Sexton SP gun. See *Command Tank, Sexton* and *Sexton GPO.*

Ram OP — See *Ram Observation Post.*

RAMR — Royal Artillery Mounted Rifles. See *Artillery Mounted Rifles.*

RAMRI — Royal Artillery Manning and Records Instructions.

RAMRO — Royal Artillery Manning and Records Office.

Ramsay's Day — Battery Day of H Parachute Headquarters Battery (Ramsay's Troop) RHA .

Ramsay Troop — One of the Troops in 39 Roberts Bty Junior Leaders Regiment RA. See *Alanbrooke Troop, Ironside Troop* and *Porteous Troop.*

Ramsay's Troop — Battery Honour Title of H Parachute Headquarters Battery (Ramsay's Troop) RHA which was granted on 18 October 1926 under authority of 20/ARTY/4544/AG6a. See *Battery Honour Titles.*

RAMTS — Royal Artillery Mechanical Traction/Transport School.

RA MT School — Royal Artillery Mechanical Traction/Transport School.

Ram Wallaby Ammunition Carrier	A redundant ram tank from which the turret had been removed and the opening for the main armament had been plated over. A hatch was fitted in the plate to provide access, and racks for 25-pdr ammunition were fitted in the side sponsons. Ram Wallabies gave ammunition carriers the same performance as the supported Sexton self-propelled guns, and offered a great deal more protection to the detachment. (Royal Canadian Artillery). See *Ram Observation Post* and *Sexton*.
Rancid	Nickname given by 45 Field Regiment Royal Artillery to a mortar-locating radar mounted on a half-track vehicle, a predecessor of Green Archer and Cymbeline. Rancid, together with an identical radar nicknamed 'Ringworm' was used during the Korean War. See *Cymbeline, Green Archer, Radar No.1 Mk 1* and *Ringworm*.
Randy Cats	Nickname of the Bengal Rocket Troop, derived from the Battery badge which depicts a seated tiger with a rocket between its legs.
Rangiriri Day	Battery day of 94 (New Zealand) Bty RA. Held to celebrate the Battle of Rangiriri in 1863.
Range	The actual distance between two points.
Range Spread	The technique used to distribute fire along the gun-target line. (Royal Canadian Artillery.) See *Lateral Spread*.
Range Tables	These provide data to set up the correction of the moment graph and make other corrections for use when employing predicted fire.
Ranging	The process by which the observer directs artillery fire onto the target. This is achieved by establishing a bracket which is progressively halved until the target is hit.
RAO	Regimental Administration Officer.
RAOA	Royal Artillery Officers Association.
RAOC	Royal Army Ordnance Corps. Now part of the Royal Logistic Corps.
RAOWO	Regimental Administration Office Warrant Officer.
RAP	(i) Recognised Air Picture. (ii) Regimental Aid Post. (iii) Rocket Assisted Projectile.
RAPA	Royal Artillery Parachute Association.
RAPDT	Royal Artillery Parachute Display Team.
Rapier	Surface-to-air anti-aircraft missile system. See *Rapier Field Standard B1, Rapier Field Standard B2, Rapier Field Standard C* and *Tracked Rapier.*
Rapier FSB1	Rapier Field Standard B1.
Rapier FSB2	Rapier Field Standard B2.
Rapier FSC	Rapier Field Standard C.
Rapier Field Standard B1	Each launcher had four missile launch rails, and was towed by a Land Rover.
Rapier Field Standard B2	Each launcher had six missile launch rails and was towed by a 4 tonne truck.
Rapier Field Standard C	An advanced short range air defence system. It has 24-hour, all weather capability, with the primary role of providing limited area air defence coverage against fixed wing aircraft, helicopters and unmanned aerial vehicles. FSC is capable of engaging two targets at once. The system comprises four components and two types of missile. (i) The Launcher: The launcher holds 8 missiles. With a thermo-optical sight for real time thermal video feed contained within the body of the launcher, it can be deployed independently with one command and control Unit to engage aircraft. (ii) The Tracker Radar:

Capable of tracking, locking on and guiding a missile to a target with an accuracy rate of 99.9%. The Tracker Radar is also capable of being set on its own independent search pattern to look for targets.
(iii) The Surveillance Radar:
Real time overhead pictures are sent from the surveillance radar to the command and control Units. Able to display anything up to 75 potential targets, the radar is capable of interrogating all the targets and identifying friendly or hostile aircraft.
(iv) The Command and Control Unit:
Thermal pictures from the launcher and an overhead radar picture from the surveillance radar are displayed on the command and control unit, which permits the operators to control Rapier FSC engagements by way of simple menu options.
(v) The Missiles:
There are two versions of the Rapier FSC missile, both of which travel at over twice the speed of sound and look very similar.
The mark 2A is a commonly referred to as a hittile, having just a simple explosive that will detonate when coming in to contact with a target.
The mark 2B however, has a proximity fuse which detonates the warhead when near the target, showering the immediate area with over 1000 tungsten cubes which are capable of shredding any target in close proximity.
Detachment: 8 (9 on operations)
Guidance: Command to Line of Sight
Missile Diameter: 13.3 cm
Missile Length: 2.35 m
Rocket: Solid Fueled
Warhead: High Explosive
Launch Weight: 42 kg.
Speed: Mach 2+
Ceiling: 5000 m
Maximum Range: 500 metres to around 8 kms
Fire Unit: Height 2.13 m
Fire Unit Weight: 1,227 kg
Radar Height (in action): 3.37 m
Radar Weight: 243 kg
Generator Height: 0.91 m

RAPSO Royal Artillery Personnel Selection Officer.

RAPT Royal Artillery Presentation Team.

RAP Tp Recognised Air Picture Troop.

RA RA Royal Artillery Range Assistant.

RARA Royal Artillery Rifle Association.

RARC Royal Artillery Review Committee.

RARDE Royal Armaments Research and Development Establishment (pronounced 'Rah-Dee').

RARFC Royal Artillery Rugby Football Club.

RARH Royal Artillery Range Hebrides.

RARM Royal Artillery Range Manorbier.

RARO Royal Artillery Reconnaissance Officer.

RARS Review of Ammunition Rates and Scales. See *Battle Attrition Study* and *Daily Ammunition Expenditure.*

RAS Rocket Assembly Specialist (Royal Canadian Artillery).

RASA Royal Artillery Sailing Association.

RASC Royal Army Service Corps. Now part of the Royal Logistic Corps.

RASDAS Rapier Site Data Store.

RASM Royal Artillery Sergeant-Major.

RA Specialist Pool (V)	Royal Artillery Specialist Pool (Volunteers). See *CVHQ RA, All Arms Staff Officers Liaison & Watchkeepers Group* and *LCSP (V).*
RASSPT	Royal Artillery Soldier Schools Presentation Team.
RASST	Royal Artillery System Support Team.
RA Survey	Artillery survey undertaken by survey units of the Royal Artillery. RA surveyors generally used theodolites and conducted surveys over longer distances and therefore worked to greater precision than regimental surveyors needed to. See *Regimental Survey.*
RAT	Record As Target.
RATB	Royal Artillery Training Board.
RATD	Royal Artillery Training Depot.
RATDT	Royal Artillery Training Development Team.
RATDU	Royal Artillery Trials and Development Unit.
RATDU (Fd)	Royal Artillery Trials and Development Unit (Field).
Rate	Named rates of fire (intense, rapid, normal, slow and very slow) in rounds per minute, the actual number of rounds varied with the type of gun. Intense rate was the maximum sustained rate that the gun could fire without overheating.
RATE	Royal Artillery Training Establishments, a formation made up of training regiments.
Ratio of Movement	In an autosight the difference between the movement of the sight and the movement of the gun. See *Autosight* and Gun *Auto-Sight*.
RATSG	Royal Artillery Training Standards Group. See *TSG RA.*
RATT	Royal Artillery Training Team.
RAU	Range Administrative Unit.
RAWFC	Royal Artillery Women's Football Club.
RAWCF	Royal Artillery War Commemoration Fund.
RAWO	Regimental Administrative Warrant Officer.
RBAA	Reserve Brigade Australian Artillery.
RBD	Reinforcement Base Depot.
RBL	(i) Rifled Breech Loading. (ii) Rocking Bar Sight Layer.
RBSD	Reduced Burst Safety Distance.
RCA	Royal Canadian Artillery.
RCAA	Royal Canadian Artillery Association.
RCB	Regular Commissions Board.
RCFA	Royal Canadian Field Artillery.
RCGA	Royal Canadian Garrison Artillery.
RCHA	Royal Canadian Horse Artillery.
RCL	Recoilless.
RCMO	Regimental Career Management Officer.
RCO	Range Conducting Officer.
RCP	(i) Regimental Command Post. (ii) Radar Command Post.
RCPO	Radar Command Post Officer.
RCS	(i) Rapier Control System. (ii) Radar Control Set. Part of the Rapier AD system. (iii) Radar Cross Section.
RCSA	Royal Canadian School of Artillery.
Rct	Recruit.
RCU	(i) Rides Course and Upgrading (run each winter at St Johns Wood to increase pay). (ii) Radar Collimation Unit. Part of the Rapier AD system.
RCWO	Regimental Catering Warrant Officer.
RD	(i) Regimental Duty. (ii) Range Detail.
rd	Round.

RDA	Range Danger Area.
RDM	Remotely Delivered Mine.
Rd Mr	Riding Master. (Rank no longer in use).
RDMV Camera	Research Development Muzzle Velocity Camera.
Rdr	Radar.
rds	Rounds.
Rds C	Rounds Complete.
Rds FFE	Rounds Fire For Effect.
RDSS	Rapidly Deployable Surveillance System.
RDU	Remote Display Unit (Part of the ADAD system).
RDX	Research Department Formula X. A type of explosive used in artillery shells.
Rdy	Ready.
Reach	The deployment range of a weapons system plus its munition range.
Readiness State 0	Units placed on this readiness state must be able to deploy immediately.
Ready	The term used to indicate that a gun/launcher is aimed, loaded and prepared to fire.
Ready Use Area	In air defence units, this area is used to store missiles, prior to firing.
Rear Headquarters	Usually only operated by larger formations' headquarters for their personnel and logistic staff and associated services. Artillery logistic staff are usually at Rear Headquarters. See *Alternate Headquarters, Battery Headquarters, Main Headquarters, Regimental Headquarters Step-Up* and *Tactical Headquarters*.
Rebel Chasers from America	See *Royal Canadian Field Artillery.*
Rebro	Rebroadcast.
Rebroadcast	A radio technique whereby signals from one radio communicates to another set, which is adjacent and directly connected to another more powerful radio that rebroadcasts the signal on a different frequency. Rebroadcast stations are established to increase the range over which communications can be sent and to overcome line of sight problems. The technique is also used by forward observation officers, who go forward using man pack radios and rebroadcast to their command posts via the more powerful radios in their OPVs. See *Command Post, FOO* and *Warrior OPV.*
Recce	Reconnaissance.
Receiving Hatch	In coast artillery an opening in the door or wall of a cartridge or shell-filling room, through which empty shell or powder in bulk was passed.
Reciprocating Sights	A dial sight carrier that enabled the dial sight to be cross levelled to keep it vertical when the trunnions were tilted due to the terrain being uneven. For example, a gun situated on a slope with one wheel higher than the other. All British Second World War guns had reciprocating sights. See *Calibrating Sights* and *Dial Sight Carrier.*
Recognised Air Picture	An electronically produced display compiled from primary and secondary radar sources, together with electronic support measures sources covering a three dimensional area of interest in which all detected air contacts are evaluated against specific threat parameters and then assigned a recognition category and track number.
Recoil	The rearward movement of an ordnance. Prior to the introduction of recoil systems in the late nineteenth century the entire gun moved backwards, necessitating the relaying of the gun after each round, with an associated reduction in the rate of fire. Recoil systems comprise a

buffer that absorbs the recoil of the ordnance and a recuperator that returns it to its firing position on the carriage or mounting. This absorbs most of the recoil force leaving a residual amount to be transferred to the ground by the gun's carriage or mounting. Almost all British recoil systems use hydraulic buffers and hydraulic-pneumatic recuperators. Muzzle brakes also reduce recoil forces.

Reconnaissance and Interdiction Planning Line — NATO air power coordination line, between Corps or Army Group and independent air operation areas.

Reconnaissance Party — During the early 1980s the Battery Reconnaissance Party consisted of the Golf and Jig 2 Tac Signs. See *Golf* and *Jig 2*.

Record As Target — The fire order command used to denote that the target is to be recorded for future engagement or reference. See *...Recorded.*

... Recorded — The report used to indicate that the action taken to 'record as target' has been completed. It is preceded by the appropriate target number. See *Record as Target.*

Recorded Range — An alternative name for Predicted Range. See *Predicted Range.*

Recuperator — The part of the recoil mechanism that controls run-out. Usually a hydraulic-pneumatic cylinder where the recoil force compresses air (or another gas), which then expands to return the ordnance to its firing position. A spring was used on both the Bofors 40/60 and 40/70.

Redesdale — Artillery range in Northumberland, originally known as Ad Fines.

Red Hat — The name given by the King's Troop RHA to the No1 Dress Hat.

Rednecks — Nickname of 88 (Arracan) Battery RA.

Red Sea — A heavy anti-aircraft gun predictor, intended for use with the Green Mace heavy anti-aircraft gun. The project was abandoned in 1956 due to time and cost.

Red Star — See *NG*[2].

Reduced Bearing — See *Bearing.*

Reduced Charge — A charge which gives a lower pressure and hence lower velocities than any normally issued charge.

Reduced Range — See *Map Range.*

Reduction — The process by which map coordinates are derived for a registered target. Variations for non-standard conditions are removed to give map data, from which the target location is calculated by bearing and distance from the pivot gun. See *Registration.*

Reference Line — A line marked on the ground in such a way that a director may be set up on it and angles measured to other objects from the direction defined by the reference line. The line can be marked by two or more aiming posts or banderoles placed in the neighbourhood in which the director is to be used. Alternatively, the reference line can be extended from these near marks to a distant object which forms a further mark to define the reference line. See *Aiming Post, Banderole, Director* and *Reference Object.*

Reference Object — A Reference Object is used for artillery survey. It may be one of the following:
(i) A point to which a bearing has been determined.
(ii) A point to which the angle from the centre of arc or bearing of fire has been measured and recorded.
(iii) A point selected from which to measure angles to other points in a round of angles.
(iv) Any point to which the bearing is known.
See *Centre of Arc, Reference Line* and *Round of Angles.*

Reference Point	A prominent, easily located point in the terrain. (Royal Canadian Artillery.) See *Reference Object.*
Reg	Registration.
Regiment	The Royal Regiment of Artillery is itself composed of a number of regiments. An artillery regiment is a battalion-sized unit composed of a number of batteries. Until 1938 these regiments were known as brigades and were designated by type, for example, 'field brigade', 'medium brigade', etc.
Regimental Controller/ Comptroller	Usually a colonel commandant appointed by the Master Gunner, Saint James's Park to act as controller of the Royal Artillery Institution and comptroller of the Royal Artillery charitable fund and the Royal Artillery Association. He is the chairman of the RAI committee and of the board of management of the RACF and the RAA. He also oversees the affairs of the Retired Regiment and acts as the link between it and the Master Gunner Saint James's Park and the DRA. See *Colonels Commandant* and *Master Gunner Saint James's Park.*
Regimental Grid	Fixation and orientation of the guns which originated at regimental level and brought all the batteries within the regiment onto the same grid. See *Battery Grid, Fixation, Orientation* and *Theatre Grid.*
Regimental Headquarters	Depending on the type of regiment, may only be used for the peacetime location. During the Second World War regimental commanders of direct support regiments were increasingly located away from their regiments at brigade HQ. This led to RHQ near the gun areas being called Main Headquarters and the CO's Party at brigade HQ being Tac HQ. Not all field artillery batteries are direct support. See *Alternate Headquarters, Battery Headquarters, Main Headquarters, Rear Headquarters, Step-Up* and *Tactical Headquarters.*
Regimental Method R	See *Rumpus.*
Regimental Secretary	The Regimental Secretary is responsible for the management and supervision of the regimental secretariat, the day to day business of the RAI and coordination of the Master Gunner's activities.
Regimental Signals Officer /Unit Training Officer	The RSO and UTO posts were combined in the 1980s, due to the perceived lack of RSOs. By combining the two roles, it was felt that there was less likelihood of either post being disestablished in the event of force reductions.
Regimental Survey	Artillery survey undertaken by the gun regiments as opposed to RA Survey which was conducted by survey units of the Royal Artillery. Regimental surveyors generally used directors as opposed to theodolites for measuring angles. See *RA Survey.*
Regimental Survey Officer	Responsible to the regimental commander for all aspects of survey work conducted by the regimental survey party. Known as the Brigade Survey Officer prior to 1938, the position ceased to exist in about 1970 when regimental survey parties were disbanded and distributed to batteries.
Regimental TAC	Centred around the commanding officer's hard vehicle, Regimental TAC deploys at brigade headquarters. See *Brigade TAC* and *TAC Party.*
Regimental Tie	The Regimental Tie is a zigzag red line on a blue background. The line represents the lightning which, according to legend, killed Dioscorus in retribution for beheading his daughter Barbara who refused to marry a

heathen suitor. It should be remembered that each regiment and battery within the Royal Artillery, together with the various regimental organisations, have their own individual ties. See *Appendix 1 – The Legend of Saint Barbara* and the *Gunpowder Tie.*

Reginald — A trench mortar introduced around Christmas 1914. It comprised a gas pipe which formed the rear leg of a tripod and fired a tin canister containing gun cotton and old iron. A patent wooden cone carrying a detonator and a length of safety fuze fitted into the base of the canister. Black powder was used as the propellant. Once loaded, the mortar was placed at the correct elevation, ascertained from the accompanying range table, a specially shaped piece of safety fuze was inserted into the vent and lit with a match. The firer then had to retire to cover hurriedly as it was prone to bursting. As a result of this, provision was made to fire the mortar using electric detonators fired via a small electric battery. See *3-inch Stokes Trench Mortar, Cuthbert, Percy,* and *Toby.*

Registration — Now known as 'adjustment for future engagement'. Registered targets were ranged or predicted. Silent registration meant not shooting at the target ('silent marking' in modern terms). During the Second World War targets were given numbers which were prefixed by a letter that showed the level at which the target had been registered. Battery targets were given the prefix 'P' to 'T', regimental targets were prefixed 'M' and divisional targets 'U'. Thus a target 'M5' would be recorded in all batteries within a regiment, and different regiments would have the same number for different targets. If it became a divisional target, a new target number would be allocated by HQRA and the prefix, would become 'U', this new target number would then be circulated to all batteries in the division. Targets were reduced unless they were expected to be short-lived, such as those for a quick fire plan. See *Reduction.*

Registration Fire — Fire delivered in order to obtain accurate data for subsequent effective engagement of targets. See *Registration.*

Registration Point — A terrain feature or other designated point on which fire is adjusted for the purpose of obtaining corrections to firing data. See *Registration Fire.*

Regn — Registration.

Regt — Regiment.

Regtl — Regimental.

Regt Net — Regimental Net.

Releasing Commander — The commander who has the authority to authorise the release of nuclear weapons for use. See *Executing Commander*.

Relief Mules — Additional mules provided in mountain artillery regiments to relieve those mules of the gun group which carried the more difficult loads.

Rel Pt — Release Point.

Remaining Velocity — The velocity of a projectile at any specified point on its trajectory. If a specific point is not mentioned, or implied by context, it is taken to refer to the point of graze. See *Point of Graze*.

REME — Royal Electrical and Mechanical Engineers. REME personnel attached to RA Regiments provide either 1st line or 1st and 2nd line support in the form of either light aid detachments or workshops. A rough guide to the level of support offered by attached REME personnel is the title of the attached unit. A LAD will provide 1st line support (and possibly some limited 2nd line support), whilst a

	workshop will provide both 1st and 2nd line support. Units that were formally equipped with US equipment were always provided with workshops. See *Light Aid Detachment* and *Workshop*.
Remote Range Display Unit	Part of the Osprey combined day/thermal/laser system. See *Osprey*.
Remotely Delivered Mine	A scatterable mine delivered by rocket or shell. See *AT2*.
Remount	Young horse not yet broken to a Gun Team.
Rendezvous	The location to which tactical groups or parties are ordered to move pending further orders.
Replen	Replenishment.
Report All Gone	A request from the observer to the gun position officer to be informed when the last ordered round of fire for effect has been fired. See *All Gone* and *Fire for Effect*.
Repository Work	The art of moving large pieces of ordnance using cordage and timber, without the use of conventional cranes. From the name given to the original store in Woolwich.
Representative Colonel Commandant	Each year the Master Gunner Saint James's Park nominates one of the colonels commandant to act as Representative Colonel Commandant Royal Regiment of Artillery. The tour of duty is from 1st April to 31st March. The duties include visiting Royal Artillery stations and units and representing the Regiment at public events. He may also be asked to deputise for the Master Gunner on appropriate occasions. See *Colonels Commandant, Honorary Colonels Commandant* and *Master Gunner Saint James's Park*.
RERA	Riding Establishment Royal Artillery.
RERHA	Riding Establishment, Royal Horse Artillery.
Reserve Ammunition	This may be authorised by command/divisional/district or equivalent formation headquarters in order to meet special requirements. See *First Line Ammunition, Second Line Ammunition, Training Ammunition* and *With Weapons Scales*.
Reserve of Instruction	Established at Woolwich following the Napoleonic War and in the wake of the disbandment of the Corps of Artillery Drivers. Artillery companies were sent in turn to the Reserve of Instruction to learn the requisite skills of horse management and driving. The Reserve of Instruction was provided with six field batteries of artillery equipment and horses for the role.
Residency, The	Battery Honour Title of 55 (The Residency) Headquarters Battery RA which was granted on 23 July 1930 under authority of 20/ARTY/4735/AG6a. See *Battery Honour Titles*.
Rest	Order whereby an engagement is temporarily suspended, guns are made safe but detachments may not withdraw from the guns.
Restricted Operations Zone	An airspace control measure/air defence term.
Restrictive Fire Line	A line between converging friendly forces, across which fire cannot be directed without coordination between the affected units.
Resup	Resupply.
Retard	Part of a naval gunfire support message from a forward observer to indicate that the illuminating projectile is to burst later in relation to subsequent high explosive projectile (Royal Canadian Artillery).
Review of Ammunition Rates and Scales	Along with the Battle Attrition Study, this study was completed in 1981 Rates and Scales and resulted in recommendations for large increases in daily ammunition

expenditure rates for all natures of artillery. In the case of the M109, it was recommended that the Daily Ammunition Expenditure Rate be trebled. See *Battle Attrition Study* and *Daily Ammunition Expenditure Rate*

RF Radio Frequency.

RFA (i) Royal Field Artillery.
(ii) Restricted Fire Area (FSCM).

RFFE Round(s) Fire For Effect.

RFL Restricted Fire Line (FSCM).

RFO Net Regimental Fire Orders Net. The term was employed during the period 1960–70. The Net was subsequently known as the Tech Net.

Rft (i) Reinforcing.
(ii) Reinforcement.

RFU (i) Rapier Fire Unit(s).
(ii) Remote Firing Unit.

RFWO Regimental Families Welfare Officer.

RGA Royal Garrison Artillery.

RGCIs Radar Group Critical Items. Part of the COBRA system. See *COBRA.*

RGF (i) Round(s) of Gun Fire.
(ii) Royal Gun Factory.

Rhayader Heavy Artillery range in Wales, first used in 1903.

RHA (i) Royal Horse Artillery.
(ii) Rolled Homogenous Armour.

RHAMR Royal Horse Artillery Mounted Rifles.

RHA(TF) Royal Horse Artillery (Territorial Force) (Royal Australian Artillery).

RHI Residual Humidity Indicator.

Rhine Troop One of the troops in 3rd Squadron Honourable Artillery Company. See *Aden Troop, Gaza Troop* and *Honourable Artillery Company.*

R Hour The time at which the use of nuclear weapons is authorised.

RHQ Regimental Headquarters. See *BHQ* and *THQ*.

RHQ RA That element of the DRA's staff responsible for domestic regimental matters.

RIA (i) Royal Indian Artillery (A now disbanded regiment).
(ii) Royal Irish Artillery.
(iii) Restricted Impact Area.

RIATC Royal Indian Artillery Training Centre.

RICSO Regimental Information, Communications and Signals Officer.

Ride and Drive The Gun Team horses (The King's Troop RHA).

Riding Establishment RA Formed on 20 December 1802 under the title of the Riding House Troop, RHA, colloquially referred to as 'The Troop'. 'The Troop' consisted of one captain superintendent, three lieutenants, approximately twenty men and twelve horses. Other ranks were known as riders to distinguish them from the drivers of the driver corps from whom the horses and rank and file were drawn. The name for the riders was changed to Rough-Riders in the 1820s. Under an order dated 30 August 1808 the troop became a unit in its own right, up until 1856 it formed part of the Horse Brigade, which was under command of the master general of the ordnance.

In 1857, the Establishment has thirty-five horses on strength and in the following year, a second captain and a riding master were added. In 1861–62 the Troop was renamed the Riding Establishment RA and greatly expanded with no fewer than twenty-one riding masters. During 1874 there were 144 horses on strength. For no apparent reason, the Troop was transferred to the Royal Field Artillery in 1887, and in 1897 the establishment was severely cut back to one major superintendent, two riding masters, one sergeant-major, four sergeants, eighty other ranks and 77 horses.

On 1st April 1903, without a change to the establishment, the Troop reverted to the Royal Horse Artillery. Following the First World War, the purpose of the Troop was expanded and it was split into two branches. The Cadet Branch at Woolwich was responsible for training cadets at the Royal Military Academy whilst the officer's and NCO's branch at Weedon could accommodate thirty-six officers and seventy-two NCOs on courses extended over thirty-six months. The Weedon Branch was short-lived merging with the newly formed School of Equitation on 2nd September 1922.

In 1924 the Troop had an establishment of one captain, two lieutenants, one BSM instructor, four sergeant instructors, two bombardier instructors, one artificer, five farriers, one saddler, 75 other ranks and 136 Horses.

However, the introduction of mechanisation spelt the end for the Troop, although its title and heritage lives on in the shape of the King's Troop, RHA. See *King's Troop, RHA, The.*

Riding House — Colloquial name for the Riding Establishment Royal Artillery. See *Cab Yard and Riding Establishment Royal Artillery.*

Riding House Troop, RHA — See *King's Troop, RHA. The* and *Riding Establishment RA.*

Rifled Portion — That part of the bore, which may be either parallel or tapered and in which is cut a system of spiral grooves. See *Bore* and *Lands.*

Rifling — Designed to impart the correct amount of spin and therefore stability to the projectile. On ramming, the driving band partially engages with the rifling. On firing the projectile is forced forward and the driving band engages the rifling. The driving band then follows the twist of rifling and spins the projectile as it passes up the bore. See *Bore* and *Twist of Rifling.*

Rifter — Material used to clean metal work of harness (The King's Troop RHA).

Rifting — To clean the polish from metal work (The King's Troop RHA).

Rifting Belt — Belt worn around the waist whilst rifting (The King's Troop RHA).

Rigger/Marshaller — Unit personnel trained by a Helicopter Handling Instructor to work under the supervision of either an HHI or LPC. They are qualified to rig and prepare unit equipment for internal and external carriage by helicopter. They may be employed as primary or secondary marshallers and hook-up personnel. See *Helicopter Handling Instructor* and *LPC.*

Right — (i) A directional deviation used by an observer in adjusting ground or naval gunfire. See *Left.*

(ii) Fire correction used by an observer to indicate that a lateral shift to the mean point of impact perpendicular to the observer-target line is required. See *Left.*

Right of the Line — A title by which the Regiment is sometimes known. It refers to the order of precedence in which the Royal Horse Artillery, when on parade with its guns, takes precedence over all other regiments and corps of the British Army and therefore parades on the right of the line. Otherwise the precedence is as follows: Life Guards and Royal

	Horse Guards/Dragoons, Royal Horse Artillery, Royal Armoured Corps and the Royal Artillery followed by other arms and services.
Ring Shell	Used during the latter half of the nineteenth century, ring shell were constructed from rings welded together. On detonation each ring broke into small segments. See *Common Shell*.
Ringworm	Nickname given by 45 Field Regiment Royal Artillery to a mortar locating radar mounted on a half-track vehicle, a predecessor of Green Archer and Cymbeline. Ringworm, together with an identical radar nicknamed 'Rancid' it was used during the Korean War. See also *Rancid*.
RIPL	Reconnaissance and Interdiction Planning Line (pronounced 'ripple').
RISTA	Reconnaissance, Intelligence, Surveillance and Target Aquisition.
Rkt	Rocket.
RL	Rocket Launcher.
RLB	Radio Line Box.
RLC	Royal Logistic Corps.
RLG	Ring-Laser Gyro.
RLGS	Ring Laser Gyroscope.
RLO	Range Liaison Officer.
RLT	Ruggedised Laptop Computer.
R/M	Rigger/Marshaller. See *HHI* and *LPC*.
RMA	(i) Royal Military Academy. (ii) Royal Malta Artillery. (iii) Regimental Medical Assistant. (iv) Royal Marine Artillery (A now disbanded regiment).
RMAA	Royal Malta Artillery Association.
RMFA	Royal Malta Fencible Artillery.
RML	Rifled, Muzzle-Loading.
RMO	Regimental Medical Officer.
RMS	Radar Module Set. Part of the COBRA system. See *COBRA*.
RMT	Representative Military Tasks.
RMTWO	Regimental Military Transport Warrant Officer.
RMV	Reduced Muzzle Velocity.
RNZA	Royal Regiment of New Zealand Artillery.
RO	(i) Retired Officer. (ii) Reference Object. (iii) Regimental Order.
Robert	Long range ground surveillance radar, GS No. 9, fitted in Saracen AFV (1960s).
ROBG	Rear Operations Battle Group.
ROCC	Review of Officers' Career Courses.
Rocket Assembly Specialist	A position within a Honest John Battery (Royal Canadian Artillery).
Rocketeer	Nickname for a member of O Battery.
Rocket Jockey	A member of an MLRS Battery.
Rocket Pod Container	There are two RPCs to an MLRS launcher, each holding six rockets. Rockets can be fired individually or in a ripple of two to twelve in less than one minute. The two RPCs contain a total of 7728 M77 bomblets, which is approximately equivalent to eighteen 155 mm guns firing five HE rounds FFE.
Rockets	Nickname of O Battery RA.
Rocket Troop, The	Battery Honour Title of O Headquarters Battery (The Rocket Troop) RHA which was granted on 18 October 1926 under authority of 20/ARTY/4544/AG6a. See *Battery Honour Titles*.
ROE	Rules of Engagement.

Roger	Radio Procedure used as an acknowledgement and indicating that the individual concerned has received the message. See *Through.*
Rogers's Company	Battery Honour Title of 30 Battery (Rogers's Company) RA which was granted on 7 May 1937 under authority of 20/ARTY/5023/AG6a. See *Battery Honour Titles.*
Rolled Homogenous Armour	In this, the oldest form of armour, the steel has been rolled in order to spread weakening impurities evenly and thus make it homogeneous, which simply means 'of a similar nature throughout'.
Roller Handspike	See *Handspike.*
Rolling Barrage	See *Barrage.*
Rolling Replen	A form of replenishment where the battery vehicles do not stop moving. Various supply points (water, rations, ammo etc.) are established along a path, the battery vehicles are driven along this path and the various items of supply are passed to them.
Romeo 1	Tactical sign for a battery FOO party. See *Romeo 2, Romeo 3* and *Tactical Sign.*
Romeo 2	Tactical sign for a battery FOO party. See *Romeo 1, Romeo 3* and *Tactical Sign.*
Romeo 3	Tactical sign for a battery FOO party. See *Romeo 1, Romeo 2* and *Tactical Sign.*
RONCO	Regimental Orderly Non-Commissioned Officer. See *BONCO.*
ROP	Restriction of Privileges.
ROS	Regimental Orderly Sergeant.
Ross Troop	With Alkmaar Tp one of the two troops forming A Battery (The Chestnut Troop) RHA.
Rotator	Nickname for a member of a locating battery.
Rough	Abbreviated form of address for a rough-rider.
Rough Ex	See *Rough Exercise.*
Rough Exercise	Exercising horses, generally before breakfast with one rider controlling up to three horses. The horses would wear watering bits and stable headcollars whilst the riders used blankets instead of saddles. Rough exercise usually lasted for three-quarters of an hour and was conducted at the walk.
Rough-rider	Prior to mechanisation, unit establishments included rough-riders who instructed recruits in horsemanship. The term was replaced in 1923 by Riding Instructor.
Rough Terrain Fork Lift	Coming in two versions, 1841 kg or 2400 kg, the Rough Terrain Fork Lift was used to move ammunition on gun positions.
Round	The complete projectile. Shell, fuze, propelling charge and the initiating explosion which fires the charge. The term is used informally to refer to the projectile and its fuze only. See *Charge.*
Round of Angles	The process of relaying on the reference object after measuring horizontal angles in order to ensure that the reading scale of the director has not moved and that additionally the lower plate has not been disturbed. Used in Artillery Survey. See *Reference Object.*
Round of Vertical and Horizontal Angles	A series of observations of horizontal and vertical angles opening and closing on the same reference object. Used in artillery survey.
... Rounds	A fire order command used to indicate the number of projectiles per barrel to be fired on a specific target.
Rounds Complete	Message from the gun position to the CP and OP indicating that the required number of rounds have been fired. This phrase replaced 'All Gone'. See *All Gone.*

Round Shot	The name given to the original iron cannonballs used in smoothbore artillery. The name, not unusually, derives from the shape of the projectile.
Rover Group	A Commander's mobile group without staff officers, however, it normally includes the artillery commander. Rover Groups were widely used during the Second World War and later.
Roving Position	A position occupied for a comparatively short time to carry out a task. Examples of tasks undertaken from these positions are: deep harassing fire, harassing fire in enfilade, destruction of suspected observation posts and to confuse the enemy as to the location of the main position. Roving positions are used so that the enemy can gain no information from such shoots about main or temporary positions. They will seldom be occupied by more than a troop and indeed will often be occupied by a section or a single gun. See *Alternative Position, Main Position* and *Temporary Position.*
Rowanex	A PBX filling for shells created by BAE, and introduced into service in 2005 to meet insensitive munitions requirements. See *PBX.*
Royal Artillery Association	Formed in 1920 to provide, where feasible, a network in every part of the British Isles and Commonwealth to assist with welfare of artillery men and women, their families and dependants. It is a registered charity whose patron is Her Majesty the Queen. Branches are located throughout the world.
Royal Artillery Association Prize	Introduced in 1971 the prize is awarded to the young officer who makes the greatest effort to take part in sport and other outside activities on the course for newly-commissioned artillery officers at the Royal School of Artillery.
Royal Artillery Band	One of eight state bands, the Royal Artillery Band is commanded by a director of music with the regimental colonel as its president.
Royal Artillery Charitable Fund	Established in 1839 when it provided relief for wives and children, non commissioned officers and privates of the Royal Artillery embarked on foreign service. The fund now acts as the welfare agency for all serving and retired gunners and their families in need.
Royal Artillery Headquarters	A generic term used pre-Second World War, but generally replaced by HQRA.
Royal Artillery Institution	Founded in 1838, the Royal Artillery Institution is responsible for funds, property and support to the serving regiment including sports, the band, historical affairs, ceremonies and events, management, publications, direct support to units, recruiting and education.
Royal Artillery Medal	Awarded each year, by the Master Gunner's Committee, to any rank, serving or retired (Regular or Territorial Army) and civilians for outstanding service to the Royal Regiment as a whole, and not simply to just one unit. It can be awarded for a single act or for service over a prolonged period.
Royal Artillery Mechanical Traction/Transport School	Formed at Lydd but moved to Rhyl in 1940. The schoolTraction/Transport School trained instructors on all types of vehicle as well as RA MT tradesmen.
Royal Artillery Mounted Rifles	See *Artillery Mounted Rifles.*

Royal Artillery Personnel Selection Officer
Reporting directly to the SO2 Soldier recruiting at the Artillery Centre, Larkhill. The RAPSO is responsible for nurturing and tracking all RA soldier applicants, the interviewing and selection of all transfer applicants to the RA, the coordination of RA 'Insight' courses for potential applicants at Larkhill, the production of RA marketing material and the control and design of the RA website.

Royal Artillery School of Survey
Located in Catterick, North Yorkshire during the Second World War. The school is now closed and the teaching of Royal Artillery Survey methods has been transferred to the Royal School of Artillery, Larkhill.

Royal Artillery Sergeant Major
The senior Warrant Officer rank in the Royal Artillery. The RASM is on the General Duties List and is not part of the Gunnery Staff.

Royal Artillery Specialist Pool (Volunteers)
The Royal Artillery Specialist Pool is part of CVHQ RA and provides a pool of individual reinforcements for gunner formations and regiments as well as providing centralised training courses for gunner TA regiments. The Pool is made up of individuals who are trained in one of the many gunner disciplines and who, having left the regular Army, wish to remain in uniform. Or, TA gunners who wish to stay in the TA but find they can no longer meet the additional commitment of the Independent TA. See *CVHQ RA, All Arms Staff Officers Liaison & Watchkeepers Group* and *LCSP (V).*

Royal Artillery Survey
See *RA Survey*.

Royal Artillery Training Board
This Board, which consists of gunner one star officers and commanders, is used by the DRA to ensure that both individual and special arm collective training meets the operational requirement at the strategic level.

Royal Artillery Training Team
Formerly known as the Warrant Officer Training Team, the RATT Comprises the RASM, RA BSM and a staff sergeant and is based at the Artillery Centre, Larkhill. Its core function is the training and education of the Regiment's WOs and SNCOs. See *WOTT*.

Royal Artillery War Commemoration Fund
Established in 1918, the chief objects of the fund were to benefit those who had served during the First World War; their wives and dependents and the erection of a permanent memorial in London. (The Royal Artillery Memorial at Hyde Park Corner was erected through the actions of this committee). Sub-committees were formed to deal with employment, relief and education.

Royal Canadian Field Artillery
The RCFA shoulder badges worn by the Brigade Division RCA in the Karoo Campaign of the Second Anglo-Boer War were said to stand for 'Rebel Chasers from America' by the others troops in the column.

Royal Carriage Department
One of the three main branches of the Royal Arsenal at Woolwich. Responsible for the development and production of gun carriages.

Royal Gun Factory
One of the three main branches of the Royal Arsenal at Woolwich. Responsible for the production of ordnance.

Royal Laboratory	One of the three main branches of the Royal Arsenal at Woolwich. Responsible for the development of ammunition, fuzes etc.
Royal Malta Artillery	The title of the army unit(s), raised in Malta for employment in the artillery arm.
Royal Malta Fencible Artillery	The predecessors of the Royal Malta Artillery.
Royal Military Academy	Originally located at Woolwich where training was provided for Royal Artillery and Royal Engineer officer cadets but now based at Sandhurst where officers from all arms are instructed.
Royal Regiment of Artillery	Usually shortened to 'Royal Artillery' and abbreviated as RA. See *Regiment.*
Royal School of Artillery	Formed at Larkhill in 1919. In the Second World War comprised HQ, Gunnery, Equipment, Tactics, Air and Survey Wings, Radar Section and Photographic Research Branch. Trained officers and NCOs as Instructors.
ROZ	Restricted Operations Zone.
RP	(i) Reload Point. (MLRS). (ii) Rocket Pod. Part of the MLRS system. See *Multiple Launch Rocket System* and *Rocket Pod Container.* (iii) Repair Pool. Of equipment. (iv) Regimental Police. (v) Restriction of Privileges. (vi) Replenishment Park. (vii) Registration Point.
RPC	Rocket Pod Container.
RPG	Rocket Propelled Grenade.
rpg	Rounds Per Gun.
rpgpd	Rounds Per Gun Per Diem.
rpgpm	Rounds Per Gun Per Minute.
RPL	Ramp Powered Lighter (form of nautical transport).
rpm	Rounds per Minute.
RPO	Release Point Orderly.
RPOL	Rearward Passage of Lines. See *FPOL.*
Rpt	Repeat.
RP/T	Rocket Pod Trainer. Part of the MLRS system. See *Multiple Launch Rocket System* and *Rocket Pod Container.*
RPV	Remotely Piloted Vehicle. An alternative name for an unmanned aerial vehicle. See *Phoenix.*
RQ	Abbreviated form of RQMS. Used in general conversation when talking about the RQMS.
RQMS	Regimental Quartermaster Sergeant.
RQMS (T)	Regimental Quartermaster Sergeant Technical.
RQT	Reliability Qualification Trial.
RR	(i) Right Ranging. See *LR.* (ii) Artillery Code used during the First World War meaning 'More Right'.
RRB	Radio Rebroadcast (Generally used in conjunction with a number, i.e. RRB3 to denote a Radio Rebroadcast Site).
RRDU	Remote Range Display Unit. See *Osprey.*
RRPR	Reduced Range Practice Rocket (for MLRS).
RRT	Regimental Recruiting Team.
RRTT	Regimental Recruit Training Team.
RRV	Radar Repair Vehicle.
RS	Range Selector.
RS80	Multinational rocket system on a tracked launcher involving UK, Germany and France. Cancelled when the partners decided to adopt MLRS. See *Multiple Launch Rocket System.*
RSA	Royal School of Artillery.
RSAAM	Regimental Skill At Arms Meeting.

RSAGS	Royal School of Artillery Golf Society.
RSC	(i) Right Section Commander (The King's Troop RHA). (ii) Rear Support Command.
RSCP	Regimental Survey Control Point. (Royal Canadian Artillery).
RSD	(i) Reduced Safe Distance. (ii) Reduced Safety Distance.
RSE	Range Safety Equipment.
RSG	Rear Support Group.
RSI	(i) Regimental Signalling Instructor. (ii) Range Safety Instructor.
RSM	Regimental Sergeant-Major.
RSO	(i) Regimental Survey Officer. (ii) Regimental Signals Officer. (iii) Range Safety Officer.
RS of A	Royal School of Artillery (more commonly RSA).
RSO/UTO	Regimental Signals Officer/Unit Training Officer.
RSS	Range Safety Set. Part of the HVM LML system. See *HVM* and *LML*.
RSU	Remote Switching Unit.
RSV	Radar System Vehicle. Part of the COBRA system. See *COBRA*.
RSWO	Regimental Signals Warrant Officer.
R/T	Radio Telegraphy, voice radio (Second World War).
RT	(i) Radar Tracker. (ii) Range Table. (iii) Recognition Trainer.
RT20	Radio Theodolite 20. See *BILD*, *BMETS* and *MDP*.
RTA	Radio Telegraph Adaptor. FACE.
RTF	Round(s) Troop Fire. See *RPG*.
RTFL	Rough Terrain Fork Lift.
RTM	Railway Truck Mounting. See *Boche-Buster* and *Scene-Shifter*.
RTMC	Reserves Training and Mobilisation Centre.
RTO	(i) Regimental Training Officer. (ii) Regimental Transport Officer.
R Toc	Radio Telegraphy.
RTU	Returned to unit i.e. discharged from CRS or BMH.
RUA	(i) Range Use Area. (ii) Ready Use Area.
RUF	Artillery Code used during the First World War meaning 'Are you firing?'.
Rumble Buggies	Nickname given to the M109 by the gun detachments of 27 Med Regt RA in 1969.
Rumpus	Developed by the artillery of the 2nd New Zealand Division, and used exclusively by the New Zealand Artillery during the Second World War. Rumpus was a divisional artillery variation of the original Regimental Method R. Rumpus went through several standardisation stages. The first regiment would cover a normal frontage of 600 yards with the other regiments 100 yards apart on the vertical axis. If more than one round of gunfire was ordered, the regiments searched 50 yards by 25s. This procedure was modified later at which time it used two regiments side by side with a further regiment superimposed on a frontage of 1200 yards. All regiments searched on the vertical axis 150 yards by 50s covering a depth of 300 yards. See *Method B* (Royal New Zealand Artillery).
Run-out	The position of the gun barrel, prior to firing, or following recoil.
Rupert	Nickname given to commissioned officers.

Rushton Target	Towed behind an aircraft at a safe distance and used for air defence and anti-aircraft firings.
Rusty Brigade	Nickname of 15 Brigade RA in 1938/39. Thought to derive from the batteries in the brigade, namely, R, S and T (Shah Sujah's Troop).
RV	Rendezvous.
RVD	Residual Vapour Detector.
RW	Rotary Wing (aircraft).
RWO	Regimental Welfare Officer.
RWWO	Regimental Welfare Warrant Officer.
RX	(i) Right Section. (First World War.) (ii) Receiver.

S – Esses – 1904
Sugar – 1927/1943
Sierra – 1956

S	Artillery code used during the First World War meaning 'Short'.
S1	Shot One.
S2	Shot Two.
S15	The Javelin air defence missile. See *Javelin.*
S404	The Type 88 height finder radar used with the Thunderbird II Heavy Air Defence missile. See *Thunderbird.*
SA	(i) Situational Awareness. (ii) Small Arms. (iii) Suspended Animation. (iv) Semi-Automatic. (v) Selective Availability. (vi) Simple Alert.
SA80	See *L85 Individual Weapon.*
SAA	Small Arms Ammunition.
SAAA	School of Anti-Aircraft Artillery.
SAAFR	Standard Use Army Aircraft/Aviation Flight Route.
SAAI	Skill At Arms Instructor.
SAB	Smoke Arm Box.
Sabot	(i) In muzzle-loading artillery terms this was a wooden base which was attached to the projectile, with the intention of keeping the shot in the axis of the gun, thereby improving accuracy. (ii) 6 alloy sheath surrounding a hardened projectile. On firing, the sheath is discarded on leaving the muzzle. The projectile thus achieves a higher velocity owing to the greater forces exerted on the base of the projectile base in the gun.
SACA	Sub-area Airspace Control Authority.
SACC	Supporting Arms Coordinating Centre.
SACEUR	Supreme Allied Commander Europe.
SACLOS	Semi-Automatic Command to Line of Sight.
SACLOS(BR)	Semi-Automatic Command to Line of Sight (Beam Riding).
Saddle	Part of the superstructure of the carriage that pivots on the basic structure of the carriage or mounting and enables the trunnions attached to the cradle to pivot.
SAE	Services Assisted Evacuation.
SAF2	Safety and Assessment Facility.
SAFU	Safety, Arming and Firing Unit.
SAGW	Surface to Air Guided Weapon.
Sahagun Troop	Named after the Battle of Sahagun, which took place on 21st December 1808 during the Peninsula War in Spain; together with Downman's Troop, El Tamar Troop and

	Corunna Troop, it is one of the four troops in B Battery Royal Horse Artillery.
Saint Barbara	The Patron Saint of Gunners. See *Appendix 1.*
Salamanca Troop	With Gardiner's Tp, one of the two troops forming E Battery RHA.
Salisbury Plain Range Detachment	The personnel of this detachment are responsible for maintaining the ranges on Salisbury Plain. Their roles include, amongst other things, painting targets and manning the control points.
Salisbury Plain Training Area	Located in south-west England, close to Salisbury, the training area, measuring 40 km East to West and 20 km North to South, comprises over 38,000 hectares. The Royal School of Artillery, Larkhill, is located within the Training Area.
Salvage	Recovered reusable items that require accounting for, such as cartridge cases.
Salvo Fire	A method of gunfire. Guns are fired simultaneously on the orders of the GPO, the interval between salvos being indicated by the BC.
SAM	Surface to Air Missile.
SAMOC	Surface to Air Missile Operations Centre.
Sample Matrix	A FACE button enabling the operator to select the required processing function. See *FACE.*
Sandham's Company	Battery Honour Title of 16 Battery (Sandham's Company) RA which was granted on 18 October 1926 under authority of 20/ARTY/4544/AG6a. See *Battery Honour Titles.*
Sands Graph	Army Form B2596, the Concentration and Position Correction Chart. Introduced during the 1940s, this was a graph showing the deployment of the guns on the gun position, which was used to calculate corrections in order for all the rounds to land at the same impact point. It was also used to calculate concentrations. The Sands Graph remained in service until it was replaced by the Displacement Calculator in the late 1950s.
SANIE	Stand Alone Net Interface Equipment. See *BATES, MONIE* and *NIE.*
Sanna's Post	Battery Honour Title Q (Sanna's Post) Headquarters Battery RA which was granted on 18 October 1926 under authority of 20/ARTY/4544/AG6a.
SAO	Squadron Artillery Officer (forerunner of the GLO).
SAP	Semi Armour Piercing. A type of coast artillery projectile.
SAR	Synthetic Aperture Radar.
SARA	Staff Assistant Royal Artillery.
SARB	See *SAR Bde.*
SAR Bde	Siege Artillery Reserve Brigade.
SAS	Special Ammunition Supply.
SASP	Special Ammunition Supply Point.
SAS Site	Special Ammunition Storage Site.
SAT	(i) Systems Approach to Training. (ii) Stand-by Alert Team.
SAU	Safety and Arming Unit. Part of the HVM LML system. See *HVM* and *LML.*
SAWES	Small Arms Weapons Effect Simulator.
SAWOCU	Surface to Air Weapons Operational Conversion Unit (Formerly FSCOCU).
SB	Siege Battery (First World War).
SBA	(i) Sovereign Base Area. (Cyprus). (ii) Scanner Blind Arc.
SBALO	Shipborne Air Liaison Officer.
SBBL	Smooth Bore Breech Loading (gun).

SBLO — Senior Bombardment Liaison Officer (Second World War).

SBMM — Standard Ballistic Meteorological Message. See *BMETS* and *SCMM*.

SBSD — Special Burst Safety Distance.

SC — (i) Special Corridor.
(ii) Section Commander.
(iii) Artillery code used during the First World War meaning 'Smoke screen obscuring infantry'.

SC&AT — Shelling Connectivity and Activity Trace.

Scale — Each gun of the batteries/troops in a concentration of guns would fire the number of rounds specified and then stop. If a gun was out of action or engaging another target its fire would be made up by the other guns of its troop, battery or regiment. Therefore in the case of Scale 4, each gun would fire four rounds plus any necessary to make up for any missing guns.

SCAO — Shelling Connection and Activity Overlay (1972 and later). Replaced the Shelling Connection and Activity Trace, an overlay placed on the Hostile Battery Chart.

SCAT — Shelling Connection and Activity Trace.

SCATMIN — Scatterable Mine(s).

Scatterable Mine(s). — A sub-munition used with the Multiple Launch Rocket System.

SCD — Staff College Demonstration.

Scene-Shifter — The name given by 471 Siege Battery RGA to a 14-inch, 270-ton railway gun, capable of firing a three-quarter ton shell to a range of 20 miles during the First World War. See *Boche-Buster.*

Scheduled Target — A planned target on which fire is to be delivered at a specified time. See *On-Call Target.*

School of Aircraft Recogniton — Originally formed near Bishop's Stopford, but moved to Deepcut in 1944. The school trained instructors in aircraft recognition.

School of Anti-Aircraft Artillery — Initially established at Biggin Hill, the school moved to Manobier in 1939. Comprising gunnery, radar and searchlight wings, the school trained instructors and mixed anti-aircraft regiments. At its peak in 1944, the school had an establishment (including students) of approximately 4,700 personnel, with a headquarters based at Penn (near High Wycombe) and six wings based as far apart as Sheerness, Watchet, Rhyl and Manorbier.

School of Artillery — See *Royal School of Artillery*.

Shelling Connection and Activity Trace — A pictorial record that shows the areas into which hostile batteries are firing; which of them are most active and the type of fire they are delivering. Used from the Second World War until 1972 when it was replaced by the SCAO. See *Bearing Report Trace, Hostile Battery, Hostile Battery Chart* and *SCAO.*

Sherman Observation Post/Command Post Tank — A standard Sherman tank, which depending on its function, was used either by a Forward Observation Officer or a Command Post Officer. The main armament was removed and replaced by a dummy gun in order to make room for additional radios and a plotting table. See *Command Tank, Ram Observation Post* and *Sexton GPO.*

Sherman OP/CP Tank — See *Sherman Observation Post/Command Post Tank.*

School of Anti-Aircraft Artillery — Originally based at Biggin Hill in Kent, the School later moved to Manorbier, Pembrokeshire, South Wales.

School of Coast Artillery	See *Coast Artillery School.*
School of Super Heavy Artillery	Located in Catterick, North Yorkshire during the Second World War, the school has now closed.
Schooly	A member of the Army Education Corps.
SCMM	Standard Computer Meteorological Message. See *BMETS* and *SBMM.*
Scotch Up	Nickname for repository work.
Scotches	These were large timber blocks which were placed under the gun in stages as it was gradually raised by the gun, prior to mounting or dismounting from or to its carriage. See *Gyn, Scotch Up* and *Repository Work.*
SCP	Survey Control Point.
SCRA	(i) Single Channel Radio Access for entry into Ptarmigan area communications system. (ii) Staff Captain, Royal Artillery.
Screaming Eagles, The	(i) Nickname of 49 (Inkerman) Headquarter Battery RA. (ii) Nickname of N Battery (The Eagle Troop) RHA.
Screw Guns	(i) A popular term adopted to describe a jointed gun in which the barrel came in two halves, being joined together by a screwed collar. This facilitated the transport of the gun on pack-saddles for use in mountainous areas. Screw guns were used by both the British and Indian Army mountain batteries, with the last model, the 3.7-inch Mountain Howitzer, being declared obsolete in 1960. (ii) A poem by Rudyard Kipling which has become the unofficial artillery anthem. Sung to the tune of the Eton Boating Song. It sounds best when sung at a social gathering at which the participants have been sufficiently inspired by regimental spirit, not all liquid.
SCS	Static Close Surveillance.
SCU	Supply Control Unit. FACE.
SD	(i) Safe Distance. (ii) Safety Distance. (iii) Self Destruct. (iv) Staff Duties. (v) Service Dress.
SD-1	Abbreviation for the AN/USD-1. The first Remotely Piloted Vehicle used by the Royal Artillery (1960s).
SDC	Service Driver Conversion.
SDG	Special Defence Group.
SDHQ	Seaward Defence Headquarters (coast artillery, Second World War and later).
SDI	Surface Data Instrument. See *BMETS* and *MDP.*
SDP	Surveillance Data Processor. Part of the Rapier FSB2 Air Defence system.
SDPD	Surface Data Portable Display. See *BMETS* and *SDPU.*
SDPU	Surface Display Portable Unit. See *BMETS* and *SDI.*
Sdr QMS	Saddler Quartermaster Sergeant. (Rank no longer in use).
SE	Synthetic Environment.
SEAD	Suppression of Enemy Air Defence.
Seagull	Radio appointment title. This title was used army-wide by second G Staff Officer, however, in the Royal Artillery the following officers used the title. (i) At HQRA level the G3 (See *G3*). (ii) At a Regimental Headquarters level the Assistant Adjutant. See *Appointment Titles.*
Seagull Minor	Radio appointment title. This title was used army-wide by a unit commander, however, in the Royal Artillery the following officers used the title. (i) At HQRA level the commander Royal Artillery.

(ii) At a regimental headquarters level the commanding officer.
(iii) At Battery level the battery commander.
See *Appointment Titles*.

Search — In order to increase the effectiveness of fire, it is sometimes necessary to artificially increase the size of the beaten zone for line. This is achieved by the observer or the relevant HQ giving the amount of search along the line of fire, to the nearest fifty metres. Successive rounds are then fired at the current elevation, and then at elevations greater and less than the current elevation, by the amount of search ordered. Elevations are set on the range scale of the sights and guns are laid in the normal manner. Thus, if the order '6000, five rounds gunfire, 20 seconds, search 200 by 100s' is given, the guns will fire first at 6000, then at 6100, 6200, 5800 and 5900. See *Sweep*.

Searchlight Control (Radar) — Known by the nickname 'Elsie', this was a radar set fitted to a searchlight in order to direct its beam.

Sec — Section.

Sec Cmdr — Section Commander.

Second Captain — The Second Captain was the second in command of a troop, company or battery of artillery. The rank fell between that of captain and lieutenant. When the rank of major was reinstated in 1872, with the consequential demise of the rank of first captain, that of second captain also disappeared. See *First Captain*.

Second Degree Safety Line — The minimum safe distance from a nuclear strike for unwarned exposed troops. See *First Degree Safety Line* and *Troop Safety Line*.

Second Line Ammunition — Quantities of ammunition held in support echelons to replenish First Line Ammunition. See *First Line Ammunition, Reserve Ammunition, Training Ammunition* and *With Weapons Scales*.

Secraphones — Scrambler telephones provided at divisional and higher headquarters during the Second World War.

Section — Half a battery together with its associated guns, gun towers (if applicable), detachments etc. Dependant on the layout of the gun position, sections are known as Left and Right or Front and Rear. Often in the RGA a section of heavy and siege equipments would consist of one gun only. See *Section Commander* and *Sub Section*.

Section Commander — Prior to the Second World War this title had been used for the three subaltern officers in a battery, each of whom commanded a section of two guns, both in barracks and in the field. The term ceased to be used in 1938, however it was resurrected in 1942 with a different meaning. From that date it has been used to describe any officer, warrant officer or NCO temporarily appointed to supervise a section of two guns in action.

A Section Commander assists the gun position officer in the following duties:
(i) Transferring line to the guns.
(ii) Checking and maintaining parallelism.
(iii) Passage of orders.
(iv) Supervising the service of the guns in action.
(v) Supervising the daily servicing of guns and ammunition.
(vi) Supervising the sight tests carried out by the Nos. 1.
(vii) Rest periods and routine administrative duties.
(viii) The command of his/her section in the event of enemy attack.
See *Section, Subaltern* and *Battery Guide*.

Section Control	A type of fire control whereby the fire of a battery was controlled at section level by the section commander, as opposed to centrally when it would have been controlled by the battery commander. See *Battery Commander* and *Section Commander.*
Section Left	A method of fire in which weapons are discharged from the left, one after the other, at five-second intervals unless otherwise specified. See *Battery Left, Battery Right,* and *Section Right.*
Section of Defence	In coast artillery, this was a sub-division of a fortress for purposes of organization and fighting. Sections of defence were only found in the larger coast defence fortresses.
Section Right	A method of fire in which weapons are discharged from the right one after the other, at five-second intervals unless otherwise specified. See *Battery Right, Battery Left* and *Section Left.*
Sector Commander	Coast artillery officer commanding a sector of defence, a sub-division of a large fortress. (Second World War and earlier.)
Sector of Defence	A sub-division of a large fortress in the coast artillery.
Sector Searchlight Commander	The officer responsible for controlling searchlights in order to assist with fighter interception at night.
Secundra Gunge Day	D Battery RHA Battery day.
Secure Weapons Storage Site	A site used for the storage of confiscated weapons during the various Balkan peacekeeping operations.
Seen	A report that the indicated target has been seen.
Segment Shell	A Victorian item of ordnance. Segment shell consisted of a thin cast iron cylindro-conical shell, about two calibres or twice the diameter of the bore in length, which was lined with cast iron segments, built up in layers, surrounding a cylindrical powder chamber in the centre.
SEL	Safety Element Lock. Part of the MLRS system. See *Multiple Launch Rocket System.*
Selector Engagement Zone	A part of the Rapier FSB1 Air Defence system.
Selector Firing Sequence Unit	Part of the Rapier FSB2 system. The SFSU selected the relevant missile for firing and on receipt of the fire signal, it initiated a controlled firing sequence. Should a misfire have occurred, the SFSU automatically selected and fired a second missile, whilst providing the operator with a visual indication of the misfire. It was also capable of stopping the firing sequence completely should a system fault have occurred. See *Rapier FSB2.*
Self-Propelled	An artillery piece mounted on a tracked or wheeled chassis. The original self-propelled guns were mounted on adapted tank chassis, although modern versions are purpose built. This term should not be confused with Portee, which referred to a small artillery piece carried on and capable of being fired from the rear of a lorry. See *Abbot, Achilles, Archer, AS90, Portee, Priest* and *Sexton.*
Self-Propelled High Velocity Missile	A HVM launcher mounted on tracked vehicle. See *Stormer.*
Semi-Automatic Breech	A breech which, without intervention from the detachment, opens after the gun has been fired and ejects the spent cartridge case.
Semi-Automatic Command to Line of Sight	A form of missile guidance system. Used with the Rapier FSC. See *Rapier FSC* and *Semi-Automatic Command to Line of Sight (Beam Riding).*

Semi-Automatic Command to Line of Sight (Beam Riding)	A form of missile guidance. Used with the Javelin S15 air to defence missile. See *Semi-Automatic Command to Line of Sight.*
Semi-covered position	Semi-covered positions are located close behind some form of protective cover that protects the gun and its detachment from direct fire. However, whilst the guns are screened from direct observation, the smoke or flash of the weapons firing can still be seen. See *Covered Position* and *Open Position.*
Semi-Fixed Ammunition	See *Quick Firing Ammunition.*
Semper vigilantes	Always vigilant. The Battery motto of 269 (West Riding) Battery Royal Artillery (Volunteers) RA.
Senior Reporting Officer	Senior signatory above the reporting officer for Annual Confidential Reports.
Senior Responsble Officer	An appointment usually at 2 star level responsible for overseeing a major procurement program, introduced in 2005 at the direction of the Office of Government Commerce.
SENTA	Sennybridge Training Area.
Separate Ammunition	See *Quick Firing Ammunition.*
Sergt Major (AC)	Sergeant Major (Artillery Clerk). This abbreviation was subsequently replaced by SMAC.
Series Of Targets	A number of targets and/or group(s) of targets planned to support a manoeuvre phase. It may be indicated by a nickname. (Royal Canadian Artillery).
Seringapatam	(i) Battery Honour Title of 34 (Seringapatam) Battery RA which was granted on 18 October 1926 under authority of 20/ARTY/4544/AG6a. See *Battery Honour Titles.* (ii) Battery Honour Title of 38 (Seringapatam) Battery RA which was granted on 12 October 1933 under authority of 20/ARTY/4735/AG6a. See *Battery Honour Titles.*
Serjeant	Original/alternative spelling of Sergeant. It appears, from referring to copies of *The Gunner* from the 1960s, to have been used during this period, although it is now no longer used by the Royal Artillery.
Serrefile	In a mounted unit the officers, NCOs and others whose posts are in rear of the battery when in line.
Service Charge	The normal full charge for a gun.
Service Designation	This comprises the basic name and model numbers. It may include some general characteristics such as calibre and role. The following parts may be included: Basic Name – A noun which governs the model number. There is always a name, for example: Gun Equipment or Carriage. Essential Characteristics – These follow the basic name, and are used to distinguish particular items, for example, Pack or 105 mm. When the calibre is included, it is generally given in millimetres, although older ordnance was given in inches. Nickname – This is the commercial name of a trade item approved for introduction into service, it may be included after the essential characteristics. Model Number – This is always included and comprises a series of letters and figures to indicate the model and subsequent modifications. An example of a Service Designation is: Gun Equipment, 105mm, L5; (Howitzer, Pack 105 mm, L10A1 on Carriage 105 mm Howitzer, L3A1). See *Model Number.*
Serving Room	In coast artillery a chamber from which cartridges are issued to the guns.

Serving the Vent When a smooth-bore gun was being loaded, the ventsman was responsible for closing the vent by placing his thumb over it. This was to prevent smouldering fragments of powder being ignited whilst the charge was being rammed. The ventsman was provided with a leather thumb guard for this.

Setting-Up Data A punched tape that could be used to quickly reload FACE, if it was switched off, or to load the same information into another FACE. See *Field Artillery Computer Equipment.*

SEUT System Evaluation and User Trials (Thunderbird II system).

Seventy Kilometre Snipers Nickname given to the Guided Multiple Launch Rocket System and its long range precision strike capability. The nickname is a direct derivation of the earlier nickname for the Royal Artillery, the Long Range Snipers. See *Guided Multiple Launch Rocket System.*

Sexton Based on the Canadian Ram tank, but altered to take a 25-pdr. This design was very similar to the US M7 Priests then in service with the Royal Artillery. The driver sat on right and gun was offset to the left. There was an ammunition loading hatch on the left side and the floor space was designed so that floor plates could be removed to access lockers where up to 87 HE or smoke rounds and 18 armour-piercing rounds were stored. In adverse weather the fighting compartment could be covered with a canvas. The gun was installed in a special cradle. Sexton Batteries were used almost exclusively for artillery support of armoured divisions. Early vehicles had welded superstructure. Later models had cast nose, towing hook for ammo trailer, auxiliary generator and mounts for anti-aircraft machine guns.
Country of Origin: Canada.
Type: Self-propelled artillery.
Entered Service: 1941.
Retired from Service: Late 1950s.
Detachment: 6 (Commander, driver, gunner, gun layer, loader, radio operator).
Engine: One nine-cylinder Continental radial piston engine 400 or 484hp.
Range: 290 km.
Width: 2.72 m.
Primary Gun Armament: 1x 25 pounder.
Secondary Armament: 2 Bren 0.303 in, and One 0.50 Browning.
Armour: 6 mm.
Ammunition: 112 x 25-pounder shells, 1,500 x.303 in rounds.
Speed: 40.2 kph.
Length: 6.12 m.
Height: 2.44 m.
Combat weight: 25,650 kg.
See *Sexton GPO* and *Ram OP.*

Sexton GPO During late 1943 the gun was removed from some examples of the Sexton and extra radios, map tables, telephone cables and a tannoy unit were added for Gun Position Officers of Sexton batteries. See *Sexton* and *Ram OP.*

SEZ Selector Engagement Zone.

SF (i) Special Forces.
(ii) Sustained Fire. See *GPMG.*
(iii) Artillery Code used during First World War meaning 'Fire by single guns or Range afresh'.

SFF Self Forging Fragment.

SFM	(i) Sensor Fuzed Munitions. (ii) Self-Forging Fragment Munitions.
SFSU	Selector Firing Sequence Unit.
SFTA	Safe False Target Area.
SH	(i) Super Heavy. (ii) Support Helicopter.
Shah Sujah's Day	Battery day of T Headquarter Battery (Shah Sujahs Troop) RA.
Shah Sujah's Troop	Battery Honour Title of T Headquarters Battery (Shah Sujah's Troop) RA which was granted on 18 October 1926 under authority of 20/ARTY/4544/AG6a. See *Battery Honour Titles.*
Sheath	The pattern and dimensions of gun aimpoints on a target. Introduced with the Artillery Fire Data Computer in the early 1980s, it replaced parallel lines of fire reflecting the layout of the guns. The Sheath was designed to achieve optimum spread whilst allowing guns to be tactically sited in a battery position.
Sheldrake	Artillery Radio Appointment Title.
Shell Bearer	In fortifications and coast artillery batteries a device used for lifting a shell from the top of a shell lift or shell store to the muzzle of the gun.
Shell Block	Found in shell filling rooms of fortifications and coast artillery batteries this was a block of hard wood with a conical hole in it, which held a shell whilst it was being filled.
Shell Filling Room	In coast artillery, a chamber in a laboratory, where shells were filled. See *Laboratory.*
Shell Issuer	In coast artillery a hatch or opening in a wall through which shells were passed. See *Cartridge Issuer.*
Shell Lift	In fortifications and coast artillery batteries this was a shaft together with its associated equipment for raising shells from the basement stores to the gun floor. See *Cartridge Lift, Shell Store* and *Shell Serving Room.*
Shell Passage	In coast artillery a passage along which shell was transported. See *Powder Passage.*
Shell Recess	In coast artillery a small receptacle for the storage of a few shells for the immediate service of the gun. See *Cartridge Recess.*
Shell Serving Room	In coast artillery a chamber on the same level as the gun into which the shell lifts lead. See *Shell Lift* and *Cartridge Passage.*
Shell Store	In coast artillery a chamber in which all filled shells, tubes and fuzes were stored.
Shell Trucks	A special truck, not unlike those used by railway porters, which was used to move shells in fortifications and coast artillery batteries.
Shelling Connection and Activity Trace	A pictorial record that shows the areas into which hostile batteries are firing, which of them are most active and the type of fire they are delivering. See *Bearing Report Trace, Hostile Battery* and *Hostile Battery Chart.*
Shelling or Mortaring Plot	See *Shelling Plot.*
Shelling Plot	Used during the Second World War and later, it consisted of a trace over CB chart showing shelling and mortaring reports, it became the Shelling or Mortaring Plot in 1950s. It was replaced by Bearing Report Trace during the 1960s. See *Bearing Report Trace.*
Shelrep	Shelling Report. The term is often found spelt 'Shellrep'.
Shelrep OP	An observation post which had the responsibility of listening and watching for enemy guns firing. On hearing the sound or seeing the flash of a gun, the Shellrep OP reported the bearing to the counter bombardment officer

so that retaliatory fire could be brought to bear (Second World War). See *Counter Bombardment.*

Shg/Smith Shoeing Smith.

Shifting Lobby See *Shifting Room.*

Shifting Room The chamber or portion of the entrance passage devoted to the putting on or removal of laboratory or magazine clothing. See *Laboratory, Magazine* and *Shifting Lobby.*

Shiny Arse Derogatory nickname for a battery clerk.

Shiny Bottoms Derisive nickname given to command post staff by those on the gun line.

Shiny E Nickname of E Battery RHA.

Shiny K Nickname of K (Hondeghem) Battery RA.

Shiny Six Nickname of 6 Battery RA.

Shitehawks Common derogatory nickname for any battery in the Royal Artillery which has an eagle in its battery crest.

SHMA Suspected Hostile Mortar Area.

Shooie Shoeing Smith.

Shooting Corrections These are the differences between the centre-to-centre data and the bearing, angle of sight and range at which the guns fired, or will fire. For example, position corrections, line and range displacements for linear concentrations, or indeed any individual corrections which may be ordered by the Observation Post Officer. See *Centre-to-Centre Data*

Shooting Rights Rights granted to an observer to engage – without reference to higher or flanking authority – any target lying within the area of influence of that formation of which the artillery unit is in direct support (Royal Canadian Artillery).

Shop, The The original RMA at Woolwich (Slang).

SHORAD Short Range Air Defence.

SHORADEZ Short Range Air Defence Engagement Zone.

Short A round which falls short of the target, as seen from the Observation Post. See *Over* and *Target Grid Corrections.*

Short Base Usually consisting of four sound ranging microphones laid in a straight line for both speed and survey. The Short Base is used for rapid mortar location. See *Long Base.*

Short Term Deployment A quick action whereby guns deploy from a fire base to a prepared and surveyed position.

Shot Gauge During the muzzle-loading period, a shot gauge would be placed over the shot to see which projectile best suited which gun.

Shot Seating The conical portion of the bore where the chamber diameter is reduced to join the rifled portion. The rifling develops within the shot seating in a portion known as the development of rifling. The commencement of rifling is the point at which the grooves first reach maximum depth and marks the end of the shot seating. The depth of rifling is measured from the top of a land to the bottom of a groove.

Shot Start Pressure When the propellant charge is ignited, gases are evolved and as a consequence, pressure in the chamber increases until the resistance of the projectile is overcome.

Shot Tower A tower used during the smoothbore period to make shot for guns. In order to create the lead shot, molten lead was dropped from the melting chamber at the top of the tower through sieves down to water at the bottom, where it hardened and formed into balls of shot. An example of a Shot Tower, built in 1826, stood for many years on the south bank of the River Thames near Waterloo Bridge in London.

Shot Travel The distance from the base to the muzzle is known as the Shot Travel. When a shell is rammed the driving band

	engages in the shot seating and is deformed to fit the rifled portion.
Shrapnel	Invented in the early 1800s by Lieutenant Henry Shrapnel RA and first known as 'Spherical Case' it became known by its inventor's name after its adoption by the Royal Artillery. Shrapnel was an anti-personnel weapon comprising a hollow spherical projectile filled with musket balls and an explosive charge. A shell was activated by means of a time fuze to project a cone of lead bullets forward in a shot-gun like manner. In the early twentieth century Shrapnel shells contained the following: 13-pdr: 236 bullets at 41 to the pound 18-pdr: 374 bullets at 41 to the pound 4.5-inch Howitzer: 492 bullets at 35 to the pound 60-pdr: 990 bullets at 35 to the pound. The bullets, known as 'mixed bullets' were made of lead with the addition of a small amount of antimony to increase hardness. Finally withdrawn from UK service in the 1930s. The term is often widely misused to refer to the fragments from a bursting HE shell. See *Percussion Shrapnel* and *Time Shrapnel.*
Shrapnel Troop	One of the Troops in 33 Campbell Bty Junior Leaders Regiment RA. See *Borgard Troop, Gunn Troop* and *Wingate Troop.*
Shrapnel, Zero	Part of a fire order specifying that shrapnel shells should be fired with the time and percussion fuze set to zero. This resulted in the shell event occurring on discharge and therefore acting as a form of case shot. See *Case Shot, Shrapnel* and *Time and Percussion Fuze.*
SHS	Split Hairpin Shelter.
S Hy Regt	Super Heavy Regiment.
SI	Senior Instructor.
SIA	Sight Infra-Red Assembly (part of the HVM equipment).
SIAD	Senior Instructor Air Defence.
SIAP	System Intergration and Assurance Phase. (Part of a new system introduction package.)
SIBUA	Survival in Built Up Areas.
Side Slap	This phenomenon arises when the shell passes through a worn gun, vibrating from side to side, the greater the wear of the gun, for a given muzzle velocity, the greater the magnitude of side slap.
Sidi Rezegh	Battery Honour Title of J (Sidi Rezegh) Battery RHA which was granted on 26 April 1954 under authority of 20/ARTY/6271/AG6a. See *Battery Honour Titles.*
Sidi Rezegh Day	Battery Day for J (Sidi Rezegh) Battery RHA, celebrates the battle fought 21–25 November 1941.
Siege Artillery Reserve Brigade	Forming part of the Royal Garrison Artillery during the First World War. There were four Siege Artillery Reserve Brigades in the RGA, namely No. 1 at Shoreham, No. 2 at Catterick, No. 3 at Prees Heath in Shropshire and No. 4 at Aldershot.
Siege Park	Central Depot, usually on a Corps basis, where Army Service Corps lorries would be found parked (First World War).
Siege Platform	A form of portable platform used to mount a siege gun, mortar, or field gun during siege operations when the ordnance was to be fired from the same spot for any length of time. See *Dwarf Platform, Mortar Platform, New Pattern Traversing Platform* and *Traversing Platform.*
Siege Train Unit, Heavy	Circa 1878 a Heavy Siege Train Unit comprised eight 64-pdr guns and fourteen 8-inch howitzers. Circa 1884–1899

a Heavy Siege Train unit comprised four 40-pdr RML, two 6.6-inch RML howitzers and ten 8-inch RML howitzers.

Siege Train Unit, Medium — Circa 1884–1899 a Medium Siege Train Unit comprised six 40-pdr RML and ten 6.6-inch RML howitzers.

Siege Train Unit, Light — Circa 1878 a Light Siege Train Unit comprised ten 40-pdr guns, ten 25-pdr guns and ten 6.3 inch howitzers. The 6.3-inch howitzers were replaced by the 6.6-inch as soon as they became available. Circa 1884–1899 a Light Siege Train Unit comprised eight 25-pdr RML and eight 6.3-inch RML howitzers.

SIF — Service Institute Fund.

SIFF — Successor Identification Friend or Foe. See *TCWI, HVM* and *SPHVM.*

Sigex — Signals Exercise.

Sight Clino — See *Clinometer.*

Sight Line Diagram(s) — A means of demonstrating the path followed by the axes of the bore and of the sight while laying for various combinations of sight type and trunnion tilt. It is often believed by gunners that its major function is to frustrate students on technical gunnery courses.

Sight Unit Infantry Trilux — A x3 magnification sight used on the self-loading rifle.

Sight Unit Small Arms Trilux — The x4 sight used with the 5.56 mm L85A2 rifle and the L86 Light Support Weapon. Most L85s issued to the Royal Artillery are fitted with iron sights, however, SUSATs are issued when the unit deploys out of role.

Signal Terminal — The battery signallers located at either the observation post or the battery command post during the 1920/30s. They were equipped with D3 field telephones, signal flags, heliographs and daylight signalling lamps (Lucas Lamps). Signal terminals at observation posts were responsible only for communications with their own battery command post, whilst those at the battery command post had the additional responsibility of maintaining communications with the observation post and brigade headquarters. Sometimes referred to simply as Terminals. See *Terminal.*

Signature Equipment — Items of equipment that are unique to a particular unit or formation. Such equipment allows ready recognition of divisional artillery, army level reconnaissance assets and similar formations.

Silent Marking — The production of data from the map of possible enemy routes/locations. This data is used to bring fire onto the target if it is used by the enemy. Formally known as Silent Registration. See *Registration.*

Silent Position — An artillery position from which the guns (anything from a single gun to a full battery) do not fire until the commencement of the specific operation for which they have been placed in that location or for some other unforeseen emergency. This is in order to preserve surprise, and deny the enemy intelligence.

Silent Practice — A form of drill, whereby all the actions required to engage a target are carried out, without actually firing any live ammunition at the target. The term was in use during the 1950s.

Silent Registration — Now known as Silent Marking. See *Registration* and *Silent Marking.*

SIMAMMO — Simulated Ammunition (used to practise ammunition handling).

SIMMO — Simulated Ammunition (used to practise ammunition handling).

Simple Alert — The middle rung in NATO's non-emergency alert state hierarchy. See *General Alert* and *Military Vigilance.*

Simple Concentration — The general term given to the engagement of targets by fire units (sections, batteries, regiments, etc.) with line of fire parallel and without the application of position corrections. See *Linear Concentration* and *Converged.*

SIMRAD — A Norwegian-made laser range finder used in the observation post. With a range of six kilometres it was said to be accurate to ten metres.

Simultaneous Position and Azimuth Detecting Equipment — Intended to replace the Sperry Navigator, it worked by inertial means and was said to be very accurate. See *Precision Indicator Meridian.*

Sine Rule — Used in triangulation for survey. The log sine of an included angle in a triangle equals the log length of the opposite side of the triangle.

Site Guards — The name given to the force guarding a SAS Site in Germany during the Cold War. The Guard duty was for a week and rotated among units of all arms and services. See *SAS Site.*

Sit — Situation.

Sitrep — Situation Report.

Sjt — Serjeant.

SK — (i) A First World War British gas shell filling consisting of Ethyl Iodoacetate. The name being derived from South Kensington, where it was developed at the Imperial College of Science.
(ii) Socket.

Skeddy's Day — Battery day of 28/143 Battery (Tomb's Troop), celebrated in March to commemorate the forming of 28 Battery.

Skeddys Troop — One of the two gun troops in 28/143 Battery (Tomb's Troop) RA. See *Cassino Troop* and *Hills Troop.*

Skidding — A system of wooden shelving found in magazines on which barrels of powder (or metal lined cases) were stored.

Skid Target — A towed target consisting of a superstructure mounted on a type of sleigh which was towed behind a launch as a practice target for coast artillery batteries.

Sky Hooks — These were and possibly still are used to hook D10 communications wire into trees and high places to get it off the ground at road crossings etc.

SL — (i) Shoulder Launched.
(ii) Start Line, now Line of Departure.
(iii) Safe Lane.
(iv) Searchlight. See *S/L.*
(v) Swing Left. See *SLTR* and *Swinging.*

S/L — Searchlight. See *SL.*

SLC — Searchlight Control (Radar).

SLE — Spearhead Land Element.

Sleeve — Common name for the Rushton Target. See *Rushton Target.*

Sleeve Target — An anti-aircraft practice target, made of canvas and cylinderical in form, it was towed at a safe distance behind an aircraft, in order for anti-aircraft guns to engage it with live ammunition. See *Sleeve* and *Rushton Target.*

Slew — The change in angle applied during change of grid.

Slide — See *Traversing Platform.*

Slidex — A general purpose code introduced in late 1943, consisting of a set of subject-specific cards printed with words and short phrases relevant to the subject concerned on a grid/table. Each cell of the grid/table was identified by a two-letter bigram which was read from 'slides' along the top and down one side. The alignment of the slides was different depending on the message. Slidex was used for messages classified up to confidential. Messages above confidential were encrypted using One Time Pads. See *One Time Pad*.

Sling — Either a rope or chain, with thimbles attached, which was used to assist with lifting ordnance. The length of the sling varied according to its use.

Sling Cart — A two-wheeled cart used to move heavy ordnance over short distances. The barrel being slung underneath the cart. See *Sling Wagon*.

Sling Wagon — A four-wheeled wagon, sometimes known as a 'devil's carriage', which was drawn by six horses. It was used to transport a gun barrel by slinging it underneath the axle trees.

SLO — (i) Suspension Lockout. Part of the MLRS system. See *Multiple Launch Rocket System*.
(ii) Senior Liaison Officer.

SLRA — (i) Staff Lieutenant Royal Artillery.
(ii) Sierra Leone Company Royal Artillery.

SLTR — Swing Left Traverse Right, procedure with Number 6 and 7 Directors.

SM — Sample Matrix.

SMAC — Sergeant-Major Artillery Clerk.

Small Arms Ammunition — During the nineteenth and early twentieth century the supply of Small Arms Ammunition to the infantry was the responsibility of the Royal Artillery divisional and brigade ammunition columns.

Small Port Carriage — In fortifications and coast artillery batteries this was a mounting which was designed to allow the gun to be raised and lowered to different heights to achieve the required elevation or depression.

SMART — WO1 Sergeant-Major Artificer.

SMC — Sub Machine Carbine.

SME — Subject Matter Expert.

SMIG — Sergeant-Major Instructor in Gunnery. Term replaced AIG.

SMIS — Sergeant-Major Instructor of Signals.

Smiths and Fitters Shop — Found in fortifications and coast artillery batteries, this building contained a forge and other articles required to make repairs to the ordnance and mountings. It was classified as an artillery store.

smk — Smoke.

Smoke Ball — A paper shell, used in smooth-bore ordnance which contained a burning composition designed to emit large volumes of smoke. It was used in the same way as a modern day smoke shell.

Smooth Bore — A term used to describe an item of ordnance which has no rifling in its barrel. The term is also used to refer to the period during which such ordnance was in service.

SMP — Safe Maximum Pressure.

SMS — Sergeant-Major Signals.

Smuffs — Smoke Puffs. Used by air observation posts during the Korean War to report the location of hostile guns firing to the counter bombardment staff.

SNCO — Senior Non-Commissioned Officer.

SNH — South Nottinghamshire Hussars.

SNITs — Soldiers Not In Training.

Snooker — New recruit at the Royal Military Academy Woolwich.

Snots, The — Nickname of 307 (South Nottinghamshire Hussars Yeomanry RHA) Battery.

Snout — The nickname by which the Ordnance QF 25-pdr Short (Aust) Mk I on Carriage Light (Aust) Mks I and II was known by the Royal Australian Artillery. This had a barrel

	of just four feet in length and weighed just one-and-a-quarter tons, it also had a new design of cradle, trail and axles. There was a small jockey wheel at the rear to assist with manoeuvring the gun into position, but this was raised during transport. The gun could be broken down into thirteen (or fourteen depending on which manual you read) loads, all of which after packing in cartons could be parachuted from a C-47. An example of this gun can be seen in Firepower, the museum of the Royal Artillery at Woolwich.
SNVT	Short No Voltage Tester. Part of the MLRS system. See *Multiple Launch Rocket System.*
SO	Staff Officer. i.e. SO2 Staff Officer grade 2.
SOA	Sultan of Oman's Artillery.
SO Arty Ops	Staff Officer Artillery Operations.
SOB	Staff Officer Bombardment (Second World War).
SOC	Sector Operations Centre.
SOCs	Secure Orders Cards.
Soda Water Bottles	See *Woolwich Infant.*
S of A	School of Artillery
S of AA Arty	School of Anti-Aircraft Artillery.
S of E	Superintendent of Experiments.
SOHB	Staff Officers Handbook.
SOIs	(i) Standard Operating Instructions. (ii) Signals Operating Instruction.
SOME	Senior Ordnance Mechanical Engineer. Coast Artillery. See *OME.*
Somme Troop	Originally one of the Troops in 1st Squadron Honourable Artillery Company, after 1994 transferred to Signal Squadron with Aden Troop and Cassino Troop. See *Aden Troop, Cassino Troop, Honourable Artillery Company, South Africa Troop* and *Ypres Troop.*
Sonde	An electronic device attached to a weather balloon to observe the atmospheric conditions in the upper atmosphere. Used as part of the BMETS system. See *BMETS.*
Sophie	A hand-held thermal imaging device used by forward observers. See *OTIS.*
SOP	(i) Standard Operational Procedure. (ii) Section Observation Post. Coast artillery Second World War and later.
SOR	State of Readiness.
SORAS 6	Sound Ranging System 6. (Royal Canadian Artillery).
Sortie Day	Battery Day of 22 (Gibraltar 1779-1783) Battery RA. Celebrating the Great Sortie in defence of Gibraltar on 27 November 1781.
Sortie Troop	One of the three troops in 22 (Gibraltar 1779–1783) Battery RA. Named after the Great Sortie of 27 November 1781. See *Dover's Troop* and *Koehler's Troop.*
SOS	(i) Save Our Souls, the international distress signal. See *SOS Lines* and *SOS Task.* (ii) Artillery Code used during the First World War meaning 'Barrage fire'.
SOS Lines	Line or bearing (and elevation) upon which guns were laid on pre-arranged targets, usually by night, to enable them to respond to an SOS call without delay.
SOS Rockets	Coloured rockets fired by front line troops to indicate to supporting batteries that they are under attack and that the batteries should fire their defensive fire tasks (First World War). See *Defensive Fire.*
SOS Task	Defensive fire task fired in front of your own troops during an enemy attack, usually pre-arranged.
Sound Banging	A colloquial name for Sound Ranging. See *Sound Ranging.*

Sound Ranging	A method developed during the First World War, whereby hostile artillery was located by using a line of microphones and recording the different times of arrival of the sound wave at each microphone. These differences are then used to deduce the guns' position. Originally developed by the Royal Engineers, but now the prerogative of the Royal Artillery. See *ASP* and *Flash Spotting*.
Sound Ranging System 6	An obsolete sound ranging system used by the Royal Canadian Artillery.
South Africa Troop	One of the Troops in Signal Squadron Honourable Artillery Company. See *Aden Troop, Cassino Troop, Honourable Artillery Company* and *Somme Troop*.
SP	(i) Self-Propelled. See *Abbot, Achilles, Archer, AS90, Portee, Priest* and *Sexton*. (ii) Special Proficiency. (iii) Start Point. (iv) Strong Point. (v) Shelling Plot.
Sp	Support.
SP70	The self-propelled follow-on to the FH70 which was designed in collaboration with Italy and Germany. The project was eventually cancelled leading to the UK selecting the AS90 and the German development of PzH2000. See *AS90* and *FH70*.
SPADDET	Self Propelled Air Defence Detachment Engagement Trainer. See *CADDET*.
SPADE	Simultaneous Position and Azimuth Detecting Equipment. See *PIM*.
Spade	A blade fitted beneath the gun trail and designed to bite into the ground in order to resist any rearward movement of the gun caused by recoil. Usually located at the end of the trail.
Spaghetti Gun	See *Mussolini's Revenge*.
SPE	Service Protected Evacuation.
Special Ammunition Storage Site	A storage site at which nuclear weapons were held.
Special Corridor	An Airspace Control Measure / Air Defence term.
Special Defence Group	The Special Defence Group was a specialist infantry unit within the Royal Artillery and was unique to 50 Missile Regiment. Its role was to provide ground security for the missile batteries and in particular the Lance missile system. Members of the SDG completed infantry training on courses run internally by 50 Missile Regiment and also externally. The courses covered such areas as infantry tactics, field craft, weapon handling, first aid, and nuclear biological and chemical warfare. There were three Special Defence Group troops in the Regiment, each missile battery had its own SDG troop of approximately thirty men, with an organisation comparable to that of a standard infantry platoon. Each troop was broken down into three sections, with each section consisting of eight men, commanded by a bombardier. The section generally operated from light-skinned vehicles such as Land Rovers and had an array of fire power, including rifles, light support weapons, machine guns (in both the light and sustained fire roles), mortars and various anti-tank weapons. The three sections came under the command of a troop headquarters, commanded by a warrant officer or a lieutenant who in turn was assisted by a troop sergeant. The section commanders and troop sergeants attended the section commanders and platoon sergeants battle courses

run by the school of infantry which encouraged leadership, weapon handling and tactics; these courses were particularly physically demanding.

Specialist Personal Global Positioning System Receiver	Pronounced 'Spugger'. The SPGR is capable of tracking twelve satellites at any one time and selects the five optimum ones for position calculation. The basic model is issued to gun regiments. Variants include the gun laying system and the differential global positioning system software. See *Gun Laying System* and *Differential Global Positioning System.*
Special Needs Battery	(i) Derogatory nickname for 4/73 (Sphinx) Special Observation Post Battery RA. (ii) Also used as a derogatory nickname for any battery whose role is even slightly different from that of the rest of the regiment.
Special Proficiency	A qualification denoted by the letters 'SP' above a laurel spray, worn on the lower left arm.
Special Service Sections	In the early twentieth century Special Service Sections were formed, these were made up of volunteer artillery men who agreed to serve, for a period of one month, with specified coast defences in case of emergency. These sections were formed in order to avoid increasing the establishment of existing garrisons. Their role was to assist in the manning of the anti-torpedo boat defences during the time between mobilisation and the arrival of the regular reservists.
Special Weapons	Used as part of a unit title to denote a nuclear capability.
Sperry Navigator	An item of survey equipment which combined a milometer with a compass, it was found to be insufficiently accurate to be used in survey. See *Navigator* and *SPADE.*
Sperwer TUAV	Tactical Unmanned Aerial Vehicle employed by the Royal Canadian Artillery. Used in Afghanistan.
Sp Gp	Support Group.
SPGR	Specialist Personal Global Positioning System Receiver.
Spherical Case	See *Shrapnel.*
Sphinx	(i) Battery Honour Title of F (Sphinx) Parachute Battery RHA which was granted on 18 October 1926 under authority of 20/ARTY/4544/AG6a. See *Battery Honour Titles.* (ii) Battery Honour Title of 4 (Sphinx) Battery RA which was granted on 18 October 1926 under authority of 20/ARTY/4544/AG6a. Now amalgamated with 73 Battery RA to form 4/73 (Sphinx) Special Observation Post RA Battery RA. See *Battery Honour Titles.* (iii) Battery Honour Title of 7 (Sphinx) Commando Battery RA which was granted on 18 October 1926 under authority of 20/ARTY/4544/AG6a. See *Battery Honour Titles.* (iv) Battery Honour Title of 11 (Sphinx) Headquarters Battery RA which was granted on 18 October 1926 under authority of 20/ARTY/4544/AG6a. See *Battery Honour Titles.* (v) Battery Honour Title of 73 (Sphinx) Observation Post Battery RA which was granted on 16 March 1934 under authority of 20/ARTY/4943/AG6a. Now amalgamated with 4 (Sphinx) Battery RA to form 4/73 (Sphinx) Special Observation Post RA Battery RA. See *Battery Honour Titles.*
Sphinx Day	11 April, celebrated by 11 (Sphinx) Headquarters Battery RA.
SPHR	Standard Predicted Horizontal Range (1950s–1970s).
SPHVM	Self-Propelled High Velocity Missile.
Spider	An eight-legged barrack block.

Spin Stabilization	As the projectile leaves the muzzle, the rotation imparted by the driving bands engaging the rifling is maintained in the form of spinning. This spin, in conjunction with gravity and air resistance, ensures that the projectile remains pointing along its trajectory throughout its flight.
Spiral Ranging	The term used to describe the fall of shot during a mission fired by an inexperienced or incompetent observer. It is sometimes called 'spiral ranging onto and along the line OU.'
SPIT	Smallest Possible Impact Trace.
SPL	Standard Predicted Line (1950s–1970s).
Splash	A fire discipline phrase, generally used when air observation is in use or high angle fire has been ordered. It is reported to the observer five seconds before shell impact or airburst. The five-second interval can be altered using for example, 'report splash ten seconds'.
Splinter Bar	The wooden bar at the front of a horse-drawn limber that attached to the traces of the horses and also connected the futchells and axletree. See *Axletree*, *Futchell* and *Limber*.
Splintex	Name given to US-origin shells filled with several thousand small darts fired forward shrapnel-style. US forces often refer to these rounds as 'Beehive'. In Vietnam they were available for both the 105 mm Howitzer and 90 and 106 mm Recoilless Rifles.
SPLL	Self Propelled Loader Launcher (MLRS).
SPLL LST	SPLL List.
SPOD	Seaport of Departure.
Sponge	Used with smooth bore artillery, this was a wooden stave with a sheepskin attachment used to clean the bore of a gun after firing and before loading. The sheepskin would be dipped in a bucket of water before sponging, to extinguish any burning embers in the bore. During the period 1868–1876 and probably before this date, sponges used for RML guns had sponge staves of ash, with a head of elm. The elm head was covered with a coating of woven wool, fastened on with marine glue (fish glue), and choked round a groove in the head with strong string. Sponges for Armstrong's RBLs had a coating of hemp and canvas woven and fastened round the sponge stave with string. Painted canvas caps were issued with sponge heads to keep them clean and in good order. Also spelt 'spunges'. See *Rammer, Serving the Vent* and *Ventsman*.
SPOS	Special Purpose Operational Stores.
Spotting Line	In Naval Gunfire Support, either the gun-target line, observer-target line, or a reference line used by the spotter in making corrections. (Royal Canadian Artillery.)
SPRDE	Salisbury Plain Range Detachment. Pronounced 'sperde'.
Spreading Fire	A notification by the spotter or naval gunfire ship, depending on who is controlling fire, to indicate that fire is about to be distributed over an area (Royal Canadian Artillery).
SPS	Standard Positioning System.
SPTA	Salisbury Plain Training Area.
SPTA(C)	Salisbury Plain Training Area (Centre).
SPTA(E)	Salisbury Plain Training Area (East).
SPTA(W)	Salisbury Plain Training Area (West).
Spunges	See *Sponges*.
Spyglass	L5/L6A1 lightweight thermal imager system, may be mounted on a tripod together with a laser rangefinder for use by OP parties.
SQ	Super Quick, US direct action fuze used with US-origin ammunition.

Squash Head	Anti-tank fuse for a high explosive plastic (HEP) shell.
SR	(i) Sound Ranging. (ii) Superintendent of Research. (iii) Stadia Rod. (iv) Swing Right. See *SRTL and Swinging.*
SRCP	Sound Ranging Command Post.
SRg	Sound Ranging.
SRHQ	Sound Ranging Headquarters.
SR(L)	Service Requirement (Land).
SRO	(i) Special Regimental Order. (ii) Senior Reporting Officer. (iii) Senior Responsible Officer.
SRP	(i) Survey Reference Point. (ii) Stabilization Reference Package. Part of the MLRS system. See *Multiple Launch Rocket System.*
SRPC	Surveillance and Reconnaissance Patrol Course.
SRP/PDS	Stabilisation Reference Package and Position Determining System. See *Multiple Launch Rocket System.*
SRR	Surveillance Radar Receiver. Part of the Rapier FSB2 air defence system.
SRRA	Singapore Regiment Royal Artillery.
SRTL	Swing Right Traverse Left, procedure with number six and seven directors.
SS	Servicing Schedule.
SSA	Staff Support Assistant.
SSC	Sector Searchlight Commander.
SSD	(i) Safe Splinter Distance. (ii) Special Safety Distance.
SSF	Standard Safety Factor. Added to crest height. FACE.
SSGT	Staff Sergeant.
S/SGT	Staff Sergeant.
SSGW	Surface to Surface Guided Weapon.
SSM	Surface to Surface Missile, for example, the Honest John and Lance missiles.
SSTE	Special to System Test Equipment.
SSTO	SAM SHORAD Tactical Order. See *SAM* and *SHORAD.*
ST	(i) Suffix added to siege company numbers in the early twentieth century to denote their role. Presumably standing for 'Siege Train'. (ii) Surface Target. (iii) Status.
ST(L)	Service Target (Land).
STA	(i) Surveillance and Target Acquisition. (ii) Sennybridge Training Area. (iii) Sennelager Training Area. (iv) Safe Target Area. (v) Shell Transfer Arm.
STAA	Signal Training (All Arms). Generally followed by the number of the relevant pamphlet.
Stabilisation Reference Package and Position Determining System	The onboard navigation and survey system for the MLRS system. See *Multiple Launch Rocket System.*
Stables	Daily grooming parade 1100–1200 hrs (The King's Troop RHA).
Stadia Rod	Introduced soon after the Second World War, these vertical poles enable distances up to 400 metres to be measured using the vertical graticules in the eyepiece of a director set against marked lengths on the pole. They were used for single leg measurement from a surveyed battery director. Stadia rods were used to mark battery centre when this was introduced in the 1950s. See *Banderole.*

Staff	Abbreviated title by which staff sergeants are often addressed.
Staff Assistant Royal Artillery	An Artillery clerk with additional training. (1970s–1980s).
Staff Employed	Soldiers working in a trade e.g., Saddler, MT Dept, Gd Room.
Staff Parade	Usually held weekly by the regimental sergeant-major on a Monday, but different regiments have diffrent arrangements. Some RSMs prefer to hold a daily staff parade. The parade is attended by all duty-nominated staff for the week, for example the regimental orderly officer, orderly sergeants and BONCOs etc. It is the RSM's forum for briefing the duty staff on the week (or day) ahead. See *BONCO.*
Staff Ride	A euphemism for a battlefield tour.
Stag	A period of sentry duty.
Stalwart	HMLC ammunition vehicle used in self-propelled regiments 1960s–1980s. See *Alvis Stalwart.*
STAMET	Safe Target Area Adjusted for Meteorological Conditions.
STANAG	Standardisation Agreements (NATO).
Stand Alone Net Interface Equipment	The vehicle mounted net interface equipment to the radio set in the BATES system. See *BATES, MONIE* and *NIE.*
Standard Ballistic Coefficient	A mathematical formula used to describe the ability of a projectile to overcome air pressure by reason of its mass and shape. It is a measure of the carrying power of the projectile. The greater the Standard Ballistic Coefficient the further the projectile will travel, under given conditions of projection. See *Ballistic Coefficient.*
Standard Ballistic Meteorological Message	Used with the BMETS system. See *BMETS* and *SCMM.*
Standard Barrage	The standard barrage consists of a series of linear concentrations providing a moving belt of fire. See *Barrage* and *Linear Concentration*
Standard Computer Meteorological Message	Used with the BMETS system. See *BMETS* and *SBMM.*
Standard Predicted Horizontal Range	The range found by adding the correction of the moment to the map range. It is the range required to hit a target under the prevailing conditions of barometric pressure, air temperature, wind and charge temperature; provided that the standard projectile is used, the target is in the same horizontal plan as the gun and the firing gun used is of range table muzzle velocity. See *Predicted Horizontal Range.*
Standard Predicted Line	The bearing found by adding the correction of the moment to the map line. It is applied to the sight so that the target can be hit under the prevailing conditions. No corrections for drift are taken into account with this bearing. See *Correction of the Moment.*
Stand-by Alert Team	Part of the security force at a field storage site or special ammunition supply site. The team consisted of two men immediately available to respond to anything reported by a sentry.
Stand Fast	Order whereby all activity is suspended until 'Go on' is ordered.
Stand Easy	Order whereby an engagement is suspended, cartridges are unloaded and detachments may withdraw from the guns. Stand easy is cancelled by 'Take Post'. See *Take Post.*
Stand To	(i) The highest state of alert where all troops are ready for immediate action with weapons at the ready. In the British

	Army troops generally stand to at sunrise and sunset, the most common time for a surprise attack. (ii) To take up positions for action.
STANEVAL	Standards Evaluation.
STAP	Surveillance and Target Acquisition Plan.
STAPD	Safe Target Area Point Detonating.
Starge	Nickname given to a Quick Barrage by the Divisional Artillery of 56th (London) Division in 1941 It should not be confused with the a 'Stonk'. See *Stonk* and *Quick Barrage*.
Star Shell	A parachute flare delivered by base ejection (BE) shell, known in modern terms as an illumination round. Star shells were of the carrier type and contained a star case, filled with an illumination composition, which was connected to a parachute. The shell was burst high in the air, at which point the star composition was ignited and descended slowly to the ground illuminating a wide area below. See *Carrier Shell, Illumination* and *Illuminating Round.*
Starstreak	Known as the High Velocity Missile or more usually simply as HVM, Starstreak is a laser guided surface to air missile. It continues the development path of both Blowpipe and Javelin. The HVM can be shoulder-launched, fired from the lightweight multiple launcher (LML) or vehicle borne on the Alvis Stormer APC which has an eight-round launcher (twelve reload missiles are carried inside the vehicle). Designed to counter threats from very high performance low flying aircraft and fast pop-up type strikes by attack helicopters. The missile employs a system of three dart type projectiles which allows multiple hits on the target. Missile Length: 1.39 m. Missile Diameter: 0.27 m. Missile Speed Mach: 3+. Maximum Range: 5.5 kms. Minimum Range: 1500 m.
Startex	The beginning of an exercise.
Static Unit Trainer	Part of the BATES system, it is used for classroom-based training. See *BATES, TUT* and *UT*.
Station Practice	Firing drill conducted by coast artillery units.
Station Radio A13	Manpack HF set, which whilst not forming part of the Larkspur system was first issued in 1965 to select units in FARELF including RA. It is believed to have been, if not the first, certainly one of the first to be fitted with a hand generator for battery charging.
Station Radio A14	HF radio issued in late 1960s.
Station Radio A41	A manpack radio used for communication between the forward observation officer and the supported infantry battalion. Operating in the Royal Armoured Corps/ Infantry frequency band, it was a copy of US AN/PRC-9. Issued to RA for communications with supported arm units. The set had a range of three to five miles and a battery life of twenty-four hours.
Station Radio A42	A VHF FM manpack transceiver which was part of the Larkspur family of radios. It was used by Royal Artillery observation post for communication to Station Radio C45, in addition it could be used for radio rebroadcast. It had a range of from three to five miles. The A42 No.1 had 118 channels in 100 kHz steps between 26.3 to 38 MHz whilst the A42 No. 2 had 235 channels in 50 kHz steps. A copy of US AN/PRC-10.
Station Radio A43R	A manpack ground to air UHF transceiver issued to forward air controllers, with a frequency range of 240 to 300 MHz. It had 6 pre-set crystal controlled channels.

range depending on altitude aircraft but varied between 4 and 100 miles.

Station Radio A510 — A HF set that fitted into two ammunition pouches, it used exchangeable crystals to set the frequency. Produced in Australia, it was issued to selected units in FARELF including RA. It is believed that it was only capable of continuous wave transmission.

Station Radio B43/R220 — A VHF AM static transmitter receiver which was part of the Larkspur range of radios. It was employed by the Royal Artillery for anti-aircraft command communications.

Station Radio B44 — A VHF AM man portable transceiver in the Larkspur range of radios. Employed by the Royal Artillery for communication within light anti-aircraft regiments. With three crystal controlled channels the radio had a range of up to fifteen miles.

Station Radio B47 — Larkspur VHF radio covering RAC/infantry frequencies, equivalent of the Station Radio B48.

Station Radio B48 — A VHF vehicular transceiver in the Larkspur range of radios, used by the Royal Artillery for observation post and forward observation officer communication. It could be employed in the man portable role, and had a rebroadcast facility. It Had 121 channels with a range of from 3 to 5 miles when transmitting to an A42 set. The standard radio fitted to all self-propelled guns.

Station Radio C11/R210 — Used as a rear link radio to brigade and/or the commander Royal Artillery. The set had a range of twenty-five miles and a battery life of eight hours.

Station Radio C13 — Used for battery commander/commanding officer to commander Royal Artillery communications. The set had a range of 20 miles, with a battery life of 17½ hours. It operated in the high frequency bands.

Station Radio C42 — Issued to the Royal Artillery for communications with supported arm units. It had a range of from twelve to fifteen miles.

Station Radio C42Z — Radio for use with BID 150, used on formation command nets.

Station Radio C45HP — A VHF high power transceiver in the Larkspur range of radios which was used for general purpose artillery communications from corps to division. The radio had a range of thirty miles and comprised a Station Radio C45 and Amplifier RF No. 10.

Station Radio C45Z — Radio for use with BID 150, used on formation artillery command nets.

Station Radio BCC 46U — A VHF manpack transceiver. It was used by the ASSU to provide ground to air communications with close support aircraft and by Amphibiious Observation units to communicate with Naval Gunfire Support ships. It was replaced by the Station Radio A43R. See *ASSU* and *Station Radio A43R*.

Station Unit — Part of the gun tannoy system (Royal Australian Artillery).

Stbd — Starboard.

STC — Sennelager Training Centre.

STD — Short Term Deployment.

Steam Sapper — The name given to a type of traction engine used to haul heavy artillery at the beginning of the twentieth century. Like the elephants in the bail batteries, it was not suitable for bringing the guns into action.

Step-Up — A mode of operating whereby an element of a headquarters moves to the next position and sets up to become the new main headquarters. When an alternate headquarters exists it usually acts as step-up. In post 1958 field artillery, the two battery command posts move by step-up.

See *Alternate Headquarters, Battery Headquarters, Main Headquarters, Rear Headquarters, Regimental Headquarters,* and *Tactical Headquarters.*

Sterling L2A3 Submachine Gun — Produced in the United Kingdom between 1953 and 1988, the L2A3 entered service with the British Army in 1956. The L2A3 could be fired from the shoulder with the stock extended, or from the hip, with the stock folded under the barrel. Due to its compact size when folded, it was issued as the personal weapon of self-propelled detachment members. It is no longer in service with the British Army.
Cartridge: 9 x 19 mm Parabellum.
Operation: blowback, selective fire.
Feed: magazine.
Weight: empty, 2.72 kg (6 lbs).
Length: butt folded, 483 mm (19 in); butt extended 690mm (27.2 in).
Barrel length: 198 mm (7.8 in).
Muzzle velocity: 390 metres per second (426 yards per second).
Rate of fire: cyclic, 550 rounds per minute.

Stevens Graph — Graph to show the current meteorological data, to calculate the corrections of the moment to be applied to map data for predicted fire.

Stick Man — Of the gunners detailed for guard duty, the stick man was deemed the smartest and excused duty and dismissed the parade.

Sticks and String — Nickname for repository work.

STID — Synthetic Target Injection Device.

Stiffkey Camp — Anti-aircraft practice camp opened in May 1938. The camp, located on the north-east coast of Norfolk, operated throughout the Second World War and closed in April 1955. It was at this camp that the Stiffkey sight for light anti-aircraft guns was developed. Pronounced 'Stookey'. See *Stiffkey Stick.*

Stiffkey Stick — Sighting arrangement used on the Bofors 40 mm anti-aircraft gun to assist with 'aim off'. This was achieved by the stick being aligned, by a third layer, with the target's course and with the estimated speed being set by a ratchet device, linkage was used to resolve deflection and offset the foresight accordingly. See *Stiffkey Camp.*

Stirling Troop — One of the Troops in 2 Baker Bty Junior Leaders Regiment RA. See *Dickson Troop, Mercer Troop* and *Milne Troop.*

S to A — Surface to Air.

Stokes Trench Mortar — See *3-inch Stokes Trench Mortar.*

Stolly — See *Alvis Stalwart.*

Stolly walk — The ability to walk along the edge of the raised drop-side of an Alvis Stalwart without falling off. See *Alvis Stalwart.*

Stonk — (i) A heavy mortar or artillery bombardment. (Second World War Slang).
(ii) A standard fixed length (575 yards) linear target engaged by any number of regiments. Introduced in 1943 as a type of engagement to replace various local versions developed in North Africa. The length standardised on 525 yards after the Second World War at which time a stonk was fired by a single regiment. See *Field Battery Linear Target, Medium Battery Linear Target* and *Heavy Battery Linear Target.*

Stookey — Alternative name for the Stiffkey stick used with the Bofors light anti-aircraft gun. See *Stiffkey Camp* and *Stiffkey Stick.*

Stool Bed	In muzzle-loading artillery this was a flat wooden plate upon which the quoin and consequently the breech of the gun rested. See *Quoin.*
Stop	Order to the guns to stop firing until cancelled by 'Go on' or a new sequence of initial orders is given.
Stop loading	Order specifying that the guns cannot be reloaded until 'Go on' is ordered. Firing should be brought to an end with the bores clear.
Stops Running Back	A bracket to prevent barrel run back during storage and transportation.
Storekeeper of the Ordnance	See *Principal Storekeeper of the Ordnance.*
Stormer	A tracked light armoured vehicle used as the self-propelled mount for the HVM system. See *HVM.*
S to S	Surface to Surface.
St P	Start Point. See *SP.*
Strange's	Battery Honour Title of 27 (Strange's) Battery RA which was granted on 16 August 1928 under authority of 20/ARTY/4544/AG6a. Battery now in suspended animation. See *Battery Honour Titles.*
Strike	One of four branches within the Royal Artillery. Strike is dedicated to the firing of lethal munitions (guns, rockets or missiles), it is itself sub-divided into two branches, namely, surface to surface and surface to air. See *Artillery Command Systems, Artillery Logistics* and *Targeting.*
Striker Case	The name given to the mechanism which holds the firing pin in the breech block. It normally consists of a spring and case assembly, which, in emergencies can be removed for the breech in order to disable the gun.
Striking Velocity	The velocity of the projectile as it strikes the point of impact. See *Point of Impact.*
STTE	Special Tools and Test Equipment.
STTT	Short Term Training Team.
STU	Services Trials Unit.
SU	(i) Step-up. (ii) Station Unit. (Royal Australian Artillery.)
SUAAFR	Standard Use Army Aircraft Flight Route.
Sub	(i) Sub-Section. (ii) Abbreviated title by which 2nd lieutenants and lieutenants are sometimes known. A contracted form of Subaltern. See *Subaltern.*
Subaltern	A general term used throughout the British Army for a commissioned officer below the rank of captain. In its true sense, it also applies to a captain, although it is not generally used in this way. In the Royal Artillery during the twentieth century it came to denote officers of the rank of 2nd lieutenant or lieutenant. The term is often contracted to 'sub'.
Sub Section	A component of an artillery battery consisting of one gun, its tractor (if not self-propelled) and the gun detachment (RA), i.e. A Sub and B Sub are each composed of one gun and its gun detachment. Generally a sergeant's command.
Subsidiary AV	A Phoenix unmanned air vehicle which has yet to have a mission allocated to it. See *Principal AV.*
Subtend	To calculate a distance, either horizontal or vertical, by using trigonometry from a known angle at a known range. The angle subtends the distance at the known range and is subtended by it.
Successor Identification Friend or Foe	A target can be interrogated manually, by using a button on the control handle or by the tactical controller via the

	TCWI keypad, or automatically when a target is acquired. If a target is identified as friendly, both a visual and audible indication is given. The audible indication is in the form of a voice in the headset announcing 'target friendly' and stating the range. See *TCWI, HVM* and *SPHVM.*
SUD	Setting-Up Data. See *FACE.*
SUDT	Staff User Data Terminal. Part of the Bowman communications system. See *Bowman.*
Suicide Club	The name given to the founding members of the trench mortar service in November 1914. Founded at Pont du Hem, near Estaires, the members were drawn from Z Battery RHA and 119 Heavy Battery RGA.
SUIT	Sight Unit Infantry Trilux.
SUL	Shell Unit Load.
Sun Barrage	Introduced in the North African campaign by 12th Anti-Aircraft Brigade, the sun barrage was designed to counter the favourite tactic of the Luftwaffe dive bombers, namely attacking out of the sun. Friendly aircraft were instructed never to approach their own landing grounds from this direction. Any aircraft doing so was automatically classified as hostile and a barrage was put up on their anticipated line of approach. LAA guns would fire 40 rounds, sweeping 5 degrees each side of the sun, whilst HAA guns would fire shells set to burst at a range of 4200 yards from the centre of the vulnerable area.
Sunderland's Gunners	An unofficial title given to 4 Regt RA. The Regiment was granted the honorary freedom of the County Borough of Sunderland in March 1974. The honour was reconfirmed by the City of Sunderland in 2000.
Sunray	Radio appointment title. This title was used army-wide by a unit commander, however, in the Royal Artillery the following officers used the title: At HQRA level, the Commander Royal Artillery. At a Regimental Headquarters level, the Commanding Officer. At Battery level, the Battery Commander. See *Appointment Titles.*
Sunray Minor	Radio appointment title. This title was used army-wide by a unit second in command, however, in the Royal Artillery the following officers used the title. At a regimental headquarters level, the second in command. At battery level, the battery captain. See *Appointment Titles.*
Sunshine Battery	Nickname given to 79 (Kirkee) Commando Battery RA. They nickname is said to have originated from their lack of arctic warfare training and their being based in Malta during the early 1970s.
Super B	Nickname of B Battery RHA.
Super Charge	A charge which gives the maximum permissible ballistics with the service weight projectile consistent with regularity.
Super Heavy	Designation given to batteries and regiments equipped with railway mounted guns.
Superimposed	Superimposed guns are those whose fire is available to be switched (by the appropriate authority) from allotted tasks to a specific fire plan, whenever necessary. Such guns are directed in a way that their removal from allotted tasks does not affect the artillery support provided to the supported arm.
Superimposed Artillery	See *Superimposed.*
Superintendent of Experiments	The commanding officer at Shoeburyness. A position formally instigated on 1 March 1855, although the title had been used unofficially for some time previous to this.

Superstructure — That part of the carriage or mounting that directly supports the ordnance. Includes the recoil system in the cradle and saddle.

Super Velocity Charge — A charge which was used with a lightweight super velocity projectile.

SupFAC — Supervisory Forward Air Controller. See *FAC* and *JFACTSU*.

Support Group — During the Second World War a support group consisted of the field, anti-tank and light anti-aircraft artillery and lorried infantry attached to an armoured division.

Surface Data Instrument — As part of the BMETS system, the SDI measures the Meteorological Datum Point. See *BMETS* and *Meteorological Datum Point*.

Surface Data Portable Display — Part of the BMETS system. See *BMETS* and *SDPU*.

Surface Display Portable Unit — Located inside the Meteorological Command Post Vehicle, the SDPU displays the meteorological data from the Surface Display Instrument together with a calculated Dewpoint. See *BMETS* and *Surface Display Instrument*.

Survey 1 — See *Svy 1*.

Survey 2 — See *Svy 2*.

Survey Control Point — The point at which artillery survey usually commences. The survey control point has known coordinates and could be either a trig point, which has been established by topographic surveyors (such as the Ordnance Survey), or a bearing picket which has been placed by artillery surveyors. This fix can the be 'carried' by traverse and/or triangulation to a point where an accurate fix is required, this will typically be a battery position or a target acquisition device. See *Trig Point*.

Survey Picket — The original title given on their introduction during the First World War, to bearing pickets. The survey picket consisted of a steel stake with a card attached which gave accurate bearings to aiming points. See *Bearing Picket*.

Survey Report Centre — A report centre originally established by the locating regiment or one of its survey troops at which data regarding the corps or divisional survey plan is available.

Survey Troop — Composed of artillery surveyors who are responsible for putting the gun lines onto an appropriate state of survey for both orientation and fixation. Battery: giving the gun position a 'rough' fixation and common orientation; regiment: all the batteries within a regiment are on a 'rough' but common fixation and orientation; division: all the regiments are on a 'rough' but common fixation and orientation; theatre: an extremely accurate state of fixation and orientation.

Surveyor-General of the Ordnance — A member of the Board of Ordnance from its constitution in 1597 and subordinate of the Master-General of the Ordnance, the holder of the position was appointed by the crown under letters patent. His duties included examining the ordnance received to see that it was of good quality and being responsible for the mapping of fortifications and subsequently for the whole of Great Britain, through the Ordnance Survey. Unlike other offices of the Board of Ordnance, the position survived the dissolution of the Board in 1855, but was for a number of years vacant, as the last holder, Lauderdale Maule, had died of cholera during the Crimean War. The office was revived under the War Office Act of 1870 which made

	the Surveyor-General responsible for all aspects of army logistics. The office remained in being until 1888. See *Board of Ordnance* and *Master-General of the Ordnance.*
SurvR	Surveillance Radar.
SUSAT	Sight Unit Small Arms Trilux.
Sustained Fire	Used as a suffix to GPMG to indicate that the weapon is either attached to its tripod or has the tripod available. See *GPMG.*
SUT	Static Unit Trainer. See *BATES, TUT* and *UT.*
SV	(i) Super Velocity. See *Super Velocity Charge.* (ii) Safety Valve. (iii) Satellite Vehicle.
Svy	Survey.
Svy1	Tactical sign for a battery survey party. See *Svy 2* and *Tactical Sign.*
Svy2	Tactical sign for a battery survey party. See *Svy 1* and *Tactical Sign.*
Svyr	Surveyor.
Svy Tp	Survey Troop.
SW	(i) Special Weapons. NATO term for non-conventional munitions. In the case of the United Kingdom, nuclear weapons. (ii) Artillery Code used during the First World War meaning 'switch'.
SWAG	Scientific Wild Arsed Guess. Not an official abbreviation, but frequently heard in such places as command posts.
Swansong	A three day live-fire exercise for young officers which is conducted at the Royal School of Artillery at the conclusion of their Young Officer's course. It is designed to confirm training and to demonstrate that all disciplines and equipment are part of the same system and fight the same battle.
Sweep	In order to increase the effectiveness of fire, it is sometimes necessary to artificially increase the size of the beaten zone for line. This is achieved by the observer or the relevant HQ giving the amount of sweep in metres, for example 'three rounds gunfire, sweep one hundred metres'. This in turn is converted by the gun position officer to the required amount of sweep in mils, rounded off to the nearest half turn of the traversing wheel, with the order to the guns being, 'three rounds gunfire, sweep ... mils'. Successive rounds are then fired on the current line and then to the right and left of the line by the amount of sweep ordered. No changes are made to dial sights, the amount of sweep being measured by counting the turns or fractions of turns of the traversing handwheel as laid down in the respective gun drills. See *Search.*
Sweep Plates	In fortifications and coast artillery batteries these were iron plates set into the floor of a gun emplacement which were used to traverse the gun.
Swingfire	Wire guided anti-tank missile used by the Royal Artillery during the 1980s, when, for a short time the Regiment again acquired the anti-tank role. Anti-tank batteries were equipped with the FV438 and the Striker anti-tank version of the CVR(T) family. Missile Length: 1.07m. Missile Weight: 27 kg. Maximum Range: 4 km.
Swinging	Directors are said to be swung when the telescope is rotated with either of the quick release levers depressed. A director is 'swung right' when rotated clockwise and

	'swung left' when rotated anti-clockwise. See *Director, SLTR, SRTL, TL, TR* and *Traversing.*
Swinglebar	See *Swingletree.*
Swingletree	A swivelling bar hooked to the footboard of the limber. The traces were hooked to the ends of the bar so that there was play to suit the movement of breast collar and the traces. Also known as a swinglebar or whippletree.
Sword, Mountain Artillery	Curved sword issued to the Indian personnel of mountain batteries.
SWSS	Secure Weapons Storage Site.
Synthetic Target Injection Device	Part of the Rapier Air Defence training system.

T – Toc – 1904/1927
Tare – 1943
Tango – 1956

(T)	Territorial.
T	Artillery Code used during the First World War meaning 'General Answer'.
T&AVR	Territorial and Army Volunteer Reserve. Formed in 1967 to replace the Territorial Army.
T&P	Time and Percussion. A type of artillery fuze.
TA	(i) Territorial Army. (ii) Target Acquisition.
TAB	Tactical Advance to Battle. Although indicating that this is a tactical move, the term 'Tabbing' is often used for long approach / route marches. Commando-based units use the term 'Yomping' in place of 'Tabbing'.
Taboo Gear	Bracket on an L118 or L119 Light Gun to restrict elevation.
Tac	Tactical.
TAC	Tactical Air Controller.
TACAS	Tubed Artillery Conventional Ammunition System.
Tac Battery	The fourth battery within a gun regiment. Tac batteries consist of the battery tac group, which comprises the BC's Party, fire planning cell and three observation post parties.
TACC	(i) Target Acquisition Coordination Centre. (Royal Canadian Artillery). (ii) Tactical Air Control Centre.
Taccon	See *Tacon.*
TacGA PRC 346	Tactical Ground To Air Portable Radio Communicator 346.
Tac Gp	Tactical Group. See *Tactical Headquarters.*
Tac Group	See *Tactical Group.*
Tac HQ	Tactical Headquarters. See *Regimental TAC, Brigade TAC* and *Tac Gp.*
Tachymetric Predictor	A predictor which worked from the measurements of rates of change of position of targets. See *Predictor.*
Tack Up	Fit bridle and saddle prior to riding. (The King's Troop RHA.)
TACOM	Tactical Command. See *OPCOM, OPCON* and *TACON.*
TACON	Tactical Control. See *OPCOM, OPCON* and *TACOM.*
TACP	Tactical Air Control Party. See *FOO, FST* and *JET.*
Tac Party	See *Tactical Headquarters.*
Tac Sign	See *Tactical Sign.*
Tactical Air Control Party	The personnel of these parties are trained in the control of fast attack aircraft and the employment of laser target markers in order to designate targets for attack by such aircraft. They work alongside the Royal Artillery forward observers and fire support teams. See *FOO and FST.*

Tactical Control — A unit under the command of a higher unit, other than its own is said to be under that unit's Tactical Control. Therefore 17/159 Battery which is part of 26 Regt RA is not TACON that Regt, but if deployed directly under the command of 40 Regt RA, would be said to be TACON 40 Regt. May also be found spelt 'Taccon'.

Tactical Controller — The commander of an SP HVM detachment.

Tactical Controller's Weapon Interface — A 10-inch LCD monitor which allows the TC to switch to operator view and monitor the operator's missile engagement. It is also the main interface with the ADAD, permitting the TC to input data and set up and monitor search arcs. The TCWI can also be employed to manually interrogate a target using the SIFF. See *SPHVM, Air Defence Alerting Device* and *Successor Identification Friend or Foe.*

Tactical Ground To Air Portable Radio Communicator 346 — A man portable multi-band radio, used for tactical ground-to-air-ground communications.

Tactical Group — Generally referred to as a 'Tac Group', the term was introduced in the late 1980s. An artillery tactical group controls the fire and provides artillery communications to those units to whom supporting fire is being given. A tac group comprises all those elements of a regiment that deploy with the supported arm, commanding officer's party and FSCC, battery commanders and their FPCs and observers' parties. See *FSCC, FPC* and *Tactical Headquarters.*

Tactical Headquarters — A general term for a small element of any HQ and comprising the commander and key staff, often only deployed when necessary but in artillery can be permanent. Tac headquarters first appeared in the First World War at the highest level and over the rest of the twentieth century were adopted at lower levels. At formation level the artillery commander is normally a member of the tac HQ. In artillery it was particularly applied to the small team accompanying the CO at an infantry or armoured brigade HQ, this expanded after the Second World War to include BC HQ Bty. Close support regiment tac HQs became called the Fire Support Coordination Cell in the 1980s. Also referred to as a Tac Party. See *Alternate Headquarters, Battery Headquarters, Brigade TAC, Main Headquarters, Rear Headquarters, Regimental Headquarters, Regimental TAC, Step-Up* and *Tactical Group.*

Tactical Recognition Flash — The Royal Artillery Tactical Recognition Flash (TRF) consists of a red over blue square worn on the right upper arm. Originally worn by 7 (Para) RHA as a drop zone patch, the TRF has now been adopted across the Royal Regiment. Some regiments added their regimental number to the TRF, for example 4 Regiment used a gold IV, 12 Regiment used a gold 12 and 26 Regiment used a gold XXVI, however, this practice has now ceased and all regiments use the standard RA TRF. During the Second World War landing zone patches were worn by airborne units, these continued to be worn after the war and have ultimately been replaced by TRF. Also during the Second World War everyone wore a horizontal strip type distinguishing flash, known as an Arm of Service Stripe on battle dress, that for the Royal Artillery was red-blue. They were not worn after the end of the Second World War when actual regt/corps names were reintroduced on shoulders.

Tactical Sign A unit identifier carried on regimental vehicles. The Royal Artillery use a tactical sign which is red over blue divided horizontally. During, and for a period after, the Second World War, unit code numbers were carried on these signs and varied between theatres, however, they bore no relation to the regimental number. Smaller signs, which were quartered differently from the main tactical sign, were displayed on Royal Artillery vehicles which signified the vehicle's role, examples of these signs are:
Commanding Officer's vehicle: Z
Battery Commander's vehicles: X
Battery Troop Commander's vehicles: RA and RB
Gun Position Officer's vehicles: GA and GB

The red over blue tactical sign has been used for many years as the Drop Zone patch for 7 Parachute Regiment RHA worn on the upper right arm. A patch similar to the drop zone patch was adopted in 2004 as the Regimental Tactical Recognition Flash. See *Hotel 1, Hotel 2, Jig 1, Jig 2, Romeo 1, Romeo 2, Romeo 3, Tactical Recognition Flash, X-Ray* and *Zulu*.

TAD Tactical Air Direction.

TADIL Tactical Digital Information Link.

TAFS Territorial Army Foundation Scheme.

TAI Target Area of Interest.

TAIGR Technical Adviser in Gunnery Research, pronounced 'tiger'.

Take Post Instruction for gun detachments to resume their positions in action. It can be given by the observer or the gun position officer. It should not be sent by the observer as a preliminary to initial orders. Also cancels 'Rest and Stand Easy.' See *Rest* and *Stand Easy*.

TALAMEF Sequence of orders to the guns; Nature of Target, Angle of Sight, Line, Ammunition, Method of ranging, Elevation, Fire. See *LARNMISS* and *TALAPFRIRF*.

TALAPFRIRF Sequence of initial orders to the guns for ranging; Target, Ammunition, Line, Angle of Sight, Position Correction (Concentration or Distribution), Fire by Order, Method of Ranging, Interval, Range, Fire. See *LARNMISS* and *TALAMEF*.

Talavera Battery Honour Title of 46 (Talavera) Headquarters Battery RA which was granted on 3 May 1937 under authority of 20/ARTY/5023/AG6a. See *Battery Honour Titles*.

TALO Tactical Air Landing Operation.

TAM Tactical Aide Memoire.

TAMA Troop Artillery Manoeuvre Area. See *AMA* and *Artillery Manoeuvre Area*.

TAMM Target Acquisition Meteorological Message. See *BMETS*.

TAN Artillery code used during the First World War meaning 'Infantry'.

Tangent Elevation The vertical angle between the axis of the bore, when the gun is laid, and the line of sight. See *Quadrant Elevation* and *TE*.

Tank Action An order to the guns indicating that an attack by tanks is considered imminent. Any other fire missions being undertaken are immediately cancelled, and the guns are loaded with a suitable anti-tank round and preparations made to defend against the tank threat. Each gun position is assigned a sector to observe and in which they will engage enemy tanks. See *Prepare for Tanks*.

Tan Yard The name sometimes given to the old Riding Establishment Royal Artillery which used to be located at Woolwich.

TAOC	Tactical Air Operations Centre.
TAOR	Tactical Area Of Responsibility.
Tap and Toe	Prepare horses' shoes prior to 'cogging up', meaning putting studs in (The King's Troop RHA.)
TAPIO	Territorial Army Press Information Officer.
TAR	(i) Tactical Air Reconnaissance. (ii) Tactical Air Request.
TARA	Technical Assistant Royal Artillery.
Tarbul	Target Bulletin.
Target	(i) The specific point at which fire is directed. The official NATO definition of Target, as given in AAP-6 *Nato Glossary of Terms and Definitions* is: 'a geographical area, complex or installation or a specified unit, or units, planned for capture, neutralization or destruction by military forces.' (ii) See *Target Grid Corrections*.
Target Acquisition Meteorological Message	A meteorological message used with the BMETS system. See *BMETS*.
Target Acquisition System 10	Together with the Global Positioning System the TAS 10 replaced PADS, the position and azimuth determining system. The GPS provided the fix whilst the TAS 10 provided the orientation. See *Position and Azimuth Determining System*.
Target Crested	Report from the gun position officer to the observer, when the guns are unable to engage a target due to being unable to clear a crest using any charge. See *Crest Clearance*.
Target Data	Target data is recorded in the AB 548 Target Record Book. Such details as target letter and number, description of target, grid reference, grid and ammunition used are included in the target data. See *Target Record Book*.
Target Effect System	The artillery projectile and/or its contents.
Target Engagement Automation Working Party	Tasked with bringing automated fire control and target engagement to the Royal Artillery, the working party was responsible for the development and implementation of BATES into the Regiment. It was commonly known during its existence as the 'Tea Party'. See *BATES*.
Target Grid	A transparent overlay for the artillery board, marked in squares of 100 yards placed over the target coordinates and aligned on the OT bearing. The OP corrections are plotted and read off the board as gun data. See *Artillery Board*.
Target Grid Corrections	Introduced in 1950 these were the corrections necessary to adjust fire onto the target. The observer corrects the fire with reference to the line OT. Rounds falling to the right of the line OT are observed as 'right' and corrected by 'go left…'. Rounds falling to the left of the line OT are observed as 'left' and corrected by 'go right…'. A round falling past the target is observed as 'over' and corrected by 'drop…'. A round falling short of the target is observed as 'short' and corrected by 'add…'. A round falling on the target is observed as 'target' and no corrections are made. See *Bracket, Line OT, Over, Short* and *Target Round*.
Target Illuminating Radar	A radar which provides the guidance signal for semi-active air defence missiles. The TIR emits a signal which illuminates the target aircraft. The missile seeker then homes in on the radar signal reflected from the target. See *Thunderbird*.
Target Letters	In order to identify the formation, unit or sub-unit registering a target, specific target letters were used. For

instance, according to 'Artillery Staff Duties 1954' these consisted of the following:
Troop Target: The letter of the troop whose guns engaged the target was used.
Battery Target: P, Q, R or S were used depending on the seniority of the battery within the regiment. An attached battery would have used the subsequent letter from the alphabet, T.
Regimental Target: M
Formation Targets
Divisional: U
AGRA: Y
Corps: V
Army: W
Counter Bombardment Targets were distinguished by the following letters:
Divisional: L
Corps: N
The identifying letter would then have been followed by the relevant Target Number, which would have been ascertained from the Target Number Pad. See *Target Number Pad.*

Target Lost — A report indicating that the target that had been acquired in the monocular field of view of an Air Defence missile system and was being tracked/engaged has been lost.

Target Map — A ready reference device used for recording grid references and OT data of targets and other objects in the zone of observation. The target map compliments the shooting map, although on occasion it can be used in place of the shooting map. It consists of two parts, the target map fan and the target map trace. Versions in both degrees and mils exist. See *OT, Target Map Fan* and *Target Map Trace.*

Target Map Fan — Shows the range arcs and bearings, and has the OT factor and a subtension angle printed against each range arc. It also has boxes for recording target information. See *OT, Target Map* and *Target Map Trace.*

Target Map Trace — A sheet of robust tracing paper gridded in metres at a scale of 1:25000. Used in conjunction with the Target Map Fan. See *Target Map* and *Target Map Fan.*

Target Mensuration — The process of obtaining target coordinates by the measurement of geometric data derived from imagery and geospatial intelligence.

Target Number Pad — A book containing 1000 four-figure numbers, each of which ended with zero, for example 0000 to 9990. These figures were arranged in a haphazard order. The pad contained twenty pages with fifty numbers on each page. Rows were numbered consecutively and the columns lettered A to E. Each number represented a block of ten consecutive numbers. Therefore, 3240 represented 3240–3249. These numbers, prefixed by a suitable target letter, were used to identify pre-registered targets. See *Target Letters.*

Target Record Book — The AB 548 consisting of a numerical index to target records together with pages for recording battery centre survey data and target data. The Target Record Book is used by the gun position officer to record all types of target. See *Battery Survey Data Target Data* and *Target Record Index.*

Target Record Index — The first ten pages of the Target Record Book (AB 548) comprise the target record index. Targets recorded in the body of the AB 548 are entered in the index against the relevant target number. See *Target Record Book.*

Target Recognition Base Ejection	A type of projectile developed for the proposed 95 mm field gun. As this gun never entered service, it is unlikely that many rounds of this nature were produced.
Target Round	A round which hits the target, as opposed to being either over or short. A target round is the equivalent of a bracket. See *Bracket, Over, Short* and *Target Grid Corrections*.
Target Winchman	See *Canberra Winchman*.
Targeting	One of four branches within the Royal Artillery, Targeting is responsible for the targeting process. See *Artillery Command System, Artillery Logistics* and *Strike*.
Tarnow Instrument	Coast artillery, graphical representation of OPs, gun and target giving range and bearing to target displayed on instrument or remotely on gun.
TAS	Training, Administration and Support.
TAS 10	Target Acquisition System 10. See *PADS*.
Task Force	Replaced brigade as the formation below division during the late 1970s.
Task Table	See *Army Book 545, Monster* and *Tiddler*.
TAT	(i) Training and Advisory Team. (ii) Technical Advisory Team.
Taxi	The main body of the Phoenix Unmanned Air Vehicle, so named in order to distinguish it from the payload. See *Phoenix*.
Taylorcraft Auster	See *Auster*.
Taylor Tables	Introduced in 1944 as an amendment to range tables to simplify calculation of correction of the moment data.
TB	Terminal Block.
TBI	Target Bearing Indicator.
TC	(i) Troop Commander. (ii) Tactical Command (as in Tactical Command Post). (iii) Troop Captain (The King's Troop RHA). (iv) Tactical Controller. (v) Transit Corridor. (vi) Tactical Control (Radar). (vii) Troop Centre.
TCC	Turret Control Computer.
TCM	Top Charge Module. See *BCM*.
TCO	Tactical Control Officer.
TCOA	Tactical Control Officer's Assistant.
TCO Ack	See *TCOA*.
TCP	Troop Command Post.
TCR	Tactical Control Radar.
TCU	(i) Tactical Control Unit. (ii) Turret Control Unit.
TCW	Thermal Camouflage Woodland.
TCWI	Tactical Controller's Weapon Interface. See *SPHVM, ADAD* and *SIFF*.
TD	Tactical Doctrine.
TDA	(i) Target Damage Analysis. (ii) Trajectory Danger Area.
TDED	Tactical Data Entry Device.
TDL	(i) Tactical Data Link. (ii) Training Datum Level.
TDP	Tie Down Point.
TDS	Temporary Duty Staff.
TDT RA	See *RATDT*.
TE	Tangent Elevation.
Tea Party	See *Target Engagement Automation Working Party*.
Tea Trolley	Cart used to carry ammunition in coastal artillery (and possibly fortress) batteries.

TECA	Technical Assistant (Post became known as TARA from 1951) See *TARA*
Tech Net	See *RFO Net.*
Technical Adjutant	The officer responsible for replacement, maintenance and documentation of transport. Generally found in armoured units.
Technical Assistant Royal Artillery	Commonly referred to as a TARA. This position dates from 1951, prior to this the post was known as TECA. RA Notes No. 22 para 1295 October 1944 stated: 'It has been decided that the following specialists will in future be tradesmen and be known as Technical Assistants RA: OPA, CPOA, GPOA'. The trade lasted until 1970 when the role was split into Command Post Assistant and Observation Post Assistant. See *Command Post Officers Assistant, Gun Position Officer's Assistant* and *Observation Post Assistant*.
Technical Instructor in Gunnery	A late entry (formerly QM Commission) officer commissioned from the Gunnery Staff.
Technical Manual	US equivalent of User Handbooks and other UK technical publications, Technical Manuals are issued with US-origin equipment, although User Handbooks are sometimes also written.
Teddy-Bear Coat	A fur coat, similar to a modern parka, but with the fur on the outside, which was issued to auxiliary territorial service members of searchlight units during the Second World War for wear in cold weather.
TEGWRA	Trials Establishment Guided Weapons Royal Artillery.
Tel-El-Kebir Day	Battery day of 171 (The Broken Wheel) Battery RA. Celebrated on or near the anniversary of the battle of Tel-El-Kebir which was fought in Egypt on 13th September 1882. The Battery is currently in suspended animation.
Telemeter, Marks 1–4	An artillery survey device, introduced prior to the First World War and used throughout that conflict. The telemeter was capable of finding a distance mechanically using the angles between internal mirrors and trigonometry. The scales could be any unit of measurement, for example, yards, metres, or even half or double-yards. The maximum range on the scale for the earlier marks of Telemeter was 6,000 yards whilst that for the later marks was 10,000 yards.
TELIC	The name given to the British deployment for the Second Gulf War 2004. It is jokingly said to stand for Tell Everyone Leave Is Cancelled. Subsequent deployments to Iraq have been identified by the addition of a numeric suffix.
Tellurometer	A survey device used for measuring distances of up to approximately eighty kilometres. The tellurometer was invented by Dr Wadley and functioned by measuring microwaves. Two tellurometers were set up at each survey point, one as a master and the other as a remote. Its use revolutionised the survey world and led to the introduction of a new survey practice, trilateration, which is the measuring of survey triangles instead of the previous method of measuring angles with a theodolite.
TEO	Tracker Electro Optical.
Temporary Minimum Risk Routes	An Airspace Control Measure / Air Defence term.
Temporary Position	Guns may fire from a temporary position in order to avoid disclosing the location, prior to its occupation, of the main position to the enemy. They may also be used during the

preliminary phases of an operation to bring fire to bear on areas not within range or arc of fire of the main position. See *Alternative Position, Main Position* and *Roving Position.*

TERA — (i) Trials Establishment Royal Artillery.
(ii) Terrain Analysis.

Terminals — A term used during the 1920s–30s to identify the battery telephone operators who maintained communications between observation posts and the guns. Also referred to as signal terminals. See *Signal Terminal.*

Territorial Army — Formed in 1920, mobilised for the Second World War, suspended in 1946 and reconstituted in 1947. In 1967 it was drastically reduced and renamed the Territorial and Army Volunteer Reserve. Artillery regiments were particular reduced in number and renumbered starting at 100. The name Territorial Army was re-adopted in 1978.

Territorial Force — Formed in 1907 as a new second line force for home defence subsuming the Yeomanry and the Volunteers. It was mobilised in 1914 and sent to overseas theatres alongside the regular army. It was disbanded in 1918.

TESEX — Test Exercise.

TESTEX — Test Exercise.

Test of Elementary Training — Basic all-arms military skill tests covering weapon handling, anti-gas and physical fitness. Lasted until the end of national service.

Test Set First Line — A test set for HVM Air Defence system.

Test Set Launcher Firing Circuit — The firing circuit test set for the Rapier A and B1 Air Defence systems.

TET — Target Engagement Team.

Tetley Fan — Introduced in 1940 as Fan, Protractor, No 4 for use with artillery boards as a method of converting the control troop's ranged firing data into data for other troop(s) in the battery. It replaced the Plotter DW. See *Artillery Board* and *Plotter DW.*

TEWT — Tactical Exercise Without Troops.

TF — (i) Territorial Force.
(ii) Time of Flight.
(iii) Task Force.

TFA — Temporary Field Accommodation.

TFAD — Task Force Acceptance Date.

TFAIO — Task Force Artillery Intelligence Office (late 1970s).

TFSU — Theatre Fleet Support Unit.

TFT — Tabular Firing Tables.

TG — (i) Troop Guide.
(ii) Training Gap.

TGC — Target Grid Correction.

TGM — Terminally Guided Missiles.

TGSM — Terminally Guided Sub-Munition.

Tgt — Target.

Tgt R — Target Record.

TH — Transport Helicopter.

Thales' Shield — Awarded annually to the best air defence battery in the Territorial Army. Formally known as the BP Trophy.

Theatre Grid — Fixation and orientation accurate to the map grid which was used by all regiments within the theatre of operations. See *Battery Grid, Fixation, Orientation* and *Regimental Grid.*

THQ — Troop Headquarters. See *BHQ* and *RHQ*.

Three Seven — The 3.7-Inch quick firing heavy anti-aircraft gun. See *3.7-Inch QF AA Gun* and *Quick Firing.*

Three Square — See *Two Square.*

Through — (i) A report from a member of a party/detachment to his/her OIC that a message has been passed successfully.

It should not be confused with the use of 'Roger' in radio procedure. There is also a visual version which is used from a non-radio gun position, this signal consists of the right arm being raised above the head and then dropped sharply to the side. See *Roger*.
(ii) Communications, whether by line or radio, are said to be 'through' once contact has been established between both parties.

Thunderbird — The Thunderbird I Heavy Surface to Air Missile entered service in 1959. Thunderbird II, with improved velocity and more advanced controls replaced Thunderbird I in the mid-1960s. The Thunderbird II missile system was retired from service in late 1976. The missile consisted of a central body containing a sustainer motor and surrounded by four booster rockets. Short wings and large tail fins were fitted to the main body. Detonation was by radio-control or via a proximity fuze.
Length: 6.35 m.
Body Diameter: 0.527 m.
Fin Span: 1.63 m.
Type of Warheads available: Continuous HE rod.
Maximum Range: 75 km.

Thunderbird Hat — Nickname sometimes given to the RA Coloured Field Service Cap.

TI — (i) Thermal Imager.
(ii) Thermal Imaging.

Tiddler — The name given, for ease of reference on the radio and telephone, to the Task Table, AB 545. See *Monster*.

Tiffy — Artificer or RA fitter.

TIG — Technical Instructor in Gunnery (*Post*).

Tiger — Nickname given to a member of 38 (Seringapatam) Battery RA.

Tiger Battery, The — Nickname for 38 (Seringapatam) Battery RA.

Tigers, The — Nickname of 38 (Seringapatam) Battery RA, the Battery badge being a tiger.

Tillings-Stephens Projector — See *Land Mattress*.

Timber Toppers — Nickname given to 84 Field Battery RA, later 166 Heavy Anti-Aircraft Battery RA. The name originated from the events on Kemmel Hill on 25 April 1918, when 84 Battery were forced to retire from their position by advancing towards the enemy. At one point a fallen tree threatened to halt the battery, but each gun was successfully galloped over the tree and they completed their withdrawal without further mishap.

Time and Percussion Fuze — A type of Artillery fuze. It functions either after a certain period of time (the time element), or on contact (the percussion element). The time element can be either igniferous (combustion) or mechanical, whereas the percussion element is provided by a graze action.

Time Fuze — Time fuzes employ either combustion (gunpowder), clockwork (mechanical time) or variable time mechanisms to measure the time from when they are fired until they initiate the shell in the flight. This period is referred to as the 'fuze length'. Combustion and Mechanical Time fuzes have to have the required length set on them before being fired. For most UK fuzes this length used an arbitrary time scale, not seconds. See *Fuze Length* and *VT Fuze*.

Time on Target — An artillery fire mission where irrespective of varying distances between firing batteries and the target, the first rounds of fire for effect are fired so as to arrive on the target at the same time. In order to achieve this batteries fire at ToT minus their time of flight.

Time Shrapnel — Used against troops in the open or where they had no overhead cover. Also during the time that observation balloons were in use, as a ranging projectile against balloons. Time shrapnel was activated by a time fuze (during the First World War the No. 80 Fuze) whilst in flight, when shrapnel is at its most effective. The battery commander would not need to order time shrapnel to be employed as specifying the fuze length made this instruction superfluous. See *Percussion Shrapnel* and *Shrapnel*.

Timothy Target — During the Second World War these targets were areas marked by coloured smoke at prearranged times to coincide with the scheduled arrival of fighter-bombers or medium bombers. Some were night-time targets for medium or heavy bombers (Royal New Zealand Artillery).

Tin Trunk — The name used for daily defensive fire (DF) plans used by the Royal Australian Artillery during the Vietnam War. These were first offered by the forward observers with the infantry and other supported arms sub-units to the battery commander with the infantry battalion in control of an area. The battery commanders then consolidated all these tin trunks and offered their tin trunk to the artillery tactical headquarters at task force (*sic* brigade) headquarters and all gun positions within range of the targets. Arty tac then consolidated the task force tin trunk, if necessary, and prepared air and ground clearances should they be required. This procedure for preparing and consolidating daily DF lists is standard throughout British and Australian Armies.

TIPEU — Thermal Imagery Processing Electronics Unit. Part of the Rapier FSB2 Air Defence system.

TIR — Target Illuminating Radar.

TL — (i) Troop Leader.
(ii) Traverse Level.

TL — (iii) Traverse Left. See *SRTL* and *Traversing*.

TLA — (i) Three Letter Abbreviation.
(ii) Travel Lock Actuator. See *Multiple Launch Rocket System*.
(iii) Troop Leader A Troop (Second World War).

TLB — Troop Leader B Troop (Second World War).

TLE — (i) Target Location Error.
(ii) Target Locating Equipment. See *LH40C TLE Laser Range Finder*.

TLM — Top Level Menu. See *BATES*.

tlr — Trailer.

TM — (i) Trench Mortar (First World War).
(ii) Temp Mobile.
(iii) Technical Manual.

TMA — Troop Manoeuvre Area. See *Battery Manoeuvre Area* and *Multiple Launch Rocket System*.

TMB — Trench Mortar Battery (First World War).

Tmpr — Trumpeter.

TMRR — Temporary Minimum Risk Routes.

TNEM — Target Neutralised, End of Mission.

TNK — Artillery code used during the First World War meaning 'Tank'.

TNT — Trinitrotoluene.

TO — Training Objective.

TOA — Transfer of Authority.

TOAD — Troop Officer Air Defence.

TOAD (TA) — Troop Officer Air Defence (Territorial Army).

TOB — Target – Observer – Battery. The first official reference to the triangle Target – Observer – Battery was made in 1906.

Toby — Name by which a type of 6-inch trench mortar was known during the First World War. Originally manufactured in the 1840s Tobys had seen service in the Crimean War. The projectile consisted of a cast iron sphere into which a hole had been drilled opposite the fuze. A wooden sabot was attached at this point by an iron bolt. Two grooves in the sabot allowed the fitting of a pair of obturator rings. The projectile was filled with black powder and actuated by a French *Siege et Montagne* punch fuze. The charge (French wood powder type C3) was poured into the mortar and the projectile pushed home. Elevation was given by using a plumb-bob and a wedge. The mortar was fired by utilising an electric detonator inserted into the vent, and fired from a safe distance. It was not unknown for an 8-inch projectile to be fired by balancing it outside the muzzle by delicate use of bricks, bits of iron or anything handy. Maximum range for the 6-inch was 300 yards, whilst the 8-inch could achieve approximately 80 yards. After Neuve Chapelle the Toby Mark II was introduced consisting of a 6-inch Toby rebored to $6^1/_{32}$-inch, making the bore almost round as opposed to oval and having the bomb and sabot replaced with a long steel shell filled with ammonal. The Toby Mark II had a medium range of from 350 to 400 yards, at which range the shells left a crater equivalent to that made by a 6-inch 100-lb shell. See *3-inch Stokes Trench Mortar, Cuthbert, Percy,* and *Reginald.*

Toc-Emmas — Members of a trench mortar battery (First World War), so named from the phonetic code of the day for TM.

TOET — Test of Elementary Training.

ToF — Time of Flight.

T of F — Time of Flight.

TOM — Type of Mission. See *BATES.*

Tombs-Benson Memorial Prize — Between 1973 and 1982 awarded to the best all-round performance by a student officer RA on the regular career course. From 1993 to date it is awarded to the Royal Artillery officer who achieves the best all-round performance whilst at the Royal Military Academy, Sandhurst. See *Benson Memorial Prize* and *Tombs Memorial Prize.*

Tombs Memorial Prize — Awarded between 1877 and 1939 to the best qualified cadet commissioned into the Royal Artillery from the Royal Military Academy, Woolwich. Between 1948 and 1973 it was awarded to the cadet commissioned into the Royal Artillery highest in Order of Merit from Sandhurst. Intakes 1–52. The award was then suspended until revived in 1987 when it was reallocated to the best all-round performance by a student officer cadet commissioned into the Royal Artillery on the standard military course. See *Tombs-Benson Memorial Prize*

Tombs's Troop — Battery Honour Title of 143 Battery (Tombs's Troop) RA which was granted on 18 October 1926 under authority of 20/ARTY/4544/AG6a. Battery now amalgamated with 28 Battery RA to form 28/143 Battery (Tombs's Troop) RA. See *Battery Honour Titles.*

Tonfanau — Anti-aircraft practice camp located near Towyn, Merionethshire, Wales. Now no longer in use.

Top Level Menu — Part of the BATES system. See *BATES.*

Top Traverse — The traverse achieved by rotating the saddle on the saddle support, that is to say, without moving the trails.

TOT — Time on Target.

Touring Battery — See *Coast Artillery Practice Camp.*

TOW — (i) Tracked Over Wire.
(ii) Tube Launched, Optically Tracked, Wire-guided. An American anti-tank missile used by the Army Air Corps on their Lynx armed helicopters. See *Lynx*.

Towing Vehicle Navigation Display Unit — A large flat panel, touch sensitive display provides the in-cab display and control of navigation data. The NDU also provides a reversionary pointing capability in the event that the layers display and control unit is unavailable, or a primary display function in a less harsh vehicle environment. See *Layers Display and Control Unit* and *Laser Inertial Automatic Pointing System.*

Toxrep — Hostile toxic attack report.

Tp — Troop.

Tp Ex — Troop Exercise. (The King's Troop RHA).

TPT — Tactical Psychological Operations Team.

Tptr — Teleprinter.

TPU — Tracker Processing Unit. Part of the Rapier FSB2 Air Defence system.

TR — (i) Tracking Radar (rapier system).
(ii) Transit Route.
(iii) Traverse Right. See *SLTR* and *Traversing.*

TR1143 — A VHF radio set used during the Second World War by batteries and artillery headquarters to communicate with Royal Air Force aircraft in the artillery reconnaissance role. This became necessary when the responsibility for ground-air communication was transferred from RAF to the Army. It was possible to connect the TR1143 to a HF radio to facilitate re-broadcasting of messages. See *Artillery Reconnaissance* and *Rebroadcast.*

Traces — Leather covered steel ropes running from breast collars to vehicles by which the vehicles were moved.

Tracked Rapier — The mobile tracked version of the Rapier Air defence system which provided organic air cover for the mobile armoured brigades.
Detachment: 3.
Engine: GMC Model 6V-53T Diesel engine developing 210hp at 2,100rpm.
Internal Fuel Capacity: 398 litres.
Speed: 48 kph.
Range: 300 km.
Width: 2.8 m.
Length: 6.4 m.
Height with tracker raised: 2.78 m.
Combat weight: 14,010 kg.
Ground clearance: 0.41 m.
Armaments: Eight Rapier Surface to Air Missiles and Smoke Dischargers.
Ammunition Carried: 8 ready to fire Rapier SAMs.
Main Armament traverse horizontal 360°.
Armour: Proof against small arms fire and backwash from missiles.
Now removed from service, an example can be seen in Firepower, the Royal Artillery Museum. See *Rapier* and *Rapier FSC.*

Tracker Electro Optical — Rapier SAM System tracker which uses Thermal Imagery for target tracking.

Trafalgar Battery — Unofficial title by which members of 16 Field Battery RA (The Old Rooks) referred to themselves during the First World War.

Trail — The lower rear portion of a gun carriage which rests on the ground when unlimbered. Various types of trail exist. See *Box Trail.*

Trail Ape — Nickname given to a member of a gun detachment. See *Gun Bunny, Grunt* and *Muzzle Maggot.*

Train of Artillery — Prior to the establishment of the two permanent companies of artillery in 1716; when an emergency requiring artillery support arose a royal warrant would be issued authorising the raising of a train of artillery. The warrant would lay down the establishment and rates of pay of the personnel, define the types of ordnance to be collected and list the stores to be collected from his Majesty's storehouses. The train was then formed by drafting in specified officers, master-gunners and gunners from the various garrisons, mobilising the necessary administrative personnel and artificers from the offices and workshops in the Tower of London, issuing guns and stores required and hiring horses and drivers from civilian sources. There was invariably a deficiency in trained men to complete the laid-down establishment, it was therefore necessary temporarily enlist additional officers, bombardiers, petardiers, gunners, matrosses and any others necessary to enable the train to take the field. Once the emergency was over, the train was disbanded; the permanent soldiers and administrative staff returned to their normal duties, whilst the remainder were discharged with some type of monetary compensation, usually half-pay. The first known reference to a train of artillery in the United Kingdom dates from 1544. See *Bombardier, Matross* and *Petardier.*

Training Ammunition — This includes operational ammunition and explosives which have been released for training together with specific ammunition types such as blank ammunition, pyrotechnics, and explosives which are only suitable for use in training. Training ammunition is sometimes referred to as practice ammunition. See *First Line Ammunition, Reserve Ammunition, Second Line Ammunition* and *With Weapons Scales.*

Training and Advisory Team — A specialist team tasked with providing training in a defined field. The specific field is identified by an appropriate prefix. Examples include: Air Manoeuvre Training and Advisory Team (AMTAT), Artillery Training and Advisory Team (ARTAT), Close Observation Training and Advisory Team (COTAT), Northern Ireland Training and Advisory Team (NITAT) and United Nations Training and Advisory Team (UNTAT).

Training Gap — The gap between the training objectives and the operational performance standard.

Training Objective — A precise statement of the skills and knowledge required at the end of the period of training to perform the tasks specified for a job.

Trainings — The term applied to the graduations marked on the traversing-arc used by coast artillery for indirect laying. They were so named to distinguish them from bearings which run clockwise, whereas trainings ruun counter-clockwise. See *Traversing-Arcs.*

Trajectory — Describes the curve of a shell in its flight.

Trans — (i) Transmit.
(ii) Transmitter.

Transit Corridor — An Airspace Control Measure / Air Defence term.

Transit Route — An Airspace Control Measure / Air Defence term.

Transom — A stout beam or bulkhead connecting two parts of a gun carriage.

Transport Wagon	Device used to move parts of heavy equipments between positions (Royal Canadian Artillery).
Transportable Unit Trainer	Part of the BATES system, unlike the static unit trainer, the TUT can be deployed into the field on a specially provided box body vehicle. See *BATES, Static Unit Trainer* and *Unit Trainer*.
Travelling Lock	A device which is used whilst the gun is being moved. It is designed to clamp the elevating parts of the gun in position and thus prevent them being damaged.
Travel Lock Actuator	Part of the MLRS system. See *Multiple Launch Rocket System*.
Traverse Level	An airspace control measure/air defence term.
Traversing	A director is said to be traversed when the telescope is rotated by either of the slow motion spindles. 'Traverse right' indicates the director is to be swung clockwise, whilst 'traverse left' indicates anti-clockwise. See *Director, SLTR, SRTL, TL, TR* and *Swinging*.
Traversing-Arc	Used for indirect laying by coast artillery; in combination with a pointer on the carriage, the traversing-arc allowed the gun to be directed horizontally to any point of the compass. Graduations on the traversing-arc ran counter-clockwise, thus when the gun pointed due north, the indicator would be at 0°, whilst when pointed due east the indicator would be at 270°. These were termed 'trainings' in order to distinguish them from bearings.
Traversing Platform	In fortifications and coast artillery batteries a wooden or metal platform, sometimes known as a slide, which supported a gun and its carriage and which could be traversed on racer tracks. See *Dwarf platform, Gun Platform, Mortar Platform, New Pattern Traversing Platform*, and *Siege Platform*.
Trawsfynydd	Field artillery range in Wales, in use between 1902–1962.
Tray Toggle Loading	A means of ramming a shell into the breech of a gun operated on a loading tray by a steel cable pulled by a toggle.
TRBE	Target Recognition Base Ejection.
Treasurer of the Ordnance	Created in 1670, the post holder was a member of the Board of Ordnance under the Master-General of the Ordnance. The Treasurer's duties were merged with that of several others in 1836 to form the office of Paymaster-General. See *Board of Ordnance* and *Master-General of the Ordnance*.
Trench Mortar	A mortar used for trench warfare in the First World War with a calibre of 3-inches to 9.45-inches. Used defensively or offensively from trench positions. The most successful British version was the 3-inch Stokes mortar (1915).
Trench Pig	Derogatory nickname for a member of an observation post party or a regimental tac group. See *Cloudpuncher* and *Gun Bunny*.
TRF	Tactical Recognition Flash.
Trg	Training.
Trials	These are specific requests by such establishments as RARDE to conduct trials for the research and development of current or future equipments. Trials are conducted using radar, (to obtain trajectory data and fuze timing), high speed photography at up to 20,000 frames per second (to study events) and flash X-ray (behind armour effects). Velocities of projectiles and fragments, spin, yaw, fuze delay, chamber pressures and even fragment temperature can also be measured.
Trials Establishment Royal Artillery	Located at Ty-Croes on the island of Anglesey, off the north-west coast of Wales. TERA was responsible for con-

ducting trials for all new equipments being introduced into the Royal Artillery. The establishment no longer exists.

Triple Trig — One of the triangulation exercise stations on the now defunct RA survey course. It was located at grid reference SU 1788 5048, just up the road from Netheravon Airfield.

Trig Point — Trigonometry Point. See *Survey Control Point*.

Trigonometry Point — An accurately surveyed and documented position which has been established by topographic surveyors and from which fixation can be taken. Within the United Kingdom a typical trig point is a concrete post set on a high point such as a hill which has a metal disc inset in the top to which a theodolite can be mounted. See *Survey Control Point*.

Trinitrotoluene — A form of explosive used in artillery shells.

Triple A — (i) Anti-Aircraft Artillery.
(ii) Artillery Administration Area (see also AAA).

Triple Base Propellant — A relatively flashless and non-erosive propellant produced by the combination of Nitroguanidine (Picrite) with Nitrocellulose and Nitroglycerine. Wear and coppering in the gun is reduced by the addition of various additives.

Trl — Trailer.

TRLV — Tracked Rapier Launch Vehicle.

TRO — Troop Reconnaissance Officer.

Troop — A sub-division of a battery.

Troop, The — Colloquial name given to the Riding House Troop, RHA and latterly the King's Troop, RHA.

Troop Captain — The title given to the second in command of the King's Troop RHA.

Troop Centre — Introduced during the 1950s, this was a point identified as being at the 'centre of mass' of a troop's guns, it replaced the pivot gun as the basis for calculations. See *Battery Centre* and *Pivot Gun*.

Troop Exercise — The morning exercise for all lines horses, usually a ninety minute walk and trot (the King's Troop RHA).

Troop Fire — Each gun fires in turn with an interval between.

Troopie — Troop Commander.

Troop Leader — Following the Second World War this role was undertaken by the second subaltern in a troop. He was responsible during a move, for leading the troop gun groups and acted, if required, as battery leader. In action he assisted the gun position officer and acted as his relief. See *Battery Leader*.

Troop Manoeuvre Area — Three TMAs make up a MLRS battery manoeuvre area. TMAs contain close hides for the MLRS launchers, survey points, where the accuracy of the launchers on-board navigation system can be confirmed and reload points where empty rocket pods can be exchanged (in under five minutes) for full ones. See *Battery Manouevre Area* and *Multiple Launch Rocket System*.

Troop Picket — An illuminated aiming point. The troop picket must be visible to all guns in the troop, and at least 150 yards from the guns. It should, preferably, be positioned in front of or to the rear of the guns. See *Aiming Point* and *Bearing Picket*.

Troop Reconnaissance Vehicle — The Stormer TRV is the companion vehicle to the HVM, and is designated as a troop recce vehicle (TRV), but also carries reload missile rounds for the HVM battery. The vehicles have identical mounting points on the hull so that a TRV can be converted to an HVM if required. Both of these vehicles have seen service in Germany and Bosnia amongst other deployments.

Troop Safety Line	The minimum safe distance from a nuclear strike for warned, protected troops. See *First Degree Safety Line* and *Second Degree Safety Line.*
TRSV	Tracked Rapier Support Vehicle.
TRT	Tracker Radar Truck. Part of the Rapier AD system.
Truck Lever	A roller handspike which was used in the running-up of guns. See *Handspike* and *Roller Handspike.*
Trucks	The small iron or wooden wheels on which a gun carriage or platform sits. See *Garrison Standing Carriage* and *Chocks.*
Truck Utility Heavy	The Reynolds Boughton RB44 is a high power-to-weight ratio, helicopter-portable medium load carrier. It is used in the Royal Artillery as a command post vehicle, a gun towing vehicle and for general utility purposes.
Truck Utility Light	Commonly known as the Land Rover, the TUL is used in the fitted for radio (FFR) version as a reconnaissance and command post vehicle. The general service version is also in wide use.
Truck Utility Medium (Heavy Duty)	Commonly known by its commercial name of Pimzgauer, this vehicle is used primarily by the airborne and commando units of the Royal Artillery in the following roles: command post, observation post and as a gun tower. 47 Regiment RA use the TUM(HD) as a lightweight multiple launcher (LML) detachment vehicle.
Trunnions	Trunnions are horizontal cylindrical projections from the barrel that rotate vertically in the saddle. They provide the rotational axis for elevating the barrel in its cradle.
TRV	Troop Reconnaissance Vehicle.
TS	Time Slot.
Ts&As	Tests and Adjustments, daily maintenance on radars.
TSA	(i) Training Safety Authority. (ii) Trigger Switch Attachment.
TSFL	Test Set First Line.
TSG RA	Training Standards Group Royal Artillery. See *RATSG.*
TSI	Tripod Scanner Infra-Red.
TSLFC	Test Set Launcher Firing Circuit.
TSLFU	Test Set Launcher Firing Unit. Part of the Rapier AD system.
TSM	Troop Sergeant-Major.
TSO	Technical Staff Officer.
TSS	(i) Thermal Sighting System (part of the HVM equipment). (ii) Target Selection Standard. (iii) Training Support Services.
TST	Time Sensitive Target.
TSU	Target Selection Unit.
TT	Troop Target.
TTB	Trunnion Tilt Bubble.
TTBR	Time To Be Ready.
TTF	Time To Fire.
TTG	Trunnion Tilt Graph.
TTI	Turret Traverse Indicator.
TTO	Turret Traverse Override.
TTOT	Timed Time on Target. Sometimes listed as TTT. See *TOT.*
TTT	(i) Timed Time On Target. Sometimes listed as TTOT. See *TOT.* (ii) Time To Target.
TTU	Telegraph Terminal Unit. FACE.
TTW	Transition to War.
TUAAM	Tuning Unit Automatic Antenna Matching.
TUAV	Tactical Unmanned Aerial Vehicle. See *MUAV* and *UAV.*

Tube	The tube is the separate percussion 'primer' which is used with breech loading ammunition. A tube is about the size of a rifle cartridge and is used by being inserted in the 'lock' fitted to the outside rear of the breech block.
TUH	Truck Utility Heavy. *See Truck Utility Heavy.*
TUL	Truck Utility Light. See *Truck Utility Light.*
TUM	Truck Utility Medium. See *Truck Utility Medium.*
TUM(HD)	Truck Utility Medium (Heavy Duty).
Turn In	Time to arrive at work.
TUT	Transportable Unit Trainer. See *BATES, Static Unit Trainer* and *Unit Trainer.*
TVAA	Tynemouth Volunteer Artillery Association.
TVE	Tube Vent Electric.
TVGU	TV Gathering Unit. Part of the Rapier AD system.
TWI	Thermal Warning Indicator.
Twiggy	A slimmed down version of the Night Observation Device. See *NOD.*
Twist of Rifling	This it the rate of turn in the rifling. It is usually expressed as 1 in 'n' calibres. Therefore, 1 in 20 calibres means that the projectile performs one revolution in twenty calibres length of the bore. Twist is usually uniform and indicates that the angle of twist remains constant. See *Bore, Calibre, Calibre Length* and *Rifling.*
Two Headed Shite Hawks	Nickname of 156 (Inkerman) Battery RA. The nickname is derive from the Battery insignia, a double-headed Russian eagle.
Two One Charlie	The second in command, derived from the regimental second in command's call sign on the regimental call sign matrix.
Two Person Rule	Fundamental rule of nuclear weapon handling which specified that any operation on a weapon should only be performed by two persons of equal competence.
Two Square	Part of fire orders, this refers to the marking of squares on shells to indicate their weight. A standard weight shell would be two square, whilst three square would indicate a heavier than standard weight shell. Thus a standard weight HE shell is referred to as HE Two Square.
TWR	Timed When Ready.
TX	Transmitter.
Ty Croes	Missile firing range in Anglesey, North Wales. Now closed.
Type 88 Height Finder Radar	See *S404* and *Thunderbird.*
Type H	See *(H)* (Royal Canadian Artillery).
Type L	See *(L)* (Royal Canadian Artillery).
Type LS	See *(LS)* (Royal Canadian Artillery).
Type M	See *(M)* (Royal Canadian Artillery).
Type of Mission	Part of the BATES data entry process. See *BATES.*

U – Uncle – 1927/1943
Uniform – 1956

U/A	Used in regards to promotion, this stood for Unpaid Acting, and would be written as per the following example U/A/L/Bdr. During the Second World War a gunner would be promoted to Unpaid Acting for twenty-one days, after which he would be Paid Acting (P/A) for three months, shown as P/A/L/Bdr, and finally would become War Substantive (W/), W/L/Bdr, which meant that one could only be demoted by a courts martial.
UAD	Universal Automatic Director. Coast artillery, Second World War.

UAPM — Unit Accident Procedure Manager.

UAV — Unmanned Aerial Vehicle. See *Desert Hawk, Phoenix* and *Watchkeeper*.

Ubique — 'Everywhere'. A general regimental order published in 1833 stated that the word 'Ubique' was to be substituted for all other terms of distinction hitherto borne on any part of the dress of appointments, throughout the whole Regiment. The motto 'Ubique' therefore took the place of all battle honours conferred on the regiment prior to that date and all that have been earned since then. The Regiment proudly refers to 'Ubique' as its battle honour.

UBRE — Unit Bulk Refuelling Equipment.

UCADMIN — Under Command for Administration (Command State).

UCD — User Control Device (Bowman).

UCDM — Under Command for Daily Maintenance (Command State).

UCLA — Uncontrolled Loss of Altitude.

UCM — Urban Camouflage Material.

U Co-ordinates — Uncorrected Co-ordinates. See *C Co-ordinates*.

UDT — User Data Terminal (Bowman)

UDTA — Urban Deployment Training Area.

UE — (i) Unit Equipment Establishment.
(ii) See *UE Call*.

UE Call — Call for fire from arty/R aircraft, one battery, stationary target, ranging with first salvo then individual rounds.

UEI — Unit Equipment Inspection.

UFH — Ultralightweight Field Howitzer.

UFO — Unit Fire Officer.

UGL — Under slung Grenade Launcher.

UGS — Unattended Ground Sensor.

UH — Unit Holdings.

UHB — User Handbook.

UIN — Unit Identification Number.

UK/PRC-343 — The Personal Role Radio. See *Personal Role Radio*.

ULC — Unit Load Container (Holds 17x155mm shells plus charges).

ULOTC — University of London Officer Training Corps.

ULS — Unit Load Standard.

Umbrella Shoot — A concentration of fire by light anti-aircraft guns during the Second World War. Whereby the concentration was fired overhead. It was not considered to be very effective and was also wasteful in ammunition. See *Curtain Shoot*.

UMS — Unit Mobile Stocks (of ammunition).

UNCIVPOL — United Nations Civilian Police (Cyprus).

Uncle Light — Affectionate nickname by which U Battery was known during the 1950s.

Uncle Percy — Unrotated Projectile.

Uncle Target — Quick concentration of fire by the guns of an entire division onto one target. Second World War until NATO phonetic alphabet in 1950s when it became Uniform Target.

Uncontrolled Loss of Altitude — Used to describe the loss of control of a UAV, resulting in a crash landing. See *Desert Hawk, Phoenix, UAV* and *Watchkeeper*.

Uncorrected Co-ordinates — That data which is required to hit the target under the prevailing conditions. Corrections for abnormal conditions are, therefore, included automatically by the process of ranging, and uncorrected data is therefore the same as predicted data.

Under Command — Artillery works with the formation named; that formation will have priority call on their fire.

Under slung Grenade Launcher Designed to be mounted beneath the barrel of the L85 Individual Weapon. It is issued to infantry fire teams on a scale of one to each team. This scale of issue also applies to gunner units operating in an infantry role. The UGL is capable of firing 40 mm high explosive (HE), smoke and illuminating rounds out to a range of 350 metres.

UNFICYP United Nations Forces in Cyprus.

Uniform Target See *Uncle Target.*

Unit Trainer Part of the BATES system. There are two types available; the Statitc Unit Trainer and the Transportable Unit Trainer. See *BATES, Static Unit Trainer* and *Transportable Unit Trainer*.

Unit Training Officer Position in RHQ introduced in the 1970s. Usually occupied by a TIG. See *TIG.*

Unitary Warhead A warhead, used for example, in conjunction with the GMLRS system, which comprises a single explosive charge. See *Guided Multiple Launch Rocket System.*

United States Army Artillery Detachment US custodial detachment assigned to nuclear artillery units. Replaced the earlier term United States Army Field Artillery Detachment when nuclear armed air defence missiles were withdrawn from NATO.

University Officer Training Corps There are nineteen UOTCs in the country, eight of which have a gun troop. Gun troops train with the L118 Light Gun, and the organisation and deployment of a gun troop is the same as that of a regular army light gun battery, e.g. gun group, recce party, CP and FOO. Every member of the troop has a specific function within one of these units, requiring specialist training and qualification by the Royal School of Artillery. The Regiment supports the gun troops and provide a WO2 for each. The WO2 undertakes the role of battery sergeant-major and also assists with OTC training throughout the year. The Regiment views the gun troops as a resource for future officers and actively encourages officer recruitment within the troops by having a weekend at Salisbury Plain training area where every item of kit used by the Regiment is displayed. The other main event in the gun troop calendar is the two weeks course held at Otterburn every September, where new members gain qualifications and the necessary safety certificates, before undertaking live firing. See *KGVI.*

Unobserved Fire Artillery fire which is brought to bear without the benefit of preliminary ranging but as a result of a knowledge of the coordinates of the gun and the grid reference of the target in association with information concerning the prevailing meteorological and ballistic conditions.

UNPROFOR United Nations Protection Force.

Unrotated Projectile One which is not stabilised in flight by being spun about its longer axis. It is normally stabilised by fins.

UNTAT United Nations Training and Advisory Team.

UOR Urgent Operational Requirement.

UOTC University Officer Training Corps. See *KGVI.*

UP Unrotated Projectile.

UP-3 3-inch rocket employed by Z batteries in the air defence role during the Second World War. The UP-3 had a lethal radius of 70 feet. The main body of the rocket was white, whilst the warhead was yellow with a green band to indicate a TNT filling. See *Unrotated Projectile, UP* and *Z Battery.*

UPO	Unit Press Officer.
Upper Register	Refers to firing an artillery piece at angles in excess of 45°. Now known as High Angle.
Urban Operations	Current British Army name for what was formally known as FIBUA (qv).
U/S	Unserviceable, useless.
USAAD	United States Army Artillery Detachment.
USAFAD	United States Army Field Artillery Detachment. See *United States Army Artillery Detachment.*
UT	Unit Trainer. Part of the BATES system See *BATES, SUT* and *TUT*.
UTM	Universal Transverse Mercator.
UTO	Unit Training Officer.
UTR	Unit Telecommunications Repair.
UVB	Unverified Short Bracket. See *VSB*.

V – Vic – 1904/1927 Victor – 1943/1956

(V)	Volunteer, used as part of a unit title.
VA	(i) Vulnerable Area. (ii) Vertical Angle.
Vaisala Meteorological System	Currently used by 29 Commando Regiment Royal Artillery instead of the BMETS system used by other Regiments of the Royal Artillery. See *BMETS*.
Vaisala RT20	See *RT20*.
Varied by Observation	Fire plan that may be changed on the initiative of the artillery observer. (Second World War).
VARO	Valve Adjusting Run Out.
Vaudrey Range	A .22 rifle superimposed on a 25-pdr field gun and used in conjunction with a moving target in order to practise anti-tank shooting on a miniature range.
VBIED	Vehicle-borne Improvised Explosive Device. Pronounced 'Vbed'.
VDU	Visual Display Unit.
veh	Vehicle.
Vel	Velocity.
Vehicles to the Mile	Used in the calculation of road space requirements for convoy movement.
Vehicle Tactical Sign	See *Tactical Sign*.
Vehicle User Data Terminal	Part of the Bowman communications system. See *Bowman*.
Vent	The hole, which is usually located in the top, but possibly in the side or cascable of a gun into which a tube was fitted or powder was poured in order to fire the gun.
Vent field	In muzzle-loading artillery pieces, this was an area on the breech where the vent was drilled. Usually consisting of a raised metal rectangle through which the vent was drilled and to which the firing lock could be was attached.
Vent Plug	See *Fid* and *Vent*.
Ventsman	The member of a smooth-bore gun detachment who was responsible for 'serving the vent' whilst the gun was being loaded. See *Serving the Vent*.
Verified Short Bracket	When the plus and minus rounds of a Short Bracket are repeated for verification and they fall on the same spots as the original short bracket.
Vertex	The highest point reached by a projectile during its flight from the gun to the target.
Vertical Ballistic Angles	See *Ballistic Angles*.
Vertical Gun Angles	See *Gun Angles*.

Vertical Plane of Sight	The vertical plane which contains the line of sight. See *Line of Sight.*
VFSO	Visual Flight Safety Officer.
VHF	Very High Frequency.
Vickers 75 mm gun	See *Millimetre Gun.*
Vickers Range Clock	See *Coventry Clock.*
Vic Tock	Visual Telegraphy.
Victor Target	Quick concentration of fire by the guns of an entire corps onto one target.
VIDS/VEDS	Vehicle Internal and External Distribution Systems (Radio).
Visual Telegraphy	Signalling by flag or lamp. Flag signalling had a range of about 2 miles by day, whereas lamp had the same range by day, but 6 miles by night.
VLAP	Velocity Enhanced Long-Range Artillery Projectile.
VLLAD	Very Low Level Air Defence.
VL Shoot	An air shoot, where the pilot would fire a Very Light before signalling his altitude, while the GPO followed the aircraft along the edge of his protractor, his ack reading the final angle of sight.
VM	Vehicle Mechanic.
VMS	Vaisala Meteorological System. See *BMETS.*
VN	A First World War British gas shell filling consisting of Prussic Acid Gas. The name being derived from *Vincennite*, the French name which was in turn derived from the location of their factory at Vincennes.
VO	(i) Veterinary Officer (the King's Troop RHA). (ii) Artillery Code used during the First World War meaning 'Salvo'.
V of D	Velocity of Detonation.
Voice Procedure	The way to speak clearly and concisely on the radio net.
VOL	Volume.
Volunteer Artillery	Part of the auxiliary artillery, originally raised as part of the volunteer force in the Napoleonic War and revived in 1859. Became part of the territorial force in 1907.
VP	(i) Vulnerable Point. (ii) Vital Point. (iii) Voice Procedure.
VPA	(i) Visual Priority Arc. (ii) Visible Primary Arc.
VP/ADCIS	Vulnerable Point/Air Defence Control Information System.
VRC	Vehicle Radio Communicator. The abbreviation is followed by the number of the type of radio in question. See *PRC.*
VRSD	Variable Range Safety Distances.
VRSDTO	Variable Range Safety Distances Troops in Open.
VSB	Verified Short Bracket. See *UVB.*
VSHORAD	Very Short Range Air Defence.
VSM	Vickers Sons and Maxim.
VT	(i) Visual Telegraphy. (ii) Variable Time. See *VT Fuze.*
VT Fuze	Variable Time. A type of artillery fuze which first became available in 1944. In fact, despite being given a degree of legitimacy in Artillery Training Pamphlets, the VT fuze is not in fact a time fuze at all. The term 'Variable Time' was chosen during its developmental stages in order to disguise the true nature of the fuze. It was in point of fact a Proximity Fuze which used miniature valves within the fuze itself to emit radio signals as the round approached a target. The echo or return pulse from the target caused the fuze to detonate the round when it was a few feet from the target.
VTM	Vehicles to the Mile.
VUDT	Vehicle User Data Terminal. See *Bowman.*

W – William – 1927/1943
Whiskey – 1956

W	Artillery Code used during the First World War meaning 'Shot unobserved or washout.'
W7	Nuclear weapon in Corporal warhead.
W31	Nuclear weapon in Honest John warheads M27, M47 and M48.
W33	Nuclear weapon in 203 mm M422 shell.
W48	Nuclear weapon in 155 mm M454 shell.
W70	Nuclear weapon in Lance warhead.
W/	War substantive. See *U/A*.
Wadhook	See *Worm*.
Wadmiltilt	A strong woollen cloth covering which was placed on the floor of a magazine to prevent damage to the gunpowder barrels.
WAGE	Wide Area Global Positioning System Enhancement.
Wagon	A two-wheeled cart similar in appearance to a limber in which extra ammunition was carried in horse-drawn batteries. A sub-section consisted of the actual gun detachment, a gun and limber and a wagon and limber each drawn by a team of horses.
Wagon Lines	The name given to the location where towing and other vehicles are kept whilst the guns are in action. In horse drawn days, the gun teams would also have returned to the wagon lines.
Wagon Supply	The normal method of supplying ammunition to the gun. The gun limber would return to the wagon lines and one of the two ammunition wagons forming part of a sub-section would be dropped at the gun to provide ammunition. Ammunition wagons carried greater amounts of ammunition than the gun limber. See *Limber Supply*.
WAGs	Wives and Girlfriends.
Walt	The name given to anyone who gives an inflated impression of themself. Someone who is not averse to telling tall stories. Derived from the short story and film character Walter Mitty, a fantasist.
WAP Battery	West Aden Protectorate Battery.
Wardrop	Nickname of 40 Battery RA. This is not an honour title, and as it is not an official part of the battery title, it is not included on battery signs, letterheads etc.
War Office Controlled Stores	Standard issue items such as watches and binoculars. Now known as Ministry of Defence Accountable Controlled Stores (MODACS).
Warrant Officer Class 1	For example a regimental sergeant-major or a master gunner. See *Master Gunner*.
Warrant Officer Class 2	For example a battery sergeant-major.
Warrant Officer Class 3	Introduced in 1938, however the class was placed into suspension in 1940, although it has not been officially abolished.
Warrant Officers Training Team	Now known as the Royal Artillery Training Team. See *Royal Artillery Training Team*.
Warrior OPV	A Royal Artillery variant of the Warrior infantry fighting vehicle. The turret and fighting compartment are equipped with a thermal imaging (TI) and image intensification (II) sight, laser range finder (LRF), and azimuth positioning and elevation system (APES). The turret does not mount a 30 mm cannon, but is equipped with a dummy gun. The

enhanced turret suite is fully aligned with APES, enabling the bearing, range and angle of sight to be measured and the subsequent coordinates displayed. The OPV is also equipped with MSTAR, which is mast mounted onto the rear of the vehicle and operated from inside.
Weight loaded: 24,500 kg.
Length: 6.34 m.
Height to turret top: 2.78 m.
Width: 30 m.
Max Road Speed: 75 kph.
Road Range: 500 km.
Engine: Rolls Royce CV8 diesel.
Detachment: 3–4.
See *MSTAR*.

Warrior Target — A type of butt target used for comparative tests of guns and shot during the 1860s. Consisting of 4½-inch iron plates fastened together with 1¼-inch diameter bolts and backed by 18-inches of teak and a ½-inch iron inner skin supported by iron ribs 18-inches apart. The name derives from the fact that the target simulated the hull construction of HMS *Warrior*.

Watchkeeper — The Watchkeeper unmanned aerial vehicle is the replacement for the Phoenix UAV system. Although not in service at the time of writing, it will be operated by 32 Regiment RA. It forms part of the UK's plans for a network-enabled capability, and will provide UK commanders with accurate, timely and high quality information, including imagery. See *Phoenix*.

Waterloo Day — (i) Battery day of G Battery (Mercer's Troop) RHA, celebrated on or as near as possible to 18 June each year. Also known as Mercer's Day.
(ii) Battery Day of 30 (Rogers's) Battery RA, celebrated on or as near as possible to 18 June each year.

Waterproofing Supervisor — Each Battery in 29 Commando Regt RA holds a number of waterproofing supervisors, who have been trained at Royal Marines Poole. They are responsible for supervising the waterproofing of vehicles and guns prior to amphibious operations.

Waxy — Slang term for a cobbler or saddler.

WCO — Weapon Control Order. See *WCS*.

WCS — Weapon Control Status. See *WCO, Weapons Free, Weapons Hold* and *Weapons Tight*.

WD — War Department.

WDA — Weapon Danger Area.

Wdr — Withdraw.

WDT — Weapon Density Trace. (1960s and later) Replaced GDT.

WE — War Establishment.

Weapon Control Order — The order whereby a weapons control status is imposed. See *Weapon Control Status*.

Weapon Control Status — Used by air defence units, the three weapons control states are Weapons Free, Weapons Hold and Weapons Tight. They define within the Rules of Engagement when fire units can engage airborne targets. They may be further defined by the addition of a suffix fixed wing, UAV or helicopter, indicating the type of aerial target to which the WCS applies. See *Weapon Control Order, Weapons Free, Weapons Hold* and *Weapons Tight*.

Weapon Density Trace — In use from the 1960s, it replaced the Gun Density Trace. See *Gun Density Trace*.

Weapon Engagement Zone — In air defence, an area of airspace of defined dimensions within which the responsibility for engagement normally rests with a particular weapon system.

Weapon Holding Area Field storage facility for reserve stocks of nuclear weapons. It formed part of the Weapon Support Group. See *Weapon Support Group.*

Weapons Free An air defence weapons control status under which weapon systems may engage all aircraft not positively identified as friendly. This is the normal weapons control status in clear airspace. Engagement of targets may take place if any of the following parameters are met: (i) In visual only systems if the target is either not visually recognized or if it commits a hostile act. (ii) With systems fitted with IFF, if no response is received from the target, the fire unit may engage the target using either a visual, thermal or radar engagement sequence. See *IFF* and *Weapon Control Status, Weapons Hold* and *Weapons Tight.*

Weapons Free Zone An airspace control measure/air defence term.

Weapons Hold An air defence weapons control status under which weapon systems may only fire in self-defence, in response to a formal order, or if it is seen that friendly troops/installations are under direct air attack. See *Weapon Control Status, Weapons Free* and *Weapons Tight.*

Weapons Mount Installation Kit A pintle mounting for Land Rovers suitable for large calibre automatic weapons such as the .50 calibre machine gun.

Weapon Support Group Originally the Royal Malta Artillery regiment and subsequently 8 Regiment Royal Corps of Transport after Malta became independent. The Weapon Support Group operated the ammunition supply point and the weapon handling area with 570th USAAG and was responsible for nuclear weapon resupply. See *570th USAAG, Ammunition Supply Point* and *Weapon Holding Area.*

Weapons Technical Staff Field Forces Known colloquially as Wheatsheaf, the unit originated as a weapons technical staff, which at the beginning of the Second World War served the British expeditionary forces as the technical wing of the MGRA's staff. There were similar units with 21 Army Group and in the Mediterranean. Its personnel were responsible for maintaining personal touch with formations and units in the theatre covered. This bypassed normal channels of communications in a bid to reduce to a minimum the delays which would otherwise have hampered effective action between those who developed and produced the weapons and the end user. All members of Wheatsheaf were highly trained experts with personal user experience of the weapon or weapons of his particular department.

Weapons Tight An air defence weapons control status under which weapon systems may only engage aircraft which are positively identified as hostile or which are committing, or have committed a hostile act. IFF must therefore be supplemented by either thermal or visual recognition. Weapons Tight is the normal WCS in a controlled airspace. See *IFF, Weapon Control Status, Weapons Free* and *Weapons Hold.*

Wear The life of the barrel depends mainly on the condition of rifling as gas action is concentrated behind the driving band as the projectile passes up the bore. Wear is generally greatest close to the commencement of rifling. The amount of twist, the shape and number also affect wear. See *Bore, Commencement of Rifling* and *Twist of Rifling.*

Webbing 37 Pattern 1937 pattern webbing used in the Second World War, it replaced the 1908 pattern.

Webbing 44 Pattern	1944 pattern webbing, limited use in the Second World War but became standard FARELF webbing until late 1960s. Had the most practical mug ever issued to UK troops.
Webbing 58 Pattern	1958 pattern webbing, replaced 1937 pattern and some 1944 pattern. It was itself replaced by PLCE.
Wedge Wad	A wedge shaped pad which was placed in the bore of an RML gun designed to hold the projectile in place so that it was centred in the bore.
Wee Gee Corps	Nickname given to the Corps of Royal Artillery Drivers during the Napoleonic Wars. See *Corps of Royal Artillery Drivers.*
wef	With effect from.
Welin Thread	The thread used with a screw breech, it is a non-tapering thread with 3 steps, each covering an arc of about 40 degrees.
Welsh Gunners	Regimental title of the now disbanded 22 Regiment RA, now adopted by 39 Regiment RA. Identifies the Regimental recruiting area.
Wendy House	Nickname given to the detachment compartment on the Foden gun towing vehicle.
WEPC	Weapons and Equipment Policy Committee.
WER	War Establishment Reinforcement.
WES	Weapons Effect Simulator.
Wessex Troop	The unofficial name given to the air defence troop of CVHQ RA. See *CVHQ RA.*
West Aden Protectorate Battery	During the 1960s batteries of the Royal Artillery provided support to the Federal Regular Army in Aden. The deployed Battery was known as the West Aden Protectorate Battery and deployed in three sections of two guns each in support of Federal Regular Army battalions at the Yemeni border garrisons of Dhala, Mukeiras and Beihan, with BHQ remaining in Aden.
West Midland Gunners	Regimental title of 26 Regiment RA. Identifies the regimental recruiting area.
WEZ	Weapon Engagement Zone.
WF3M	Officially referred to as the Radar FA No 19, this was a balloon tracking radar that formed part of the 1970s AMETS meteorological system and replaced the Radar AA No 3 Mk 2 which had previously been used in the balloon tracking role. See *AMETS.*
WFE	War Fighting Experiment.
WFM	Whole Fleet Management.
WFZ	Weapons Free Zone.
WHA	Weapon Holding Area.
WHE	Warhead Event.
Wheatsheaf	Weapons Technical Staff, Field Forces (Second World War).
Wheeled Vehicle Mounted Inertial Navigation System	A system whereby an Inertial Navigation Unit from APS would have been fitted into either a signals or survey land rover. This system would then have been used in the same way as PADS to provide fix in the event of GPS denial. See *Automatic Positioning System* and *Position and Azimuth Determining System.*
Wheelers	The horses nearest the wheel of the limber in a gun team, they act as the brakes of the gun team.
Whippletree	See *Swingletree.*
White Star	A First World War British gas shell filling consisting of a Chlorine-Phosgene mixture.
Whlr QMS	Wheeler Quartermaster Sergeant (rank no longer in use). The abbreviation was used alongside Whr/QMS for the same rank, often in the same publications. See *Whr/QMS.*

Whr | Wheeler.
Whr/QMS | Wheeler Quartermaster Sergeant. (Rank no longer in use). The abbreviation was used alongside Whlr/QMS for the same rank, often in the same publications. See *Whlr QMS.*
Whr/S/Sgt | Wheeler Staff Sergeant (rank no longer in use).
WHS | Warhead Section.
WI | (i) War Increment.
(ii) Working Instructions.
William Target | A target engaged by all the guns within range in a field army.
Windage | The difference between the bore of the piece and the diameter of the projectile. The greater the difference, the more the propellant force could escape, thus reducing range and effectiveness. Wear is generally greatest close to the commencement of rifling. The amount of twist, the shape and number also affect wear. See *Bore, Commencement of Rifling* and *Twist of Rifling.*
Windage Area | The difference between the cross-sectional area of the projectile and the bore. See *Windage.*
Wind Correction Graph | A graph giving corrections to range and line per 10 feet/second for wind. Wind details were provided in the meteor telegram. The data was used by the command post to either calculate a correction or, with temperature correction data, to set up a 'correction of the moment graph' for the current meteor period. See *Meteor Telegram* and *Correction of the Moment.*
Wind Set | AN/MMQ-1B, trailer mounted elevating mast with sensor to measure low level wind speed and direction for Honest John.
Wingate Troop | One of the Troops in 33 Campbell Bty Junior Leaders Regiment RA. See *Borgard Troop, Gunn Troop* and *Shrapnel Troop.*
Winger | Slang for a round fired wide of the target as a result of the application of incorrect settings to the gun or ammunition.
WINS | Wheeled Vehicle Mounted Inertial Navigation System.
Wireless Set No 18 | A man pack transmitter/receiver developed in 1940 for short range communication (about 5 miles using a tactical antenna) in forward areas between battalion HQ and company HQ. It was used by forward observation officers and observation post officers to communicate with infantry units. Frequency range 6–9 MHz.
Wireless Set No. 19 | A mobile transceiver developed in 1941. It was the standard armoured vehicle radio but was later used additionally as a general purpose set in truck station and ground station. Range for the 'A' set was up to 15 miles; whilst that for the 'B' set was 3/4 mile. Using the RF Amplifier No. 2 increased the range to 45 miles. Frequency range 'A' set: 2–8 MHz; 'B' set: 229–241 MHz.
Wireless Set No. 21 | The range of this set was, realistically too short for artillery use, although it saw considerable use during the middle years of the Second World War. It was replaced by the Wireless Set No. 22 or in units using armoured vehicles, by the Wireless Set No. 19.
Wireless Set No. 22 | A portable transceiver developed in 1942 and used throughout the British Army. Generally resembling the Wireless Set No. 19 in appearance, it was used as a general purpose low-power vehicle and ground station with facilities for man pack usage. With a range of up to 20 miles, it was widely used in artillery regiments and formations, and as well as being fitted to air observation post aircraft. Frequency range 2–8 MHz.

Wireless Set No. 38	A man pack transceiver developed in 1942. With a range of up to 1 mile using a long 12 ft rod aerial, it was used mainly within infantry companies for short range communication. It was issued to forward observation officers and fitted to observation post tanks for communications with supported infantry. Frequency range 7.4–9.2 MHz
Wireless Set No. 46	A special crystal controlled and water-proofed radio designed for use during amphibious landings, it is likely that some artillery observers used it.
Wireless Set No. 62	Introduced towards the end of the Second World War as a replacement for the Wireless Set No. 22. The No. 62 comprised a two man load and was considered unusual as its front panel was labelled in both English and Russian. It remained in service until the mid 1960s.
Wireless Set No. 68	A man pack transmitter/receiver developed in 1943 and used by members of the forward observer units (airborne) RA. The set had a maximum range of 10 miles. See *Airborne Support Net* and *Forward Observer Unit RA (Airborne).*
WIRGA	West Indian Battalion Royal Garrison Artillery.
With Weapon Scales	A guide to the quantity of first line ammunition which should accompany a weapon on deployment, the balance of the first line ammunition is carried in follow-up echelons. See *First Line Ammunition, Reserve Ammunition, Second Line Ammunition* and *Training Ammunition.*
Witness Point	A point some distance from a target, but accurately located in relation to it, which can be ranged without losing surprise against the target and the correction applied to data for the target.
Wkpr	Watchkeeper.
WKSP	Workshop.
WL	Wagon Line.
WLO	Wagon Line Officer.
WLR	Weapons Locating Radar.
WMIK	Weapons Mount Installation Kit.
WMR	War Maintenance Reserve.
Wng	Warning.
WNGO	Warning Order (Royal Australian Artillery).
WO	(i) Warrant Officer. (Either a I or a II, WOI would be an RSM or a MG, a WOII would for example be a BSM or a SMIG). (ii) War Office.
WO1	Warrant Officer Class One.
WO1 (Master Gunner)	See *Master Gunner*.
WO2	Warrant Officer Class Two.
WO3	Warrant Officer Class Three.
WOCS	War Office Controlled Stores. Standard issue items such as watches and binoculars. Now known as Ministry of Defence Accountable Controlled Stores (MODACS).
WOF	Weight of Fire.
WOI	See *WO1*.
WOIC	Warrant Officer in Charge.
WOII	See *WO2*.
WOIII	See *WO3*.
Wolverine	The official British Army designation for the American M10 self-propelled 3-inch anti-tank gun. The full designation being 3-inch SP Wolverine. The Wolverine had an open-topped turret, leaving it vulnerable to artillery and mortar fire and infantry assault. By 1945 its armour proved too thin to provide adequate protection from the new German tanks and anti-tank guns. A major disadvantage for the Wolverine was the fact that it was not provided with a power traverse, which resulted in a

	very slow hand cranked turret traverse. Indeed, it took approximately two minutes to traverse a full 6400 mils. Some of the Wolverines in service with the Royal Artillery were re-armed with the more effective 17-pdr gun and re-designated the 17-pdr SP Achilles. See *Achilles*. Detachment: 5 (Commander, (3x) gun Detachment, driver). Length: 6.83 m (22.41 ft) (w/ gun) 5.97 m (19.6 ft) (w/o gun). Width: 3.05 m (10 ft). Height: 2.57 m (8.43 ft). Weight: 29.6 tonnes (65,000 lb). Armour: 9–57.2 mm (0.3–2.3 in). Main armament: 3 in (76.2 mm) Gun M7. Ammunition carried: 54 rounds. Secondary armament: .50 cal Browning M2HB m/gun. Ammunition carried: 300 rounds. Power plant: General Motors 6046 Twin Diesel 6-71 375 hp (276 kW). Suspension: Vertical Volute Spring Suspension. Road speed: 51 km/h (32 mph). Power/weight: 12.5 hp/tonne. Range: 300 km (186 miles).
WOMBAT	Weapon of Magnesium Battalion Anti Tank Gun. See *BAT* and *MOBAT.*
Wood, The	Abbreviated title for Saint John's Wood Barracks, London. Home of the King's Troop, Royal Horse Artillery.
Wood's Troop	Together with Desbrisay's Troop, and Lucknow Troop, one of the three troops in 76 (Maude's) Battery Royal Artillery.
Woolwich Groove	See *Woolwich Pattern Rifling*.
Woolwich Infant	The name given to the 12-inch, 35-ton Victorian RML guns constructed at the Woolwich Arsenal, owing to the large girth at the breech of the guns. They were found to be inaccurate when tested on the ranges. Also known as 'Soda Water Bottles', presumably due to their resemblance to Victorian soda water bottles. Also a public house in Woolwich, which derives its name from the gun.
Woolwich Pattern Rifling	Introduced in the 1880s this type of rifling was used in R.M.L. guns. The groove of the rifling was rounded off at the sides to prevent any tendency of the steel to split along the edge of the groove. The number of grooves depended on the nature of the piece. The 7-inch R.M.L. had three grooves whilst the 9-inch R.M.L. had six. See also *Palliser Conversion.*
WOPSI	Warrant Officer Permanent Staff Instructor.
WOPV	Warrior Observation Post Vehicle Trainer.
Workshop	A REME unit tasked with providing both 1st and 2nd line repair and recovery support to Artillery Regiments. See *Light Aid Detachment* and *REME.*
Worm	In muzzle-loading artillery this was a sidearm used to scour the inside of the barrel to remove burning embers or blockages. It consisted of a wooden staff with a spiral iron hook on its end. Also known as a *wadhook.*
WOSB	War Office Selection Board.
WOTT	Warrant Officers Training Team. See *Royal Artillery Training Team.*
WP	(i) White Phosphorus. (ii) Waypoint.
WP LIB	Waypoint Library.
WPNF	Artillery Code used during the First World War meaning 'Many Batteries in square…' This would be followed by the map square location.

WRA	Weapon Restricted Arc.
WRAT	West Riding Artillery Trust.
WRE	Weapons Research Establishment.
WS 18	Wireless Set No 18.
WS 19	Wireless Set No 19.
WS 21	Wireless Set No 21.
WS 22	Wireless Set No 22.
WS 38	Wireless Set No 38.
WS 46	Wireless Set No 46.
WS 62	Wireless Set No 62.
WS 68	Wireless Set No 68.
WSG	Weapon Support Group.
W/T	Wireless Telegraphy, non-voice radio (Second World War).
WTLHA	Wet Target Laser Hazard Area.
WTLHAT	Wet Target Laser Hazard Area Trace.
WTSFF	Weapons Technical Staff, Field Force.
WWS	With Weapon Scales.
WWT	Winter Warfare Tactics. Part of winter training in Norway.
WZ	Artillery Code indicating 'Stop'. See *Artillery Code.*

X – X-Ray – 1927/1943/1956

X	Artillery Code used during the First World War meaning 'Change to...'.
XC	Section Commander (First World War).
X-Day	Two days before the start of an operation (First World War). Now referred to as D minus 2. See *Y-Day* and *Z-Day.*
X-Hour	Firing time for a nuclear shell or rocket (i.e. ToT – ToF). See *N-Hour.*
XLWB	Extra Long Wheel Base.
Xmas Barrage	An anti-aircraft barrage devised in Malta over the Christmas 1941 period as a replacement for the Chevron Barrage. The Xmas Barrage was fired in the form of an X. Each of 5 HAA regiments fired into squares in the sky, the location of each square was calculated by the GPO who passed range, bearing and height to the guns. The five squares formed the X in the shape of a five on a dice. This form of barrage became the main defence against mass bomber raids on Malta during 1942. See *Chevron Barrage, GPO* and *HAA.*
XP	Experimental Establishment.
X-Ray	Battery Commander's Tactical Sign. See *Zulu* and *Tactical Sign.*

Y – Yorker – 1927
Yoke – 1943
Yankee – 1956

y	After an officer's name in the Army List, this signified attendance on the Long Observation Course.
Y Class	See *Yellow Class.*
Y-Day	One day before the start of an operation (First World War). Now referred to a D minus 1. See *X-Day* and *Z-Day.*
Yellow Class	Choking gas filled munitions. Second World War and later.
Yellow Dog	Nickname of F (Sphinx) Para Battery RHA.
Yellow Fever	FCE No 7 used with Bofors L40/70 AA gun.

Yellow Star — A First World War British gas shell filling consisting of 70 per cent Chlorine and 30 per cent Chloropicrin.

YO — Young Officer.

Yoke Target — A target engaged by guns of an AGRA.

Yorkshire Gunners, The — Battery Title of 269 (West Riding) Battery RA (V). It identifies the recruiting area of the Battery. See *North, East and West Yorkshire Gunners.*

Ypres Troop — One of the troops in 1st Squadron Honourable Artillery Company. See *Honourable Artillery Company, Somme Troop* and *Ypres Troop*.

Z – Zebra – 1927/1943
Zulu – 1956

Z — Artillery Code used during the First World War meaning 'Smoke shell'.

Z-Car — The commanding officer's vehicle, the title is derived from the commanding officers tactical sign – Zulu. See *Tactical Sign*.

Z-Day — The day on which an operation commenced. Also referred to as Zero Day. (First World War) Now known as D-Day. See *X-Day* and *Y-Day*.

Zap Number — A personal identification number made up from the first 2 letters of a soldiers surname and the last 4 digits of his/her army number. Thus, the Zap number for 12345678 Gunner Les Smith would be SM5678. They are used when personnel, and in particular casualties, need to be identified over insecure communications.

ZB298 — Radar GS No 14 battlefield surveillance system. A short range (6.2 miles (10 km) man-portable radar, used by OP parties, manufactured by Marconi Avionics. Could be fitted to the FV432 personnel carrier or mounted in the rear of a Land Rover. Forerunner of MSTAR. See *MSTAR*.

Z Battery — A Second World War anti-aircraft battery armed with 3-inch rockets, which were originally referred to as Unrotating Projectiles. Batteries could be equipped with either single or multiple launchers. Eventually, the battery launchers, or projectors as they were more correctly known, were linked to radar and predictors to predict the flight path of planes. The first Z Battery was formed in October 1940, by Major Duncan Sandys with the task of defending Cardiff. By December 1942 there were 91 Z batteries in existence within the UK.

Zenda — A multinational gun/mortar locating radar involving several European nations in the early 1970s. In UK service it would have been carried by 2 x FV432.

Zero — Controlling callsign on a radio net.

Zero Alpha — The callsign of the battery commander on the battery callsign Matrix.

Zero Day — See *Z-Day*.

Zero Hour — The time at which an operation commences and attacking troops cross their start line. Known in current terminology as H-hour.

Zero Length Launch — A method of launching the Falconette target drone by using attached rocket motors.

Zero Length Launcher — The launcher for the Falconette target drone. The name was also applied to the light weight launcher M740 for the lance missile. See *Lance, LWL* and *Zero Length Launch.*

Zero Line — An imaginary line from a gun position, usually the 'centre of arc' to the expected target area. The guns were oriented relative to the zero line, which could be different for every battery. When the dial sights were set to zero and azimuth corrections to the guns were given as 'more' or 'less' degrees and minutes or mils. The layer would use the right hand to turn the right sight knob away for a 'more' correction, and the left hand to turn the left sight knob towards him for a 'less' correction. The zero line remained in use until 1956 when bearings were adopted. See also *Centre of Arc*.

Zero Point — An identifiable feature somewhere near the centre of the battery's zone of fire. If visible through the sights of the gun, it could be used as an aiming point, although this was unlikely. It was introduced at the beginning of the twentieth century. See *Aiming Point*.

Z-Jeep — See *Z-Car*.

ZL — Zero Line.

ZLL — Zero Length Launch.

Z Location. — During the Second World War a hostile battery was located by sound ranging or flash spotting to a degree of accuracy categorised as either Z, A, B, C or Area Location. The most accurate location being a Z Location which meant the position of the hostile battery had been established to within 50 metres.

ZM — The artillery code equivalent of 'Out'. See *Artillery Code* and *ZT*.

Zone Call — During the First World War the zone call was established as a method by which aircraft could call for fire from artillery units. Maps of the period were not gridded, but divided into squares, identified by a letter, each of these squares covered an area of 6000 square yards. Each square was in turn quartered and given an identifying letter of A, B, C or D. This sub square had sides of 3000 yards and was known as a Zone. Batteries were assigned to engage targets in a particular zone. In order to employ a Zone Call, an aircraft of a Corps Wing Royal Flying Corps would use squared maps, which were normally overprinted with the locations of known hostile batteries. Each of these locations was identified by a number. If a pilot saw a hostile battery firing he would broadcast a 'NF' call giving the zone (for example PJ) and the relevant hostile battery number. The batteries allocated to that zone would then engage by ascertaining the target co-ordinates from their HB list. In addition a number of two-letter codes existed which were used to identify the type of target and pass additional information/instructions to the batteries concerned. For example, instead of sending a Morse message indicating 'six enemy guns now firing from the north east edge of Delville Wood,' an aircraft could send '6 NF PJ A', where NF represents Guns Now Firing, PJ is the Map Square and A the Zone in question, all batteries assigned to engage targets in that zone would then fire when ready. The Zone Call was considered to be quite fast, although it was not as fast as the Mike, Uncle and Victor Target procedures introduced during the Second World War. A system existed whereby zones were divided into tenths and possibly hundredths but its not clear whether this was much used by aircraft against opportunity targets. See *Mike Target*, *NF*, *Uncle Target* and *Victor Target*.

Zone of Fire — The area over which a battery or a single gun must be able to fire. See *Zone of the Gun*.

Zone of the Gun — A series of shells from a gun firing at a given elevation will not fall in exactly the same spot but will be spread around the theoretical impact point; this rectangular area is known as the zone of the gun. The 50% zone is the rectangular area into which 50% of the shells fired will fall, this is shown in firing tables for every 100 yards of range. The 100% zone is that into which all shells fired by the gun will fall, it is four times the size of the 50% zone. It is impossible to guarantee to hit a precise spot and gunners need to be mindful of the zone of the gun when ranging onto a target. See *Ranging*.

ZP	(i) Zero Point. (ii) See *Zulu Papa*.
ZQ	See *Zulu Quebec*.
ZR	See *Zulu Romeo*.
Z Rocket Battery	An unofficial title for a Z Battery. See *Z Battery*.
ZS	See *Zulu Sierra*.
ZT	(i) The Artillery Code equivalent of Over. See *Artillery Code*. (ii) See *Zulu Tango*.
ZU	See *Zulu Uniform*.
Zulu	Commanding Officer's Tactical Sign. See *X-Ray* and *Tactical Sign*.
Zulu Muster	A vehicle lager or rendezvous point where armoured personnel carriers etc. rendezvous to await their dismounts.
Zulu Papa	A target identifier followed by a four-figure number calling for the fire of the first battery in a regiment.
Zulu Quebec	A target identifier followed by a four-figure number calling for the fire of the second battery in a regiment.
Zulu Romeo	A target identifier followed by a four-figure number calling for the fire of the third battery in a regiment.
Zulu Sierra	A target identifier followed by a four-figure number calling for the fire of the fourth battery in a regiment.
Zulu Tango	A target identifier followed by a four-figure number calling for the fire of a regiment.
Zulu Time	Greenwich Mean Time. All operations in the British Army, irrespective of location in the World, are carried out using Zulu Time. This is shown as, for example, 1000 hrs Zulu, to differentiate from local time.
Zulu Uniform	A target identifier followed by a four-figure number calling for the fire of a division.
Zulu Victor	A target identifier followed by a four-figure number calling for the fire of a corps.
Zulu Whiskey	A target identifier followed by a four-figure number calling for the fire of a force, army or army group.
ZV	See *Zulu Victor*.
ZW	See *Zulu Whiskey*.
ZZ	Artillery code meaning 'Clear'. See *Artillery Code*.

APPENDIX 1
The Legend of Saint Barbara

A number of legends exist concerning Saint Barbara, but it is generally accepted that Barbara was a Greek living in Heliopolis, Egypt in either the 3rd or 4th century AD. Against her father's wishes, she converted to Christianity. Some legends say that her father, Dioscorus, wished her to marry a non-Christian. However, when she refused to do so, he had a tower built to imprison her. Barbara ordered three windows to be made in it, as a symbol of the Holy Trinity and an outward demonstration of her faith. Her actions further angered her father who had her beheaded (some versions of the legend say he did this himself). Suddenly, a violent storm broke out and he was struck by a bolt of lightning which killed him outright.

It would appear that Barbara had been canonised by the 7th century and her story is reported to have been introduced to Britain during the time of the Crusades.

Saint Barbara is generally portrayed standing by a tower with three windows, and carrying the palm of a martyr in her hand. She can often be seen holding a chalice and a sacramental wafer and sometimes cannon are displayed near her.

Saint Barbara was invoked to grant safety from lightning. When the use of gunpowder became widespread in the Western world, Saint Barbara was invoked for aid against accidents resulting from the explosions often associated with this material; it being an all too common occurrence for early artillery pieces to explode rather than fire their projectile. As a result of this, Saint Barbara became the Patron Saint of gunners, and consequently of the Royal Regiment of Artillery.

Saint Barbara's day is celebrated on the 4th of December.

APPENDIX 2

Origins of the Lanyard by Brigadier K. A. Timber

There has long been a tale about the gunners wearing a white lanyard for cowardice, allegedly for deserting their guns, but the story is nothing more than a piece of leg-pulling. However, it is time to put this particular story to rest.

Lanyards came into use in the late nineteenth century when field gunners manned the 12- and 15-pounder equipments, ammunition for which had a fuze set with a fuze key. The key was a simple device, and every man had one, attached to a lanyard worn around the neck. The key itself tended to be kept in the breast pocket until needed. The lanyard was simply a piece of strong cord, but in time it was a typical soldier's reaction to turn it into something a bit more decorative. It was smartened up with white ink or even blanco, and braided, gradually taking its present form.

Prior to the South African War, gunners were issued with steel folding hoof picks, carried on the saddle or in the jacket. In about 1903 these were withdrawn and replaced by jack-knives, which were carried in the left breast pocket of the service dress attached to the lanyard over the left shoulder.

During the two World Wars, the lanyard could be used as an emergency firing lanyard for many of the guns, because they had a firing mechanism which operated like a trigger. The lanyard could be attached to the trigger mechanism and allowed the gunner to stand clear of the gun's recoil.

The question of which shoulder bore the lanyard depends on the date. There is no certainty about this, but the change from the left shoulder to the right probable took place at about the time of the Great War, when the bandolier was introduced, because it was worn over the left shoulder. But there are some who insist that 1924 was the year of the change, when the sloping of rifles over the left shoulder would soil the white lanyard.

Eventually, in 1933, the end of the lanyard was simply tucked into the breast pocket without the jack-knife, though many will remember that it was often kept in place with the soldier's pay-book! On the demise of battledress, the lanyard disappeared for a short time, but returned as part of the dress of the Royal Regiment of Artillery in 1973.

For those still plagued by jokers, the simplest answer to any leg-pulling is to invite the comedian to produce evidence, as no change can take place to any of the Army's dress regulations without an appropriate order, and since no such evidence exists, the story falls flat on its face.

One might even ask why other arms and corps wear lanyards – they say that imitation is the sincerest form of flattery!

APPENDIX 3

Master Gunners Whitehall & St. James's Park

Captain Thomas Silver	1678–1710
Lieutenant Colonel Jonas Watson	1710–1741

Master Gunners St. James's Park

Lieutenant Colonel James Deal	1742–1760
Captain Joseph Brome	1760–1769
Held by a Non-Commissioned Officer	1770–1783
Lieutenant Colonel Joseph Walton	1783–1808
Lieutenant General Sir John McLeod GCH	1808–1833
Major General Sir Alexander Dixon KCH	1833–1840
General Sir Robert Gardiner GCB KCH	1840–1864
Field Marshal Sir Hew Dalrymple Ross GCB	1864–1868
General William Wylde CB	1868–1877
General Sir John Bloomfield GCB	1877–1880
General Poole Valency England	1880–1884
General Sir John St. George GCB	1884–1891
General Sir Collingwood Dickson VC GCB	1891–1904
Field Marshal The Earl Roberts VC KG KP GCB OM GCSI GCIE	1904–1914
General Sir Robert Biddulph GCB GCMG	1914–1918
Major General Sir Francis William Ward CB	1918–1919
General Sir Edward Francis Chapman KCB	1919–1926
General The Lord Horne GCB KCMG	1926–1929
Field Marshal The Lord Milne GCB GCMG DSO	1929–1946
Field Marshal The Viscount Alanbrooke KG GCB OM GCVO DSO	1946–1956
General Sir Cameron Nicholson GCB KBE DSO MC	1956–1960
General Sir Robert Mansergh GCB KBE MC	1960–1970
Field Marshal Sir Geoffrey Baker GCB CMG CBE MC	1970–1976
General Sir Harry Tuzo GCB OBE MC	1977–1983
General Sir Thomas Morony KCB OBE	1983–1988
General Sir Martin Farndale KCB	1988–1996
Field Marshal The Lord Vincent GBE KCB DSO	1996–2000
General Sir Alex Harley KBE CB	2001–

Defence Select Commitee, 19 January, 2000:

Michael Colvin MP: *Last year you monitored 'nights out of bed' for Army personnel, which showed that every soldier is out of bed about 27 per cent of the time. Do you regard that as acceptable?*

General Sir Alex Harley: *No, we do not, but everybody is clear that when operational commitments … have to be undertaken, they get on with it and do it.*

APPENDIX 4

Members of the Royal Artillery awarded the Victoria Cross

Name	**Date**	**Campaign (Battle)**	**Regt / Bty**
Bt Lt Col C. Dickson	17 Oct 1854	Crimea (Sebastapol)	Rt Siege Train RA
CSM A. Henry	5 Nov 1854	Crimea (Inkerman)	4 Coy 11 Bn RA
Lt F. Miller	5 Nov 1854	Crimea (Inkerman)	4 Coy 12 Bn RA
Capt M. C. Dixon	17 Apr 1855	Crimea (Sebastapol)	5 Coy 9 Bn RA
Sgt G. Symons	6 Jun 1855	Crimea (Sebastapol)	6 Coy 11 Bn RA
Gnr & Dvr T. Arthur	7 & 18 Jun 1855	Crimea (Sebastapol)	1 Coy 5 Bn RA
Bdr D. Cambridge	8 Sep 1855	Crimea (Sebastapol)	8 Coy 11 Bn RA
2/Capt G. Davis	8 Sep 1855	Crimea (Sebastapol)	2 Coy 5 Bn RA
Lt C. C. Teesdale	29 Sep 1855	Crimea (Kars)	Staff (ADC) RA
Gnr W. Connolly	7 Jul 1857	Indian Mutiny (Jhelum)	1 Tp 3 Bde Ben HA
Lt J. Hills	9 Jul 1857	Indian Mutiny (Delhi)	2 Tp 1 Bde Ben HA
Bt Major H. Tombs	9 Jul 1857	Indian Mutiny (Delhi)	2 Tp 1 Bde Ben HA
Capt G. A. Renny	16 Sep 1857	Indian Mutiny (Delhi)	5 Tp 1 Bde Ben HA
Capt W. Olpherts	25 Sep 1857	Indian Mutiny (Lucknow)	2 Coy 3 Bn Ben Arty
Bdr J. Thomas	27 Sep 1857	Indian Mutiny (Lucknow)	4 Coy 1 Bn Ben Arty
Sgt B. Diamond	28 Sep 1857	Indian Mutiny (Boolundshur)	2 Tp 3 Bde Ben HA
Gnr R. Fitzgerald	28 Sep 1857	Indian Mutiny (Boolundshur)	2 Tp 3 Bde Ben HA
2/Capt F. C. Maude	25 Sep 1857	Indian Mutiny (Lucknow)	3 Coy 8 Bn RA
Lt H. E. Harrington	14-22 Nov 1857	Indian Mutiny (Lucknow)	3 Coy 1 Bn Ben Arty
R Rider E. Jennings	14-22 Nov 1857	Indian Mutiny (Lucknow)	1 Tp 1 Bde Ben HA
Gnr J. Park	14-22 Nov 1857	Indian Mutiny (Lucknow)	2 Coy 4 Bn Ben Arty
Gnr T. Laughnan	14-22 Nov 1857	Indian Mutiny (Lucknow)	2 Coy 6 Bn Ben Arty
Gnr H. McInnes	14-22 Nov 1857	Indian Mutiny (Lucknow)	3 Coy 1 Bn Ben Arty
Lt F. S. Roberts	2 Jan 1858	Indian Mutiny (Khodagunge)	Staff (DAQMG) Ben Arty
Bt Maj R. H. Keatinge	17 Mar 1858	Indian Mutiny (Chundairee)	Political Offr Bom Arty
Bdr J. Brennen	3 Apr 1858	Indian Mutiny (Jhansi)	5 Coy 14 Bn RA
Lt A. F. Pickard	20 Nov 1863	New Zealand (Rangiri)	C Bty 4 Bde RA
Asst-Surg W. Temple	20 Nov 1863	New Zealand (Rangiri)	C Bty 4 Bde RA
Asst-Surg W. G. N. Manley	29 Apr 1864	New Zealand (Tauranga)	1 Bty 4 Bde RA

Sgt P. Mullane	27 Jul 1880	Afghanistan (Maiwand)	E Bty B Bde RHA
Gnr Collis	28 Jul 1880	Afghanistan (Maiwand)	E Bty B Bde RHA
Gnr A. Smith	17 Jan 1885	Soudan (Abu Klea)	1 Bty 1 Bde S Div RA
Capt H. N. Schofield	15 Dec 1899	S. Africa (Colenso)	Staff (ADC) RA
Capt H. L. Reed	15 Dec 1899	S. Africa (Colenso)	7 Bty RFA
Cpl G. E. Nurse	15 Dec 1899	S. Africa (Colenso)	66 Bty RFA
Maj E. J. Phipps-Hornby	31 Mar 1900	S. Africa (Sanna's Post)	Q Bty RHA
Sgt C. E. H. Parker	31 Mar 1900	S. Africa (Sanna's Post)	Q Bty RHA
Gnr I. Lodge	31 Mar 1900	S. Africa (Sanna's Post)	Q Bty RHA
Dvr H. H. Glasock	31 Mar 1900	S. Africa (Sanna's Post)	Q Bty RHA
Dvr F. H. Bradley	27 Sep 1901	S. Africa (Itala)	69 Bty RFA
Shoe Smith A. E. Ind	20 Dec 1901	S. Africa (Tafel Kop)	11 Pom-Pom Sect RHA
Lt Col E. W. Alexander	25 Aug 1914	WW 1 (Elouges)	119 Bty RA
Capt D. Reynolds	26 Aug & 9 Sep 14	WW 1 (Le Cateau)	37 Bty RFA
Dvr J. H. C. Drain	26 Aug 1914	WW 1 (Le Cateau)	37 Bty RFA
Dvr F. Luke	26 Aug 1914	WW 1 (Le Cateau)	37 Bty RFA
Capt E. K. Bradbury	1 Sep 1914	WW 1 (Nery)	L Bty RHA
BSM G. T. Dorrell	1 Sep 1914	WW 1 (Nery)	L Bty RHA
Sgt D. Nelson	1 Sep 1914	WW 1 (Nery)	L Bty RHA
Bdr E. G. Horlock	15 Sep 1914	WW 1 (Vendresse)	113 Bty RFA
Capt G. N. Walford	26 Apr 1915	WW1 (Gallipoli)	Staff (BRMRA)
A/Sgt J. C.. Raynes	11–12 Oct 1915	WW 1 (Fos 7 de Bethune)	A Bty 71 Bde RFA
Capt L. W. B. Rees	1 Jul 1916	WW 1 (Flying Duties)	Attached to RFC
Sgt W. Gosling	3 Apr 1917	WW 1 (Vimy)	V/51 Trench Mortar)
2/Lt T. H. B. Maufe	4 Jun 1917	WW 1 (Feuchy)	124 Siege Bty RGA
T/Lt S. T. D. Wallace	30 Nov 1917	WW 1 (Cambrai)	C Bty 63 Bde RFA
Sgt C. E. Gourley	30 Nov 1917	WW 1 (Cambrai)	D Bty 276 Bde RFA
Gnr C. E. Stone	21 Mar 1918	WW 1 (St Quentin)	C Bty 83 Bde RFA
Lt E. S. Dougall	10 Apr 1918	WW 1 (Messines)	A Bty 88 Bde RFA
T/Lt R. V. Gorle	1 Oct 1918	WW 1 (Ledgehem)	A Bty 50 Bde RFA
Maj J. C. Campbell	21-22 Nov 1941	WW 2 (Sidi Rezegh)	Staff
2/Lt G. W. Gunn	21 Nov 1941	WW 2 (Sidi Rezegh)	J Bty RHA
Lt P. A. Porteous	19 Aug 1942	WW 2 (Dieppe)	No 4 Commando

APPENDIX 5

Directors Royal Artillery

Major General W. J. Eldridge CB CBE DSO MC	1942–1944
Major General O. M. Lund CB DSO	1944–1946
Major General C. G. G. Nicholson CB CBE DSO MC	1946–1948
Major General S. B. Rawlins CB CBE DSO MC	1948–1950
Major General K. F. Mack. Lewis CB DSO MC	1950–1954
Major General R. W. Goodbody CB DSO	1954–1957
Major General R. G. S. Hobbs CB DSO OBE	1957–1959
Major General E. D. Howard-Vyse CB CBE MC	1959–1961
Major General E. J. H. Bates OBE MC	1961–1964
Major General G. F. de Gex CB OBE	1964–1966
Major General P. J. Glover CB OBE	1966–1969
Major General H. C. Tuzo OBE MC	1969–1971
Major General H. Janes CB MBE	1971–1973
Major General R. Lyon OBE	1973–1975
Major General T. L. Morony OBE	1975–1978
Major General T. S. C. Streatfield CB MBE	1978–1981
Major General M. J. Tomlinson CB OBE	1981–1984
Major General C. G. Cornock MBE	1984–1986
Major General P. R. F. Bonnet MBE	1986–1989
Major General B. T. Pennicot	1989–1991
Major General M. T. Tennant	1991–1994
Major General I. G. C. Durie CBE	1994–1996
Brigadier M. G. Douglas-Withers CBE ADC	1996–2000
Brigadier J. B. A. Bailey MBE	2000–2002
Brigadier C. C. Brown CBE ADC	2002–2003
Brigadier C. C. Wilson	2003–

APPENDIX 6
Royal Artillery Sergeant-Majors

WO1 (RASM) L. C. Wilson May	1989–Jun 1991
WO1 (RASM) R. A. McPhearson	Jun 1991–Aug 1993
WO1 (RASM) L. Place MBE	Aug 1993–Jul 1995
WO1 (RASM) N. A. Ashford	Jul 1995–Jan 1997
WO1 (RASM) A. Durrant	Jan 1997–Mar 1998
WO1 (RASM) J. E. Le Feuvre	Mar 1998–Feb 2000
WO1 (RASM) C. Broadfoot	Feb 2000–Mar 2002
WO1 (RASM) D. J. Gilbert	Mar 2002–Mar 2004
WO1 (RASM) G. McIntosh	Mar 2004–Mar 2006
WO1 (RASM) A. Harvey	Mar 2006–Mar 2008
WO1 (RASM) N. Kenny	Mar 2008–

Bibliography

Barnes, Leslie W.C.S. — *Canada's Guns. An Illustrated History of Artillery*

B Battery RHA — B Battery History as shown on the 1 RHA website.

Callwell, Major-Gen. Sir Charles & Headlam, Major-Gen. Sir John — *History of The Royal Artillery From The Indian Mutiny To The Great War: Volume I 1860-1899*

Cleaveland, RA. Colonel — *Notes on The Early History of The Royal Regiment of Artillery (To 1757)*

Franklin C E — *British Rockets of the Napoleonic and Colonial Wars 1805–1901*

Graham DSO, OBE, DL, *psc.* Brigadier-General C A L — *The History of the Indian Mountain Artillery*

Gunner Magazine — Various issues

Headlam Major-Gen. Sir John — *History of The Royal Artillery From The Indian Mutiny To The Great War: Volume II 1899–1914*
History of The Royal Artillery From The Indian Mutiny To The Great War: Volume III Campaigns 1860–1914

Hogg Ian V. — *Allied Artillery of World War One*
Allied Artillery of World War Two
Anti-Aircraft Artillery
Coast Defences of England and Wales 1865–1956
The Illustrated Encyclopaedia of Artillery

Hogg, Ian V. & Thurston, L. F. — *British Artillery Weapons & Ammunition 1914–1918*

Jocelyn. Col. Julian R. J. — *History of The Royal Artillery (Crimean Period)*
History of The Royal And Indian Artillery In The Mutiny of 1857

Journal of the Royal Artillery — Various issues

NATO — *AAP 6 – NATO Glossary of Terms and Definitions*

Nicholson CD, Colonel G. W. L. — *The Gunners of Canada*

Rollo, Denis — *The Guns and Gunners of Malta*

Royal Artillery Historical Committee — *Some Outstanding Episodes of Regimental History*

War Office/Ministry of Defence — *Artillery Training Volume 1 Drill, 1934*
Artillery Training, Volume 1, Artillery in Battle, Pamphlet No. 2A, Locating and Artillery Intelligence, 1964
Artillery Training Volume 1 Artillery in Battle, Pamphlet No. 6 Artillery Staff Duties (Field Branch), 1954
Artillery Training Volume 1 Artillery in Battle, Pamphlet No. 6 Field Artillery Staff Duties, 1964
Artillery Training Volume 11 Gunnery, 1934
Artillery Training, Volume I, Artillery in Battle, Pamphlet 1, Organization, Command and Employment, 1948
Artillery Training, Volume I, Artillery in Battle, Pamphlet 6, Artillery Staff Duties (Field Branch), 1954
Artillery Training, Volume II, Handling Units in the

Field, Pamphlet No. 1, Field Branch Artillery, 1948
Artillery Training, Volume III, Field Gunnery, Pamphlet No. 1, Ballistics and Ammunition, 1948
Artillery Training, Volume III, Field Artillery, Pamphlet No. 1A, Ordnance, Carriages and Mountings, 1965
Artillery Training, Volume III, Field Gunnery, Pamphlet No. 1B, Ballistics and Technical Aspects of Field Gunnery, 1959
Artillery Training, Volume III, Field Gunnery, Pamphlet No. 3, Duties at RHQ and the Guns – General, 1955
Artillery Training, Volume III, Field Gunnery, Pamphlet No. 4, Duties at the OP. 1956
Field Artillery Training 1914
Garrison Artillery Training, Volume I, 1914
Wyndham Malet, Major G. E. — *History of "J" Battery Royal Horse Artillery*
Whinyates Col. F. A. — *From Coruna To Sebastopol: The History Of 'C' Battery, 'A' Brigade (Late 'C' Troop), Royal Horse Artillery*

Useful Internet Sites

British Artillery in World War II	http://members.tripod.com/~nigelef/
Firepower, Museum of the Royal Artillery	http://www.firepower.org.uk/home/home.cfm
Palmerston Forts Society	http://www.palmerstonforts.org.uk
Royal Artillery Historical Society	http://www.army.mod.uk/rahistoricalsociety/
Royal Artillery	http://www.army.mod.uk/royalartillery/
Royal Artillery Association, The	http://www.theraa.co.uk/
The Garrison	http://www.thegarrison.net
The Royal Artillery 1939-45	http://www.ra39-45.pwp.blueyonder.co.uk
Royal School of Artillery	http://www.army.mod.uk/royalartillery/units/royal_school_of_artillery/
Trux Models	http://truxmodels.co.uk/

Also Available from The History Press

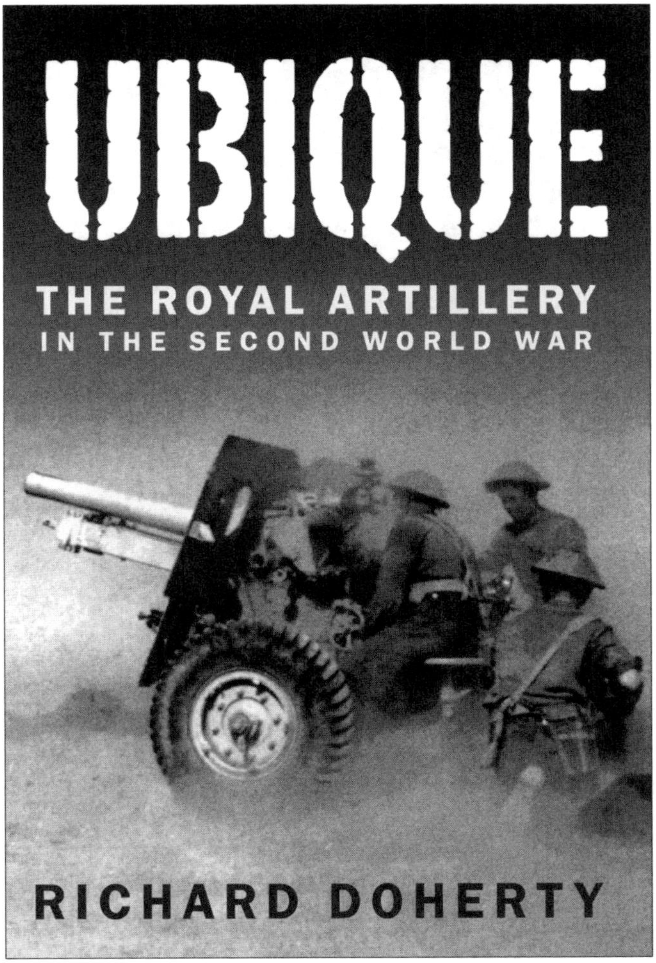

During World War II the Germans assessed the Royal Artillery as the most professional arm of the British Army. British gunners were accurate, effective and efficient, and provided fire support for their armoured and infantry colleagues that was better than that in any other army. In *Ubique*, Richard Doherty looks at the wide-ranging roles of the Royal Artillery, examining its state of preparedness in 1939, the many developments that were introduced during the War, including aerial observation and self-propelled artillery, the growth of the regiment and its effectiveness in its many roles.

ISBN 978-1-86227-492-1

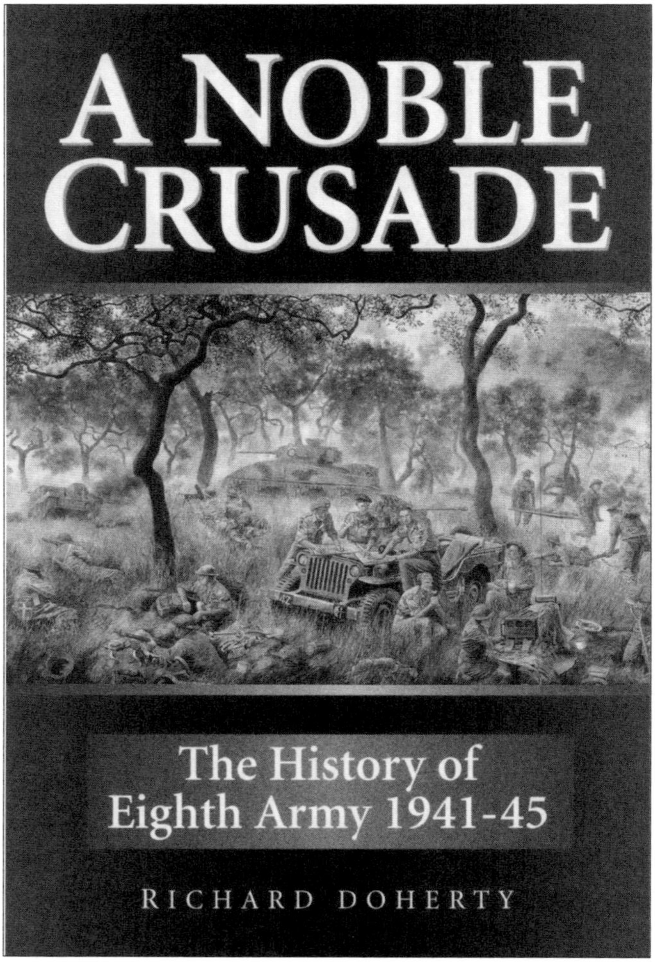
A NOBLE CRUSADE
The History of Eighth Army 1941-45
RICHARD DOHERTY

A Noble Crusade provides a comprehensive history of the Eighth Army, one of the most famous of all British armies. Richard Doherty uses official records, personal accounts and Victoria Cross winners' stories to deliver a complete tale of the Eighth Army from its beginnings in the sands of North Africa through the victory of El Alamein to the end of the War and victory. Under the inspiration of Montgomery the army launched a major offensive in El Alamein before taking part in the successful invasion of Sicily and the long and bloody campaign to defeat the Axis forces in Italy.

ISBN 978-1-86227-479-2

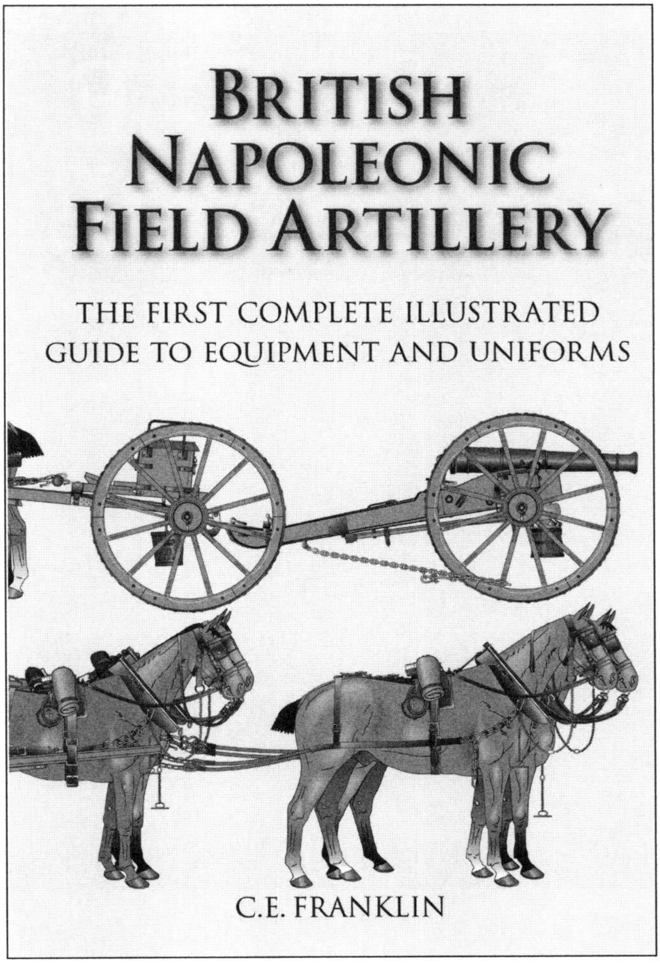
BRITISH
NAPOLEONIC
FIELD ARTILLERY
THE FIRST COMPLETE ILLUSTRATED
GUIDE TO EQUIPMENT AND UNIFORMS
C.E. FRANKLIN

This beautifully illustrated compendium by master draughtsman and Napoleonic expert Carl Franklin draws together extensive research with previously unpublished information to provide a fresh insight into the field equipment and uniforms of the period. The role of field artillery to support the army as part of its organisation and use in tactics is examined in great detail, with specific reference to the fighting arms of the Royal Regiment of Artillery, the Royal Artillery and the Royal Horse Artillery. See page 1 of the picture section for an example of Carl Franklin's artistry.

ISBN 978-1-86227-373-3